Law and the Social Order

ESSAYS IN LEGAL PHILOSOPHY

BY

MORRIS R. COHEN

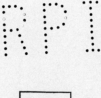

HARCOURT, BRACE AND COMPANY

NEW YORK

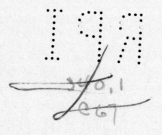

PRINTED IN THE UNITED STATES OF AMERICA
BY QUINN & BODEN COMPANY, INC., RAHWAY, N. J.
Typography by Robert S. Josephy

To Mary

PREFACE

THE meaning of law in the lives of men and women is a theme to which my earliest reflective thought was directed; for I could not help seeing the effects of legal rules and judicial decisions on the daily life of those nearest to me. At first I used to think that the havoc-working opinions of our courts in labor cases were simply the product of a lack of sympathetic understanding of the actual conditions under which most men and women work and live. But when I came to study the history of human thought I found that the road of relief for the oppressed and the needy was also barred by an old philosophy whose limitation had often been demonstrated in the purely intellectual realm. As the teaching of philosophy became my daily occupation, I found that legal material gave new and pointed significance to old issues in logic, ethics, and metaphysics. Sound methods and logical errors seem strikingly illustrated in the reasons courts give for their decisions, as well as in the writings of their critics. The craving for absolute moral distinctions and the confused effort to apply them to practical life— the source of so much of our spiritual grandeur and misery—appear nowhere more clearly than in the history of the law. And even the most elementary questions of metaphysics, such as the grounds of materialism and subjectivism, find revealing light thrown on them by a consideration of the nature of *things* in the law of property and of *will* in the law of contract. Law, philosophy, and social justice have thus become merged in an absorbing theme of reflection.

Occasions for the partial expression of my reflections on this theme have brought forth these essays, originally printed in various periodicals. Members of the bench and bar, colleagues and former students, have urged me to put these scattered offerings together in some more permanent form. I have hitherto hesitated to take the latter course because I have not yet abandoned the hope of completing a systematic exposition of the field of legal philosophy, and I fear that I may prejudice a good cause by the publication of what are only occasional and therefore inadequate fragments. But repeated references to these papers in recent legal literature put me under some obligation to make them more readily accessible.

With few exceptions these essays have been written either for popular periodicals or for law reviews, and I feel that I have dealt rather sketchily with philosophical issues which, in a different context, would have called for a fuller and more explicit statement. I can only trust that the thoughtful reader will note the traces and suggestions of the philosophy of realistic rationalism which unites all these fragments. I have tried, in my book *Reason and Nature*, to outline the major elements of this view. The use there made of the principle of polarity, particularly in the chapter on "Natural Rights and Positive Law," offers to the interested reader some light upon the perspective from which I have viewed the subjects of these collected papers.

Reflection on the nature and function of legal institutions has never completely lost attraction for keen and generous minds; and there has recently arisen in the law schools of our great universities an interest in this field so free, vigorous, and lively as to have seemed unbelievable in the years before the war, when the Conference on Legal and Social Philosophy could not interest more than a handful of law-teachers. But in law as in other social fields the very vitality of our interests makes us passionately espouse half-truths and zealously exclude the vision of those who see the opposing and supplementary half-truth.

In opposing the narrowness of those who conceive of the law, especially our constitutional law, as a body of abstract and unchanging principles, we are apt to forget the fixed in the flux, the constant elements that give changes their meaning. In opposing exclusive preoccupation with the historical past we are apt to impoverish our view of the present. In turning our backs on the study of abstract rules *in vacuo* we are apt to fall into a blind empiricism that leads nowhere. In rejecting the imposition of arbitrary ideas as to what the law ought to be and in pleading for a scientific study of the facts of the law *wie es eigentlich ist*, we are apt to forget that the law is a human product and can be remoulded nearer to the heart's desire. Such partiality gives our opponents a vantage-ground from which to attack us.

It may be, as I have heard Justice Holmes assert, that such partiality is our inevitable fate or destiny, because of our mortal finitude. It does certainly seem that those who wish to restore the helm of thought to its right position must first push with all their might in one direction, regardless of the danger of passing beyond the right mark. But the function of intelligence is not only to recognize but also to evaluate opposing forces, and to determine their resultant with the highest attainable accuracy. Only in that way can we, in part at least, mitigate the perpetual and cruel swing from one extreme error to its opposite. In calling attention to the necessity of this intellectual task, the principle of polarity offers no ready solution to our ancient difficulties. But in making us aware of real difficulties that otherwise we are likely to ignore, it points to the kind of consideration necessary to overcome our partiality. The recognition of our limitation is the beginning of progress in real understanding.

The essays included in this volume were written at intervals that all together cover twenty years. I am reluctant to believe that those years have been for me altogether devoid of growth in knowledge and insight. But I am not conscious of any radical change in fundamental point of view. And as it is the latter that gives these essays whatever value they may have for the reader today, it has not seemed necessary to bring them "up to date" by taking account of subsequent events in the course of legal decisions and juristic thought.

They are therefore reprinted substantially in the original form except for an occasional recasting or expansion to make the meaning clearer.

As the essays are somewhat diverse in scope and style, a word on their arrangement in this volume may be in order. The first book, "The Social Scene," contains short comments on books and personalities that embody some of the significant current attitudes towards the law. The second book, "Law and the Social Order," surveys the part played by fundamental legal institutions in maintaining the present social and economic order and in blocking the road to a better one. Those papers concerned with the permanent philosophical problems that permeate the fabric of the law find a place in the third book, "Law and Reason." In the fourth book, "Contemporary Legal Philosophy," I have offered critical appraisals of several outstanding legal thinkers.

That a layman should persist for more than twenty years in grappling with the problems of the nature of the law is explained by the encouragement of many friends, especially Professor Felix Frankfurter, Dean Roscoe Pound, Professor Harold J. Laski, and Justice Oliver Wendell Holmes. The law schools of Columbia and Yale and of St. John's College and my alma mater, the College of the City of New York, have aided me by the opportunity to give courses on the philosophy of law for some of the keenest students in our country. Almost all of the more popular essays were extracted from me by the gentle pressure of the early editors of the *New Republic*, Walter Lippmann, Francis Hackett, Alvin Johnson, Philip and Robert Littell, and especially their leader Herbert Croly. The judicious character of Croly's attitude to legal and social problems drew my profound admiration and I regret deeply that this tribute comes when he is, alas, no longer with us.

Acknowledgment for permission to reprint the essays included in this volume is gratefully made to the editors of *The American Law Review*, *The American Law School Review*, *The American Political Science Review*, *The Columbia Law Review*, *The Cornell Law*

Quarterly, The Harvard Law Review, The International Journal of Ethics, The Journal of Criminal Law, The Journal of Philosophy, The Nation, The New Republic, and *The Philosophical Review.*

Lastly I must acknowledge the aid of my colleague, Dr. Ernest Nagel, of my son, Dr. Felix S. Cohen, and of my daughter-in-law, Lucy Kramer, in seeing this volume through the press.

M. R. C.

CONTENTS

BOOK ONE

THE SOCIAL SCENE

Judge Parry on The Law and the Poor [1]

T HE rich have many law books written to protect their privileges, but the poor who are the greater nation, have but few."

This, gentle reader, is not the utterance of one of our legal muckrakers, but the opening sentence of a commentary on *The Law and the Poor* written by his honour Judge Parry, for over twenty years judge in English urban county courts. Judge Parry is peculiarly gifted with that rare imagination which enables him to see mortal men and women where others see cases, litigants, or parties before the court. Hence his volume is a rare document, especially useful as a corrective to the tendency to lose sight of actual living conditions in the logical pursuit of abstract legal doctrines.

A good part of the book deals with imprisonment for debt, which the reading of the English statute-books leads one to suppose was abolished in 1869, but which we here learn still forms a deplorable factor in the social life of the poor in England, especially in breaking up homes. Imprisonment for debt, of course, affects only the poor; the rich man, aided by expert counsel, has the privilege, on payment of ten pounds, of filing a petition in bankruptcy and thus wiping out his debts. Though some of the conditions treated in this connection fortunately no longer prevail in this country,[2] the book may serve as a powerful antidote against foolish complacency which supposes that equality before the law is an accomplished fact. The thesis that in the legal race the poor man is the scratch-man, and the greater the wealth the larger the advantage is made out in many fields. It is shown in a strikingly suggestive way in the realm of

NOTE: Footnotes appear at the end of the volume, pp. 371-390.

3

divorce law, where the relief that the court offers can be obtained only at a cost prohibitive to the poor. Not only has the one who can hire the better counsellor the greater chance in the legal lottery, but the whole machinery of appeal makes litigation a rich man's game. Unless the poor workman belongs to a union and his case is a test case, he stands little chance. The professional code of the "better-class" lawyers which discourages taking cases on contingency also militates against the poor man. As to the criminal law, all men may be equal once they are in the dock, "but one may harbour a suspicion whether all men have equal opportunities of getting there." [3]

Unlike Dante's Inferno, our penal system punishes violence and brutality more than fraud and deceit, and yet "crimes of violence and brutality are naturally the crimes of the less fortunate of mankind," [4] and while the law is old and decrepit, the modern well-to-do swindler is quite up to date. The imposition of fines means imprisonment for poverty, but freedom for those whose purses are long enough. It is only natural for judges to treat the kleptomaniac lady or derelict young man of "good family" with greater consideration. "The wrong doing of a man or woman of our own class naturally appeals to our bump of forgiveness more readily than that of a slum dweller whose temptations and environment we know nothing about." [5] A judge is not a legal slot-machine, but a human being. "He has toddled about in the same nursery, learned in the same school . . . and lived in the same society as the rest of the middle class." [6]

The main trouble, however, is not with the judge, but with the "old derelict law made by slaveowners for slaves, by masters for serfs, by the landlords for the landless." [7] If only there were a "lethal chamber" where laws could retire as soon as they had outlived their usefulness! Still it is true that most improvements in the law have had to be won against the opposition of the bench and the bar.

The saloon problem is properly part of this book, since the ale-house, like the poor-house, is for the poor only. The rich enjoy at their clubs or hotels privileges denied to their less prosperous brethren. In Germany, "A workingman and his wife and children spend their evening listening to the band in a German beer-garden with as little sense of impropriety as Lord and Lady De Vere and the Hon. Gladys De Vere take their lunch at the Ritz," [8] but in England (and in the United States) the wife of a labourer is "looked upon as degraded if she joins him at the only place where he can spend his leisure, and the rich lawgivers put the true stamp on their own invention by enacting that it is an unfit place for little children to enter." [9] "The first step you have to take is to convince the unenlightened puritan that the Alehouse is, or ought to be, as worthy a public house as the church or the school." [10]

The account above does little justice to the human and readable qualities of this book. The author, unlike most propagandists, has a real sense of humour, and his comments on Biblical precepts are well worth remembering: "On Sunday we intone on slow music our desire to forgive our enemy his trespasses; on Monday we go down to our solicitor to issue a writ against him for the trespasses we have failed to forgive." [11] Characteristic also is the following on the minimum wage: "If a man has a smoking chimney, or pollutes a river, or goes about in public with an infectious disease, we fine or imprison him for his anti-social misconduct. Surely a man who pursues an industry that does not make a living wage for the workers in it is equally an enemy of the people, to be dealt with as such by the law!" [12] As to the "scientific" sociologists who are afraid that "if the law were to protect the fool the effect would be to increase and multiply the breed of fools, whereby the human race would become a bigger fool race than already it is," the reply is made "that the law as it now stands makes the trade of knavery such a lucrative one that the business of it is fast becoming overcrowded." [13]

With all his radicalism Judge Parry is still, as he tells us, a member of the cultured upper class, and he would not counsel any harsh or hasty action. His consolation is that it will all turn out right if we are willing to wait centuries rather than months. He shares the prevailing faith that nature is like a plumber who delays and sputters about his job, but in the end somehow manages to have it done. His instances, however, do not always bear this out. Thus, not only is the English law of divorce far behind the Roman, but the confusions of the Archbishop of York in 1912 are far behind those of Archbishop Cranmer of 1550. In the introduction, Judge Parry mentions a more encouraging incident. For many years, as is well known, Mr. Plimsoll carried on an agitation against the practice of the " 'ship-knackers,' who bought up old unseaworthy vessels and sent them to sea overloaded and overinsured." [14] It was only when in unparliamentary fashion he began to give the names of the parliamentary gentlemen engaged in the business of sending poor men to death that he was called to order, and made to leave the House, but his measure passed. Sometimes it is better not to wait for nature or the plumber, but to tackle the job at once.

Herbert Hoover's Myth of Individualism [1]

MR. HOOVER is one of the very few who emerged from the World War with any credit to human nature; and though his glory was somewhat dimmed by the frailties of his presidential ambition in 1920 and by outbursts of intemperate words that he injected into his good deeds in Europe and Russia, he is still one of the most significant characters in our public life. For there can be little doubt that our rulers will in the future be drawn more and more from the class that he represents, viz., the engineers. Indeed, it seems at first most amazing that a civilization so fundamentally dependent on the physical scientists and engineers should so long have continued to be governed by professional diplomats, lawyers, and financiers. But our amazement at this diminishes when we reflect that human nature is still a factor in human affairs and that the training of the engineer has not as yet, despite cheap cant about social psychology and motivation, prepared the engineer to replace those who, with less knowledge of the material facts, are more sensitive and have a better prophetic sense of what will go with multitudes of men. Thus it is that the Lloyd Georges have proved more successful than the Kitcheners. Still, though technical ability alone can never elevate a man to supreme leadership, it is to be expected that, as the engineering profession expands, more of its members will find their training a great advantage in the struggle for the rulership of human affairs. Will the engineer then bring with him the mathematical accuracy and the scrupulous regard for actual facts that his training and occupation make him exercise in the management of material things? If you think an affirmative answer to this is self-evident, you will do well to consider Mr. Hoover's expression of his philosophy in his little book entitled *American Individualism.*

Haziness about the meaning of fundamental ideas such as individualism, carelessness in making assertions of fact, and, what is worse, an ungenerous disinclination to consider whether our opponents might not be honest and possessed of some intelligence are things that we have grown to expect of the ordinary Fourth of July oration. It is painfully surprising to find them in one who has shown a remarkable combination of perspicacity and human sympathy in the organization of vast systems of relief, as well as the qualities of a careful scholar in his book on Agricola.

I, for one, have no quarrel with the usual Fourth of July oratory. It is a service to people and it compensates them for the dreary drudgery of life to be told that they alone have the right system of government, philosophy, etc. But Mr. Hoover intimates that it is only demagogues who feed the mob with emotional phrases.[2] True leadership is of the intellect, deliberate consideration, etc.[3] Judged by the latter standard, we have a right to demand that Mr. Hoover attach some definite meaning to words like "individualism" and "equality of opportunity," that he define or throw some light on the issue between individualism and socialism rather than merely add to the plentiful amount of heated utterance. But, alas, Mr. Hoover has never deigned to read any of the classical works on the socialism that he so vehemently rejects—witness his silly argument [4] that all breeds of socialism "contemplate a motivation of human animals by altruism alone." (Shades of Karl Marx and the economic interpretation of history!)

Mr. Hoover identifies individualism with the force which colonized this country and has been its primary force for three centuries.[5] One wonders whether he means to include in individualism the Puritan theocracy with its fierce intolerance of all forms of morals or worship other than its own, or the old Southern squirearchy dating back to Governor Berkeley's gratitude to God that there were no free schools or printing-presses in Virginia? Can it be that Mr.

Hoover is so ignorant of United States history as to ignore the fact that political equality and manhood suffrage are not older than Jacksonian democracy, which came only with the opening of the West in the nineteenth century, and that equality of opportunity has not yet in fact been extended to ten million coloured men? Mr. Hoover's instincts, at least, are wiser than his orthodox professions, and he rejects the identification of individualism with the old laissez-faire that dominated orthodox thought in this country up to the days of Theodore Roosevelt and is still too much alive.

In one section of his book ("Philosophic Grounds"), Mr. Hoover begins bravely enough by laying it down as an axiom that intelligence, character, etc., "do not lie in agreements, in organizations, in institutions, in masses or in groups. They abide alone, in the individual mind and heart." [6] But a little reflection enables one to see that civilization rests on accumulated group experience, that the intelligence of the individual, the language he uses, the ideas that he imbibes, the ideals that he cherishes or tries to imitate, his manners and morals, do depend on the group in which he lives and on the institutions of his country. Organized or group action is therefore not necessarily antagonistic to individual initiative or development. It may be the only effective way of giving it expression. Indeed, in view of many of Mr. Hoover's strictures on the old conception of individualism as laissez-faire, his insistence that no civilization can rest on unrestrained self-interest, it would not be difficult for patriotic heresy-hunters to make excerpts that would convict Mr. Hoover's booklet of being socialistic. When, however, fervid patriots denounce free seeds to farmers as socialism and see no objection to subsidies for shipowners, when individualism is held compatible with high protective tariffs but not with minimum-wage legislation, it is as clear as a pikestaff that the popular use of the words "individualism" and "socialism" denotes nothing beyond an emotional explosion of approval or disapproval, depending on whose ox is gored. Under these circumstances, it is useless to assert that we must be willing to experiment "in the remedy of our social faults," [7] and then block such experiment with the blind dogma that the vexed problems of economic and social life "can be solved within our social theme and under no other system." [8]

A few illustrations may not be amiss to show that Mr. Hoover the engineer is as unfortunate in his statements of fact as in his speculative generalizations. I pass over the flat assertion that "none of us is either hungry or cold or without a place to lay his head." [9] Mr. Hoover himself refutes it when, on a subsequent occasion, he speaks of children in this country who are undernourished and overworked. (The number of them may be much larger than Mr. Hoover guesses.) Recent experience, also, will enable every reader to judge the statement that the United States has succeeded beyond all others in keeping open the channels of free speech. [10] To Mr. Hoover's assertion that we have given more to Europe than we have received from it, [11] it is sufficient to utter the words literature, art, science, philosophy, or spiritual teachings. When Mr. Hoover said "taxation will reduce relatively excessive individual accumulations," [12] he paid little attention to the taxation policies of the Republican administration of which he was a part. Nor is it true that small stockholders control our great corporations. [13] The histories of the Morgan control of the New Haven railroad and Judge Gary's autocracy in the steel industry are still fresh in people's minds. Mr. Hoover swallows popular impressions and gives them out as facts just as he swallows the vulgar error that Frankenstein was a monster [14] instead of an experimentalist who created one. As an engineer he surely could not get very far with such loose, unverified statements.

Devoid of responsible meaning, also, are such statements as: "The war itself in its last stages was a conflict of social philosophies." [15] After the rejection of the peace offers of 1917 it was clear that France wished to crush Germany as Germany wished to crush France—not much difference of social philosophy. Unfortunate for Mr. Hoover is the statement that socialism has "proved itself with rivers of blood and inconceivable misery to be an economic and spiritual fallacy." [16] It is unfortunate because it enables the socialist to retort that *he* did not bring about the World War and, indeed, that he was blamed for protesting against it. Nor did even the Russian Bolsheviki excel in invading the territory of former allies and in sending arms and ammunitions to promote civil war.

The inaccuracies thus culled from a thin booklet may not be of much inherent importance, but they are the little straws that show the currents which swamp even generous minds away from their moorings in common-sense. Even in this booklet Mr. Hoover amply shows that when he forgets the fear of radicalism he can say sensible things. The discipline of the forum and the market place may enable men to excel in specific situations; but without the impartial reflection of the study they are the worst victims of doctrinaire phrases.

The Legal Calvinism of Elihu Root[1]

CONCERNING Mr. Root there are current two distinct legends. One paints him as "undoubtedly the ablest man in the United States," the greatest lawyer and statesman of our time. The other pictures him as the typical corporation lawyer, the defender of Tweed and the legal servant of the traction and whisky trusts. Few of us really know how much truth underlies these legends. Mr. Root organized our Philippine government and re-organized our army. How many of us really know enough of the facts in each case to judge what he did or should have done? How many of those who denounce him as a tool of Ryan in the traction scandals know exactly what was Root's specific part in those trans-actions? But we dare not admit our ignorance when all our neigh-bours speak with the undisturbed confidence that comes from not knowing anything to the contrary. Hence we clutch at the first avail-able straw of evidence that comes our way; and rumour, hearsay, or chance impression becomes the basis of our emphatic belief. In this situation it is well to turn to Mr. Root's published addresses to examine the quality of his mind and his fundamental views.

To assert, for instance, that Mr. Root is entirely devoid of crea-tive insight on the general nature of government may shock and call to arms Mr. Root's ardent admirers; but they will find it diffi-cult to point out a single original idea in the five hundred and forty-two pages of the volume entitled *Addresses on Government and Citizenship*. So, also, will the reading of this volume discomfort those who confidently assert that Root is nothing but a shrewd law-yer, using legal and technical subtleties to bolster up the interests of the propertied classes. These addresses do not show him to be of the

12

common brood of hirelings who bay at the rising tide of democracy. There is in his utterance a rugged rustic simplicity and strength that comes only of a thorough, naïve acceptance of a very simple doctrine. Indeed, in spite of obvious differences of temperament, experience, and sympathy, Mr. Root appears here essentially like Mr. Bryan, a preacher of evangelical faith in the traditional American individualism. To Mr. Root, it is true, the gospel appears in its harder form, as an eternal law condemning in advance all varieties of Western insurgency; whereas to Mr. Bryan the gospel is essentially a human liberation, and specifically a liberation from the sway of the Wall Street that employs men like Mr. Root. But it would be a radical error to overlook the fact that Mr. Root's thought starts not from his experience in Wall Street, but from his naïve faith in the rural Puritanic individualism that he imbibed in his native Oneida.

The outlines of this faith are as simple as they are familiar. It begins with the Calvinistic belief in the total depravity of human nature in politics, especially when it comes to ordinary legislation. "Our natures are weak, prone to error, subject to fall into temptation and to be led astray by impulse." [2] On the other hand, there is an abounding grace in man's unrestricted individual economic activity. All that is valuable in civilization is simply "the sum total of intelligent selfishness in a vast number of individuals, each working for his own support, his own gain, his own betterment." [3] To protect each individual in this right to pursue his happiness in his own way, constitutional restraints must be imposed on the majority and especially on the legislature. These restraints can be enforced only by an independent judiciary, which alone is always free from human passion and interests, and decides always in accordance with the eternal principles of justice and reason.

The professed theorist or closet philosopher is seldom a doctrinaire. He knows too well the difficulty of making theories fit the obstinate facts, and he is apt to have a very keen sense of his practical inexperience. The successful man of affairs, whose mind is not

trained to question first principles, is not conscious of such limitations, and when he is committed to a theory the poor facts of life
have no chance at all. Thus Mr. Root is so committed to the old
doctrinaire individualism that he can see nothing in the World
War but the fight of the individual against the claims of the state,[4]
and he does not stop to ask whether it was Germany or Russia that
fought for the view that the rights of the individual are superior to
those of the state. So, also, to Mr. Root the American constitutional
system is not simply the historic result of Colonial experience, to be
justified only so long as it works well. It is the embodiment of absolute eternal laws of justice and liberty,[5] valid for all generations to
come,[6] and no experience to come will justify any amendment of it.[7]
Not to mar the lyric intensity of this refrain, the editors have wisely
omitted all reference to Mr. Root's activity on behalf of the Income
Tax amendment.

Like other preachers, Mr. Root does not prove or justify his
"principles." He treats them as if they were universally admitted.
The only doubters he recognizes are the vague tribe of socialists
(whose writings have never contaminated his mind), immigrants,
who are sure to be converted sooner or later, and certain perverse
professors in our colleges and law schools, "half-baked and con-
ceited theorists." Despite, however, this display of temper, pardonable in an old man, we may be sure that Mr. Root has too much of
the American spirit to adopt the attitude of Torquemada to students
of history who find his historical learning obsolete, or to students
of philosophy and political science who find that his method of ele-
vating all his assumptions into "eternal principles" has become
hopelessly antiquated since modern experimental science has replaced the method of Scotch intuitionism that prevailed in the days
of Mr. Root's youth.

Obsolete learning about Anglo-Saxons, Witenagemot, and Magna
Carta may be pardonable in a man of affairs, and even total ignorance when he speaks of Roman law. But why should an intelligent
man today speak of the Fathers of 1789 in the manner of the Chi-

nese, as if they were semi-divine beings not subject to the limitations of human nature? Surely the world has learned a great deal since 1789. The writers of the *Federalist* could surely have improved their knowledge of Greek federalism if they had read Polybius instead of relying on Mably. Mr. Root also confuses the restraints on popular will embodied in the Constitution with the doctrine of popular sovereignty embodied in the Declaration of Independence. Conservative historians like McMaster, Ford, or President Wilson have repeatedly pointed out that the Federal Convention was organized not by democrats like Jefferson, Patrick Henry, or Samuel Adams, who were prominent in the Revolutionary movement, but by the commercial and propertied classes, who were frightened at the excesses of the popular state governments. The Federal Convention, however, agreed not on eternal principles, but on practical compromises which did not completely satisfy any party. These compromises worked until the slavery issue became so acute that men refused to compromise any longer, and the constitutional system broke down. The Dred Scott decision had to be recalled by a frightful civil war.

It is not creditable to Mr. Root's knowledge of European democracies that he should repeat the vain boast that they all envy us our constitutional system. Neither in France nor in England would liberal public opinion for a moment tolerate giving the final word in matters of railroad or labour legislation to a small number of elderly judges. The Swiss are surely a liberty-loving people and they have a federal form of government, but they have explicitly prohibited their courts from declaring acts of their federal legislature unconstitutional.

Lawyers get so in the habit of relying on legal fiction that they become incapable of distinguishing it from fact. Thus to Mr. Root constitutions "are made impersonally, abstractly, dispassionately, impartially, as the people's expression of what they believe to be right and necessary, etc." [8] But in point of fact constitutions are made by conventions of delegates in which lawyers of a certain type frequently predominate. That they are not always free from partisan bias may be seen in the way in which they often gerrymander the state in the interests of their own political party. Mr. Root himself admits that the New York State constitution was a complicated affair which took the convention five months to work out, and that ordinary business men, farmers, or working-men could not be expected to determine what it meant. Indeed, if there is one thing certain about the American legal system it is that not even trained lawyers know how, in a new case, the courts will interpret "due process" or "equal protection" of laws.

Mr. Root, one of the authors of the New York State constitution of 1894, apparently disagrees with the Court of Appeals upon the constitutionality of workmen's compensation.[9] Courts, as Mr. Root admits, are certain to vary and differ and conflict in their decisions, so that the plain, unmistakable fact is that government by bills of rights has produced a reign not of law, but of the higher lawlessness, in which judges have through ignorance, apathy, or class bias frequently defeated the just demands of the community.

Both the political opponents and the friends of Mr. Root are united in referring to him as "a cold, clear intellect." The contents of this volume certainly do not bear out this legend. The clear mind does not abound in glaring contradictions. Thus, when Mr. Root argues against the public dissatisfaction with the quality of judicial decisions, he says "it is not his [the judge's] function or within his power to enlarge or improve or change the law." [10] But when he talks to lawyers of what is actually going on, he points out how the courts are now making administrative law and retiring the constitutional doctrine against the delegation of legislative power. Again, the broad general principles that Mr. Root invokes so often turn out to be most vague when we press for their precise meaning. It is impossible, for instance, to obtain any clear idea of what Mr. Root means by "representative government," about which he always speaks with rapture. All that we can gather is that he believes that some of our rulers should be elected by a limited body of voters, but that after election they should represent their own judgment. It seems that "the people" have "unerring insight" in their judgment of men,[11] but cannot be trusted on important measures. The truth indeed is that all these attempts to settle complicated problems by direct appeal to broad principles are transactions with blank checks. To say that "it is injurious for the government to attempt too much" sounds sententious, but it is just as true that it is injurious for the government to attempt too little. Mr. Root himself, when he is not arguing for laissez-faire, amply indicates the danger of the latter course in an age when men cannot protect themselves against many dangers except through their government. Indeed, when Mr. Root is not thinking of his fundamental theory he states rather clearly what all intelligent men now recognize as the shortcomings of government by law and lawyers.[12] But his adherence to his theory and his devotion to the established order are too passionate to allow mere facts to influence him.

The passionate intensity of Mr. Root's utterance convinces the reader that to his friends Mr. Root must be a model of personal loyalty. For forty years he unprotestingly watched his native State ruled by an "invisible government." [13] Nay, he was himself a part and defender of this government, which he knew to be unconstitutional and wrong. His own naïve explanation is embodied in the following: "I don't criticize the men of the invisible government. How can I? I have known them all and among them have been some of my dearest friends." [14] A cold, clear intellect would surely have distinguished between loyalty to friends and loyalty to the state or civic righteousness. Perhaps the habits of the paid advocate, accustomed to defending questionable interests in accordance with the rules of the legal game, blunt a man's moral initiative. But whether Mr. Root did or did not originally possess the capacity for moral initiative, it is clear that he has never had the illuminating experience of life which makes a man become a Pilgrim himself instead of remaining proud of the fact that his ancestors were.

One whose gaze is directed to the future will look in vain in this volume for any light on the vexed problems of industrial and social reform or of racial and religious adjustment. Such a reader will be impressed with the pathos of so much native energy and moral zeal wasted in trying to prevent the inevitable and crushing hand of time from falling on ancient beliefs. Nor is there lacking a certain nobility in this defence of a cause intellectually as antiquated as was chivalry in the days of Don Quixote.

As I was reading Mr. Root's elaborate but futile speech against the popular election of United States senators, I must have dozed off. For I thought I was on Olympus, where Rabelais, Cervantes, Molière, Heine, Dickens, and Mark Twain were drinking ambrosial beer and filling the air with thunderous laughter. Soon Mr. Root came along, his body erect, his head thrown back, reciting a speech in which could be heard "eternal principles," "popular passion," "constitutional restraints," and "separation of powers." He walked by, not paying the least attention to the jolly company. Some one— it sounded like Mark Twain—called after him: "I'd change that song, Elihu! It's getting stale and it doesn't work any more. Why don't you learn the new songs? Throw in something about evolutionary philosophy, social psychology, and social uplift and progress. Men of wealth and power can play the new tunes as well as the old, and have the additional comfort of not being laughed at by their own young fellows who have had a little more schooling." But Mr. Root walked on unperturbed.

The Conservative Lawyer's Legend of Magna Carta [1]

TO THOSE who believe that there is some sort of difference between the new and the true, it is a genuine disappointment to find the writings of our American conservatives so monotonously devoid of force and distinction. It is of course true that our conservatives are in an unusually bad predicament intellectually. The conservative abroad has a comparatively easy time holding on to the good old ways and denouncing the reformer as one who would subvert our ancient glory. But in this country the conservative is a Son of the Revolution and has to defend the established order by the eighteenth-century revolutionary philosophy. It is certainly difficult to use the fact that our forefathers revolted in 1776 as an argument why we should forever maintain the status quo, just as it is hard to reconcile the refusal of self-government to the Philippines with the doctrine of the Declaration of Independence about "the consent of the governed." But an intellectually resourceful class like the old theologians could easily have overcome such difficulties. Perhaps the basic trouble with our conservatives is that their leaders have been lawyers who have been busy defending the interests of property before elderly judges, and have not had the chance to realize that there has grown up an intellectual public in this country—a public that is not satisfied with the archaic rhetoric and the obsolete learning on which the conservative has so long been resting his case. This may well be seen in a book called *Magna Carta and Other Addresses*, by William D. Guthrie, one of the leaders of the New York bar.

The first essay of this volume deals with Magna Carta, a medieval legal document whose precise meaning has recently been

the object of laborious research by scholars like Maitland, Vinogradoff, and McKechnie. But Mr. Guthrie will have nothing to do
with their painful efforts to determine the exact meaning of medieval
technical terms. It is not necessary for him to know that the social
structure of the thirteenth century was so different from ours as to
make it dangerous to transfer our present notions of government
and legislative power to medieval conditions. The traditional learning of a hundred years ago is good enough to show the lesson of
Magna Carta to be that we should forever remain satisfied with the
American system, in which the courts have the power to veto legislation interfering with private rights.

Mr. Guthrie accepts unquestioningly the tradition that magnified
the importance of Magna Carta because it was extracted from a king.
But modern students of history, and readers of thirteenth-century
chronicles like those of Walter of Coventry, know that the people
at large had little to do with Magna Carta, that it was the outcome
of a struggle between an Angevin king and Norman barons (lay,
clerical, and mercantile) in which the common people suffered from
both parties, that very few of its provisions could have been of any
use to the great mass of the people, who were villeins or serfs and
certainly not "freemen" in any sense that the word had in 1215.[2]
Moreover, some of its provisions for the administration of justice
were distinctly reactionary and detrimental to the common people
oppressed by the local barons—against whom the court of a powerful king like Henry II offered some protection.

The oft-quoted clause 39, "No freeman shall be imprisoned . . .
save by the lawful judgment of his peers," did not originate or
guarantee jury trial, despite pious assurances to the contrary by
Lord Coke, Edmund Burke, and the United States Supreme
Court. It did guarantee that no "peer of the realm" should be
tried by the king's judges who were not themselves peers, and that,
similarly, clerics should be tried in their own court ("benefit of
clergy"). In that respect there is some justice in Jenks's characterization of Magna Carta as a "reactionary document and a great

nuisance and stumbling block to the generation which came after it."

The light of secular history fails, also, to bear out Mr. Guthrie's rhetorical statement that Magna Carta "saved England from becoming one of the arbitrary and degrading despotisms which arose in Europe after the overthrow of the feudal system." [3] That document was certainly of no use in preventing the Statute of Labourers and the grinding-down of the workers by the local lords fixing the legal rate of wages. It did not prevent the granting of monopolies, the wholesale branding and hanging of the unemployed, or the confiscations of the common lands for the individual benefit of favoured landowners. One would suppose that a lawyer like Mr. Guthrie would be sufficiently acquainted with English legal history to know that in spite of some dicta and the dubious case of Dr. Bonham, English courts never did have the power of declaring acts of Parliament void as contrary to Magna Carta. But busy lawyers have no time for these matters, which are usually left to minor clerks in the office.

Mr. Guthrie's predilection for quasi-historical arguments prevents him from dealing with any issue on its merits. However, in the essay on the income tax, he clearly shows his moral bias in his condemnation of a graduated income tax. Such a tax, he argues, violates the principle of equality that is the essence of justice. But what does the principle of equality mean? Does it mean that rich and poor should pay equal sums, or does it mean that they should bear equal burdens? Will any one maintain that to pay 5 per cent of an income of $800 a year is no greater burden than to pay 5 per cent of an income of $100,000? Mr. Guthrie, as an ardent advocate of the protective tariff, has no objection to having the poor pay a greater proportion of their income in the form of indirect taxes.

While Mr. Guthrie admits in a general way that secular human judges are not absolutely infallible, he is not willing to admit that they have actually been wrong in any single case; and he tries hard to defend nearly all the decisions that have been the object of popular criticism. The result is a remarkable example of what a respectable lawyer considers fair advocacy. Thus the Ives case [4] (in which a workmen's compensation law was declared unconstitutional) is defended by showing that certain critics misrepresented the facts of the case. Mr. Guthrie is satisfied to show that Ives was hurt "probably through his own carelessness," [5] that the injury was not very serious, and that the railroad company, after winning the case, paid him fifty dollars. But Mr. Guthrie knows that the Ives case was a regular test case and that the Court of Appeals in its decision took no notice at all of the specific facts of this particular case, but considered only the general principle of the statute; and that by declaring the latter unconstitutional the court imposed upon thousands of seriously injured workmen the hardships that Theodore Roosevelt and other critics of the court erroneously attributed to Ives personally. Mr. Guthrie's defence is one of those befogging literal half-truths which are infinitely more deceiving than Roosevelt's wildest exaggeration. That the author of such a defence can serve as a leader of the legal profession is perhaps a sufficient explanation of the popular dissatisfaction with the working of our legal system.

An American Judge on the Nature of Justice[1]

JUDGES are commonly supposed to decide controversies not only according to the law of the land but also in accordance with the principles of justice. And it is often urged in favour of our system of government by the judiciary, or aristocracy of the robe, that it leaves the final word to those who have a trained sense of justice. However that may work out in practice, we may still ask whether it necessarily follows that a long and honourable experience on the bench will enable one to throw light on the general question as to what justice is and how it may be secured in actual administration. A book on the nature of justice by a chief judge of the State of Maine, giving the content of a series of Storrs Lectures (Lucilius Emery, *Concerning Justice*), tempts one who is interested in that ancient question. Philosophers are often rebuked (and should be) for leaving the realm of theory and dogmatizing in realms where their factual knowledge is inadequate. But a judge occupying a seat among the mighty may generalize about law and justice without much fear of criticism or protest. A mere philosophic onlooker can only report the results.

In the first chapter of this book we learn that the question of justice "has engaged the thought and fired the imagination of the greatest minds,"[2] but what precisely the problem is about it is hard to say. To the numerous questions that have been or can be asked about justice, the author tells us he is "not so presumptuous as to venture an answer."[3] One question, however, whether justice is a reality, he answers categorically by an "appeal to our consciousness, to our innate convictions, etc."[4] This way of settling questions, formerly taught in American colleges by the old Scotch "realistic" philosophy, certainly has the advantage of sparing us the labour of analyzing our question or of making clear to ourselves what precisely we mean by the much-suffering word "reality."

On the basis of instinctive feeling we come to the acceptance of the view that justice consists in giving every one his due or his rights. But what are each one's rights?

This "problem of rights," which, we learn, "is also centuries old," [5] is not directly answered in the next chapter, which is devoted rather to a polite mention of different opinions on the subject from "patriarchal times" [6] down to Mill—the last philosopher, it seems, whom American jurists may mention by name. Here Judge Emery startles us by telling us that though the doctrine of natural rights has been "formally and officially iterated in the constitutions of many American states and has been proclaimed and invoked as an impregnably established political truth . . . nevertheless the doctrine is only a theory, not yet demonstrated nor undoubted." [7] On the next page we are somewhat reassured by learning that "despite the vigorous arguments against the doctrine there remains the innate feeling and a general belief that society abridges individual rights instead of conferring them." [8]

But even this "innate feeling" does not quite satisfy the author, and in the third and fourth chapters he passes on from "the region of theory" to "the region of facts," seeking to show that justice is the equilibrium between the freedom of the individual and the safety of society or the like freedom of other individuals. Just wherein the equilibrium between the freedom of the individual and the safety of society consists, or how we are to determine whether a given law embodies such an equilibrium, we are not told. Modern philosophers who have no special fund of "innate convictions" will doubtless find it hard to discern the freedom of the individual "which would be his if he were alone in the world," [9] but the difficulty probably does not exist for those who have power to take judicial notice of such matters. In general, the "region of facts" in which the author's discussion moves is that of the general powers with which nature has endowed us,[10] and these powers it seems any gentleman of the bench or bar may describe without that vulgar intimacy with the experimental details or quantitative determinations that modern science regards as essential. At one point, indeed, Judge Emery tells us that the question how far society should go in regulating the conduct of individuals is "largely a question of expediency which may safely be left to sociologists and economists"[11] —but not altogether so. "It is also a question of rights, and hence of justice, since every action or non-action of society affects the freedom of the individual in the gratification of his desires or, in other words, in his pursuit of happiness."[12] Presumably, then, questions as to what will promote human happiness are not to be answered by social science, but are to be left either to the innate convictions or the judicial notice of our courts.

The remaining chapters of this book proceed from the assumption that justice can thus be secured only by a government in which there are constitutional limitations on the legislative power, enforced by an independent judiciary. The argument, with its implication that no other civilized nation—not even Anglo-Saxon England—enjoys the blessing of liberty and just government, proceeds along the usual lines, which a hundred years of faithful reiteration have made somewhat familiar. The monotonous repetition is doubtless sweet and soothing music to the orthodox among us, though it must be confessed that it has lately lost the power to charm those into whom the virus of strange doubts and new ideas has entered.

The style of this book embodies the best tradition of the American literary essay. Despite the author's conviction that "in any inquiry into the nature of justice we get little help from the wisdom of the ancients,"[13] there is a generous amount of ornamental learning concerning the various opinions of different philosophers, written from a respectful distance and unmarred by undue intimacy with the subject-matter. Why a great university, which is sometimes supposed to exist for the advancement of knowledge, should publish a book which contributes so little that is new to the subject, it is rather hard to say. Possibly it is to show us the actual state of juristic learning and thought on the basis of which the leaders of the American bar have undertaken to educate the public as to the just solution of current political issues.

The Birthright of Esau[1]

A TEACHER of ethics who wanted to warn his class against the dangers of answering foolish casuistical questions according to their folly recently asked why it was wrong of Esau to sell his birthright for a mess of pottage. The members of the class were somewhat mature urban college students. Many of them called themselves radicals. Yet not one of them thought of suggesting that the ethical blame, if any, should rest rather on the tricky exploiting Jacob. Instead they ingeniously invented all sorts of reasons why Esau should be condemned for preferring to be saved from immediate exhaustion even at the expense of a future interest in a presumably large amount of property. The reason that found most favour with members of this class was that it was Esau's duty to accumulate as much property as possible to leave to *his* children. This incident, perfectly authentic, is characteristic of the large extent to which primitive tribalism still dominates the prevailing moral attitude in such questions as those of inheritance. Generations of Bible readers have evinced no moral indignation at the atrocious way in which Joseph used his control of the food market to acquire all the money, cattle, land, and bodies of the Egyptians. He did not do it to his own people, but to the Egyptians, and for that he deserved a double portion of his father's inheritance.

There can be no doubt that our ideas of inheritance date back to the tribal organization of society, and are supported today by social inertia even more than by the sentiment that puts individual family loyalty above the larger public good. The fact that this tribalism is largely ingrained and unavowed does not diminish its potency, a potency that makes the attempt of Mr. Read, in *The Abo-*

lition of Inheritance, to discuss the question on purely rational grounds seem pathetically futile. On purely rational grounds Mr. Read proves his case beyond a shadow of a doubt. The inheritance [2] of wealth means the rule of the living by the dead. The substance inherited consists, for the most part, not of goods for the nourishing and protection of the young, but of legal power whereby the favoured beneficiaries may continue to tax the labour of the rest of the community (in the form of dividends, rents, and interest charges). Inherited wealth, therefore, involves inherited poverty. The unconscionable sophistries by which this is so often supported are mercilessly refuted by Mr. Read. He does not seem to realize, however, that the arguments usually adduced in justification of our inheritance system are just intellectual exercises in the realm of apologetics, and have little to do with the real origin and maintenance of the system.

While books of arguments, like Mr. Read's, cannot directly overthrow a system based on established habits and prejudices, they are none the less useful in knocking off the protective paint of moral and intellectual respectability that always covers the ugly features of reigning iniquities.

So accustomed have we become to see property transferred by will or testament that we find it difficult to imagine any civilized society without laws that protect this custom. In this state of mind, any argument which seems to justify or show the necessity of this legal institution is apt to seem valid. But the right to dispose of property in this way is a relatively recent one in human history, and the reasons given for its necessity today will not withstand critical reflection.

So well established today is the law giving men who have any property the right to direct what shall be done with it after their death that the idea has arisen that the law of intestacy, directing how the property shall be distributed when there is no will, is a sort of afterthought of the law of wills, and jurists often discuss it as if it were an attempt of the legislature to do that which the deceased would have done if he had made a will. This view, however, is a perversion of the facts of history. It is rather the law of testamentary disposition that represents a relatively modern invention. Among the Romans, it seems to have originated as a substitute or extension of the custom of adopting a son when there were no sons to continue the family worship. In England the right to make a will to dispose of land—the basic form of property—did not come into being until the reign of Henry VIII, and this right has generally been in effect restricted by the entailing of estates. Historically the original and universal idea of inheritance is not at all concerned with the power or natural right of the deceased individual. It is simply a consequence of the fact that ownership is vested in the family as a whole, so that when any individual dies there must be some adjustment between the remaining members as to the use of the property. It is only in the recent régime of extreme individualism, when property has become very mobile and the economic solidarity of the family weakened, that the testamentary disposition of one's goods has become normal. In Europe, where land is more limited than in America and the economic solidarity of the family is greater, there are still important restrictions on the right to dispose of one's patrimony by will.

This historical perspective of the conditions of inheritance puts us in a clearer position to discuss the merits of any proposal to restrict or modify the legal institution. The classical argument is that a man's property is his own and that therefore he has an absolute right to dispose of it as he pleases. This, however, simply begs the whole question. The institution of the last will and testament is a creation of positive law, and is nowhere entirely unrestricted. If it is to be defended at all, it must be on the ground that it serves some desirable social end. This is what the individualistic philosophy maintains in the following argument:

The productivity of goods necessary for human welfare depends on individual exertion. One of the strongest incentives to such exertion is the desire to provide for one's children or to build up a large family fortune to continue the glory of the builder. Hence any restriction on the right to dispose of our goods after death will diminish the motive for the productivity that is necessary for the economic welfare of any society.

The first observation to make is that this argument considers only those who make a fortune and not those who inherit it. It is also well to note in passing that mere productivity is not necessarily conducive to social welfare. But, waiving these two points, we must clearly distinguish between socially desirable productivity and the individual profit that can lead to the accumulation of any considerable fortune under modern conditions. Great fortunes are nowadays generally made through financial manipulations in which the productive powers of others largely enter, or through the unearned increment brought about by increased social demand and rising prices. And even in the manufacture of goods, no man is productive alone, and great fortunes are made through the fact that some get a larger share of the collective output than others do. The argument that men would not work efficiently without the hope of leaving a fortune ignores the vast rôle that non-pecuniary incentives play in men's working lives. Consider the soldier, the priest, or the judge, or the activities of the ordinary man in which love or hate, pride or the esteem of his fellow men, or even the mere desire to be active, is the driving force. The more we reflect in this direction, the more does the notion that pecuniary profit on a large scale is the major incentive to productive work seem the expression of a provincialism that never ventures beyond the narrow boundaries of the contemporary business world.

The argument that men would not work enough unless motivated by the hope of leaving a fortune to their relatives or friends gives to the anticipation of death a greater rôle than it plays in the daily conduct of most men. Men commonly act as if the contention of some idealistic philosophers were true, namely, that the world could not exist without us. The important choices in our lives are made in the light of considerations more immediate and pressing than the disposition of our wealth after our death.

In recent years a great many people have come to speak of property as a public trust. The owner of property is under modern conditions a ruler of those men who are dependent on the things over which he has dominion. Why may not such rulership be held for life only? Formerly it was thought that hereditary monarchy was the only stable and efficient government. But now we elect our rulers for limited periods or in the case of certain officials, like judges, for life. Why may not a man administer his public trust as efficiently if his office terminates with his natural life?

The argument that every one wishes to provide for his children, and fears to leave them in a condition of economic insecurity, moves in a vicious circle. For this fear itself springs from the present order of property distribution. Any social arrangement that protects the interests of all children naturally removes this necessity for providing for a few.

It is, of course, true that any sudden abolition of our laws of inheritance, like any other sudden change, would be a social shock and defeat the natural expectations of a large part of the community. But the result can be, and in a measure is being, achieved through steeply graduated inheritance taxes. Such taxes are not only just in themselves, but offer the least disturbance to the business life of any community.

New Leadership in the Law[1]

IN ELECTING Roscoe Pound the dean of its law school, Harvard has chosen not only a man who is fit to continue the splendid tradition of Langdell and Ames, but, what is still better, one who is bound to create a new and vital tradition on his own account. Scholars may debate whether the new dean has Langdell's power of seemingly unanswerable logical analysis, or Ames's rare combination of logical subtlety with creative historical imagination. But for all-around comprehensive knowledge of the law and juristic thought in their diverse branches and phases, including Roman and modern European law as well as our own legislation and common law, Professor Pound has set a new standard of legal scholarship.

Scholarship is an unfortunate and much misunderstood term. It suggests to most people insensibility to immediate vital interests and a morbid preference for things long dead. Hence, though people generally admit that scholarship has some value, they think of it as a necessary evil. Nor is this view altogether unfounded. Scholarship does withdraw men from the common life, and frequently distorts their perspective of it. The man who spends years as do our Ph.D. candidates, on a topic sufficiently minute to have escaped the attention of all previous writers, cannot help attaching undue importance to the subject-matter of his particular investigation. The outside world knows that while the thorough mastery of details may be the beginning of wisdom, it is not or ought not to be its end. But art is long while life is short, and most of those who set out with the ideal of scholarly mastery of details have to quit the scene before they have learned the bare alphabet in which life's problems are written. Only rarely does a scholar arise who not only is able to dig out the stones of learning but also knows how to put them together to make a more commodious home for the human spirit. Anglo-American legal scholarship has produced few men of this type, but Roscoe Pound is surely one of them.

The sea of legal learning is deep and wide, and most difficult of navigation are many of its currents. Much wasted experience has persuaded legal scholars that it is futile to pay attention to philosophers, sociologists, or political scientists who, on the basis of some distant glimpse, attempt to chart the whole of that difficult sea. It is easy to convert past failures into dogmas. Hence the prevailing attitude among legal scholars that the consideration of the aim of the law falls in the hazy realms of philosophy and politics, outside the proper domain of accurate legal scholarship. Professor Pound, however, has been convinced that a general view of the law, its function, resources, and limitations, is indispensable for a sound administration of justice, the end for which law and law schools exist. To this end he seems in a most astonishing way—for a man who has been teacher, captain of militia, botanist, practising lawyer, and judge—to have utilized all the available legal and extra-legal sources. So thoroughly has he worked both on details and on principles that his utterances command the highest respect of the hard-headed practical lawyers who compose our various bar associations, as well as the despairing admiration of students of legal and social philosophy. The mere attempt at so thorough and comprehensive a view of the law as an integral part of life is notable, apart from any specific results.

Thorough legal scholars have never fully subscribed to the loud proclamation of the politician-lawyers that our law is the embodiment of perfect reason and justice, the envy of all peoples, etc. But legal scholars have always tended to regard the main features of the traditional common law as fixed principles by which human affairs must eternally be governed. Even as keen and sensitive a mind as Ames's viewed the distinction between equitable and common-law remedies as something inherent in the very nature of things, which no demands of justice or social need could override. One of the achievements of Professor Pound is to have challenged this dogma of the finality of the common law as the beginning of wisdom and the eternal jural order. Law is a means, not an end. The end is a just life between living human beings here and now. As social conditions change, the law must keep pace. Our law received its present form in a rural economy uncomplicated by conditions of extreme inequality, where there was little need and, considering how widely people were scattered, little opportunity for governmental interference. But "in our modern industrial society, this whole scheme of individual (legal) initiative is breaking down. Private prosecution has become obsolete. Mandamus and injunction have failed to prevent rings and bosses from plundering public funds. Private suits against carriers for damages have proved no preventive of discrimination and extortionate rates. The doctrine of assumption of risk becomes brutal under modern conditions of employment. An action for damages is no comfort to us when we are sold diseased beef or poisonous canned goods. At all these points, and they are points of everyday contact with the most vital public interests, common-law methods of relief have failed." [2]

Professor Pound calls attention to the fact that "in intervals of work the farmer, remote from the distractions of city life, found his theatre in the court house and looked to politics and litigation for amusement." [3] Hence arose what he calls the sporting theory of justice. "The common law theory of litigation is that of a fair fist-fight, according to the canons of the manly art, with a court to see fair play and prevent interference. . . . We strive in every way to restrain the trial judge and to insure the individual litigants a fair fight, unhampered by mere considerations of justice. To give them this fair play we sacrifice public time and money; incidentally also —for if all men are equal, their pocketbooks are not—giving certain litigants a conspicuous advantage in reality, through a theoretical equality." [4] "The individual, in short, gets so much fair play that the public gets very little." [5]

Popular dissatisfaction with the administration of justice in this country has in the past decade found a good deal of rather crude expression, and some of our legal muck-rakers have made the judicious grieve by the carelessness or even the dishonesty of their reports. But they are poor doctors who become vexed with their patient because he makes a wrong diagnosis of what is really troubling him or suggests an unscientific remedy. Professor Pound has been very outspoken in regard to cheap diagnosis and worse remedies, but he has always kept in mind that "in large part this dissatisfaction has a real basis and is well founded." [6] Whenever and wherever things go wrong, popular habit attributes it to "bad" men—"bosses," "reactionary judges," etc.—and seeks for ways of getting rid of them. Pound has shown that the fundamental difficulty with our administration of justice has its roots in our national tradition and organization—the individualistic tradition of our bills of rights, which up to recently held almost complete sway, and our judicial organization, whereby the administration of law for urban communities is reviewed and thus dictated by men who have no experience or knowledge of the social problems of those communities.[7] "Both by bills of rights and by separation of powers and checks and balances, the eighteenth century and the pioneer or rural communities of the nineteenth century, from which our constitutions so largely proceed, sought to hold down all the activities of government. On the contrary, the conditions of modern city life call upon us to set them free and to make government an instrument of securing social interests which are endangered by individual freedom of action." [8] The old law has been defended on the ground that it makes for self-reliant character. But this, Professor Pound has shown, is not historically or actually true. The old tradition simply serves now to defeat "the right of society to stand between our labouring population and oppression." [9] To persist in applying the individualist philosophy of our common law to modern urban and industrial conditions is reckless and cruel injustice.

"Law," Langdell once said, "is to be found in books"; and that has been the basis of the improved as well as the old system of legal education. Roscoe Pound is, as far as I know, the first of our legal scholars to direct attention to the fact that the cases reported in printed books represent the law as it is only for those who can afford the expense of long litigation culminating in appeal. For the great mass of our urban population law is administered by police and municipal courts. The amount of money involved in a case may determine the lawyer's fee, but not the inherent importance of the matter in controversy to the parties. Two weeks' wages may be less than twenty-five dollars and still be of greater importance to the worker's family than a debt of a million is to the United States Steel Corporation. Yet our whole legal system has its energy directed to the higher courts, and the judge of our lower court is frequently an "oriental cadi administering justice at the city gate by the light of nature tempered by the state of his digestion for the time being." [10] It is a denial of justice to make poor people hire lawyers, and "it is a shame to drive them to legal aid societies to get as a charity what the state should give as a right." [11] The lower courts are entitled to judges just as good as those sent to the highest.

The public is vitally affected by the work of our law schools, for it is they "that preserve our old legal philosophy and prevent the best educated of our Bar from being children of the present." [12] "So long as the one object is to train practitioners who can make money at the Bar, and so long as schools are judged chiefly by their success in affording such training, we may expect nothing better." [13]

The modern teacher of law "should know not only what the courts decide and the principles by which they decide, but quite as much the circumstances and conditions, social and economic, to which these principles are to be applied; he should know the state of popular thought and feeling which make the environment in which the principles must operate in practice. Legal monks who pass their lives in an atmosphere of pure law, from which every worldly and human element is excluded, cannot shape practical principles to be applied to a restless world of flesh and blood." [14]

Langdell revolutionized the teaching of law and raised the standard of the legal profession by insisting on the simple principle that law is a science. Mr. Pound is sure to produce an equally important and beneficent revolution by insisting on the more obvious principle that law is a social science.

BOOK TWO

LAW AND THE SOCIAL ORDER

Property and Sovereignty [1]

PROPERTY and sovereignty, as every student knows, belong to entirely different branches of the law. Sovereignty is a concept of political or public law and property belongs to civil or private law. This distinction between public and private law is a fixed feature of our law-school curriculum. It was expressed with characteristic eighteenth-century neatness and clarity by Montesquieu, when he said that by political laws we acquire liberty and by civil law property, and that we must not apply the principles of one to the other.[2] Montesquieu's view that political laws must in no way retrench on private property, because no public good is greater than the maintenance of private property, was echoed by Blackstone and became the basis of legal thought in America. Though Austin, with his usual prolix and near-sighted sincerity, managed to throw some serious doubts on this classical distinction,[3] it has continued to be regarded as one of the fixed divisions of the jural field. In the second volume of his *Genossenschaftsrecht* the learned Gierke treated us to some very interesting speculations as to how the Teutons became the founders of public law just as the Romans were the founders of private law. But in later years he somewhat softened this sharp distinction;[4] and common-law lawyers are inclined rather to regard the Roman system as giving more weight to public than to private law.

The distinction between property and sovereignty is generally identified with the Roman discrimination between *dominium*, the rule over things by the individual, and *imperium*, the rule over all individuals by the prince. Like other Roman distinctions, this has been regarded as absolutely fixed in the nature of things. But early Teutonic law—the law of the Anglo-Saxons, Franks, Visigoths,

41

Lombards, and other tribes—makes no such distinction; and the state long continued to be the prince's estate, so that even in the eighteenth century the Prince of Hesse could sell his subjects as soldiers to the King of England. The essence of feudal law—a system not confined to medieval Europe—is the inseparable connection between land tenure and personal homage involving often rather menial services on the part of the tenant and always genuine sovereignty over the tenant by the landlord.

The feudal baron had, for instance, the right to determine the marriage of the ward; as well as the right to nominate the priest; and the great importance of the former as a real property right is amply attested in Magna Carta and in the Statute Quia Emptores. Likewise was the administration of justice in the baron's court an incident of landownership; and if, unlike the French up to the Revolution, the English did not regard the office of judge as a revenue-producing incident of seigniorage to be sold in the open market (as army commissions were up to the time of Gladstone), the local squire did in fact continue to act as justice of the peace. Ownership of the land and local political sovereignty were inseparable.

Can we dismiss all this with the simple exclamation that all this is medieval and we have long outgrown it?

Well, right before our eyes the Law of Property Act of 1925 is sweeping away substantial remains of the complicated feudal land laws of England, by abolishing the difference between the descent of real and that of personal property, and by abolishing all legal (though not equitable) estates intermediate between leaseholds and fees simple absolute. These remains of feudalism have not been mere vestiges. They have played an important part in the national life of England. Their absurdities and indefensible abuses were pilloried with characteristic wit and learning by the peerless Maitland. The same thing had been done most judiciously by Joshua Williams, the teacher of several generations of English lawyers brought up on the seventeen editions of his great text-book on real property law. Yet these and similar efforts made no impression on the actual law.

What these great men did not see with sufficient clearness was that back of the complicated law of settlement, fee-tail, copyhold estates, of the heir-at-law, of the postponement of women, and other feudal incidents, there was a great and well-founded fear that by simplifying and modernizing the real property law of England the land might become more marketable. Once land becomes fully marketable it can no longer be counted on to remain in the hands of the landed aristocratic families; and this means the passing of their political power and the end of their control over the destinies of the British Empire. For if American experience has demonstrated anything, it is that the continued leadership by great families cannot be as well founded on a money as on a land economy. The same kind of talent that enables Jay Gould to acquire dominion over certain railroads enables Mr. Harriman to take it away from his sons. From the point of view of an established land economy, a money economy thus seems a state of perpetual war instead of a social order where son succeeds father. The motto that a career should be open to talent thus seems a justification of anarchy, just as the election of rulers (kings or priests) seems an anarchic procedure to those used to the regular succession of father by son.

That which was hidden from Maitland, Joshua Williams, and the other great ones, was revealed to a Welsh solicitor who in the budget of 1910 proposed to tax the land so as to force it on the market. The radically revolutionary character of this proposal was at once recognized in England. It was bitterly fought by all those who treasured what had remained of the old English aristocratic rule. When this budget finally passed, the basis of the old real property law and the effective power of the House of Lords was gone. The legislation of 1925-26 was thus a final completion in the realm of private law of the revolution that was fought in 1910 in the forum of public law, i.e., in the field of taxation and the power of the House of Lords.

As the terms "medievalism" and "feudalism" have become with us terms of opprobrium, we are apt to think that only unenlightened selfishness has until recently prevented English land law from cutting its medieval moorings and embarking on the sea of purely money or commercial economy. This light-hearted judgment, however, may be somewhat sobered by reflection on a second recent event—the Supreme Court decision on the Minimum Wage Law.[5] Without passing judgment at this point on the soundness of the reasoning whereby the majority reached its decision, the result may still fairly be characterized as a high-water mark of law in a purely money or commercial economy. For by that decision private monetary interests receive precedence over the sovereign duty of the state to maintain decent standards of living.

The state, which has an undisputed right to prohibit contracts against public morals or public policy, is here declared to have no right to prohibit contracts under which many receive wages less than the minimum of subsistence, so that if they are not the objects of humiliating public or private charity, they become centres of the physical and moral evils that result from systematic underfeeding and degraded standards of life. Now I do not wish here to argue the merits or demerits of the minimum wage decision. Much less am I concerned with any quixotic attempt to urge England to go back to medievalism. But the two events together show in strong relief how recent and in the main exceptional is the extreme position of the laissez faire doctrine, which, according to the insinuation of Justice Holmes, has led the Supreme Court to read Herbert Spencer's extreme individualism into the Fourteenth Amendment, and according to others, has enacted Cain's motto, "Am I my brother's keeper?" as the supreme law of industry. Dean Pound has shown [6] that in making a property right out of the freedom to contract, the Supreme Court has stretched the meaning of the term "property" to include what it has never before signified in the law or jurisprudence of any civilized country. But whether this extension is justified or not, it certainly means the passing of a certain domain of sovereignty from the state to the private employer of labour, who now has the absolute right to discharge and threaten to discharge any employee who wants to join a trade-union, and the absolute right to pay a wage that is injurious to a basic social interest.

It may be that economic forces will themselves correct the abuse which the Supreme Court does not allow the state to remove directly, that economic forces will eliminate parasitic industries which do not pay the minimum of subsistence, because such industries are not as economically efficient and profitable as those which pay higher wages. It was similarly argued that slavery was bound to disappear on account of its economic inefficiency. Meanwhile, however, the sovereignty of the state is limited by the manner in which the courts interpret the term "property" in the Fifth and Fourteenth Amendments to the Federal Constitution and in the bills of rights in our state constitutions. This makes it imperative for us to consider the nature of private property with reference to the sovereign power of the state to look after the general welfare. A dispassionate scientific study of this requires an examination of the nature of property, its justification, and the ultimate meaning of the policies based on it.

I. PROPERTY AS POWER

Any one who frees himself from the crudest materialism readily recognizes that as a legal term "property" denotes not material things but certain rights. In the world of nature apart from more or less organized society, there are things but clearly no property rights.

Further reflection shows that a property right is not to be identified with the fact of physical possession. Whatever technical definition of property we may prefer, we must recognize that a property right is a relation not between an owner and a thing, but between the owner and other individuals in reference to things. A right is always against one or more individuals. This becomes unmistakably clear if we take specifically modern forms of property such as franchises, patents, goodwill, etc., which constitute such a large part of the capitalized assets of our industrial and commercial enterprises.

The classical view of property as a right over things resolves it into component rights such as the *jus utendi, jus disponendi,* etc. But the essence of private property is always the right to exclude others. The law does not guarantee me the physical or social ability of actually using what it calls mine. By public regulations it may indirectly aid me by removing certain general hindrances to the enjoyment of property. But the law of property helps me directly only to exclude others from using the things that it assigns to me. If, then, somebody else wants to use the food, the house, the land, or the plough that the law calls mine, he has to get my consent. To the extent that these things are necessary to the life of my neighbour, the law thus confers on me a power, limited but real, to make him do what I want. If Laban has the sole disposal of his daughters and his cattle, Jacob must serve him if he desires to possess them. In a régime where land is the principal source of obtaining a livelihood, he who has the legal right over the land receives homage and service from those who wish to live on it.

The character of property as sovereign power compelling service and obedience may be obscured for us in a commercial economy by the fiction of the so-called labour contract as a free bargain and by the frequency with which service is rendered indirectly through a money payment. But not only is there actually little freedom to bargain on the part of the steel-worker or miner who needs a job, but in some cases the medieval subject had as much power to bargain when he accepted the sovereignty of his lord. Today I do not directly serve my landlord if I wish to live in the city with a roof over my head, but I must work for others to pay him rent with which he obtains the personal services of others. The money needed for purchasing things must for the vast majority be acquired by hard labour and disagreeable service to those to whom the law has accorded dominion over the things necessary for subsistence.

To a philosopher this is of course not at all an argument against private property. It may well be that compulsion in the economic as well as the political realm is necessary for civilized life. But we must not overlook the actual fact that dominion over things is also *imperium* over our fellow human beings.

The extent of the power over the life of others which the legal order confers on those called owners is not fully appreciated by those who think of the law as merely protecting men in their possession. Property law does more. It determines what men shall acquire. Thus, protecting the property rights of a landlord means giving him the right to collect rent, protecting the property of a railroad or a public-service corporation means giving it the right to make certain charges. Hence the ownership of land and machinery, with the rights of drawing rent, interest, etc., determines the future distribution of the goods that will come into being—determines what share of such goods various individuals shall acquire. The average life of goods that are either consumable or used for production of other goods is very short. Hence a law that merely protected men in their possession and did not also regulate the acquisition of new goods would be of little use.

From this point of view it can readily be seen that when a court rules that a gas company is entitled to a return of 6 per cent on its investment, it is not merely protecting property already possessed, it is also determining that a portion of the future social produce shall under certain conditions go to that company. Thus not only medieval landlords but the owners of all revenue-producing property are in fact granted by the law certain powers to tax the future social product. When to this power of taxation there is added the power to command the services of large numbers who are not economically independent, we have the essence of what historically has constituted political sovereignty.

Though the sovereign power possessed by the modern large property owners assumes a somewhat different form from that formerly possessed by the lord of the land, they are not less real and no less extensive. Thus the ancient lord had a limited power to control the modes of expenditure of his subjects by direct sumptuary legislation. The modern captain of industry and of finance has no such direct power himself, though his direct or indirect influence with the legislature may in that respect be considerable. But those who have the power to standardize and advertise certain products do determine what we may buy and use. We cannot well wear clothes except within lines decreed by their manufacturers, and our food is becoming more and more restricted to the kinds that are branded and standardized.

This power of the modern owner of capital to make us feel the necessity of buying more and more of his material goods (that may be more profitable to produce than economical to use) is a phenomenon of the utmost significance to the moral philosopher. The moral philosopher must also note that the modern captain of industry or finance exercises great influence in setting the fashion of expenditure by his personal example. Between a landed aristocracy and the tenantry, the difference is sharp and fixed, so that imitation of the former's mode of life by the latter is regarded as absurd and even immoral. In a money or commercial economy differences of income and mode of life are more gradual and readily hidden, so that there is great pressure to engage in lavish expenditure in order to appear in a higher class than one's income really allows. Such expenditure may even advance one's business credit. This puts pressure not merely on ever greater expenditure but more specifically on expenditure for ostentation rather than for comfort. Though a landed aristocracy may be wasteful in keeping large tracts of land for hunting purposes, the need for discipline to keep in power compels the cultivation of a certain hardihood that the modern wealthy man can ignore. An aristocracy assured of its recognized superiority need not engage in the race of lavish expenditure regardless of enjoyment.

In addition to these indirect ways in which the wealthy few determine the mode of life of the many, there is the somewhat more direct mode that bankers and financiers exercise when they determine the flow of investment, e.g., when they influence building operations by the amount that they will lend on mortgages. This power becomes explicit and obvious when a needy country has to borrow foreign capital to develop its resources.

I have already mentioned that the recognition of private property as a form of sovereignty is not itself an argument against it. Some form of government we must always have. For the most part men prefer to obey and let others take the trouble to think out rules, regulations, and orders. That is why we are always setting up authorities; and when we cannot find any we write to the newspaper as the final arbiter. But although government is a necessity, not all forms of it are of equal value. At any rate it is necessary to apply to the law of property all those considerations of social ethics and enlightened public policy which ought to be brought to the discussion of any just form of government.

To do this, let us begin with a consideration of the usual justifications of private property.

II. THE JUSTIFICATION OF PROPERTY

1. *The Occupation Theory*

The oldest and until recently the most influential defence of private property was based on the assumed right of the original discoverer and occupant to dispose of that which thus became his. This view dominated the thought of Roman jurists and of modern philosophers—from Grotius to Kant—so much so that the right of the labourer to the produce of his work was sometimes defended on the ground that the labourer "occupied" the material that he fashioned into the finished product.

It is rather easy to find fatal flaws in this view. Few accumulations of great wealth were ever simply found. Rather were they acquired by the labour of many, by conquest, by business manipulation, and by other means. It is obvious that today at any rate few economic goods can be acquired by discovery and first occupancy.[7] Even in the few cases when they are, as in fishing and trapping, we are apt rather to think of the labour involved as the proper basis of the property acquired. Indeed, there seems nothing ethically self-evident in the motto "Findings is keepings." There seems nothing wrong in a law that a treasure trove shall belong to the king or the state rather than to the finder. Shall the finder of a river be entitled to all the water in it?

Moreover, even if we were to grant that the original finder or occupier should have possession as against any one else, it by no means follows that he may use it arbitrarily or that his rule shall prevail indefinitely after his death. The right of others to acquire the property from him, by bargain, by inheritance, or by testamentary disposition, is not determined by the principle of occupation.

Despite all these objections, however, there is a kernel of positive value in this principle. Protecting the discoverer or first occupant is really part of the more general principle that possession as such should be protected. There is real human economy in doing so until somebody shows a better claim than the possessor. It makes for certainty and security of transaction as well as for public peace—provided the law is ready to set aside possession acquired in ways that are inimical to public order. Various principles of justice may determine the distribution of goods and the retribution to be made for acts of injustice. But the law must not ignore the principle of inertia in human affairs. Continued possession creates expectations in the possessor and in others, and only a very poor morality would ignore the hardship of frustrating these expectations and rendering human relations insecure, even to correct some old flaws in the original acquisition. Suppose some remote ancestor of yours did acquire your property by fraud, robbery, or conquest, e.g., in the days of William of Normandy. Would it be just to take it away from you and your dependents who have held it in good faith? Reflection on the general insecurity that would result from such procedure leads us to see that as habit is the basis of individual life, continued practice must be the basis of social procedure. Any form of property that exists has therefore a claim to continue until it can be shown that the effort to change it is worth while. Continual changes in property laws would certainly discourage enterprise.

Nevertheless, it would be as absurd to argue that the distribution of property must never be modified by law as it would be to argue that the distribution of political power must never be changed. No less a philosopher than Aristotle argued against changing even bad laws, lest the habit of obedience be thereby impaired. There is something to be said for this, but only so long as we are in the realm of merely mechanical obedience. When we introduce the notion of free or rational obedience, Aristotle's argument loses its force in the political realm; and similar considerations apply to any property system that can claim the respect of rational beings.

2. *The Labour Theory*

That every one is entitled to the full produce of his labour is assumed as self-evident both by socialists and by conservatives who believe that capital is the result of the savings of labour. However, as economic goods are never the result of any one man's unaided labour, our maxim is altogether inapplicable. How shall we determine what part of the value of a table should belong to the carpenter, to the lumberman, to the transport worker, to the policeman who guarded the peace while the work was being done, and to the indefinitely large numbers of others whose coöperation was necessary? Moreover, even if we could tell what any one individual has produced—let us imagine a Robinson Crusoe growing up all alone on an island and in no way indebted to any community—it would still be highly questionable whether he has a right to keep the full produce of his labour when some shipwrecked mariner needs his surplus food to keep from starving.

In actual society no one ever thinks it unjust that a wealthy old bachelor should have part of his presumably just earnings taken away in the form of a tax for the benefit of other people's children, or that one immune to certain diseases should be taxed to support hospitals, etc. We do not think there is any injustice involved in such cases because social interdependence is so intimate that no man can justly say: "This wealth is entirely and absolutely mine as the result of my own unaided effort."

The degree of social solidarity varies, of course; and it is easy to conceive of a sparsely settled community, such as Missouri at the beginning of the nineteenth century, where a family of hunters or isolated cultivators of the soil might regard everything that it acquired as the product of its own labour. Generally, however, human beings start with a stock of tools or information acquired from others and they are more or less dependent upon some government for protection against foreign aggression, etc.

Yet despite these and other criticisms, the labour theory contains too much substantial truth to be brushed aside. The essential truth is that labour has to be encouraged and that property must be distributed in such a way as to encourage ever greater efforts at productivity.

As not all things produced are ultimately good, as even good things may be produced at an unjustified expense in human life and worth, it is obvious that other principles besides that of labour or productivity are needed for an adequate basis or justification of any system of property law. We can only say dialectically that all other things being equal, property should be distributed with due regard to the productive needs of the community. We must, however, recognize that a good deal of property accrues to those who are not productive,[8] and a good deal of productivity does not and perhaps should not receive its reward in property. Nor should we leave this theme without recalling the Hebrew-Christian view—and for that matter, the specifically religious view—that the first claim on property is by the man who needs it rather than the man who has created it. Indeed, the only way of justifying the principle of distribution of property according to labour is to show that it serves the larger social need.

The occupation theory has shown us the necessity for security of possession, and the labour theory the need for encouraging enterprise. These two needs are mutually dependent. Anything that discourages enterprise makes our possessions less valuable, and it is obvious that it is not worth while engaging in economic enterprise if there is no prospect of securely possessing the fruit of it. Yet there is also a conflict between these two needs. The owners of land, wishing to secure the continued possession by the family, oppose laws that make it subject to free financial transactions or make it possible that land should be taken away from one's heirs by a judgment creditor for personal debts. In an agricultural economy security of possession demands that the owner of a horse should be able to reclaim it no matter into whose hands it has fallen. But in order that markets should be possible, it becomes necessary that the innocent purchaser should have a good title. This conflict between static and dynamic security has been treated most suggestively by Demogue.[9]

3. Property and Personality

Hegel, Ahrens, Lorimer, and other idealists have tried to deduce the right of property from the individual's right to act as a free personality. To be free one must have a sphere of self-assertion in the external world. One's private property provides such an opportunity.

Waiving all traditional difficulties in applying the metaphysical idea of freedom to empirical legal acts, we may still object that the notion of personality is too vague to enable us to deduce definite legal consequences by means of it. How, for example, can the principle of personality help us to decide to what extent there shall be private rather than public property in railroads, mines, gas-works, and other public necessities?

Not the extremest communist would deny that in the interest of privacy certain personal belongings such as are typified by the toothbrush must be under the dominion of the individual owner, to the absolute exclusion of every one else. This, however, will not carry us far if we recall that the major effect of property in land, in the machinery of production, in capital goods, etc., is to enable the owner to exclude others from *their necessities,* and thus to compel them to serve him. Ahrens, one of the chief expounders of the personality theory, argues: "It is undoubtedly contrary to the right of personality to have persons dependent on others on account of material goods." [10] But if this is so, the primary effect of property on a large scale is to limit freedom, since the one thing that private property law does not do is to guarantee a minimum of subsistence or the necessary tools of freedom to every one. So far as a régime of private property fails to do the latter it rather compels people to part with their freedom.

It may well be argued in reply that just as restraining traffic rules in the end give us greater freedom of motion, so, by giving control over things to individual property owners, greater economic freedom is in the end assured to all. This is a strong argument, as can be seen by comparing the different degrees of economic freedom that prevail in lawless and in law-abiding communities. It is, however, an argument for legal order rather than for any particular form of government or private property. It argues for a régime where every one has a definite sphere of rights and duties, but it does not tell us where these lines should be drawn. The principle of freedom of personality certainly cannot justify a legal order wherein a few can, by virtue of their legal monopoly over necessities, compel others to work under degrading and brutalizing conditions. A government that limits the right of large landholders limits the rights of property, and yet may promote real freedom. Property owners, like other individuals, are members of a community and must subordinate their ambition to the larger whole of which they are a part. They may find their compensation in spiritually identifying their good with that of the larger life.

4. *The Economic Theory*

The economic justification of private property is that by means of it a maximum of productivity is promoted. The classical economic argument may be put thus: The successful business man, the one who makes the greatest profit, is the one who has the greatest power to foresee effective demand. If he has not that power his enterprise fails. He is therefore, in fact, the best director of economic activities.

There can be little doubt that if we take the whole history of agriculture and industry, or compare the economic output in Russia under the *mir* system with that in the United States, there is a strong *prima facie* case for the contention that more intensive cultivation of the soil and greater productiveness of industry prevail under individual ownership. Many *a priori* psychologic and economic reasons can also be brought to explain why this must be so, why the individual cultivator will take greater care not to exhaust the soil, etc. All this, however, is so familiar that we may take it for granted and look at the other side of the case, at the considerations which show that there is a difference between socially desirable productivity and the desire for individual profits.

In the first place, let us note that of many things the supply is not increased by making them private property. This is obviously true of land in cities and of other monopoly or limited goods. Private ownership of land does not increase the amount of rainfall, and irrigation works to make the land more fruitful have been carried through by governments more than by private initiative. Nor was the productivity of French or Irish lands reduced when the property of their landlords in rent charges and other incidents of seigniorage was reduced or even abolished. In our own days, we frequently see tobacco, cotton, or wheat farmers in distress because they have succeeded in raising too plentiful crops; and manufacturers who are well informed know when greater profit is to be made by a decreased output. Patents for processes that would cheapen the product are often bought up by manufacturers and never used. Durable goods that are more economic to the consumer are very frequently crowded out of the market by shoddier goods which are more profitable to produce because of the larger turnover. Advertising campaigns often persuade people to buy the less economical goods and to pay the cost of the uneconomic advice.

In the second place, there are inherent sources of waste in a régime of private enterprise and free competition. If the biologic analogy of the struggle for existence were taken seriously, we should see that the natural survival of the economically fittest is attended, as in the biologic field, with frightful wastefulness. The elimination of the unsuccessful competitor may be a gain to the survivor, but all business failures are losses to the community.

Finally, a régime of private ownership in industry is too apt to sacrifice social interests to immediate monetary profits. This shows itself in speeding up industry to such a pitch that men are exhausted in a relatively few years, whereas a slower expenditure of their energy would prolong their useful years. It shows itself in the way in which private enterprise has wasted a good deal of the natural resources of the United States to obtain immediate profits. Even when the directors of a modern industrial enterprise see the uneconomic consequences of immediate profits, the demand of shareholders for immediate dividends,[11] and the ease with which men can desert a business and leave it to others to stand the coming losses, tend to encourage ultimately wasteful and uneconomic activity. Possibly the best illustration of this is child labour, which by lowering wages increases immediate profits, but in the end is really wasteful of the most precious wealth of the country, its future manhood and womanhood.

Surveying our arguments thus far: We have seen the roots of property in custom, in the need for economic productivity, and in individual needs of privacy. But we have also noted that property, being only one among other human interests, cannot be pursued absolutely without detriment to human life. Hence we can no longer maintain Montesquieu's view that private property is sacrosanct and

that the general government must in no way interfere with or retrench its domain. The issue before thoughtful people is therefore
not the maintenance or abolition of private property, but the determination of the precise lines along which private enterprise must be
given free scope and where it must be restricted in the interests of
the common good.

III. LIMITATIONS OF PROPERTY RIGHTS

The traditional theory of rights, and the one that still prevails
in this country, was moulded by the struggle in the seventeenth and
eighteenth centuries against restrictions on individual enterprise.
These restrictions in the interest of special privilege were fortified
by the divine (and therefore absolute) rights of kings. As is natural
in all revolts, absolute claims on one side were met with absolute
denials on the other. Hence the theory of the natural rights of the
individual took not only an absolute but a negative form: men have
*in*alienable rights, the state must never interfere with private property, etc. The state, however, must interfere in order that individual
rights should become effective and not degenerate into public nui-
sances. To permit any one to do absolutely what he likes with his
property in creating noise, smells, or danger of fire, would be to
make property in general valueless. To be really effective, therefore, the right of property must be supported by restrictions or positive duties on the part of owners, enforced by the state, as much as
by the right to exclude others that is the essence of property. Unfortunately, however, whether because of the general decline of juristic
philosophy after Hegel or because law has become more interested
in defending property against attacks by socialists, the doctrine of
natural rights has remained in the negative state and has never developed into a doctrine of the positive contents of rights based upon
an adequate notion of the function of these rights in society.[12]

Lawyers occupied with civil or private law have in any case continued the absolutistic conception of property; and in doing this,

they are faithful to the language of the great eighteenth century codes, the French, Prussian, and Austrian, and even of nineteenth century codes like the Italian and German, which also begin with a definition of property as absolute or unlimited, though they subsequently introduce qualifying or limiting provisions.[13]

As, however, no individual rights can in fact be exercised in a community except under public regulation, it has been left mainly to publicists,[14] to writers on politics and constitutional and administrative law, to consider the limitations of private property necessary for public safety, peace, health, and morals, as well as for those enterprises like housing, education, the preservation of natural resources, etc., which the community finds it necessary to entrust to the state rather than to private hands. The fact, however, that in the United States the last word on law comes from judges, who, like other lawyers, are for the most part trained in private rather than in public law, is one of the reasons why with us traditional conceptions of property prevail over obvious national interests such as the freedom of labourers to organize, the necessity of preserving certain standards of living, of preventing the future manhood and womanhood of the country from being sacrificed to individual profits, and the like. Our students of property law need, therefore, to be reminded that not only has the whole law since the industrial revolution shown a steady growth in ever new restrictions upon the use of private property, but that the ideal of absolute laissez faire has never in fact been completely operative.

(1) Living in a free land economy we have lost the sense of how exceptional in the history of mankind is the absolutely free power of directing what shall be done with our property after our death. In the history of the common law, wills as to land begin only in the reign of Henry VIII. On the Continent it is still restrained by the system of the reserve. In England no formal restriction has been necessary because of the system of entails or strict settlement. Even in the United States we have kept such rules as that against perpetu-

ities, which is certainly a restraint on absolute freedom of testamentary disposition.

Even as to the general power of alienating the land *inter vivos* history shows that some restrictions are always present. The persistence of dower rights in our own individualistic economy is a case in point. Land and family interest have been too closely connected to sacrifice the former completely to pure individualism. Though the interests of free exchange of goods and services have never been as powerful as in the last century, governments have not abandoned the right to regulate the rate of interest to be charged for the use of money, or to fix the price of certain other services of general public importance, e.g., railway rates, grain-elevator and warehouse charges, etc. The excuse that this applies only to business affected with a public interest, is a very thin one. What large business is there in which the public has not a real interest? Is coal less a public affair than gas, or electricity? Courts and conservative lawyers sometimes speak as if the regulation of wages by the state were a wild innovation that would upset all economic order as well as our legal tradition. Yet the direct regulation of wages has been a normal activity of English law; and we in fact regulate it indirectly by limiting hours of work, prohibiting payment in truck, enforcing certain periodic payments, etc.; and under the compensation acts the law compels an employer to pay his labourer when the latter cannot work at all on account of some accident.

(2) More important than the foregoing limitations upon the transfer of property are limitations on the use of property. Looking at the matter realistically, few will question the wisdom of Holdsworth's remarks, that "at no time can the state be wholly indifferent to the use which the owners make of their property." [15] There must be restrictions on the use of property not only in the interests of other property owners but also in the interests of the health, safety, religion, morals, and general welfare of the whole community. No community can view with indifference the exploitation of the needy by commercial greed. As under the conditions of crowded life the

reckless or unconscionable use of one's property is becoming more and more dangerous, enlightened jurists find new doctrines to limit the abuse of ancient rights. The French doctrine of *abus de droit*, the prohibition of chicanery in the German Civil Code, and the rather vague use of "malice" in the common law are all efforts in that direction.[16]

(3) Of greatest significance is the fact that in all civilized legal systems there is a great deal of just expropriation or confiscation without any direct compensation. This may sound shocking to those who think that for the state to take away the property of the citizen is not only theft or robbery but even worse, an act of treachery, since the state avowedly exists to protect people in those very rights.

As a believer in natural rights, I believe that the state can, and unfortunately often does, enact unjust laws. But I think it is a sheer fallacy based on verbal illusion to think that the rights of the community against an individual owner are no better than the rights of a neighbour. Indeed, no one has in fact had the courage of this confusion to argue that the state has no right to deprive an individual of property to which he is so attached that he refuses any money for it. Though no neighbour has such a right, the public interest often justly demands that a proprietor shall part with his ancestral home, to which he may be attached by all the roots of his being.

When taking away a man's property, is the state always bound to pay a direct compensation? I submit that while this is generally advisable in order not to disturb the general feeling of security, no absolute principle of justice requires it. I have already suggested that there is no injustice in taxing an old bachelor to educate the children of others, or taxing one immune to typhoid for the construction of sewers or other sanitary measures. We may go further and say that the whole business of the state depends upon its rightful power to take away the property of some (in the form of taxation) and use it to support others, such as the needy, those invalided in the service of the state in war or peace, and those who are not yet able to produce but in whom the hope of humanity is embodied. Doubtless, taxation and confiscation may be actuated by malice and may impose needless and cruel hardship on some individuals or classes. But this is not to deny that taxation and confiscation are within the just powers of the state. A number of examples may make this clearer.

(a) Slavery. When slavery is abolished by law, the owners have their property taken away. Is the state ethically bound to pay them the full market value of their slaves? It is doubtless a grievous shock to a community to have a large number of slave-owners, whose wealth often makes them leaders of culture, suddenly deprived of their income. It may also be conceded that it is not always desirable for the slave himself to be suddenly taken away from his master and cut adrift on the sea of freedom. But when one reads of the horrible ways in which some of those slaves were violently torn from their homes in Africa and shamelessly deprived of their human rights, one is inclined to agree with Emerson that compensation should first be paid to the slaves. This compensation need not be in the form of a direct bounty to them. It may be more effectively paid in the form of rehabilitation and education for freedom; and such a charge may take precedence over the claims of the former owners. After all, the latter claims are no greater than those of a protected industry when the tariff is removed. If the state should decide that certain import duties, e.g., those on scientific instruments or hospital supplies, are unjustified and proceed to abolish them, many manufacturers may suffer. Are they entitled to compensation by the state?

It is undoubtedly for the general good to obviate as much as possible the effect of economic shock to a large number of people. The routine of life prospers on security. But when that security contains a large element of injustice the shock of an economic operation by law may be necessary and ethically justified.

This will enable us to deal with other types of confiscation:

(b) Financial loss through the abolition of public office. It is only in very recent times that we have come to forget that public office is and always has been regarded as a source of revenue like any other occupation. When, therefore, certain public offices are abolished for the sake of good government, a number of people are deprived of their expected income. In the older law and often in popular judgment today this does not seem fair. But reflection shows that the state is not obligated to pay any one when it finds that particular services of his are unnecessary. At best, it should help him to find a new occupation.

Part of the prerogative of the English or Scotch landlord was the right to nominate the priest for the parish on his land. To abolish this right of advowson is undoubtedly a confiscation of a definite property right. But while I cannot agree with my friend Mr. Laski [17] that the courts were wrong to refuse to disobey the law that subordinated the religious scruples of a church to the property rights of an individual, I do not see that there could have been any sound ethical objection to the legislature's changing the law without compensating the landlord.

(c) In our own day, we have seen the confiscation of many millions of dollars' worth of property through prohibition. Were the distillers and brewers entitled to compensation for their losses? We have seen that property on a large scale is power, and the loss of it, while evil to those who are accustomed to exercise it, may not be an evil to the community. In point of fact, the shock to the distillers and brewers was not as serious as to others, e.g., saloon-keepers and bartenders, who did not lose any legal property since they were only employees, but who found it difficult late in life to enter new employments.

History is full of examples of valuable property privileges abolished without any compensation, e.g., the immunity of nobles from taxation, their rights to hunt over other persons' lands, etc. It would be absurd to claim that all such legislation was unjust.

These and other examples of justifiable confiscation without compensation are inconsistent with the absolute theory of private property. An adequate theory of private property, however, should enable us to draw the line between justifiable and unjustifiable cases of confiscation. Such a theory I cannot here undertake to elaborate, though the doctrine of security of possession and avoidance of unnecessary shock seem to me suggestive. I wish, however, to urge that if the large property owner is viewed, as he ought to be, as a wielder of power over the lives of his fellow citizens, the law should not hesitate to develop a doctrine as to his positive duties in the public interest. The owner of a tenement house in a modern city is in fact a public official and has all sorts of positive duties. He must keep the halls lighted, he must see that the roof does not leak, that there are fire-escape facilities; he must remove tenants guilty of certain public immoralities, etc.; and he is compensated by the fees of his tenants, which the law is beginning to regulate. Similar is the case of a factory owner. He must install all sorts of safety appliances, hygienic conveniences; see that the workmen are provided with a certain amount of light, air, etc.

In general, there is no reason for the law's insisting that people should make the most economic use of their property. They have a motive in doing so themselves and the cost of the enforcing machinery may be a mischievous waste. Yet there may be times, such as occurred during the late war, when the state may insist that man shall cultivate the soil intensively and be otherwise engaged in socially productive work.

With considerations such as these in mind, it becomes clear that there is no unjustifiable taking away of property when railroads are prohibited from posting notices that they will discharge their employees if the latter join trade unions, and that there is no property taken away without due or just process of law when an industry is compelled to pay its labourers a minimum of subsistence instead of having subsistence provided for them by private or public charity or else systematically starving its workers.

IV. POLITICAL VS. ECONOMIC SOVEREIGNTY

If the discussion of property by those interested in private law has suffered from a lack of realism and from too great a reliance on vague *a priori* plausibilities, much the same can be said about political discussion as to the proper limits of state action in regard to property and economic enterprise. Utterly unreal is all talk of men's being robbed of their power of initiative because the state undertakes some service, e.g., the building of a bridge across a river. Men are not deprived of opportunities for real self-reliance if the state lights their streets at night, fills up holes in the pavements, and removes other dangers to life and limb, or provides opportunities for education to all. The conditions of modern life are complex and distracting enough so that if we can ease the strain by simplifying some things through state action we are all the gainers by it. Certain things have to be done in a community and the question whether they should be left to private enterprise dominated by the profit motive, or to the government dominated by political considerations, is not a question of man versus the state, but simply a question of which organization and motive can best do the work. Both private and government enterprise are initiated and carried through by individual human beings. A realistic attitude would not begin with the assumption that all men in the government service are less or more intelligent or efficient than all those in private business. It would rather inquire what sort of people are drawn into government service and what attitudes their organization develops in contrast with that of private business. This is a matter for specific factual inquiry, unfortunately most sadly neglected. In the absence of such definite knowledge I can only venture a few guesses.

Government officials seem likely to be chosen more for their oratorical ability, popularly likable manners, and political availability, and less for their competence and knowledge of the problems with which they have to deal. The inheritance of wealth, however, may bring incompetent people for a while into control of private business. More serious is the fact that political officials have less incentive to initiate new ventures. Political leaders in touch with public sentiment are apt to be too conservative and prefer to avoid trouble by letting things alone. Their bureaucratic underlings, on whom they are more dependent than business executives are on theirs, are apt to overemphasize the value of red tape, i.e., to care more for uniformity of governmental procedure than for the diverse special needs to which they ought to minister. All business administration, however, also loses in efficiency as its volume increases. On the other hand, experience has shown all civilized peoples the indispensable need for communal control to prevent the abuse of private enterprise. Only a political or general government is competent to deal with a problem like city congestion, because only the general government can coördinate a number of activities some of which have no financial motive. Private business may be more efficient in saving money. It does so largely by paying smaller wages to the many and higher remuneration to those on top. From a social point of view this is not necessarily a good in itself. It is well to note that men of great ability and devotion frequently prefer to work for the government at a lower pay than they can obtain in private employment. There is something more than money in daily employment. Humanity prefers—not altogether unwisely—to follow the lead of those who are sensitive rather than those who are efficient. Business efficiency mars the beauty of our country-side with hideous advertising signs and would, if allowed, ruin the scenic grandeur of Niagara.

The subordination of everything to the single aim of monetary profit leads industrial government to take the form of absolute monarchy. Monarchy has a certain simplicity and convenience; but in the long run it is seldom the best for all concerned. Sooner or later it leads to insurrections. It is short-sighted to assume that an employer cannot possibly run his business without the absolute right to hire and fire his employees whenever he feels like doing so. It is interesting to note that even a modern army is run without giving

the general the absolute right to hire and fire. The Shah of Persia
was shocked when a British ambassador, Sir John Malcolm, informed him that the King of England could not at his pleasure
behead any of his courtiers. But Sir John Malcolm was equally
shocked to observe the elaborate precautions that the Shah had to
take against assassination.[18] May not democratic or limited constitutional government in industry have some human advantages over
unlimited monarchy? [19]

The main difficulty, however, with industrial and financial government is that the governors are released from all responsibility
for the actual human effects of their policies. Formerly, the employer could observe and had an interest in the health and morals
of his apprentice. Now, the owners or stockholders have lost all
personal touch with all but few of those who work for them. The
human element is thus completely subordinated to the profit motive. In some cases this even makes for industrial inefficiency, as
when railroads or other businesses are run by financiers in the interest of stock manipulation. Very often our captains of finance exercise power by controlling other people's funds. This was strikingly
shown when several millions of dollars were paid for some shares
that promised little or no direct return but which enabled the purchaser to control the assets of a great life insurance company. Professor Ripley has recently thrown Wall Street into a turmoil by
pointing out the extent to which promoters and financiers can with
little investment of their own control great industrial undertakings.

There can be no doubt that our property laws do confer sovereign
power on our captains of industry and even more so on our captains
of finance.

Now it would be unworthy of a philosopher to shy at government by captains of industry and finance. Humanity has been ruled
by priests, soldiers, hereditary landlords, and even antiquarian
scholars. The results are not such as to make us view with alarm
a new type of ruler. But if we are entering a new era involving

a new set of rulers, it is well to recognize it and reflect on what is involved.

For the first time in the history of mankind the producer of things is in the saddle—not of course the actual physical producer, but the master mind that directs the currents of production. If this is contrary to the tradition of philosophy from Plato down, we may well be told that our philosophy needs revision. Great captains of industry and finance like the late James J. Hill deal with problems in many respects bigger than those which faced Cæsar and Augustus in building the Roman Empire.

Still the fear may well be expressed that as modern life is becoming more and more complex it is dangerous to give too much sovereignty to those who are after all dealing with the rather simpler aspects of life involved in economic relations.

It may, of course, rightly be contended that the modern captain of industry is not merely concerned with the creation of things, that his success is largely determined by his judgment and ability to manage the large numbers of human beings that form part of his organization. Against this, however, there is the obvious retort that the only ability taken account of in the industrial and financial world, the ability to make money, is a very specialized one; and when business men get into public office they are not notably successful. Too often they forget that while saving the money of the taxpayer may be an admirable incident, it is not the sole or even the principal end of communal life and government. The wise expenditure of money is a more complicated problem than the mere saving it, and a no less indispensable task to those who face the question of how to promote a better communal life. To do this effectively we need a certain liberal insight into the more intangible desires of the human heart. Preoccupation with the management of property has not in fact advanced this kind of insight.

Many things are produced to the great detriment of the health and morals of the consumers as well as the producers. This refers not only to things that are inherently deleterious or enervating to those who create them and those who use them. It includes also many of the things of which people buy more than they need and more than is consistent with the peace and leisure of mind that is the essence of culture.

It is certainly a shallow philosophy that would make human welfare synonymous with the indiscriminate production and consumption of material goods. If there is one iota of wisdom in all the religions or philosophies that have supported the human race in the past it is that man cannot live by economic goods alone but needs vision and wisdom to determine what things are worth while and what things it would be better to do without. This profound human need of controlling and moderating our consumptive demands cannot be left to those whose dominant interest is to stimulate such demands.

It is characteristic of the low state of our philosophy that the merits of capitalism have been argued by both individualists and socialists exclusively from the point of view of the production and distribution of goods. To the more profound question as to what goods are ultimately worth producing from the point of view of the social effects on the producers and consumers almost no attention is paid. Yet surely this is a matter which requires the guidance of collective wisdom, not one to be left to chance or anarchy.

The Basis of Contract[1]

THE nature of contract has been much discussed by lawyers interested in specific technical doctrines, and by moralists, economists, and political theorists interested in general social philosophy. There is still need for some effort to combine these points of view. The bearings of general philosophy become more definite through its applications, and the meaning of a technical doctrine receives illumination when we see it in the light of those wider ideas of which it is the logical outcome.

This large and important task is obviously beyond the limits of a short paper. But a few suggestions may indicate something of the scope of the problem.

I. THE SOCIAL ROOTS OF CONTRACT

One of the most influential of modern saws is Maine's famous dictum that the progress of the law has been from status to contract. It has generally been understood as stating not only a historical generalization but also a judgment of sound policy—that a legal system wherein rights and duties are determined by the agreement of the parties is preferable to a system wherein they are determined by "status."

This easy assumption, that whatever happens to be the outcome of history is necessarily for the best and cannot or ought not to be counteracted by any human effort, is typical not only of the historical school of jurisprudence since Savigny, but also of the general progressive or evolutionary philosophy of Maine's generation and largely of our own. Accordingly pleas that under present conditions

69

we need certain limitations on the freedom of contract have encountered the objection that we must not go against history and
thereby revert to barbarism.

1. *Contract in History*

Before considering the validity of the last argument let us briefly
consider Maine's dictum from the point of view of the present state
of historical learning. For while the study of the past in itself is
not sufficient to determine desirable policies for today, it is necessary
to view reigning ideas in their perspective and past careers if we
are to separate them from their obsolete elements. In any case objections based on inadequate history can be fully met only on the
basis of sounder knowledge.

That Maine's generalization is not a universal and necessary law,
he himself recognized in his treatment of feudal land tenure.[2] The
rights and duties of sovereign and subject, of homage or fealty and
protecting lordship, were contractual in the early Middle Ages,
and gradually ceased to be so as they became customary and were
later replaced by the legislation of the modern national states. It
is also true, as Dicey, Hedemann, Charmont, Jethro Brown, Duguit,
and Pound have shown, that the modern state has, in all civilized
countries, been steadily increasing the scope of its functions, so
that men now do things by virtue of their status as citizens and
taxpayers which formerly they did by voluntary agreement. One
only needs to mention the fields of charity and education to make
this obvious. Moreover, in many relations in which men are more
or less free to enter into contracts, such as that between insurer and
insured, landlord and tenant, employer and employee, shipper and
carrier, the terms of the agreement are more and more being fixed
by law, so that the entering into these relations has something
analogous to the entering into the relation of marriage, trusteeship,
or public office. The specific rights and duties are not fixed by

agreement, though the assumption of the relations is more or less voluntary.

Nevertheless there is enough truth in Maine's observation to warrant a more discriminating attitude to it than that of complete acceptance or complete rejection.

Looking at the matter macroscopically rather than microscopically, there can be little doubt that legally binding agreements or promises play a smaller part in the earlier history of all known peoples. The development of contract is largely an incident of commercial and industrial enterprises that involve a greater anticipation of the future than is necessary in a simpler or more primitive economy. In the latter the solidarity of relatively self-sufficient family groups and the fear of departing from accustomed ways limit individual initiative as well as the scope and importance of what can be achieved by deliberate agreements or bargains. In some respects, however, less developed societies resort more than we do to contracts or compacts and enforce promises that we no longer enforce. Thus they preserve peace not by organized police or standing armies, but by agreements like our present treaties of peace between nations; and promises to the gods, which are now matters of individual conscience, used to be enforced by the community as a whole because it feared the undiscriminating effects of divine wrath.

It has been assumed since the days of Homer—it is involved in Montesquieu's story of the Troglodytes—that savage men make no compacts or agreements and do not attach importance to promises. This is a doubtful generalization, which modern anthropology does not confirm. We may, however, agree that while commerce in its early as in some of its later stages is connected with war and piracy—"Who would have faith in a tradesman's wares or his words?"—the main effect of widening markets has been in the long run to favour steady industry and reliance on promises as a basis for individual enterprise otherwise impossible. Extensive commerce, involving travel and contact with other peoples, leads to the observation of habits and ideas different from our own, and thus tends to introduce the disintegrating force of rational reflection into the hard crust of traditional mores and beliefs. Customary ideas and familiar ways of doing things thus lose their pristine fixity, and a certain amount of free individual thought and conduct is thus developed, despite the opposition to all innovations expressed by the conservative landed interests. In this state individual bargains or agreements necessarily receive increased attention from the law. This is repeatedly illustrated in the history of the ancient Jews, Greeks, and Romans and of medieval Europe.

The growth of the Hebrew law of contract in the Mishnah seems to have followed the expansion of commerce that came with the capture of their first seaport, Jaffa, by Simon Maccabæus. The older Deuteronomic law, that in the Sabbatical year released all debtors, naturally discouraged credit transactions at certain times. This inconvenience was overcome in the time of King Herod by the institution of the *prosbul*, a contract of record by which loans became debts to the court unaffected by the older law.[3] In general Talmudic jurisprudence favoured contracts, even in cases where religious scruples might have led to restrictions.[4] It is interesting to note that the notion of individual responsibility, a point in which religion, commerce, and ideas of contract or covenant meet, was first vigorously put forth when the Jews were settled in Babylonia, where they were largely engaged in commerce. I refer to the prophet Ezekiel. The older view held the family, tribe, or nation responsible for the acts of any one individual, whether he was a ruler like Saul or David or an ordinary rapacious soldier like Achan.[5] God visits the sins of the fathers upon the children to the third and the fourth generation. But the experience of transplantation to a foreign land led Ezekiel to the rejection of the older view that if the fathers eat sour grapes, the children's teeth are set on edge. "The righteousness of the righteous shall be upon him, and the wickedness of the wicked shall be upon him."[6] After this came the further reflection that sin is a voluntary act, an affair of the heart, and not something that can happen to you by involuntary contact with an object that is "unclean" or taboo, or even when with the most worshipful intentions in the world you touch a holy object.[7] The significance for the law of contract of this notion of individual responsibility for voluntary acts is too obvious to need development.

The same expansion of the law of free contracts under a predominantly commercial régime can be seen in the history of Greece. The Hellenic laws of contract seem to have allowed as much freedom of business transactions as any legal system known to us. This is particularly clear in Athens after the change, under Cleisthenes, from tribal organization and after the rapid expansion of commerce that followed in the fifth century B.C. The effect of commerce on the Roman law of contract can be seen in the change from the old rigid rules of the *jus civile* to those of the *jus gentium* and the prætor's edict. When, as a result of the Crusades and other influences, European trade began to expand, the law of contract was liberalized by the extensive use of the oath to bind verbal agreements [8]—a procedure to which the Church yielded support only after some reluctance in view of Christ's explicit prohibition: "Swear not at all."

The expansion of the régime of contract since the seventeenth century has been intimately related to the modern commercial revolution in northern Europe following the development of trade with India and America. The commercial revolution, even before the industrial one, served to transform a predominantly fixed land-economy into a more fluid and enterprising one on the basis of money and credit. This situation was largely responsible for the decay of the remaining feudal concepts and for the reception of the more commercial, Italianized Roman law in the period of the Renaissance. This movement, as Maitland has shown,[9] went so far even in England as to endanger the old common law—a danger from which we were "saved" by the vested interests of the practitioners who were organized in the Inns of Court. Even so, the rapid expansion of the modern law of contract took a direction in England not so widely different from that in Holland and France, and the work of Coke, Holt, and Mansfield is in many respects parallel to that of Grotius, Voet, Domat, Pothier, and the other commentators on modern civil or Roman law.

Maine's observation that the progress of the law is from status to contract is, therefore, partly true in certain periods of expanding trade. But close on the heels of expansion comes consolidation or closer organization; and in the wake of increased freedom of contract we find increased regulation, either through the growth of custom and standardization or through direct legislation. At no time does a community completely abdicate its right to limit and regulate the effect of private agreements, a right that it must exercise to safeguard what it regards as the interest of *all* its members.[10]

These very brief historic observations do not of course settle the issue. But they are sufficient to override the supposed veto of history, and to allow us to consider on their specific merits all questions as to the regulation of contract.

The support of Maine's dictum, however, did not come exclusively from legal history. It had its roots in the general individualistic philosophy that manifests itself in modern religion, metaphysics, psychology, ethics, economics, and political theory. Let us begin with the last.

2. *The Political Theory of Contractualism*

Contractualism in the law, i.e., the view that in an ideally desirable system of law all obligation would arise only out of the will of the individual contracting freely, rests not only on the will theory of contract but also on the political doctrine that all restraint is evil and that the government is best which governs least. This in turn is connected with the classical economic optimism that there is a sort of preëstablished harmony between the good of all and the pursuit by each of his own selfish economic gain. These politico-economic views involve the Benthamite hedonistic psychology, that happiness consists of individual states of pleasures and that each individual can best calculate what will please him most. Back of this faith of legal individualism is the modern metaphysical assumption that the atomic or individual mind is the supreme reality and the theologic view that sin is an act of individual free will, without which there can be no responsibility.

The argument that a régime of free contract assures the greatest amount of liberty for all is characteristic of the eighteenth-century philosophy of the Enlightenment and is still essential to the faith of Jeffersonian democracy behind our bills of rights. The older Calvinistic argument for government rested on the need of restraining the wickedness of man (due to the corruption of the flesh) by rules and magistrates deriving their power from God. Against this the deistic and bourgeois Enlightenment developed the contrary view, that men are inherently good and that their dark deeds have been due to the corruption and superstition brought about by tyrants and priests. As we get rid of the latter, the original benevolent nature of man asserts itself and history thus shows a gradual but steady progress in the direction of freedom. It was natural for the representatives of the growing commercial and industrial interests to view the state, controlled as it had been by landed barons and prelates (lords temporal and spiritual), as exclusively an instrument of oppression, and necessarily evil. But their argument overshot its mark. They forgot that not only industry but also the whole life of civilization depends on the feeling of security that the protection of the government or organized community affords.

The philosophy of freedom or liberty illustrates one of the most pervasive and persistent vices of reasoning on practical affairs, to wit, the setting up of premises that are too wide for our purpose and indefensible on their own account.

In the fierce fight against the numerous irrational, tyrannical, and oppressive restraints, men jump to the conclusion that the absence of all restraint is a good in itself and indeed the one absolute good in the political field. The error of this cult of freedom is of the same logical type as that of the tradition which it opposes. The latter argues that since our natural impulses are not free from bad consequences, therefore they are absolutely bad and must be made powerless by checks and balances or some other device. Both sets of arguments leap from the perception of what is evil under certain conditions to the affirmation of an untenable absolute. Let us consider the situation from this point of view.

Since what we want generally seems to us good, freedom, as the removal of obstacles to achievement, is a necessary part or condition of this good. But mere freedom as absence of restraint, without positive power to achieve what we deem good, is empty and of no real value. The freedom to make a million dollars is not worth a cent to one who is out of work. Nor is the freedom to starve, or to work for wages less than the minimum of subsistence, one that any rational being can prize—whatever learned courts may say to the contrary.

The tragic fallacy of supposing that mere absence of restraint or of other temporary evil can be an absolute good is poignantly illustrated when men, chafing at oppressive work or company, suppose that mere release will make them forever happy. When this release comes to us we may find ourselves abjectly miserable, not knowing what to do with ourselves. We then look for some other work that will absorb our attention or other company to fill our interests. So all revolutionists complaining against the oppression of government must as soon as they are successful—indeed, even to attain such success—set up a new government. The new work, the new company, or the new government must prove more congenial or beneficent if we are to escape or mitigate the human inclination to regret the struggle and the pain that brought about the change.

Does the state always and necessarily seek to oppress the individual? Doubtless it is true—and those who talk about democratic government or government by law should note the fact—that all government is by individual men, whether they govern as priests in the name of God, as people's commissars in the name of the proletariat, or as judges issuing orders in the name of the law. And when men are in the position of governors they cannot escape seeing the justice on the side of their own special interests when these interests conflict with those of the rest of the community. Thus governments almost always think it necessary to keep and to perpetuate their power. But even so, the interest of the governors is not always contrary to those of the governed. Even a wolf, if we may modify a parable of Santayana's, can, to insure a steady supply of sheep, become a careful shepherd of his flock.[11] The question to what extent the interests of the governor and the governed coincide and to what extent they differ is an empirical one. The answer varies under different conditions. In general, it is psychologically false to assert, as anarchistic individualists maintain, that government rests exclusively on the force of the governors. Governors exercise a certain social function, the function of making decisions. This is in fact felt to be too arduous a task by most people; and kingship or authority is thus sometimes thrust on a man as it was on Saul looking for his father's asses. It is thrust on our newspapers by those who wish an authoritative source of decision in matters of taste as to the latest books, plays, dress, proper social deportment, etc.

If the state oppresses some it also serves as a defence to those who can control it. Generally speaking, even the most tyrannical state has some interest in protecting the mass of its people against the ravages of epidemics, against disturbance of the general peace or attacks on life by those inclined to violence. But as more and more people become interested in the government, its action becomes more like that of an assembly of ambassadors where each tries to get the most for the interests he represents and yet there is some intelligence of the fact that the preservation of the common interests is the condition of the special ones' being maintained.

In the United States the Jeffersonian democrats fought against the power of the government both in the nation and in their states.

They feared that the merchants and the large landowners of the seaboard, who had controlled the older states, would control the central government. To limit the power of government by a system of checks and balances was therefore the way to assure liberty from oppression. So long as the country was sparsely settled and our people remained for the most part a nation of independent free-holders, this was a workable theory. It never, however, was carried out consistently, for the temptation to use the government for positive ends, such as education or the safeguarding of our commercial interests in the West and on the seas, could not be resisted even by Jefferson himself. In the last forty or fifty years the representatives of large industry have invoked this theory of the bills of rights to limit legislative power to regulate industry in the interests not only of the workers but also of the future manhood and womanhood of the nation. The same group, however, that protests against a child labour law, or against any minimum wage law intended to insure a minimum standard of decent living, is constantly urging the government to protect industry by tariffs. Clearly, the theory of laissez faire, of complete non-interference of the government in business, is not really held consistently by those who so frequently invoke it. A government so limited in its powers that it could do no harm would be useless, since it could do no good.

To draw a sharp line, as Mill does, between those acts which affect one person and no one else and those acts which do affect others, is impracticable in modern society. What act of any individual does not affect others?

> Nor knowest thou what argument
> Thy life to thy neighbor's creed has lent.

A contract, therefore, between two or more individuals cannot be said to be ever generally devoid of all public interest. If it be of no interest, why enforce it? For note that in enforcing contracts, the government does not merely allow two individuals to do what they have found pleasant in their eyes. Enforcement, in fact, puts the machinery of the law in the service of one party against the other. When that is worth while and how that should be done are important questions of public policy. Since no government is omniscient, some element of discretion in the conduct of affairs must be left to the individuals who make a contract. We cannot rely entirely on regulations made in advance by the legislature, or post factum by judges. In fact, how can the element of discretion ever be completely taken away from those who have to transact business? But the notion that in enforcing contracts the state is only giving effect to the will of the parties rests upon an utterly untenable theory as to what the enforcement of contracts involves. Part of the confusion on this point is due to the classical theory which views a contract as always and entirely an expression of the will or of "the meeting of the minds" of those who make it.

3. *The Economic Argument for Contractualism*

When the political argument is closely pressed, it is found to rest on the economic one that a régime in which contracts are freely made and generally enforced gives greater scope to individual initiative and thus promotes the greatest wealth of a nation. Three arguments have been used in defence of this view.

The first was based on the eighteenth-century optimism that assumed, on religious and metaphysical grounds, a preëstablished harmony between man's selfish pursuit of gain and the common good.

> Thus God and Nature planned the general frame
> And bade self-love and social be the same.

But this was soon seen to be contrary to fact when factory and mine owners began to exploit men, women, and children in a way that a nation like Great Britain could not tolerate. Factory legislation thus followed as a refutation of the optimistic dogma.

The second argument, the psychologic one of Bentham, rested

on the assumption that as happiness consists in a maximum of pleasure, and that as each man knows best what will please him most, a contract in which two parties freely express what they prefer is the best way of achieving the greatest good of the greatest number. This argument blandly ignores the fact that though men may be legally free to make whatever contract they please, they are not actually or economically free. The mere fact of litigation, of appeal to the courts for enforcement, proves that the parties did not achieve real agreement or that their compact has not been found to serve the interest of one of the parties. Men in fact do not always know what will turn out to their advantage, and some of them have a talent for exploiting the ignorance or the dire need of their neighbours to make the latter agree to almost anything.

The psychologic argument has therefore been succeeded by the biologic doctrine of natural selection and the survival of the fittest. The old Providence that rewarded the virtuous and punished the wicked became the biologic law according to which the most fit survive and those who are not fit perish. On the basis of this romantic confusion between biologic and moral categories, Spencerian liberals have opposed all intervention by the state to aid the weak in the economic struggle. This indifference to the fate of those who are economically crushed is extolled as a virtue in the Nietzschean motto: Let the weak perish that the strong may survive. But the absolute division of men into the strong and the weak collapses before critical reflection. Who are the weak and who are the strong? Those who prove weak in a state of anarchic competition may become strong in a state of wise regulation and protection.

The clearest and most convincing statement of the case for the classical theory of free competition is that of Justice Holmes.[12] Let us, he urges, get behind the fact of ownership, and look at the processes of production and consumption of goods. The men who achieve great private fortunes do not consume very much of this social wealth. Their fortunes denote rather power to control the flow of goods. And who is better fitted to command this process of production and distribution than the man who wins it in the competition of the market? The assumption behind this is that the man who succeeds in winning a fortune (not, it should be noted, the man who receives it by inheritance) has succeeded because he has been able to anticipate the largest effective demand for goods and to organize the most economical way of producing them.

One weakness of this argument is that it ignores the frightful waste involved in competition. The community as a whole ultimately pays the cost, in labour and capital goods (including their extensive sales and advertising forces), of all the economic enterprises that are allowed to compete and fail. Moreover, the greatest profits do not always come with the greatest productivity. There are monopoly profits, like the unearned increment of land value, that clearly do not arise from productivity of the owners, and there are monopoly profits that are swelled by reducing the output, so that fishermen, wheat and cotton growers, and other producers are often advised to do this. Neither can free competition prevent the paradoxical situation that our economic crises repeatedly show, viz., an overstocked food market and general destitution from inability to buy. The latter is certainly in part due to the fact that, under unrestrained competition, wages and the return for the labour of the farmer are not sufficient to enable the vast majority of the people to buy enough of what they have produced. Thus, some of the supposed greater efficiency of private over public business, to the extent that it involves lower real wages, is detrimental to the general welfare. The latter depends not only on the mass of production, but also on the kind of goods produced, on the conditions under which men work, and on the ways in which the product is distributed.

For these reasons it is rare nowadays to find any advocates of a régime of free competition except among certain lawyers and judges who use it to oppose regulation of the "labour contract" by the state. The general consensus among business men has demanded the organization of our Interstate Commerce Commission and

Federal Trade Commission, our state railway and public service commissions, our state insurance and industrial commissions, and other administrative bodies that limit and regulate certain essential business contracts. Also the great captains of industry are everywhere trying to eliminate free competition. And those who talk about "keeping the government out of business" are the last to desire that the government shall not help or protect, by proper rules, the business in which they are involved. The differences that divide men in this respect concern the questions of what interests should be protected and who should control the government.

4. Contractualism and Religion

The laws of any people, as a rule, receive not only their sanction but also a good deal of their direction from their religion. Not only is the tendency to completely separate law from religion very modern and limited to certain Protestant countries, but also it has never been perfectly carried out in practice. There are many facts to support those who, like the late Justice Brewer, insist that our law recognizes ours to be a Christian nation. A closer view shows that English and American legal ideas have been shaped not only by the Christian tradition but more especially by the effects of the Protestant Reformation. The general philosophy called individualism was certainly strengthened by the religious movement which denied the claims of the historically organized hierarchy, made salvation depend primarily upon individual faith, identified the Church with the body of the individual communicants, and led to setting up individual conscience as the final authority. For our present purpose we must limit ourselves to noting how the category of contract or covenant was broadened by the Reformation, and more especially by Calvinism.

Max Weber has made popular the idea, previously suggested in part by Thorold Rogers and others, that modern commerce and Protestantism are closely connected in their ascetic ethics, in emphasizing the virtues of industry and thrift, or saving for the future.[13] Some features of this view have been severely criticized by the veteran economic historian Brentano.[14] But still we may say that Calvinism was predominantly the faith of the commercial classes, in opposition to the Catholic Church, which, as a great international landowner or as ministering to agricultural populations, upheld the old order of a land economy. This manifested itself characteristically enough in the question of interest for loans of money and in other phases of mercantile contracts.

Leaving aside the conduct of the Popes as temporal rulers of their Italian states, we can say that the general teachings and policy of the Church were undoubtedly directed to the maintenance of social order. Commerce largely in the hands of Jews and Lombards was viewed as a possible disintegrating force. The clearest and most liberal statement of this attitude is to be found in St. Thomas's tract *De Avaritia:* "Trade is rendered lawful when the merchant seeks a moderate gain for the maintenance of his household, or for the relief of the indigent; and also when the trade is carried on for the public good, in order that the country may be furnished with the necessaries of life, and the gain is looked upon not as the object, but as the wages of his labour." [15]

Starting with the popular notion that all wealth is the product of labour applied to nature, the Church regarded the demand for interest or payment for the mere lending of money as a form of avarice, one of the mortal sins. Melancthon and especially Calvin questioned this attitude, and the Protestant theologians, even in the Church of England, soon followed them.[16] In general, the old canon law and the Doctors of the Church emphasized custom rather than the will or agreement of the parties in determining fair price and other incidents of contract. But the newer religious movement has been more subjective, and has left things more to individual conscience, without elaborating any definite rules that should govern such conscience in the very complicated situations of modern economic life. Casuistry, indeed, fell into such bad repute that the very word has become a term of opprobrium. This allowed lawyers serving the interests of their commercial clients to formulate the doctrine of complete freedom of contract.

5. Contractualism and Metaphysical Individualism

Ever since Plato employed a realistic metaphysics to defend his social philosophy against the individualistic relativism of the Sophists, theories that emphasize the rôle of compact, conventions, or agreements have relied on nominalistic metaphysics, i.e., on an emphasis on the particular as an atom or individual (the two terms are etymologically equivalent) as against the abstract universals that serve as integrating relations. The atomistic analysis of physical nature that triumphed in the seventeenth century found its analogy in the analysis of society as constituted by separate individuals who are united only by compact or convention.

The prevalent idea that there can be no individual responsibility without free will, though most often asserted by modern idealistic philosophies, involves this atomistic metaphysics. For if the individual will is only a part of the world, it cannot be absolutely autonomous but must be subject to influences from the rest of the world. But the sharp distinction between mind and nature inherent in this nominalism is hostile to the possibility of any natural science of man, and this difficulty has been a moot point in Continental social philosophy.

In England nominalism has, since the days of William of Occam, John Locke, Hume, and Mill, been carried into the field of psychology and has tended to resolve the individual mind into a number of psychic states more or less closely connected by the laws of association of ideas. On this basis, English liberalism effected a compromise between the determinism necessary for a science of man and the concept of freedom necessary for a practical social program. This viewpoint emphasizes the nominalistic analysis as between different individuals and stresses psychologic determinism as between different states of the mind.

Though this compromise, in view of its obvious theoretic difficulties, can hardly be called intellectually respectable, there is behind it some sound perception. The human mind or will is neither absolutely determined nor absolutely free. As a part of the world it is genuinely dependent and determined. But as a real and irreducible entity it has, like all other realities, a realm of relative independence. When we speak of its being influenced, we must recognize that there is an *it* to be influenced. In daily life this shows itself in our craving for the recognition of our personality as an actual factor in human relations.

In the realm of contracts this principle of polarity means that the element of will can never be eliminated from the field of law or from any other social field. But the law as part of a larger world must be regulated and determined by the nature of the larger order of which it is a part.

II. EXCESSES OF CONTRACTUALISM

As the result of the various forces that have thus supported the cult of contractualism there has been developed in all modern European countries (and in those which derive from them) a tendency to include within the categories of contract transactions in which there is no negotiation, bargain, or genuinely voluntary agreement. Let us consider a few typical situations.

A citizen going to work boards a street-car and drops a coin in the conductor's or motorman's box. This, or the buying of a ticket, is treated as a contract, and courts and jurists speak of its "terms" and of the rights and duties under it. No one claims that there is any actual "meeting of minds" of the passenger and the street railway corporation. There is no actual offer or acceptance— certainly no bargaining between the two parties. The rights and duties of both are prescribed by law and are the same no matter what, if anything, goes on in the passenger's mind, or in the corporation's, if it has any mind. Moreover, the liabilities of the railway corporation to the passenger are in many circumstances exactly the same even if he does not buy any ticket. Obviously, therefore, we have here a situation in which the law regulates the relation between different parties and it is pure fiction to speak of it as growing out of any agreement of the wills of the parties.

A more serious confusion of fact and fiction occurs when we speak of the "labour contract." There is, in fact, no real bargaining between the modern large employer (say the United States Steel Corporation) and its individual employees. The working man has no real power to negotiate or confer with the corporation as to the terms under which he will agree to work. He either decides to work under the conditions and schedule of wages fixed by the employer or else he is out of a job. If he is asked to sign any paper he does so generally without any knowledge of what it contains and without any real freedom to refuse. For we cannot freely change our crafts, and if a man is a weaver or shoe-laster, he is dependent on the local carpet or shoe factory for his livelihood, especially so if he has a family, which is not as mobile as money. The greater economic power of the employer exercises a compulsion as real *in fact* as any now recognized by law as duress. The extreme form of such duress, the highwayman's pistol, still leaves us with the freedom to accept the terms offered or else take the consequences. But such choice is surely the very opposite of what men value as freedom.

Clearly, then, the element of consent on the part of the employee may be a minor one in the relation of employment—a relation much more aptly and realistically described by the old law as that between master and servant. Down to the end of the eighteenth century this relation was in fact regulated by the government. Wages used to be regularly fixed by justices of the peace under the authority of parliamentary enactments, and even the beer that the master was to serve to the servant with his bread had its strength regulated by law. Any demand by workmen for higher wages or any accession to such demands on the part of masters was a violation of the law. Yet courts now speak as if the effort on the part of the state to regulate wages were an unheard of interference with the eternal laws of nature. As a matter of fact, it was only after the Civil War that the United States Supreme Court invented the doctrine that the "right *to* contract" is property and is thus protected against real government regulation by the Fifth and Fourteenth amendments of our Federal Constitution. But so widespread has this idea become that few have noticed its radical novelty.

The spread of contractualistic notions shows itself in the tendency to speak of marriage as itself a contract. Now there are, usually, solemn promises exchanged when the marriage ceremony is performed and there may be agreements as to dowry and other property rights. But the specific legal relations of husband and wife are by no means determined thereby. These relations are entirely fixed by law and the parties to it cannot vary its terms, just as they cannot vary the terms of their obligations to any children they may bring into the world. If there is no sense in speaking of the rights and duties between parents and minor children as contractual, neither is there in speaking of the relations of husband and wife as contractual. The fact that an act is more or less voluntary does not make its legal consequences contractual.

The extreme of contractualistic thought was reached when European publicists of the eighteenth century and American judges of the nineteenth century spoke of the social compact or contract as the basis of society and of all law.

I do not want to add to the many (in fact, too many) refutations of the social contract theory. The critics of the theory seem to me to have ignored the large voluntary element in the formation and continuance of government. This is unmistakably manifest if we consider the governance of international affairs or the formation of many of our own States as well as of our national Union. Moreover, the tradition of Hebrew history and Greek philosophy that bases government and law upon covenant or agreement has had a salutary influence in challenging all law to justify itself at the bar of reason. It is good to ask of any law whether it is such as rational beings would adopt if they wanted to establish a society. Nevertheless, there are obviously insuperable difficulties in trying to derive all legal obligations from contract. Children have certain obligations to their parents that are not contractual. Indeed, we may well ask, "Why should we obey laws that our ancestors and not we agreed to?" We may even go further and ask, "Why *should* we keep agreements that we made some time ago when we were younger and less experienced or wise than we are now?" If there is any rational answer to either of these queries it must take the form of indicating some social good or necessity that is served by our keeping our promises. But if so, why may not the same social good or necessity be served by making children obey and at times support their parents, or by making those who hold property pay for sewage, education, and other communal necessities, even if they do not agree? The merits of the issue are not really affected by introducing a fictional contract.

These attempts to stretch the category of contract err in failing to recognize a certain necessary social solidarity, especially that of any generation with its ancestors, as not the outcome but the very basis of contract itself. Indeed, the vast majority of those who formerly held that we were bound by the original contract of our ancestors also believed that we could be justly punished because of the original sin of our ancestors. The analogy of the theologic identity strengthened the legal one.

III. THE JUSTIFICATION OF CONTRACT LAW

1. *The Sanctity of Promises*

Contract law is commonly supposed to enforce promises. Why should promises be enforced?

The simplest answer is that of the intuitionists, namely, that promises are sacred *per se*, that there is something inherently despicable about not keeping a promise, and that a properly organized society should not tolerate this. This may also be said to be the common man's theory. Learned writers ignore this because of their interest in showing the evil consequences of allowing promises to be broken. But the intuitionists can well object that to judge the goodness of an act by its consequences is an obvious evasion by postponing the issue. For when we inquire which consequences are good and which are bad, we face the same question over again. If the terms "good" and "bad" have any meaning, there must be some ultimate character of action that makes them so, just as there is some ultimate character or nature of objects that makes them blue or beautiful. To say that the blueness or beauty of an object depends upon "the observer" only means that a complete answer involves an additional factor that "the observer" brings into the case. There can be no sense at all in speaking of the quality of an object that the observer beholds if there is no object or there are no qualities to behold.

Now there can be no doubt that common sense does generally find something revolting about the breaking of a promise, and this, if a fact, must be taken account of by the law, though it may be balanced by other factors or considerations. In any case, let us not ignore the fact that judges and jurists, like other mortals, do frequently express this in the feeling that it would be an outrage to let one who has broken his promise escape completely.

It is not a sufficient answer to the foregoing position to show that common sense is not consistent, that in many cases we approve the breaking of promises,[16a] that the promises which we think ought not to be broken depend on the relation in which people stand to us, and that all these factors vary from time to time. I do not always have the same appetite or aversion for the same food, but when I do like or dislike a given dish, that is a fact which is not to be read out of existence because something else was true on another occasion. If, then, we find ourselves in a state of society in which men are, as a matter of fact, repelled by the breaking of promises and feel that such practice should be discouraged or minimized, that is a primary fact which the law must not ignore.

But while this intuitionist theory contains an element of truth, it is clearly inadequate. No legal system does or can attempt to enforce all promises. Not even the canon law held all promises to be sacred. And when we come to draw a distinction between those promises which should be and those which should not be enforced, the intuitionist theory, that all promises should be kept, gives us no light or guiding principle.

Similar to the intuitionist theory is the view of Kantians like Reinach [17] that the duty to keep one's promise is one without which rational society would be impossible. There can be no doubt that from an empirical or historical point of view, the ability to rely on the promises of others adds to the confidence necessary for social intercourse and enterprise. But as an absolute proposition this is untenable. The actual world, which assuredly is among the possible ones, is not one in which all promises are kept, and there are many people—not necessarily diplomats—who prefer a world in which they and others occasionally depart from the truth and go back on some promise. It is indeed very doubtful whether there are many who would prefer to live in an entirely rigid world in which one would be obliged to keep *all* one's promises instead of the present more viable system, in which a vaguely fair proportion is sufficient. Many of us indeed would shudder at the idea of being bound by every promise, no matter how foolish, without any chance of letting increased wisdom undo past foolishness. Certainly, some freedom to change one's mind is necessary for free intercourse between those who lack omniscience.

For this reason we cannot accept Dean Pound's theory [18] that all promises in the course of business should be enforced. He seems to me undoubtedly right in his insistence that promises constitute modern wealth and that their enforcement is thus a necessity of maintaining wealth as a basis of civilization. My bank's promise to pay the checks drawn to my account not only constitutes my wealth but puts it into a more manageable form than that of my personal possession of certain goods or even gold. Still, business men as a whole do not wish the law to enforce every promise. Many business transactions, such as those on a stock or produce exchange, could not be carried on unless we could rely on a mere verbal agreement or hasty memorandum. But other transactions, like those of real estate, are more complicated and would become too risky if we were bound by every chance promise that escapes us. Negotiations would be checked by such fear. In such cases men do not want to be bound until the final stage, when some formality like the signing of papers gives one the feeling of security, of having taken proper precautions. The issue obviously depends upon such factors as the relative simplicity of a given transaction, the speed with which it must be concluded, and the availability of necessary information.

At various times it has been claimed that mere promises as such received legal force in Hebrew, Greek, early German, and canon law. None of these claims can be justified.

All Biblical references to binding promises are either to those involving an oath or promise to God or else they assume, as a matter of course, some formality such as striking of hands and pledge or security.[19] Greek covenants, or agreements, had to be in writing or to be recorded and were not free from other formalities.[20] The binding character of promises could not have been absolute to a people to whom Odysseus was a hero.

Though the great authority of Gierke, following Tacitus and Grotius, can be cited for the view that the early Germans attached great importance to keeping one's word,[21] the evidence collected by men such as Brunner, Von Amira, Heusler, and Brissaud shows that the Germans, like other peoples, held promises binding only if some real object passed hands or some formal ceremony took place.[22] Otherwise, pledge or security was required.

More substantial is the case for the canon law, which undoubtedly went further than any other system to enforce bare promises. The Council of Carthage in 348 B.C. made all written agreements binding and this later led to the action *ex nudo pacto* before the courts of the Church. But the use of the oath was a distinctive ceremony and as it was binding in conscience, i.e., in one's relation to God, it did not always afford relief to the promisee. The latter was at times even compelled by the ecclesiastical judge to release the promisor. And through the extension of the power of temporal rulers, as well as of bishops, to pass on the validity of the promise under oath, the legal effectiveness of the latter was whittled away.[23]

2. *The Will Theory of Contract*

According to the classical view, the law of contract gives expression to and protects the will of the parties, for the will is something inherently worthy of respect. Hence such authorities as Savigny, Windsheid, Pothier, Planiol, Pollock, Salmond, and Langdell hold that the first essential of a contract is the agreement of wills, or the meeting of minds.

The metaphysical difficulties of this view have often been pointed out. Minds or wills are not in themselves existing things that we can look at and recognize. We are restricted in our earthly experience to the observation of the changes or actions of more or less animated bodies in time and space; and disembodied minds or wills are beyond the scope and reach of earthly law. But while this objection has become familiar, it has not been very effective. The force of the old ideas, embodied in the traditional language, has not always been overcome even by those who like Langdell and Salmond profess to recognize the fictional element in the will theory.

Another line of objection can be found in the incompatibility of the classical theory with the consequences that the law attaches to an offer. Suppose that I offer to buy certain goods from A at a given price, and following his refusal give him a week's time to reconsider it. If I change my mind the next day but fail to notify him, a contractual obligation will none the less arise if five days later he notifies me that he has accepted my terms. Here there is never a moment of time when the two parties are actually in agreement or of one mind. Yet no one denies that the resulting rights and duties are identical with those called contractual. It does not help the classical theory to say that I am under a legal duty to notify A (the offeree) and that if I fail to perform this duty in the proper way, the law will treat my change of mind as a nullity, *as if* it had never happened. The phrase italicized indicates that we are moving in the realm of fiction (or better, rights and duties imposed by law) and not in the realm of fact. No one denies that the contractual obligation should attach in this case; but there is in point of fact no actual agreement or meeting of minds. The latter, then, is not always necessary for a legal contract.

The logical inconsistency of the classical theory is not cured if we say that the law protects not the will but the expression or declaration of the will.[24] Suppose that in the case mentioned I make a solemn declaration of the revocation of my offer, or write a letter but fail to communicate it. The law, in refusing to give effect to my declared revocation, is not protecting my expressed will, but is enforcing a duty on me in the interest of the general security of business transactions.

A more important objection to the theory that every contract expresses the consensus or agreed wills of the two parties is the fact that most litigation in this field arises precisely because of the advent of conditions that the two parties did not foresee when they entered into the transaction. Litigation usually reveals the absence of genuine agreement between the parties *ab initio*. If both parties had foreseen the difficulty, provision would have been made for it in the beginning when the contract was drawn up. When courts thus proceed to interpret the terms of the contract they are generally not merely seeking to discover the actual past meanings (though that may sometimes be investigated), but more generally they decide the "equities," the rights and obligations of the parties, in such circumstances; and these legal relations are determined by the courts and the jural system and not by the agreed will of the contesting parties.

Planiol and others have argued that while certain effects of a contract may not have been foreseen by the parties, nevertheless these are effects following from the original objective and are therefore the will of the two contractors.[25] But to argue that because the law fixes certain obligations you did foresee something that in fact you did not see is a confusion which would be too ridiculous to criticize were it not so prevalent in juristic discussions. The confusion between what exists in fact and what ought to be according to our theory occurs also in other fields of liability. An employer is held liable for the negligence of an agent, even where he may have specifically warned the agent against it. For instance a man instructs his servant to exercise his two horses in his field, since the animals are too spirited to be taken on the street. The servant takes the horses into the street, where they commit some damage. The master is held liable. Now the theory holds that the man who caused the damage is liable. Therefore, the master, being liable, is declared to be the "cause" of the damage. In truth, however, he is the "cause" because he is liable, and not vice versa. So in contracts men are liable for things that they did not actually foresee; and to say that they intended or willed these results is a fiction designed to save the will theory.

The obvious limitations of the will theory of contract has caused a reaction that takes the form of positivism or behaviourism: Away with the whole notion of will!—the only realities are specific acts to which the law attaches certain consequences, i.e., if you do something by word of mouth, by writing, or by any other act that some one else takes as a promise, then the latter can, under certain conditions, bring an action. In its extreme form, this appears in what Dean Pound calls the state of strict law, which, like everything called primitive, is always with us. A developed system of law, however, must draw some distinction between voluntary and involuntary acts. Justice Holmes thinks that even a dog discriminates between one who stumbles over him and one who kicks him. The whole of the modern law of contract, it may be argued, thus does and should respond to the need of greater or finer discrimination in regard to the intentional character of acts. The law of error, duress, and fraud in contract would be unintelligible apart from such distinction.

3. *The Injurious-Reliance Theory*

Though this seems the favourite theory today, it has not as yet been adequately formulated, and many of those who subscribe to it fall back on the will theory when they come to discuss special topics in the law of contract. The essence of the theory, however, is clear enough. Contractual liability arises (or should arise) only where (1) some one makes a promise explicitly in words or implicitly by some act, (2) some one else relies on it and (3) suffers some loss thereby.

This theory appeals to the general moral feeling that not only ought promises to be kept, but that any one innocently injured by relying on them is entitled to have his loss "made good" by the one who thus caused it. If, as Schopenhauer has maintained, the sense of wrong is the ultimate human source of the law, then to base the obligation of the promise on the injury of the one who has relied on it, is to appeal to something really fundamental.

This theory also appeals powerfully to modern legal theorists because it seems to be entirely objective and social. It does not ask the court to examine the intention of the promisor. Instead, the court is asked to consider whether what the defendant has said or done is such that reasonable people generally do rely on it under the circumstances. The resulting loss can be directly proved and, to some extent, even measured. In emphasizing the element of injury resulting from the breach, the whole question of contract is integrated in the larger realm of obligations, and this tends to put our issues in the right perspective and to correct the misleading artificial distinctions between breach of contract and other civil wrongs or torts.

Nevertheless, this theory is not entirely consistent with existing law, nor does it give an altogether satisfactory account of what the law should do.

Contractual obligation is not coextensive with injurious reliance because (1) there are instances of both injury and reliance for which there is no contractual obligation, and (2) there are cases of such obligation where there is no reliance or injury.

(1) Clearly, not all cases of injury resulting from reliance on the word or act of another are actionable, and the theory before us offers no clue as to what distinguishes those which are. There is first the whole class of instances of definite financial injury caused by reliance on an explicit promise made in social relations, such as dinner-parties and the like. Suppose I say to A: "If you agree to meet my friends and talk to them about your travels in Africa, I will hire an appropriate room in a hotel and give a dinner in your honour." A agrees but fails to come, or notifies me too late to prevent my financial loss. Here the law gives me no redress. Cases like these are often said to be properly ruled out on the ground that those who make them do not intend to be legally bound. And doubtless people generally know enough law to know that they cannot collect damages in such cases. But this argument is rather circular, since liability does not generally depend on knowledge or ignorance of the law. Men are held liable in many cases where they do not intend to be bound legally. There are doubtless good reasons why there should be no legal liability for "social" promises; but our theory does not account for them.

Even clearer are those cases where some one advertises goods for sale or a position to be filled, and, when I come, tells me that he has changed his mind. The fact that I have suffered actual loss from relying on this public statement does not in this case give me a cause of action. The law does not help every one who has relied on the word or act of another.

(2) In formal contracts, such as promises under seal, stipulation in court, and the like, it is clearly not necessary for the promisee to prove reliance and injury. Certain formalities are binding *per se*. Consider also an ordinary agreement to sell something. Suppose that the defendant, who refuses to receive the goods, offers to prove that the vendor did not expect the deal to go through and had told others that he did not care whether it did or not. Would that be a bar to recovery? Actual reliance, it seems, is not always a necessary element in the case. The reliance of the promisee may be as "constructive" or fictional as the intention of the promisor. Nor does the plaintiff have to prove actual damage through the defendant's refusal to live up to his promise and take the goods. To be sure, where the law recognizes no loss, only nominal damages are usually awarded. But the fact that the plaintiff receives judgment is of practical, as well as of theoretic, importance. Clearly, the law favours the carrying out of promises even in cases where there is no actual reliance or actual loss from non-performance.

(3) Finally, the recovery that the law allows to the injured promisee is determined not by what he lost in relying on the promise, but rather by what he would have gained if the promise had been kept. There are obviously many cases where the injured party is substantially no worse after the breach than if the contract had never been made. He has thus not been in fact injured. And yet he may recover heavy damages if he would have gained heavily by the performance of the contract. The policy of the law, then, is not merely to redress injuries but also to protect certain kinds of expectation by making men live up to certain promises.

There can be no question about the soundness of the injurious-reliance theory in accounting for a dominant phase of the law of contract, and the foregoing difficulties may thus seem petty. But they do call attention to fundamental obscurities in the very idea of "reliance" as well as in the criteria of "injury." The injurious-reliance theory, like others, calls attention to a necessary element but does not give an adequate account of the whole of the law of contract. Its merits become clearer when its claims are properly limited.

4. *The Equivalent Theory*

Popular sentiment generally favours the enforcement of those promises which involve some quid pro quo. It is generally considered unfair that after A has given something of value or rendered B some service, B should fail to render anything in return. Even if what A did was by way of gift, B owes him gratitude and should express it in some appropriate way. And if, in addition, B has promised to pay A for the value or services received, the moral sense of the community condemns B's failure to do so as even more unfair. The demand for justice behind the law is but an elaboration of such feelings of what is fair and unfair.

The equivalent theory of contract has the advantage of being supported by this popular sentiment. This sentiment also explains the primacy of *real* contracts.

While a legal theory must not ignore common sense, it must also go beyond it. For common sense, while generally sound at its core, is almost always vague and inadequate. Common sentiment, for instance, demands an equivalent. But what things are equivalent? It is easy to answer this in regard to goods or services that have a standard market value. But how shall we measure things that are dissimilar in nature, or in a market where monopolistic or other factors prevent a fair or just price? Modern law therefore professes to abandon the effort of more primitive systems to enforce material fairness within the contract. The parties to the contract must themselves determine what is fair. Thereby, however, the law loses a good deal of support in the moral sense of the community.[26]

Though legal historians like Ames are right in insisting that the common-law doctrine of consideration did not originate in the law's insistence on equivalence in every contract, the latter idea cannot be eliminated altogether. It colours the prevailing language as to consideration, and especially the doctrine that in a bilateral contract each promise is consideration for the other. If a bare promise is of no legal validity, how can it be of any profit to the promisee or of any detriment to the promisor? Clearly, two things that are value-less cannot become of value by being exchanged for each other. The real reason for the sanctioning of certain exchanges of promises is that thereby certain transactions can be legally protected, and when we desire to achieve this result we try to construe the transaction as an exchange of promises. Consideration is in effect a formality, like an oath, the affixing of a seal, or a stipulation in court.

5. Formalism in Contract

The recognition of the formal character of consideration may help us to recognize the historical myopia of those who speak of the seal as "importing" consideration. Promises under seal were bind-ing (because of the formality) long before the doctrine of consid-eration was ever heard of. The history of forms and ceremonies in the law of contract offers an illuminating chapter in human psy-chology or anthropology. We are apt to dismiss the early Roman ceremonies of *mancipatio*, *nexum*, and *sponsio*, the Anglo-Saxon *wed* and *borh*, or the Frankish ceremonies of *arramitio*, *wadiatio*, and of the *festuca*, as peculiar to primitive society. But reflection shows that our modern practices of shaking hands to close a bar-gain, signing papers, and protesting a note are, like the taking of an oath on assuming office, not only designed to make evidence secure, but are in large part also expression of the fundamental human need for formality and ceremony, to make sharp distinc-tions where otherwise lines of demarcation would not be so clearly apprehended.

Ceremonies are the channels that the stream of social life creates by its ceaseless flow through the sands of human circumstance. Psy-chologically, they are habits; socially, they are customary ways of doing things; and ethically, they have what Jellinek has called the normative power of the actual, i.e., they control what we do by creating a standard of respectability or a pattern to which we feel bound to conform. The daily obedience to the act of the government, which is the basis of all political and legal institutions, is thus largely a matter of conformity to established ritual or form of behaviour. For the most part, we obey the law or the policeman as a matter of course, without deliberation. The customs of other people seem to us strange and we try to explain them as ceremonies symbolic of things that are familiar or seem useful to us. But many of our own customs can appear to an outsider as equally non-rational rituals that we follow from habit. We may justify them as the sacred vessels through which we obtain the substance of life's goods. But the maintenance of old forms may also be an end in itself to all those to whom change from the familiar is abhorrent.

6. *Contract and the Distribution of Risks*

Justice Holmes has suggested that a legal promise may be viewed as a wager: I assure you of a certain event (which may or may not be within my control) and I pay in case of failure.

This view has not found much favour. The first objection that has been urged against it is that when men make a contract, they contemplate its performance rather than its breach. This is hardly fatal. Men can and do sometimes deliberately plan to pay damages in certain contingencies rather than carry out their legal promises. It might even be said that the law sometimes encourages that attitude. Thus, up to the period of the Reform Bill, English law definitely put obstacles in the way of the lessee of land for a term of years who wanted any relief other than damages. On the other hand, Justice Holmes fails to dispose of the objection that the law does in some cases—in civil law countries more even than in our equity courts—compel specific performance. Moreover, his theory fails to attain its expressed objective, viz., to dispose of the view that a contract is a qualified subjection of one will to another. For the paying of damages does not flow from the promisor's willingness, but is the effect of the law's lending its machinery to the promisee.

Nevertheless, when taken in a wider sense in connection with Justice Holmes's general philosophy concerning the risk in all human affairs, his theory is illuminating and important.

All human transactions are directed to a future that is never free from elements of uncertainty. Every one of our ventures, therefore, involves the taking of a risk. When I board a train to go home I am betting my life that I will get to my destination. Now a contract or agreement may be viewed as an agreement for the distribution of anticipated gains or losses. If I agree to sell certain goods or services I expect that I shall be paid in good United States money and that with this money I shall be able to acquire certain other goods. I do not generally take into account the possibility that the purchasing power of the American dollar may be radically reduced when I receive my pay. That contingency is generally not thought of or else deemed too remote, yet certain bondholders do think of it and specify payment in gold of a certain standard. Now the human power to foresee all the consequences of an agreement is limited, even if we suppose that the two parties understand each other's meaning to begin with. Disputes or disagreements are therefore bound to come up; and the law of contract may thus be viewed as an attempt to determine the rights and duties of the two parties under circumstances that were not anticipated exactly in the same way by the two contracting parties, or at any rate were not expressly provided for in an unambiguous way. One can therefore say that the court's adjudication supplements the original contract as a method of distributing gains and losses.

From this point of view, we may look upon the law of contract as a number of rules according to which courts distribute gains and losses according to the equities of such cases; and the pretense that the result follows exclusively from the agreement of the two parties is fictional. Just as the process of interpreting a statute is really a process of subsidiary legislation, so is the interpretation of a contract really a method of supplementing the original agreement by such provisions as are necessary to determine the point at issue.

If we view the law of contract as directed to strengthening the security of transactions by enabling men to rely more fully on promises, we see only one phase of its actual workings. The other phase is the determination of the rights of the contracting parties as to contingencies that they have not foreseen, and for which they have not provided. In this latter respect the law of contract is a way of enforcing some kind of distributive justice within the legal system. And technical doctrines of contract may thus be viewed as a set of rules that will systematize decisions in this field and thus give lawyers and their clients some guidance in the problem of anticipating future decisions. Thus, for instance, if the question arises as to who should suffer a loss caused by the destruction of goods in transit, the technical doctrine of when title passes enables us to deal with the problem more definitely. In any case, the essential problem of the law of contract is the problem of distribution of risks. The other phase, namely, the assurance that what the parties have actually agreed on will be fulfilled, is a limiting principle.

IV. CONTRACT AND SOVEREIGNTY

It was said of Aristotle that whenever he set up a theory he began, like an Oriental despot, by killing off all possible rivals. And this seems to be the fashion in the peaceful world of scholarship. I trust that the foregoing discussion will not appear in that light. It has not been my object to refute the various theories discussed but rather to sift the valid from the invalid elements in them. Not one of these theories logically covers the whole field of contracts. But as they are not mutually exclusive, a more adequate account is possible by utilizing the valid elements of all of them.

This task of formulating a comprehensive theory of contract that

THE BASIS OF CONTRACT

shall do justice to its many sources and various phases, is one that I shall not undertake here. But I wish to emphasize certain considerations that supplement the theories discussed so far.

The cardinal error of the traditional individualistic theories of contract is their way of speaking as if the law does nothing but put into effect what the contracting parties originally agreed on. The best that can be said for this is that it may sometimes be true. But even if that were more generally the case, we should still have to attach more importance to the factor of enforcement than the prevailing theories do. The fact that two people agree to do something not prohibited by the public criminal law and carry out their agreement, or fail to do so, does not of itself bring the law of contract into being. A large number of important agreements, even in business, as in social, political, and religious matters, are left to be directly regulated by other agencies, such as the prevailing sense of honour, individual conscience, or the like. It is an error, then, to speak of the law of contract as if it merely allows people to do things. The absence of criminal prohibition will do that much. The law of contract plays a more positive rôle in social life, and this is seen when the organized force of the state is brought into play to compel the loser of a suit to pay or to do something. Doubtless most people live up to their promises or agreements either through force of custom or because it is in the long run more advantageous to do so. But there can be no doubt that the possibility of the law's being invoked against us if we fail to do so is an actual factor in the situation. Even if the transactions that come to be litigated are atypical, their judicial determination is still influential in moulding the legal custom. For the ruling in a case that departs from the mode supports or opposes some direction of variation and thus fixes the direction of growth of what becomes customary. The fact, then, that in the general run of transactions people do not resort to actual litigation is certainly in part due to the fact that they know in a general way what will be the outcome of that process. The law of contract, then, through judges, sheriffs, or marshals puts the sovereign power of the state at the disposal of one party to be exercised over the other party. It thus grants a limited sovereignty to the former. In ancient times, indeed, this sovereignty was legally absolute. The creditor acquired dominion over the body of the debtor and could dispose of it as he pleased. But even now, when imprisonment for debt has been, for the most part, abolished, the ability to use the forces of the state to collect damages is still a real sovereign power and the one against whom it can be exercised is in that respect literally a subject.

From this point of view the law of contract may be viewed as a subsidiary branch of public law, as a body of rules according to which the sovereign power of the state will be exercised as between the parties to a more or less voluntary transaction.

The first rules of public law, generally called constitutional law, regulate the conduct of the chief state officials by indicating the scope of their powers. Within this scope legislatures use their discretion or wisdom to enact certain statutes; and judges, by following precedents, elaborate certain rules as to when and how the power of the state shall be exercised. Among these rules we have the laws of partnership, leases, agreements for services, contracts of surety or insurance, and the like. Now, just as the rules of constitutional law are general and leave blanks to be filled in by the legislature, courts, and administrative officials (whose rules and habitual practices are law to those over whom they have authority), so do the rules of contracts allow men to formulate for themselves, within the prescribed limits, certain rights and duties governing certain transactions between them; and when the parties have thus formulated their agreements, the latter become a part of the law of the land, just as much as do treaties between our nation and others, compacts between states, contracts between a state or division thereof and a private corporation, or the grant of a pension to the widow of a former President. When a state or a municipality makes a contract with a public service corporation for gas or transportation at a given price to the consumer, no one doubts that such an agreement is part of the legal order. But so are private agreements that the law sanctions. Thus, when a trade union makes an agreement with an association of employers, or even with a single employer, the result is law not only for those "represented" at the signing of the papers but for all those who wish to enter the industry at any time that the agreement is in force. This is in general true of all more or less permanently organized partnerships, companies, corporations, or other groups; and enforceable agreements between individuals, no matter on how limited a scale, are similarly part of the law by virtue of the general rules of state action that apply to them.

If, then, the law of contract confers sovereignty on one party over another (by putting the state's forces at the disposal of the former), the question naturally arises: For what purposes and under what circumstances shall that power be conferred? Adherents of the classical theory have recognized that legal enforcement serves to protect and encourage transactions that require credit or reliance on the promises of others. But we also need care that the power of the state be not used for unconscionable purposes, such as helping those who exploit the dire need or weaknesses of their fellows. Usury laws have recognized that he who is under economic necessity is not really free. To put no restrictions on the freedom to contract would logically lead not to a maximum of individual liberty but to contracts of slavery, into which, experience shows, men will "voluntarily" enter under economic pressure—a pressure that is largely conditioned by the laws of property. Regulations, therefore, involving some restrictions on the freedom to contract are as necessary to real liberty as traffic restrictions are necessary to assure real freedom in the general use of our highways.

From this point of view, the movement to standardize the forms of contract—even to the extent of prohibiting variations or the right to "contract out"—is not to be viewed as a reaction to, but rather as the logical outcome of, a régime of real liberty of contract. It is a utilization of the lessons of experience to strengthen those forms which best serve as channels through which the life of the community can flow most freely.

Consider, for instance, the position of the man who has to ship his goods. Shall we leave him to bargain with the railroad company? That would certainly not add to the security of business. Experience has shown the necessity of the government's standardizing the transaction in regard to rates and other incidents. Similar considerations hold in regard to life and fire insurance.

The notion that standardization is necessarily inimical to real freedom is a fallacy of the same type as the one that habits are necessarily hindrances to the achievements of our desires. There is doubtless the real possibility of developing bad social customs, as we develop bad individual habits. But in the main, customs and habits are necessary ways through which our aims can be realized. By standardizing contracts, the law increases that real security which is the necessary basis of initiative and the assumption of tolerable risks. Naturally, diverse interests are differently affected by this process of legal standardization. The interests of the railroads, for instance, are not always the same as those of the shippers or commuters. But issues as to justice between conflicting interests in such relations require consideration of the specific factors of the situation. For our present purpose it is sufficient to note that the law of contract in thus dealing with public policies cannot be independent of general political theory. By what has been called the method of judicial empiricism courts sometimes pretend that they avoid facing these issues. What really happens, however, is that they apply old, uncriticized, or unavowed assumptions in their interpretation of the "facts." The advantage of empiricism and of the lack of clear ideas as to the policy of the law is that it sometimes saves the community from the deplorable consequences that would follow if courts consistently carried out some of their professed theories. But the history of human tribulation does not support high expectations from the process of "muddling through."

Contracts are standardized not only by statutory enactments such as the New York legislation on life insurance, by orders of commissions such as the Interstate Commerce Commission and the like, but also by the process of interpretation that courts apply to human transactions and to their formulated agreements. All agreements, if they are to hold for any length of time, must be constantly revised or supplemented. When disputes arise and courts are appealed to, the latter, by the process of interpretation, do this work of supplementing the existing agreements, just as they generally engage in subsidiary legislation when they interpret statutes. When courts follow the same rules of interpretation in diverse cases, they are in effect enforcing uniformities of conduct.

We may thus view the law of contract not only as a branch of public law but also as having a function somewhat parallel to that of the criminal law. Both serve to standardize conduct by penalizing departures from the legal norm. Not only by decrees of specific performance or by awards of damages, but also by treating certain contracts as void or voidable and thus withholding its support from those who do not conform to its prescribed forms, does the law of contract in fact impose penalties. Thus even when certain practices like gambling, illicit sex relations, or agreements in restraint of trade are not criminal offences, the law regards them with sufficient disfavour to refuse them the protection of its enforcing machinery.

The function of the law of contract in promoting the standardization of transactions is at all times an important one. And the more developed and complicated transactions become, the more there is need for eliminating as much uncertainty as possible by standardization. This is certainly true today. Consider the case of a man who wants to publish a book, to buy an insurance policy or a letter of credit, to ship his goods or to store them in a warehouse, to lease an apartment, to have gas or electricity or telephone service supplied to him, to mortgage his house, or to obtain a surety bond—in all these and in many other relations his freedom to contract is facilitated by standard forms moulded by past law and custom.

Naturally, standardized contracts, like other laws, serve the interests of some better than those of others; and the question of justice thus raised demands the attention not only of legislatures but also of courts that have to interpret these standard forms and of administrative bodies that have to supervise their enforcement. In a changing social order these standards or forms must grow or become modified; and to make them function more serviceably it is not sufficient to wait until trouble develops and is brought before the courts for adjudication. The need of intelligent anticipation that can be affected by initiating inquiries cannot be met by our traditional court procedure, and this has compelled the joining of administrative with judicial power in the hands of bodies like the Interstate Commerce Commission and our various state public service commissions.

A realization of the growth of standard forms suggests the introduction of a point of view in the study of contract similar to what has been called the institutional approach in the study of economics. The classical method in economics starts with a theory of free competition and then seeks to qualify that theory by taking note of the hindrances to the free mobility of capital or labour in actual conditions. While this is perfectly just as a scientific procedure, it postpones an adequate account of actual economic conditions. Recently economists have begun at the other end, i.e., with the existing organized social habits involved in economic institutions such as our currency, our technical methods of increasing production, the system of distributing and marketing goods, and the like. From this point of view competition is a real and important incident, but its limitations become more clear in this context. A similar change of approach in the study of the law of contract means beginning not with the bargaining between the two parties, but with the legal form or way of doing things, with the established institution within which negotiation is possible.

One of the most suggestive treatments of the nature of contracts occurs in the few pages devoted to it in Hauriou's *Droit public*.[27]

The French master draws a sharp distinction between contracts and institutions. Contracts are voluntary, fixed, and temporary, while institutions are socially hereditary, grow, and last longer. Yet Hauriou also recognizes that contracts, especially collective ones, grow into institutions. The marriage relation shows the passage from one to the other. Attention to what I have elsewhere called the principle of polarity warns us against making irremediable antitheses or antinomies out of necessary distinctions within any living situation. Nowhere is this warning more necessary than against the absolute separation of freedom of contract from government regulation, the former conceived as purely negative and the latter as purely arbitrary. In actual life real freedom to do anything, in art as in politics, depends upon acceptance of the rules of our enterprise. As has been remarked elsewhere, the rules of the sonnet do not hamper real poets but rather help weak ones. Real or positive freedom depends upon opportunities supplied by institutions that involve legal regulation. Our legislative forces may be narrowly partisan and the rules may be poor ones. But this can be remedied not by the abrogation of all rules but by the institution of better ones.

For this reason the notion that government rests on contract—a notion that runs through both our Hebrew and Greek heritage, and largely conforms to our peculiar American experience—contains a partial truth that should not be utterly disregarded because of some poor arguments in its behalf. If we discard the notion that *all* organized society began in a voluntary contract—a proposition that few have advanced as a literal truth—we may yet recognize that as men become more enlightened they can treat government as if it were a contractual affair, i.e., judge the services of governmental rules by the price we pay for them. The great men who founded the rationalistic legal and political tradition of the Enlightenment, Althusius, Grotius, Leibniz, and Locke, may have underestimated the force of tradition, but in treating governmental rights and duties under the categories of contract, they helped to liberalize and humanize our international and our criminal law, as well as the law of private and commercial transactions.

There is no inherent reason for rejecting the view that the roots of the law of contract are many rather than one. Agreements and promises are enforced to enable people to rely on them as a rule and thus make the path of enterprise more secure; but in this connection the law must also go beyond the original intention of the parties, to settle controversies as to the distribution of gains and losses that the parties did not anticipate in the same way. Some recognition must always be given to the will or intention of those who made the contract, but the law must always have regard for the *general* effects of classes of transactions, and it cannot free men from the necessity of acting at their peril when they do not know the consequences that the law will attach to their acts—and this needs to be emphasized in any attempt to formulate a rational theory. The law is a going concern and like all social institutions is governed by habit. It therefore will continue to enforce promises and agreements for no better reason than that they have been enforced and there is no sufficient countervailing consideration to force or justify a break with the established habit that has become the basis of social expectancies. Legal and other habits are not always deliberately formed to serve a definite purpose. Certain forms or ceremonies arise under special circumstances but continue to appeal to us through the principle of economy of effort: it is generally easier to use the existing forms than to break with them and adopt new ones. Of course old forms may become inconvenient or positive hindrances. They are then whittled away by pious fiction or violently changed by revolutionary legislation. In general, however, the ancient truth that men are creatures of habit will put us on guard against the vain assumption that we can get rid of formalism in the law of contract or anywhere else. We may flatter ourselves on getting rid of seal or other ancient binding ceremony. But we must remember that these forms seemed as naturally obligatory to our fathers as the signing of papers or the administering of oaths seem to us today.

In arguing for their indispensability we may recognize that not all forms are perfectly congenial or responsive to the need of the life that pulses through them. And as men become more enlightened they become more ready to discard, as well as employ, diverse instruments or vessels. Wisdom is not attained either by blind acceptance or blind rejection. We need a discriminating evaluation of what exists and what is possible; and this is something to which we can apply Spinoza's dictum: All things excellent are as difficult as they are rare.

The Process of Judicial Legislation[1]

WHETHER because of the general overturning of ordinary interests brought about by the World War, or for some other reason, the controversy over the recall of judges and judicial decisions that raged some years ago seems to have disappeared. The leaders of the American bar claim to have settled the matter by a campaign of education. The key-note of this campaign was sounded by Elihu Root when he urged that the public be educated to an appreciation of the true function of the judge, which he expressed as follows: "It is not his function or within his power to enlarge or improve or change the law."[2] In Sharswood's "Essay on Professional Ethics," republished by the American Bar Association, judicial legislation is the one cardinal sin of which jurists must beware.[3]

In spite, however, of the apparent authority back of this theory, a philosopher need not hesitate to declare it demonstrably false, i.e., contrary to fact. If judges never make law, how could the body of rules known as the common law ever have arisen or have undergone the changes which it has?

Moreover, not only is the common law changed from time to time by judicial decisions, but we may with Professor Gray[4] go on to assert that in the last analysis the courts also make our statute law; for it is the court's interpretation of the meaning of a statute that constitutes the law. If any one needed to be convinced of this, a mere reference to the history of the Sherman Anti-Trust Act would be sufficient. The situation, however, becomes quite transparent in the realm of constitutional law. Who has made the body of law dealing with the police power of the states if not judges within the last forty years? Indeed the same men who insist that judges never make the law also tell us, as Mr. Hornblower does, how much better judge-made law is than that which we get from our legislators.[5] What respectable lawyer is not ready, at a moment's notice, to extol the work of John Marshall in shaping the national Constitution? If the judges are in no way to change or make the law, what business had Marshall to shape the Constitution?[6] Obvious as these considerations are, the theory with which we are contending is so entrenched in powerful places that we cannot afford to ignore it. We must consider the motives that make it acceptable to so many.

(1) The first reason that suggests itself is that the theory finds acceptance because it meets the daily experience of the bench and bar. Most human actions that come before courts are of the kind that repeat themselves. One case is very much like another, and for the vast majority of cases some rule or precedent can be discovered. Lawyers and judges, therefore, get into the habit of thinking and talking of every possible case in terms of some rule that ought to govern it. This explanation, however, while perfectly true so far as it goes, is not adequate; for the uncertainty of the law before the court has decided, the doubt whether it will follow or overrule precedent, or try to do both by subtly distinguishing the new case, is also an experience and ought to throw doubt on the dogma that every decision is absolutely necessitated by established principles.[7] Our text-books of logic tell us that a theory must meet all the facts; that a universal proposition is rendered false by the presence of any contradictory instances. But in the legal field (as in others) what we call facts are moulded by the theories into which they have to fit. Many of the facts, then, which seem to bear out what I shall call the phonograph theory of the judicial function—according to which the judge merely repeats the words that the law has spoken into him—seem true only because of the prevalence of the theory in question. Obstructing facts can be ignored, explained away, or denied. But theories are mental habits that cannot be

changed at will. These considerations are important in so far as they put us on our guard against the easy assumption that legal theories are like inert clothes, made to fit preëxistent facts.

(2) It may be argued that this theory of the function of the judge is necessitated by the doctrine of the division of powers embodied in our constitutions. The prevailing attitude toward this theory was well expressed by the late Justice Lurton: "Nearly a half century before our Federal Constitution emerged, Montesquieu formulated, and defended upon unanswerable philosophical and historical considerations, the dogma that neither public nor private liberty could be maintained without a division of the legislative, executive and judicial functions of the government." [8]

An examination of Montesquieu's argument [9] shows that the supposed unanswerable philosophical and historical considerations are nothing more than a misinterpretation of the British constitution of his day, and an exaggeration of a very questionable political doctrine of Aristotle.[10] Montesquieu thought that the British constitution embodied such a division of power. As a matter of fact, it did nothing of the kind. The judges of England were independent of the Crown, but not of Parliament, and there was certainly no sharp separation even then between the legislature and the executive. Montesquieu was a man of wide but inaccurate learning—witness his treatment of the Roman law. The exquisite character of his style was responsible for the spread of many a vague and false generalization, but modern political science has gone beyond his method of free and easy generalization from one or two inaccurately observed instances. Not only does history show no example of any form of government where the three powers were really sharply separated, but modern political science has learned a general distrust of the naïve rationalism which supposes that the complicated facts of government can be readily and sharply divided into airtight *a priori* compartments.

But you may say: Whatever the origin of the theory of the division of power, it has become embodied in our federal and state constitutions and is, therefore, no longer a theory but a legal fact. Unfortunately, the situation is not so simple, for not even the might of a written constitution can make a false theory work smoothly. A complete separation of the organs of government, as even the writers of the *Federalist* recognized,[11] would lead to three separate attempts at government, resulting in anarchy. The framers of the Federal Constitution gave the President a share in legislation, and one branch of Congress a share in the administration (through the power of confirming or rejecting executive appointments), but these exceptions have not been enough. The executive now makes all sorts of laws in the form of departmental regulations; and in such matters as the use of the mail, on which a man's entire business may depend, executive officers exercise almost complete judicial power. On the other hand, our legislators, by controlling appropriations, determine executive policies, while our courts control administrative matters through mandamus proceedings, and administer a large part of the business of the country through receivers. Through the power of determining what is a reasonable return on an investment, judges practically decide the price of gas, railway rates, etc. As conservative a thinker as Judge Baldwin admits that in no state are the functions of our courts purely judicial.[12]

The result of thus maintaining a theory and not allowing its logical consequences to interfere with the necessities of practice has been to breed a confusion that would be regarded as scandalous in any of the natural sciences. Marshall is seldom at ease when he approaches this topic,[13] and Story plainly flounders. Thus the latter in his *Commentaries*,[14] after laying it down as "a maxim of vital importance that these powers should be forever kept separate and distinct," goes on later to point out that the true meaning of this maxim is that "the whole power of one of these departments should not be exercised by the same hands which possess the whole power of either of the other departments." But clearly the doctrine becomes futile in this last form, for in no government can all the power be exercised by the same hands. Certainly in no case where legislative acts have been held void because of violation of this constitutional maxim has this "true meaning" of the maxim been employed. Courts, however, commonly begin by paying homage to this maxim and then quietly disregard it. Thus one court says, "While it is true that 'the executive, legislative and supreme judicial powers of the government ought to be forever separate and distinct,' it is also true that the science of government is a practical one." [15] Thus this second principle, because it is also true, takes precedence over the Constitution. We may well say, with Goethe, "Mighty is the Law, but mightier still is Necessity."

Teachers of political science assure us that the inconsistency of judges in enforcing this and other *a priori* maxims is the only thing that has made some sort of government possible. But on purely logical grounds it is hard to see any ground of preference between the anarchy of a government trying to function with three separate and distinct organs, and the higher lawlessness of courts overruling the Constitution that they profess to guard.

It has been claimed that in practice our party system has abolished the theoretical division of powers just as the extra-legal national convention system has in effect abolished the constitutional provisions for the election of the President. But the confusion of responsibility that competent observers place among the radical shortcomings of our system of government shows that we have by no means solved the problem of getting rid of the effects of our maxim in practice. Doubtless the party system has accomplished something in the way of funded responsibility, but the extra-legal character of its leadership and control has been an insuperable handicap to its efficiency. The fact that we profess the theory of the separation of powers, and of the responsibility of all officers to the people directly, gives strength to the perennial crusades of reformers against "bossism" and makes the position of the party leader unattractive to the type of man who in England or France would aspire to the position of prime minister. The double life of an extra-legal union and legal separation works as badly in the state as it does in the family.

A recent device to overcome this division of responsibility is that of government by commission. Commissions like the Interstate Commerce Commission, the Wisconsin Industrial Commission, the various public service commissions, boards of health, etc., all really combine limited administrative, legislative, and judicial power. They initiate investigations, formulate rules and regulations, and pass on the question whether these rules have been complied with. But while courts have been in the main liberal in allowing such commissions to flourish, the fact remains that if the maxim of the division of power and its corollary (that legislative power may not be delegated) were strictly enforced, the life of these commissions would be impossible. As it is they live in a sort of legal twilight.

How we are to be relieved of the difficulties resulting from thus professing a false theory while endeavouring in practice to disregard it, is a problem for the statesman rather than for the philosopher. Seeing that many other civilized nations enjoy the blessings of liberty without professing this tripartite division of powers,[16] the philosopher can view with unconcern the entire abandonment of the theory. Certainly to defend the phonograph theory of the judicial function on the basis of the dogma of separation of powers is to base an untenable theory upon one still more untenable.

(3) A third source of opposition to the view that judges make law is found in our constitutional prohibition of *ex post facto* laws and general abhorrence of retroactive legislation, which make it very disagreeable for lawyers to admit that judges make law; for all judicial legislation is literally *ex post facto* so far as the parties before the court are concerned.[17] Mr. Hornblower tries to meet this difficulty by the simple argument that since judges always make their rules in accordance with the principles of honesty and fair play, the parties before the court may be presumed to have been familiar with those rules, and to have acted at their peril.[18] This argument ignores the fact that the law deals with large regions

of acts that are morally indifferent. Surely a sense of justice and fair play will not alone enable one to predict how courts will rule on a question of equitable conversion or executory devises. Moreover, as not all principles of honesty and fair play receive legal sanction, and those which do are often limited by purely technical rules, it is clear that it is only by virtue of some process of judicial legislation that certain moral rules are selected and adapted for legal enforcement.

(4) In an article on Puritanism in American law,[19] Professor Pound contends that the Puritan view of life led to a distrust of magistrates and thus to a limitation of judicial power. This may well be disputed, but surely no thoughtful student can fail to note how deeply all our political institutions are saturated with the Calvinistic views of human nature. So certain is man to sin that the mere fact "that power might be abused was a conclusive argument against its being bestowed." [20] But it is well to note that we find this phonograph view of the judicial function prevailing also in other countries. The historical and socialistic schools in Europe apply this view also to the legislature, regarding the legislature simply as a registering machine, by means of which the *Volksgeist*, or the prevailing system of economic production, enforces its demands. Indeed, before the advent of the modern legislative industry, we find an almost universal tendency to regard law not as man-made, but as imposed by supernatural power, by Yahweh himself on Mount Sinai. In the Middle Ages it was generally felt that to find the law, appeal to supernatural power was necessary.[21] And not long ago a leader of the New York bar declared "poor, indeed, will be the lawgiver or the judge who does not . . . acknowledge that he is not a maker, but a seeker among divine sources for preëxisting truth." [22] The feeling seems to be that statute law, or anything man-made, is a mere contrivance and cannot have the virtue of true law. Men certainly find it difficult to conceive how they can be the creators of that which is binding upon them. This difficulty is by no means peculiar to the law. The situation meets us in lan-

guage, religion, and wherever else we encounter obligatory elements, the existence of which in a mechanistic system is explained by a *deus ex machina*. Thus it used to be thought that language could have originated only by a special convention (Lord Monboddo) or else by special divine intervention (De Maistre). The existence of society needed a social contract to give it birth, just as religion could have come into being only as the invention of some clever priest, or else as the result of some special revelation.

These difficulties as to origins appear only in narrowly mechanistic systems. They disappear if we think in terms of growth or development. Thus if we view language as gradually growing out of expressive gestures and cries that are organic in origin, we need no longer be troubled by the ancient and difficult question, "Which was the first human language and what was the first word uttered?" In a process of growth there need not be any absolute first term. Similarly, if we look at law or language as a fixed system, its governing rules seem eternal and dictated, as it were, by powers not ourselves. But consider any human institution as growing, and you can see how its rules, which are obligatory and which seem *a priori* at any one stage, are the outcome of previous functions.

This insight is the sound core of the opposition of the historical school of jurisprudence to the older natural-law theories which regarded the genuine rules of law as eternal. But the historical school because of its initial bias against revolutionary legislation could not or would not recognize that the rules of law are not only changing, but also changeable. Law, like language, they urged, is a growth of the folk-spirit (*Volksgeist*), which could no more be changed by deliberate human effort than could the laws of nature. This, however, still adheres to the old narrowly mechanistic view of nature as entirely external to individual human intelligence. The adherents of this view failed to realize that human effort might be, as Justice Holmes puts it, one of the ways through which the inevitable comes to pass. Thus it is true in a sense that the English common law, like the English language, was never planned by any individual mind or assembly. But each of these institutions shows, certainly in its later stages, the integrated effects of the deliberate and conscious efforts of individual men to deal with legal or linguistic policies. When society is relatively stable, law-making is carried on in a relatively minute scale and can be covered by fictions. But in a period of rapid social changes, law-making becomes more comprehensive and must thus become more deliberative and explicit—just as baseball and football, when they become highly organized, must call into being deliberative rule-making bodies. Even language, in its advanced stage, has its actual growth influenced by the resolutions of academies, and the views of critics, grammarians, and educational authorities. Judges, umpires, and the chairmen of parliamentary bodies may, in their rulings, try to meet the needs of the cases before them. But if their decisions are wise, it is because they recognize the controlling elements or factors, and to the extent that they do so, their decisions will serve as precedents and thus make law.

Typical of the old eighteenth-century preëvolutionary philosophy of law is the rather naïve view that we can draw up a final code of substantive rules to govern the affairs of men for all time to come. To be sure, in this country we do not use the word code; but is not the classical view of the Constitution from Marshall to Fuller just such a plan of government to endure forever and under which men will live happy forever afterwards? Indeed we sometimes also speak of the common law as if it were just such a code drawn by some superhuman wisdom in the dim past.[23] It is so usual to speak of our Lady of the Common Law as having a continuous existence since Anglo-Saxon days or at least since the days of Edward I, that some of us would be shocked if a sceptic questioned the identity of the Lady. Such a sceptic might, for instance, quote a recent incumbent of Blackstone's chair at Oxford: "I doubt if Blackstone, could he suddenly visit the Courts which have taken the place of those he knew, would understand enough of their law and procedure to do more than to feel occasionally shocked."[24] At any rate, if the identity of the common law since Littleton, Coke, or Blackstone is to be maintained at all, it is not as a collection of substantive rules but rather as a mode of judicial thinking, or as a method of law-making.

The theory, then, that law preëxists judicial decision, and that judges, therefore, can and should do their work without at the same time making new law, can be defended only on the assumption of the eternal self-sufficiency of the existing law. If, however, life is continually developing new and unforeseeable situations not covered by precedent, and judges are obliged to decide every case before them (these decisions serving as binding precedents), it follows that they must in the course of their work develop new rules.[25]

The process according to which this law-making takes place may be viewed under the three headings of finding, interpreting, and applying the law.

I. FINDING OR MAKING THE LAW

In the physical world no antithesis seems more justified than that between making and finding. Inventing and finding a continent are surely incompatible. When, however, we come to human affairs, the antithesis becomes less sharp. Making and finding an opportunity, making or finding time, making or finding a theory, are not so clearly antagonistic. Hence we need not be surprised that under the pressure of a prevailing theory, embodied in a current terminology, the process of law-making should be called finding the law. Some simple-hearted people believe that the names we give to things do not matter. But though the rose by any other name might smell as sweet, the history of civilization bears ample testimony to the momentous influence of names. At any rate, whether the process of judicial legislation should be called finding or making the law is undoubtedly of great practical moment.

To speak of finding the law seems to connote that the law exists before the decision, and thus tends to minimize the importance of the judicial contribution to the law or of the *arbitrium judicium* and the factors that determine it.

How is the law found? Consider, to begin with, cases of first impression that have no clear precedent. They are decided, we are told, on principle.[26] But what principle, and where does it come from? If we examine the decisions of the great creative minds in our legal history, of judges like Mansfield, Gibson, or Shaw, we find the prevailing ideas of justice, public convenience, and what is "reasonable" are always appealed to as decisive. (It has been noted that Marshall seldom cited precedents.) Moral rules or considerations of public convenience do not, of course, of themselves have the force of law. It is only when courts, balancing considerations of justice and policy, decide to enforce a moral or political rule that they transform it into a legal rule.[27] At any rate, there can be no doubt that by direct judicial legislation based on supposed principles of justice have been developed the bodies of law known as quasi contract, the common counts, the law of boycott, etc. Principles of public policy can be seen in the law of trade and other fixtures, in the doctrine of contracts void against public policy, the law of agency, the distinction between libel and slander, the law of privileged communications, the law of corporations, etc.[28] A great deal of judicial legislation also takes place under cover of finding what is "reasonable" under given circumstances. Thus our whole law of negligence consists essentially of various standards of conduct set up by courts to which people must conform at their peril. The same process can be observed in the law as to what are the reasonable necessities of an infant, what is a reasonable time for notice of dishonour of a bill, what is reasonable cause in an action for malicious prosecution or false arrest, and what is the reasonable income to which a public service corporation is entitled.[29]

It may be urged that these cases of first impression which constitute the leading cases of any branch of law are rare and must continue to become rarer as the number of precedents increases. To this we may reply that the cases of first impression are rare only because, in consequence of the prevailing theory, we tend to lose sight of them. Every case differs in some respect from previous ones. But the felt necessity of finding precedents produces the tendency to ignore or minimize these differences. Nor is it true that as the number of decided cases increases, the number of cases of first impression must necessarily diminish. The possibility of these latter cases depends not so much on the mass of adjudicated cases as on the rapidity with which conditions of life are changing. Moreover, as the number of precedents increases, skilful counsel can and do all the more readily find precedents on both sides, so that the process of judicial decision is, as a matter of fact, determined consciously or unconsciously by the judges' views of fair play, public policy, and the general nature and fitness of things. It is true that judges of a certain temperament, the so-called strong-minded judges, frequently stop short at most tempting equities with the plea that authoritative precedent or well-settled law will not permit them to mete out the justice that they would like to enforce.[30] This, however, does not mean that justice is not a ground of decision with such judges; for we find them in other cases reasoning that that which leads to unjust or monstrous consequences cannot be the law.

The same judges who could not, because of the Fourteenth Amendment or its equivalent, approve the constitutionality of an admittedly just workmen's compensation law, had no difficulty in declaring unconstitutional a primary law that for all its iniquity did not seem to run afoul of any specific constitutional provision.[31] The simple fact is that the desire to do justice is a constant motive, but the sense for juristic consistency or symmetry is another that sometimes outweighs it. The relative weight of these two, as a matter of fact, varies with the psychology or temperament of the judge. Whatever may be the constitution of the ideal judge, it is not unreasonable to suppose that the minds of most judges work like those of other mortals, that is, having in various ways been unconsciously determined to decide one way or another, they look for and find reasons or precedents for such decisions. It was not a layman but a president of the American Bar Association who said that "a judge may decide almost any question any way, and still be supported by an array of cases." [32]

Perhaps an extreme instance of establishing new rules under the guise of following precedent is seen in judicial legislation that is based on analogy, as when, for instance, the law of common carriers is applied to telegraph companies, or the rule of easement by prescription to mortgages, etc. In such legislation, the influence of text writers and what the French call "doctrine" is most apparent. The influence of general doctrines of jurisprudence is also seen clearly in the process of judicial codification, i.e., the process of generalizing from a number of cases to a general rule or definition. [33]

One of the most serious charges that can be made against the historical school of jurisprudence is that it has failed to do justice to the process whereby one nation adopts the laws of another. The reception of Roman law in Germany, of a great deal of canon and civil law in England, of the Napoleonic Code in the different countries of Europe, Spanish America, and elsewhere, of the French criminal code in Japan, and of the common law in the colonies, are not solitary phenomena. [34] They are simply extreme instances of a process that goes on more or less slowly between all nations that have cultural relations with each other. Our laws of probate, admiralty, conflict of laws, and rules of international law illustrate a constant though slow process, which takes place when judges decide to give sanction to rules prevailing in other jurisdictions, and thus introduce new rules into their own system. It is to be observed that foreign laws are not accepted merely because they are laws elsewhere. Judges exercise the sovereign prerogative of choice, and refuse to give effect to rules that in their opinion are unjust, inconvenient, or totally out of harmony with their own system. [35]

The transformation of custom into law is somewhat analogous to this reception of foreign law. Custom as such does not give one a legal right. Courts, however, do frequently give legal sanction to certain customary ways of doing things and thus transform them into legal rules. The classical instance of such judicial legislation is the creation of modern mercantile law by Lord Mansfield out of long-established customs of merchants.

Legislation generally consists not only in the making of new rules but also in the amendment or modification of old rules. Some writers seem to maintain that while judges can make law, they cannot or should not change it. It is hard to see any possible valid reason for this distinction. The making of a new rule itself changes the legal rights of people and is therefore a change in the law. As a matter of fact, the common law is constantly changed by judicial decision. Even in those branches of the law that do not directly bear on the industrial order, great changes have taken place: [36] in the law of marriage and divorce and in the law of evidence the books of Messrs. Bishop and Wigmore have caused the legal profession to entertain new views on these subjects, and the law has changed accordingly. Even in the supposed relatively fixed branches of law, such as property, contracts, equity, criminal law, and civil liability, no teacher of the law could adequately present the leading principles of his subject if he left out the leading cases of the past twenty years.

Owing to the prevalent acceptance of the phonograph theory of the judicial function and the fact that owing to many circumstances judges belong to the most conservative portion of the community, changes in the law are not introduced except when compelled by overpowering considerations and then only in gradual and piecemeal fashion. The accepted theory thus prevents judges from changing the law when they should and disguises the process when they do. For the most part, old established rules are gradually abrogated by the process of distinguishing new cases and creating exceptions, or else they are altered by stretching them to fit entirely new situations. Well known illustrations of the former process are to be found in the establishment of the fellow-servant rule as a limitation on the general rule of *respondeat superior*, in the softening of the former by the "vice-principal" doctrine and by the extension of the degree of care due the employee, and in the way the parol evidence rule has been whittled down by the doctrine of collateral contracts. Instances of change in the law by the process of stretching old terms are to be found in the law of conspiracy [37] and in the way the old law of common carriers has been applied to modern railways, telegraphs, express companies, etc.

The elasticity of legal rules is not unlimited; and when the new wine can no longer be poured into the old bottles, courts resort to fictions whereby new vessels are adopted as old possessions of the legal household. Legal fiction is the mask that progress must wear to pass the faithful but blear-eyed watchers of our ancient legal treasures. But though legal fictions are useful in thus mitigating or absorbing the shock of innovation, they work havoc in the form of intellectual confusion. The least that can be said is that they tend to make us all ignore the magnitude and character of the actual changes wrought by them.[38] The mask shuts off a great deal of needed light.

Among the various types of legal fiction we may briefly mention: (1) changes in the substantive law under the guise of passing on the sufficiency of evidence; (2) the creation of presumptions; and (3) the invention of conditions implied by law.

(1) As to the first, a single quotation from Justice Holmes's classic book will be sufficient: "When a judge rules that there is no evidence of negligence, he does something more than is embraced in an ordinary ruling that there is no evidence of a fact. He rules that the acts or omissions proved or in question do not constitute a ground of legal liability, and in this way the law is gradually enriching itself from daily life, as it should." [39] The law should by all means enrich itself from daily life, but it should do so with open eyes. The confusion between substantive rules and evidence has, as Thayer has indicated, been a fruitful source of mischief.

(2) Of the character of presumptions as rules of substantive law, and the identity in effect between the process of developing presumptions and the process of conscious legislation, it is only necessary to refer to the golden words on the subject in Thayer's *Preliminary Treatise on Evidence*.[40]

(3) The finding of conditions implied by law is amply illustrated in many branches of law. Thus the so-called contract of employment has a number of duties implied, one of which is the assumption of risk by the employee. As a matter of fact the workman actually never or seldom thinks of the risk, and surely in actual life has very little to do with determining the conditions of his employment. The assumption of risk is purely the judicial invention of Lord Abinger, Chief Justice Shaw, and Baron Alderson. Yet so powerfully do legal fictions work and so short is the legal memory of men, that a doctrine of which there is no trace before 1837 is in 1911 treated as a law of nature, and courts doubt whether a legislature has the right to abolish it.[41] It may be a law of nature that the loss should lie where it falls, but surely it is not a law of nature that the loss should forever lie where the courts happen to have put it. Indeed the same court that holds the assumption of risk on the part of the employee to be a law of nature did, in a subsequent decision, flatly overrule itself and shifted the loss from the employee to the employer in cases where the latter had violated statutory provisions.[42] The whole theory of employers' liability (which has grown to such enormous bulk and monstrous complexity) is certainly simplified by omitting all reference to implied conditions and recognizing with the late Mr. Beven that in addition to contract obligations, the master has certain other obligations prescribed by common law.[43]

In thus briefly indicating some of the ways in which courts make law under the guise of finding it, we must not forget that so far as the law of practice or procedure is concerned, there is little doubt that courts do and should enact rules as consciously as other legislative bodies. All higher common law courts also ultimately decide the limits of their jurisdiction, whether they shall or shall not overrule their own decision, etc. Under the Scotch Acts of Sederunt or in the form of the French *arrêts de règlement* this power extends to direct conscious changes in the substantive law, and our own practice permits statutes that in effect leave it to the courts to fill in the details or to determine when the statute is to go into operation.

It is characteristic of the prevailing rationalistic systems of legal philosophy that they minimize the importance of procedure by calling it adjective law, etc. But the tendency of all modern scientific and philosophic thought is to weaken the distinction between substance and attribute (based on a simile of a man in his clothes) and to emphasize the importance of method, process, or procedure. Students of legal history know the truth of the statement that "the substantive law is secreted in the interstices of procedure," nor need practitioners be reminded how frequently changes in procedure affect the substantive right of parties.

II. INTERPRETATION AS A MODE OF JUDICIAL LEGISLATION

There are few branches of the law of which the theory is so confused and disorganized as in the case of the interpretation and construction of written instruments. For this condition the theory of judicial passivity is in no slight degree responsible. This theory finds expression in the assertion that legal interpretation consists solely in finding the intention of the writer. But can any one maintain that the accepted rules of legal interpretation are simply scientific rules for the discovery of actual intention? Doubtless judges, like others, do sometimes seek and find the actual intention of parties as revealed in writings before them; but when they do so, they make use of the ordinary knowledge of language and affairs and they do not use any special rules or organon any more than they do in interpreting the oral communications of witnesses. Perhaps the day is not far distant when a scientific psychology of written language will be in a position to offer definite data to the jurist, but the prevailing technical rules of construction are not of this character. They come down to us largely from the Roman law, and their main function, so far as they partake of the nature of rules, is first, to introduce certainty by fixing a meaning in cases where conflicting meanings are otherwise possible (all questions of meaning for the court arise, of course, through the fact that two different meanings are claimed by the contending parties),⁴⁴ and, secondly, to subordinate the intention of the parties to considerations of public policy and the convenience of judicial administration. Just as the rules of evidence are, in the main, fashioned to exclude what is logically probative, so our rules of interpretation and construction of written instruments are, for the most part, rules for the exclusion of inquiry into the actual psychological intention. Considerations of public policy and of the convenient administration of justice require us to attach certain consequences to words, irrespective of the actual intention of the writer.⁴⁵ It is because of such considerations, and not in the interest of scientific truth, that the rules for the interpretation of wills differ from the rules for the interpretation of contracts or deeds, and the rule of executory from those of executed trusts.⁴⁶ Again, a blind fear of paternalism makes us say that the proper duty of the court is to interpret people's contracts, to give effect to their actual intention, and not to make contracts or impose obligations that the parties did not intend when they contracted. But as a matter of fact most of the disputes about contracts arise because of the emerging of unexpected conditions that were not in the contemplation of the parties when they made their agreement. In all such cases the courts do not enforce the real intentions of the parties, for there were none, but decide on the rights of the contestants in accordance with their sense of the equities of the case or the suggestion of analogous rules of legal obligation.

These considerations are suggestive in enabling us to avoid some confusing fiction in the theory of statutory interpretation.

Austin, Lieber, and most eminent writers after them define interpretation as the discovery of the true meaning of a statute or law. In harmony with the phonograph theory of the judicial function, this true meaning is lodged in the mind of the legislature, and the upright judge simply finds it and in no way modifies it. In actual judicial interpretation, however, this is certainly not always true. If I have any difficulty in interpreting a passage in a book, I consider myself fortunate if I can interrogate the author himself. But for the courts to ask those who actually drew up a statute what they meant would be absurd,[47] nay, even an expressed declaration by a legislature as to what was meant in a previous statute is effective not from the time of the original, but only from the time of the declaratory act.[48] In defence of this rule we are told that the rights acquired under the original act must not be presumed to be divested by a subsequent declaratory act. But if the actual intention of the legislator makes law, how could any rights be acquired contrary to the intention of the law? [49] We can get rid of this and other difficulties by recognizing that the legislative intent is an eliminable fiction. Experience amply shows that the drafters or framers of a law, the committee that reports it, the majority of the members of the two houses that, for various reasons, pass it, and the executive that signs it are by no means always agreed as to its meaning.[50] Hence the rule that parliamentary debates are of no direct value in the interpretation of statutes.[51]

Back, however, of the motives and ideas of the various individuals who constitute the legislature are the various interests concerned in the passing of a measure into law. We do not, of course, avoid fiction altogether by calling the triumph of one of these interests or the final compromise between conflicting claims "the will of the people." But such language brings us nearer to the actual procedure of courts in interpreting statutes, and helps us to understand the real significance of the statement that courts interpret not the actual intention of the legislator but the meaning of the statute before them.

What is the meaning of a statute? The rule that courts must interpret the meaning of the statute rather than the intention of the legislature is frequently conceived as if it implied that the words of a statute are sufficient to determine every question that arises under it. This would lead to a revival of the stage of strict law in which the strictly literal meaning of words is followed no matter how unjust or absurd the consequences. Doubtless there are many who still believe juristic interpretation to be a kind of magic whereby a whole body of law is made to spring out of a few words or phrases. But most modern jurists are outgrowing the superstitious awe of the printed word and its magic potency. The meaning of a statute consists in the system of social consequences to which it leads or of the solutions to all the possible social questions that can arise under it.[52] These solutions or systems of consequences cannot be determined solely from the words used, but require a knowledge of the social conditions to which the law is to be applied as well as of the circumstances which led to its enactment. Legal rules relate to human life, and grammar or formal logic alone will not enable us to deduce their juridical consequences. The proof of the fact that the interpretation of legal rules is impossible without an intimate knowledge of the factual world to which they are to be applied, is seen in the many rules of Roman law that are today unintelligible because we do not know sufficiently under what conditions they were intended to work. The meaning of a statute, then, is a juridical creation in the light of social demands. It decides not so much what the legislature actually intended, nor what the words of a statute ordinarily mean, but *what the public, taking all the circumstances of the case into account, should act on.*[53]

Consider the rules of statutory interpretation laid down in any text-book, for example, that penal statutes, or statutes in derogation of the common law, should be strictly construed, that remedial statutes should be liberally construed, and that there is an almost conclusive presumption against an unreasonable or inconvenient intention on the part of the legislator. These are not scientific rules for the discovery of actual intentions or the meanings of words, but *maxims of public policy to guide judges in the process of making law out of statutes.* It is notorious that the assumption of legislative reasonableness and regard for public welfare is one that judges privately do not hold, but public policy requires it in the administration of law. It is certainly only from this latter point of view that we can find any rationale in the rules against retroactivity. Why, for instance, can rules against retroactivity be invoked against new rights but not against new remedies, against penal legislation but not against remedial provisions? It is only by the recognition of the fact that judicial interpretation makes law that we can justify the position that decisions, like statutes, are not to be interpreted retroactively;[54] that the judicial construction of a statute is "as much a part of the statute as the text itself, and a change of decision is to all intents and purposes the same in its effects on contracts as an amendment of the law by means of a legislative act or amendment."[55] The whole Gordian knot of controversy over *Gelpcke* v. *Dubuque*, together with the seeming force of Justice Miller's dissenting opinion, is certainly removed by the recognition that courts do and must make law.[56]

It is generally stated that the reason why questions of interpretation arise at all is because of the necessary obscurity of language; and doubtless it is impossible to formulate regulations that shall be so unequivocal in all situations as to render unnecessary judicial selection from possible meanings. Reference, however, to the rules of interpretation applied by English courts, dealing with statutes very carefully drawn, shows that most of the questions of interpretation arise not so much because of the obscurities of language, but rather because the *courts have to apply a general law to a situation that could not have been foreseen by the legislature*. Take as an instance the Workmen's Compensation Act of 1906. This act was practically an extension of the act of 1897, as amended in 1900. The original act was most carefully drawn, and its workings carefully studied by the Digby Commission, whose report the framers of the act of 1906 had before them. Yet in spite of a mass of supplementary legislation, in the form of orders by the Home Secretary, volumes of court decisions have been necessary to determine whether certain situations shall be brought within the scope of the bill or not. In our own country, where statutes are not so carefully drawn (because of perennially green legislators), where we do not have anything to compare in thoroughness with the English statutory interpretation act of 1889, and where, because of the mischievous dogma that legislative powers cannot be delegated, we do not allow administrative officers ample power of supplementary legislation, all this mass of supplementary legislation has to be enacted by the courts, in the form of judicial interpretations, and no one really knows a law thoroughly unless he knows what the courts have made of it.[57]

Not only must courts supplement legislative enactments by supplying the detailed rules and regulations, but the interests of any workable justice demand that courts should also in effect exercise a limited power of amending the law. Legislatures are the commissioners of warring social interests. They can draw up general treaties of peace, but the details have at all times been and must be inserted by the courts, else we should have a constant recurrence to a state of lawlessness. Courts must necessarily attach a somewhat different meaning to statutes than do the legislators, owing to the necessarily different point of view. The conditions of legislation make legislators view even the most general statutes exclusively as measures of relief to certain social demands. Courts, however, must construe them as integral parts of the legal system that controls the whole of life. Legislators can never have in mind all the possible consequences of their enactments, and many of them would be shocked and would refuse to pass the bills they do if they could realize these consequences. Hence, every system of legal administration that is not impossibly rigorous allows the judge, who has had the chance of seeing the actual working of the statute in concrete situations, some power of amendment—hard and fast legal and political theories to the contrary notwithstanding.[58]

The process by which the terms of laws are widened or narrowed has been called spurious interpretation. Such interpretation is spurious only so far as it pretends to discover the actual intention of the legislator, but the process of extending or restricting the meaning of a statute is inevitable. Unless we are wilfully to blind ourselves by some dogma of legislative omniscience, we must recognize that supplementary legislation by judges or other administrative officials is absolutely necessary to make statutes workable.[59] Statutes must be expressed in general and more or less abstract terms. *To make a de-*

tailed description of specific human actions forbidden or allowed and their consequences would be an endless and impossible task. The judge, however, must apply the general rule to specific cases. To prevent an impossible uniformity or rigour, and to give statutes a form and content that will adapt them to the complicated needs of life, judges must classify the cases under the rule and use what is called equitable interpretation as a corrective or supplement to the abstract generality of the law before them. That equitable interpretation is not foreign to the essence of the common law can be seen in such writers as Littleton, Coke, and Sheppard. Some of our courts and text-book writers have said that the doctrine of equitable interpretation has been abandoned in modern times. But does not the well established rule and practice that an inconvenient and inequitable interpretation is to be avoided, that the spirit rather than the letter of the statute is to be given effect, amount to the same thing? The extent to which this latter rule is carried can be shown by the fact that courts will, in the interests of equitable interpretation, change the tense of a statute,[60] interpret the phrase "single man" to include widows,[61] or the term "woman" to exclude married women,[62] and the like. Nothing is more usual in the interpretation of statutes than to find them construed as operating between certain persons only, or for certain purposes only, though the language expresses no such limitation;[63] or cases where the language is extended to include things that were not known and could not have been contemplated by the legislators when the statute was passed— for example, when the word "telegraph" is held to cover the telephone invented subsequent to the law in question.[64]

Interpretation frequently appears to be necessitated by logical rigour, only because we tacitly accept the whole system of assumptions in the mind of the interpreter; thus the argument for the power to declare statutes unconstitutional, as deduced by Marshall, seems unanswerable. But that it is not at all logically necessary, that an opposite result was logically (though perhaps not historically) possible,[65] can be seen in the fact that this power is not exercised in other federal constitutions.

If the theory that judges have no share in the making of statute law breaks down, what shall we say of the theory that they have no share in the making of constitutional law? In view of the great uncertainty that always prevails not only among the educated public, but even among the members of the bar, as to how our courts of last resort will rule on a question involving, let us say the police power, how can we say that what the court does is simply to declare a preexisting will of the people? I can understand the theory that after the court has ruled, its ruling should become the will of the people. But the constitutional theory that the court always acts as the mouthpiece of a preëxisting definite will of the people is at variance with all we know of popular psychology. How can we blink at the fact that on most questions involving the constitutionality of laws the majority of the people have no will at all because they have never thought of the matter and have no opinion either way?

Moreover, the distinctions that constitutional issues involve are often of a kind that could not possibly have been present in the minds of the people. It is absurd to maintain that when "the people" in 1789 adopted the Federal Constitution, with its commerce clause, they actually intended to give Congress authority to prohibit lotteries [66] (an honourable and established institution in those days) but not to regulate life insurance [67] or the transportation of goods made by child labour,[68] to order railway companies to install all sorts of safety appliances,[69] but not to prohibit them from discharging their men for joining trade unions.[70] Secular history gives no support to the view that when the Reconstruction leaders forced through (in effect at the point of the bayonet) the Fourteenth Amendment to the Federal Constitution, presumably to protect the civil rights of the Negroes, "the people" actually intended that states should not have the rights to prohibit bakers from working more than ten hours per day [71] but should have the power to prohibit miners from working more than eight hours per day,[72] or that the states should have the power to prohibit women from working more than ten hours a day [73] but no power to prohibit them from working for less than a minimum wage.[74]

The process of adopting a constitution is frequently spoken of as if it were a magical or supernatural procedure. It is, however, subject to all the frailties of human nature. A constitutional convention meets. Various delegates are specialists in specific provisions on which they have definite views and knowledge. These views they will successfully press on those who are specially qualified to deal with other matters. Hence every part of the constitution is the work of relatively few hands. When differences of opinion arise, as they did in the federal convention, compromises are effected that leave no one completely satisfied. This constitution is then presented to the people and they must vote in most cases either to accept or reject the whole thing. How many of those who vote for approval have had the opportunity to examine carefully every provision and consider all its possible consequences? Moreover, supposing that they do so, it does not follow that because they vote for it, it expresses their will, since the voters have no power to select freely the provisions that they approve and reject those that they do not.

The matter is even worse in case of the Federal Constitution, which in spite of the fact that it begins "We, the people," was never adopted by the people directly. It was adopted as a matter of fact by specially elected conventions, which in states like Massachusetts required considerable political jockeying not much different from that which characterizes political conventions of our own day. Historians of unquestioned conservatism like McMaster, President Wilson, Ford, and others have shown that the Federal Constitution was pushed through by a well organized group of urban and wealthy people against the apathy and opposition of the lower agricultural classes. I am not now raising the issue whether our constitutional system has been of benefit to the country or whether it should or should not be continued. I am merely trying to show the fictitious nature of the argument which says that every judicial decision is the expression of the will of the people and that judges have nothing to do with making the law what it is. Surely devotion to one's country, or to the institutions which happen to be established, does not require that one should adhere to inadequate arguments on their behalf.

The reason why all these arguments must logically break down is that they ultimately involve two contradictory absolutistic conceptions of what is law. One is that the law is the will of the sovereign, and the other that law is eternal reason or immutable justice. The notion that whatever pleases the sovereign is law comes to us from the Byzantine period of Roman law. The eighteenth century writers simply put the people in the place of the absolute emperor. The notion of law as reason comes to us from the Stoic philosophy. Ever since Blackstone acquired his dominance over American legal thought, his method of simply putting these two incompatible notions side by side, in the same definition, has prevailed. Now it is possible to construct a doctrine of restraints on the popular will in the interest of justice or reason; and it is also possible to construct a doctrine that what the people want, whether it be just or not, should prevail as law. But the combination of the two in the theory that law which judges make is both just and the will of the people, is a logically impossible feat.

The doctrine that whenever a court declares a legislative enactment unconstitutional it merely declares the will of the people, implies of course that the legislature in the act in question plainly disregarded the will of the people. But the promptness with which, in New York State for instance, constitutional decisions are recalled by amendment to the constitution, as for instance *People* v. *Coler*,[75] or the Ives case,[76] shows that the legislature was a better judge of what was the actual will of the people. And if we shift the issue to the time of the adoption of the constitution, the retort can still be made that when the state constitution was adopted, probably not one in ten thousand thought of a workmen's compensation law, but that if the matter had been explained to people then, they would in all likelihood have been in favour of it in 1894 as they showed themselves in favour of it in 1912. If any one were to suggest to a court of law that before giving a decision on a constitutional point it should institute an inquiry into the actual will of the people, the suggestion would rightly be treated as absurd. Courts must decide in the interest of justice, and not in accordance with the changing will of the majorities. Nevertheless in many cases our courts have declared inquiry into the justice of a statute irrelevant, on the ground that the will of the people is absolutely binding.

Out of this dilemma between two masters, justice and the will of the people, our publicists try to escape by drawing a sharp distinction between the capricious will of the majorities as shown in elections and the deliberate solemn will of the people as embodied in constitutions or fundamental laws. This distinction, however, is not at all grounded on fact. There is no actual evidence to show that people are more deliberate and solemn when they adopt a constitution than when they vote for local representatives. As a matter of fact, statistics show that fewer people are interested in voting for or against a state constitution than in voting for or against party candidates.

As a historic fact it cannot be denied that the vast body of constitutional law has been made by our courts in accordance with their sense of justice or public policy. The whole theory of police power is a judicial invention. The term does not occur in our constitutions, and not one man in ten thousand knows its precise limitations. As our most conservative journalists admit, our constitutional courts are continuous constitutional conventions, except that their decisions do not need ratification by the people. People as a rule are willing to let elected or appointed judges exercise supreme legislative power so long as this power is not too violently abused. Thus, when the New York Court of Appeals declared parts of the infamous Levy Primary Bill unconstitutional,[77] there was a general acquiescence; and if a logician had tried to show that there is no single clause in our state constitution necessitating that decision, he would have received scant hearing from the great mass of the voters. People generally do not care much about the question of usurpation of power. They are interested not in the archæological problem how a given power arose, but in the practical question how it is exercised. Forms of government are doubtless important, but modern political science treats them as instruments for the achievement of social ends. The great difficulty with the prevailing legal theory is that these forms are treated entirely on *a priori* grounds altogether apart from the realities of human experience.

The invocation to Reason rather than to the relevant facts of the social scene has become traditional in constitutional law. Since the Dartmouth College case, it has been said that courts do not declare a statute unconstitutional unless it is so beyond a reasonable doubt. But the reason thus invoked seems to be the "artificial reason" of Coke rather than the natural reason that prevails in logic and the sciences. The orthodox view requires the good citizen to denounce the incompetency of his legislature, and to scrutinize critically the acts of the executive; but he must at all times respect and reverence the judiciary. In consequence most people are quite prepared to accept the proposition that only judges can pass on what is reasonable. But when four judges of our highest court declare that a given law has a reasonable connection with the public health, and five say that no reasonable man can suppose that there is such a connection, one begins to doubt. Not only the reason but also the sense of humour and the courtesy of our judges thus appear to be of a peculiar transcendental variety.

III. THE APPLICATION OF LAWS AS A MODE OF LAW-MAKING

The application of laws has generally been viewed as a mere mechanical process of subsuming the particular facts or case under the proper category or rule. On the shelves of the law there is an ideal set of boxes such that, no matter what set of facts comes up from the hurly-burly of life, there is always just one ready-made appropriate box into which the facts will fit perfectly without any alterations or stretching. This follows from the view that legal categories or rules have an absolute precision like those of pure mathematics, and sustain no change whatever in being applied to the changing content of life. But the uncertainties of the law in practice are certainly sufficient to throw doubt on the supposed absolute precision of actual legal categories, and the history of law sufficiently refutes the assumption that such general ideas as property, contract, etc., are unchangeable categories.[78]

The difficulty of interpreting a law without knowing the conditions under which it is to be applied shows how hard it is to distinguish sharply between the interpretation and the application of law. For practical purposes, however, we may say that the question of the application of a rule of law may arise when two or more different rules seem applicable, and the question arises, which is to prevail? A statute gives a Board of Health authority to make such regulations as are necessary for the preservation of public health from impending pestilence. The Board of Health quarantines a person who refuses to be vaccinated, thereby interfering with his liberty. The court is certain that the legislature has power to authorize measures for public health; but also that enactments which affect the liberty of the person are to be strictly construed.[79] Where does one principle begin and the other end? When conflicting principles claim our attention, which should prevail? There are few legal rules that determine this, and some of these are worse than useless. Thus it is generally said that when a conflict arises between a requirement of public policy and an express constitutional provision, the latter must prevail.

Now our Federal Constitution expressly provides that the United States shall guarantee each state a republican form of government. It also provides that the Constitution shall be the supreme law of the land, and our Supreme Court, since *Marbury* v. *Madison,* is committed to the position that the final interpretation of this supreme law is the function of the courts. It necessarily follows from these premises that the courts must decide what is and what is not a republican form of government. But this would create practical difficulties, and so the courts have evaded this assumed obligation to interpret the Constitution by labelling this issue "political." [80]

One of the most unfortunate results of the phonograph view of the judicial function is the resulting neglect of the art or technique of legal application. If the judge has nothing to do but merely declare definite, preëxisting law, then all political or social science or philosophy must be foreign to him. Consider, however, what the application of law involves. It involves, first of all, an analysis and appreciation of the different factors in the living situation to which the law is to be applied, and secondly, a comprehensive perception of the relative importance and subordination of the different possible legal principles. The former involves a definite attitude toward ethical and social problems based on some (conscious or unconscious) philosophy of life, and the latter a definite philosophy of the particular legal system, its functions and limitations.

In its application, then, law comes into most intimate contact with science and philosophy; and when our courts tell us that they are administering law, and have nothing to do with political or economic theories, they are talking from the heights of their ignorance—ignorance of the theoretic and often questionable character of the political and economic doctrines that they assume as self-evident. A few examples may not be amiss. The New York Workmen's Compensation Act was declared unconstitutional because it was a taking-away of property from the employer without due process of law. Expert economists, however, claimed that the act in question would not be at all a taking-away of property from the employer; that the expense would soon be shifted to the consumer, where it rightly belongs, as a part of the cost of production. Now whether these economists be right or wrong, it is clear that the decision cannot be justified except by maintaining the negative of that which these teachers of economics hold to be true. Again, some years ago Governor (now Justice) Hughes argued against the income tax amendment because it might have a certain unfavourable effect on state bonds. When Professor Seligman, an expert on finance, showed that an income tax would have no such economic results, it did not have any effect on Messrs. Choate, Hornblower, Guthrie, and the other leaders of the New York bar. In their appeals to the New York legislature they reiterated the argument of Governor Hughes, and dismissed Professor Seligman's testimony with the rhetorical query, "What, shall we cut loose from our constitutional restraints, and embark on the sea of theoretical economics?" The answer is, that the theoretical economics of Professor Seligman may be much safer (because founded on larger experience) than the theoretical economics that these gentlemen assume in their argument. In the Lochner case, the majority of the Supreme Court simply put their own opinion as against the expert testimony that was adduced for the fact that baking is unusually hazardous to the health of the employees. Not only Herbert Spencer's theories of government, but also a disputed theory of hygiene were necessary to make that decision what it was.

Law deals with human affairs and it is impossible to legislate or make any judgment with regard to law without involving all sorts of assumptions or theories. The issue, therefore, is not between a fixed law on the one hand and social theories on the other, but between social theories unconsciously assumed and social theories carefully examined and scientifically studied. What provision does our legal system make for the triumph of the more scientific theories? We let arbitrators, who are more or less specialists in the matter, sit for months to determine a single case. Yet we expect judges, with long calendars of all sorts of cases, without power to initiate inquiry and without power to call in experts to advise them, to settle all these matters satisfactorily. In ancient times it was comparatively easy for the court to take judicial notice of the established religion, the established Aristotelian philosophy, and various established customs of the realm. But how can judges today pretend to take judicial notice of all the findings of modern science that bear on the issues before them?

The dependence of jurisprudence on economics, politics, and sociology is now generally recognized by legal scholars.[81] Can we maintain that jurisprudence is equally dependent on general philosophy? I believe we can. Let me offer a few random suggestions.

Very few students of the law have paid sufficient attention to what might be called the principle of æsthetics in law. Judges have a regard for the abstract symmetry of the law, and frequently legislate in the interests thereof. In fact, with the advent of a class of professional jurists, the regard for logical simplicity of the legal system becomes one of the most constant and powerful factors in the transformation of the legal system and the juridical regulation of life. Legal maxims become accepted because of their apparent simplicity, or self-evidence, but the juridical consequences are unexpectedly complex and, to the layman, unnecessary. Thus the old system of common law pleading started with a few self-evident and apparently simple logical principles, but the result of constant regard for juridical system rather than for the interests of justice produced a system, at times so complex and monstrously unjust, that a wave of reform had to sweep it all away. The influence of self-evident maxims is even stronger in Continental law, in which there is even greater regard for system as such. Thus in French law, the maxim that there can be no right without some person as subject results in difficulties being put in the way of a contract of insurance for the benefit of an unborn child. Whenever judges use such expressions as: "It would be absurd," or "It would be monstrous to suppose," they are generally using this æsthetic principle. Now one of the most important contributions that recent philosophy has made to the intellectual life, and which jurists ought to take to heart, is this distrust of self-evident propositions. Our whole philosophy of mathematics has been transformed by giving up the view that Euclid's axioms are self-evident. Modern mathematical demonstration is based not on self-evident truths, but on postulates that are in effect rules of procedure, or laws of a process.[82]

The concept of self-evidence finds a most hospitable haven in discussions of justice. It is generally assumed that every one knows what justice is and that judges need pay no special attention to ethical philosophy. This is equivalent to saying that every one knows, without further study, what is best for society. If this were so, all social science would be useless. Science arises because our ordinary judgments in any one field are vague and disorganized; and the science of justice, which used to be called natural law, is a needed attempt to organize or systematize human judgments in this field. The objection that Bentham and some modern writers urge against the doctrine of natural law, viz., that it leaves each judge free to decide as he pleases, is, as Pollock has pointed out,[33] simply based on ignorance of the contents of the classical doctrine of natural law. The doctrine of natural rights in America, however, has produced a lawless jurisprudence precisely because the fiction of an all-sufficient law, anterior to all legislation, has led to the neglect of systematic natural law and the consequent unconscious importing by judges into their decisions of their own untrained notions of justice.

We must remember that there is a circumstance about our judicial system which is always tending to produce an inadequate view of social justice, and that is the fact that every case is presented as an issue between two parties. A judge looking only to the interests of the two parties before him is apt to forget that his decision will affect countless others who are not present and whose circumstances are not all identical. Human society is not so organized that a dispute between A and B can be of no concern to anybody else. The crass individualism that is based on an atomic conception of society as composed of separate individuals, each living his own life, and only occasionally touching that of his neighbour, would never have maintained itself as long as it has (no matter how adapted to the needs of a frontier country) if our judges were more familiar with some adequate philosophy of social ethics.

I cannot leave this subject without guarding myself against a serious misunderstanding. In indicating the intimate connection of philosophy and the principles of judicial legislation, I do not mean to suggest that judges should always proceed from philosophic first principles. I recognize with others that philosophic first principles crowd the graveyard of human hopes.[84] Moreover, I do not believe that law is most fruitfully developed by deduction or syllogisms. The deductive form has a powerful influence in law even more than in philosophy, but in the main it supplies the tracks rather than the motive power of the legal train. The primary motive power, both in philosophy and in law, is creative insight that will enable us to extend our knowledge. The idea may be put more positively by saying that the relation of philosophy to the technique of the jurist is analogous to the relation of philosophy to the art or technique of the dramatist. The philosophical dramatist is not necessarily the one who has studied logic and metaphysics, but is the one, rather, who has a definite plan in mind of the way human and natural forces act. Similarly, the philosophic jurist is the one who has a wide outlook on the policy of the law and the part that it plays in the human, or even in the cosmic, life. It might even be urged that a false philosophy is better than no philosophy at all, for any kind of a philosophy will eliminate hosts of contradictions and make our jurisprudence lawful, uniform, and certain. And if it is urged that the uniformity or certainty of law should not be pursued at the expense of its flexibility, I answer that there is no necessary contradiction between certainty and flexibility, between uniformity and individualization, any more than there is any contradiction in a man's remaining in one place and knowing what is going on elsewhere. All human difficulties seem contradictions before they are solved. For a man to cross the water and not get wet was a patent contradiction before the invention of boats. Human art or technique consists in solving these contradictions. Similarly, the technique of the judge, the apex of juristic technique, faces precisely such a problem. It invents or fixes boundaries between conflicting claims and thereby creates social order which allows genuine freedom by the elimination of doubt, uncertainty, and conflict. Like the other arts of civilization it may be characterized as the creation of paths or roadways in the primitive jungle of human passions and impulses. Like all other genuine arts, it waits not until imperfect human science will supply it with a complete set of rules as a guide, but generates its rules of law in the sense in which the work of the great masters can be said to generate principles of music or painting.

While judges do and must make law, it would be absurd to maintain that they are in no wise bound and can make any law they please. Every one who is engaged in making or creating something is limited by the rules of the process and by the nature of the material. But this is true also of the legislature. If the law made by judges presents a greater continuity with the past, the difference is one of degree rather than of kind. There is a great deal less novelty in legislation than is usually supposed. Fundamental changes in the law through judicial decisions all but escape general notice. Similar changes achieved through statute are brought clearly before the public eye, owing to the more dramatic or popular character of our legislatures, the excitement of frequent elections, the character of the debates, and the hearings and committee reports that generally precede important legislation. The relative importance of judicial novelty and legislative novelty is obscured by a contemporary reaction to undigested legislative statistics. Deduct from the enormous mass of legislative output the local and private acts, and the general acts that are really attempts at administration by the legislature, and the net impact of novel legislation upon the law of daily life does not loom very large. Careful studies of comparative legislation by Dicey, Jethro Brown, Charmont, Duguit, and others show that so far as legislation does change the substantive law, it is not entirely arbitrary, but moves in the main according to definite laws.[85]

The root of the fallacy underlying the phonograph theory of the judicial function consists in ignoring this difference of degree and falling back on the naïve rationalistic dilemma: either the law is the creation of man and completely arbitrary, or else it is completely determined by some mysterious non-human agency. And so the theory goes on to suppose that the work of the legislature is entirely arbitrary and that the work of courts is entirely predetermined. But human life does not present us with instances of absolute fixity or absolute mobility, any more than physics can present us with immovable bodies or irresistible forces. It is doubtless of the greatest social importance that the arbitrary element in the law, or in certain provinces of it, should be eliminated as far as possible. This, however, in no way justifies the sweeping assumption that the human element can be eliminated altogether. The idea of a government of laws without men—a sort of transcendental automaton that once wound up will go on forever without any human intervention—is one of the vainest illusions that the eighteenth century's enthusiasm for mechanical maxims imposed upon the spirit of men.[86]

The Bill of Rights Theory [1]

TO ACCUSE our statesmen and lawyers of being doctrinaire may sound strange. Freedom from academic theories passes among them as a badge of respectability. Yet if ever the affairs of a nation could show the triumphant march of an *a priori* theory over the bodies of prostrate and helpless facts, it would be the progress of the theory of the bills of rights embodied in our American constitutions.

In the seventeenth and eighteenth centuries, when people were struggling against the abuses of monarchy, the theory of natural rights proved a powerful weapon against established abuses by inducing men to appeal to rational principles of what ought to be. In their struggle against the claims of the British Parliament, American publicists elevated certain supposed common law and statute rights of Englishmen into the eternal natural rights of man.

Bills of rights were originally put into our state and federal constitutions not by the ruling classes, who believed in government by "the rich, the wise and the good," but by the popular or Jeffersonian party. They were not intended to restrain "popular passion" but rather to serve as moral checks on governments that then rested on a limited franchise, determined by property or religious qualifications. Jefferson assuredly did not believe that only judges can be trusted to protect the rights of the people against the government. "It is not enough that honest men are appointed judges. All know the influence of interest on the mind of man and how, unconsciously, his judgment is warped by that influence." [2] Our cumbrous impeachment proceedings made "our judges effectually independent of the nation. But this ought not to be." [3] The judiciary, he thought,

148

"should be submitted to some practical and impartial control: and this to be imparted, must be compounded of a mixture of state and federal authorities." [4]

So long as our judiciary continued to be drawn from the same class as the rest of our community, our bills of rights were rarely invoked to set aside popular legislation. But the individualist theory of natural rights on which they were based continued to be a cornerstone of our traditional American liberalism. Jefferson's fear of too centralized government proved—apart from the questions of states' rights over slavery—baseless. A sparsely settled agricultural people under a free land economy, without the fear of invasion by powerful neighbours, throve under a government of limited powers, and the theory of natural rights continued as the ideologic expression of general satisfaction and pride in our peculiar institutions.

But the rapid growth of industrialism after the Civil War brought into being a large industrial class in our cities whose interests are not always identical with those of the agrarian, manufacturing, and commercial classes from which our judiciary has mainly been drawn. And when legislatures, more responsive because in closer touch with the needs of our working people, began to pass measures to relieve the latter, our courts—influenced by the leaders of the bar—began to find such legislation unconstitutional. No one doubts the personal honesty of these judges. But it cannot be denied that in many of our states, such groups as railroad and mine owners were unduly influential in selecting the personnel of our courts. In any case, our judges are selected from those who are regarded as having been successful at the bar, and this generally means having served the interests of large property owners. This experience, at least, serves to make our courts more sensitive to the claims of property owners than to those of workers in shops and factories. Thus the bills of rights, originally intended to protect men against political oppression, have become the legal basis of economic exploitation. The principal device by which this has been achieved is the invention of a new legal doctrine previously unknown to jurisprudence, to wit, that the right to make contracts is itself property. The blind acceptance of this new dogma has led to the conclusion—a veritable *reductio ad absurdum*—that a minimum wage law which prevents a human being from working under conditions of starvation is a taking-away of his property.

This result has been made possible not only by lack of knowledge of actual industrial conditions, but also by an amazing ignorance of general legal and political history on the part of the American bench and bar. Only ignorance could speak of these rights as representing the principles of the social compact and the eternal basis of all free government. Thus, when students of history and political science gave up the ancient individualistic theories of inalienable rights, American courts still spoke of the natural right to take property by will, and of employers as having the natural right to make their employees utterly dependent upon them by paying them in truck or company-store orders, or prohibiting them from joining trade unions, etc.[5] Teachers of legal and social science have pointed out the intellectual poverty and narrowness of vision which underlies these conceptions. I can merely add that in most cases these decisions show ignorance of what ought to be well known legal history. Thus courts still frequently speak of trial by jury as an Anglo-Saxon right, when as a matter of fact it was introduced by the Norman kings to raise more revenue. A slight familiarity with legal history also shows that the free transfer of property by will is a comparatively modern institution in the world's history and was not fully legalized in England before the reign of Henry VIII. The notion of the free labour contract is also a historical myth. There never was a time when the relation between master and servant was not the subject of governmental regulations, except that formerly they were almost invariably and openly in the interests of the employers.

Nor are our courts more fortunate when they leave the mythical realm of history and defend their conception of natural rights on grounds of justice or public interest. Such maxims as "That government is best which governs least" have been defended on the basis of a doctrinaire mixture of political pessimism with economic optimism—a Calvinistic conception of total depravity of man's political nature and an abounding grace through man's unregulated economic activity. Both sides of this doctrine are now thoroughly discredited outside of American courts. All civilized nations have had to extend the scope of positive measures for the general welfare, and no nation ever did or could allow unlimited competition or absolute freedom of contract.

The dreadful results of the English attempt to put a régime of free labour contract into practice, the atrocious degradation of men, women, and children that resulted therefrom, shocked the humane sense of a Christian nation and soon led to the beginning of factory legislation. To insist on freedom of contract where one party is under economic pressure or compulsion is a cruel mockery.

I ought to add that I am not one of those who believe that all government regulation is necessarily just; and I have on various occasions contended that there is an element of truth in the old theories of natural rights if we divest them of their individualistic and contractualistic eighteenth-century setting. But I do not believe the terms of our bills of rights are capable of being developed into definite laws by judicial process. Over a century of judicature has left such phrases as "due process," "public purposes," "equal protection of laws," "just compensation," "republican form of government," etc. still so vague that we may well ask whether these are not really moral and political maxims of the kind that had better be left to enforcement by legislative process, controlled by enlightened public opinion. Other liberty-loving nations have put bills of rights into their constitutions, but they have regarded them rather as guides to their legislatures. They have as much faith in their legislatures as we have in our courts. Indeed, why should courts alone be deemed worthy of trust? Other nations generally feel it is safer to leave certain matters to the legislature, because the latter has greater resources of information, does not have to make all its legislation retroactive, and being more representative of the different elements of the state, is more responsive to popular need.

To American lawyers the existence of civilized government without legal (i.e., judicial) restraints on the legislature seems an impossibility. But familiarity with the government of England, France, or Switzerland shows that judicial restraints are frequently not as effective as political and general moral restraints. Certainly respect for law is not as well developed, nor crime as infrequent, here as in England. Life and property are certainly as safe in France and Switzerland as they are in this country. To be at the mercy of legislative majorities seems a horrible nightmare to the American jurist. But why should it be inherently worse than to be at the mercy of judicial majorities? A change of opinion on the part of a single judge after the rehearing in the Income Tax case in 1895 [6] dislocated our whole revenue system, brought about grave crises in government finances, and necessitated a tariff policy different from that which would have been followed if the original decision had remained.

Orators more interested in national edification than in painful accuracy speak of our form of government by written constitution as the envy of all other peoples, but though the American system has been thoroughly studied abroad, the doctrine of judicial supremacy has not commended itself to other nations. The Germans and Swiss, for instance, copied several features of the federal system, but they did not think it advisable to give the federal courts any such authority as we give ours. Those who know us best, like the English or the great British self-governing colonies, have never evinced the least desire to adopt our method of government by bills of rights interpreted by courts.

To be sure Gladstone, whose appreciation of American conditions was never very keen (witness his confident assertions about the Confederacy),[7] was persuaded to introduce a clause about life, liberty, and property, and due process of law into the Irish Home Rule Bill of 1893. But when the son of an expatriated American, Mr. Astor, proposed and introduced the same clause into the Home Rule Bill of 1912 it was vigorously rejected. Premier Asquith, with all the restraint that the responsible head of a friendly government must have felt, was compelled to point to American experience as an impressive warning against such an attempt.

The language of the proposed clause, he declared, was "full of ambiguity, abounding in pitfalls and certainly provocative of every kind of frivolous litigation. . . . What is 'equal protection of the laws'? What is 'just compensation'?" Questions raised by these phrases "are really matters of opinion, bias, or inclination and judgment, which cannot be acted on under anything like settled rules of law." [8]

To introduce the American system, said the *Manchester Guardian* on that occasion, "would choke the courts with litigation. No sooner would a law be enacted than lawyers would grow rich by resisting its enforcement upon constitutional grounds." "All administration would be checked in the American fashion," adds the *London Chronicle*, "while laws were tossed from court to court for years in a vain effort to ascertain whether or not they need be enforced. The trouble with the constitution of the United States . . . is that nobody has ever been able to find out what it means." The *London News* contained the following: "No act of Parliament could be passed which might not be taken before the courts for them to decide whether or not it was constitutional. The courts would be in Ireland, as they are in the United States, the supreme legislators, for the whole field of social and economic life. . . . Judges are not trained for that kind of function, and no man who knows the history of the exercise of this function by American judges but will agree that it would erect one of the most galling of all possible tyrannies."

Against the charge that our bills of rights are incapable of being developed into definite laws by judicial process, that they are essentially vague and productive of an enormous mass of litigation and legal uncertainty, and that they produce too great a strain on the judicial powers with a consequent degrading of our judicial standards, the defenders of our legal system bring only *a priori* arguments. Thus they argue as if all restraints were inherently good. I doubt, however, whether a single ethical philosopher, or for that matter anybody else, really considers self-restraint in itself a good. If I have the impulse to say a kind word or do a kind deed, there is nothing admirable about restraining myself. Self-restraint is a good only when applied to impulses that lead to vicious results. There is nothing virtuous about the self-restraint of the villain who subordinates all his better impulses to one vicious purpose, and the same considerations apply to national action. A good deal of the Spartan self-restraint was vicious and destructive of finer manhood. Doubtless hasty action is likely to be regretted and, in general, habits of reflection and deliberation before acting are good, provided we do not carry this deliberation to the extent of losing all opportunity to act. For nations, like individuals, must frequently make up their minds quickly if they are to grasp their opportunity and act at all. If I tie a heavy stone around my neck I shall doubtless not be able to run, and therefore may save myself from the risk of falling. But neither shall I be able to save myself when my house is on fire. I see no reason for assuming an inherent probability that modern legislatures will act too quickly rather than that they will act too slowly. But even so, greater mobility might be considered an advantage, since it enables the legislature to correct mistakes more readily.

The defenders of the doctrine of constitutional restraints ought to be able to cite more actual instances where the exercise of constitutional restraints has led to wiser and more deliberate legislation. It is notable that in the extensive discussion of the Federal Income Tax decision and the Ives case [9] no one contended that the delay of eighteen years in one case, and of four in the other, achieved any socially desirable end. If constitutional restraints are to be justified, they must, like other human works, be justified by their actual fruits in human experience.

The only argument from experience that I am familiar with in this connection is the argument from prosperity. Our American system must be the best, it is said, because under it we have prospered as no other nation ever has. But the form of this argument seems too much like the fallacy of *post hoc, ergo propter hoc*. Because prosperity has followed the adoption of our peculiar constitutional régime, it does not follow that the latter is the cause. It may well be that the unparalleled abundance of natural resources and our social rather than our political democracy is the main cause. Moreover, it is an open question whether a less individualistic theory of government would not have prevented the frightful waste of our natural resources, the depression of standards of living, and the degradation of childhood. Finally, the argument from past prosperity is a very dangerous one because of its partisan character. It appeals only to those who are satisfied with their share of the prosperity.

No one acquainted with the history of American idealism can be blind to the high sentiment of loyal devotion that our bills of rights have evoked. And no one should fail to acknowledge the noble rôle that the theory of natural rights has played in the historic process of human liberation. It may well be contended that, reinterpreted in the light of our present conditions, that ancient theory can still offer us light in our passionate struggles. But the lawyer cannot adequately serve his high calling so long as he regards it as his duty simply to defend the established system. Law is one of the essential arts of civilization. Like dikes or river works, legal forms provide or safeguard the channels through which the fitful floods of life may usefully pass. Hence the lawyer who regards his work as a liberal profession rather than as a commercial trade must not be satisfied with merely guarding the structure that has been handed over to him. He must study the stream of life and be constantly thinking of ways of improving the containing legal forms. The finest traits of the American spirit have been expressed by Emerson: "Why should we grope among the dry bones of the past, or put the living generation into masquerade out of its faded wardrobe? The sun shines today also. There is more wool and flax in the fields. There are new lands, new men, new thoughts. Let us demand our own works and laws and worship." We too are men, and we ought to live not as pall-bearers of a dead past, but as the creators of a more glorious future. By all means let us be loyal to the past, but above all loyal to the future, to the Kingdom which doth not yet appear.

Legalism and Clericalism[1]

CONFLICTS between European governments and the Catholic hierarchy call our attention to a phase of European political life that Americans seldom understand. Most of us are inclined to dismiss these matters with the comment, "Thank God, since we have adopted the policy of a free church in a free state, we have gotten rid of that trouble. Why can't the Europeans do likewise?" In passing some such judgment as this, we lightly ignore all sorts of historical and social conditions that make the complete separation of church and state impossible even in a country as liberal as England. It will help us to understand at least one phase of this difficulty, to wit, the psychology of clericalism, if we realize how much its motives are like those which in this country make for legalism. By considering how frantically the leaders of our legal profession oppose all efforts to take public issues out of the legal forum (i.e., courts) into the political forum (Congress or the electorate), we can better understand the tenacity with which the clerical profession in Europe resists the secularization of education and similar measures. As both the legal and the clerical profession serve vital functions, they inevitably fall into the attitude that salvation even in political issues can come solely through them.

Human purposes can generally be achieved only by painstaking devotion to well organized means. But the habitual attention to these means tends to make us so extol their importance that the ends themselves become remote, shadowy, and of relatively little moment. The typical illustration of this is the faithful civil servant for whom the welfare of the public is completely subordinated to the smooth functioning of his office routine. Some instances of this have become proverbial: the librarian who guards his books so faithfully that the readers have insuperable difficulty in getting at them, or the old Austrian general who complained that war spoiled the discipline of his soldiers.[2] A remarkable instance of this on a large scale is the way in which teaching and scholarship in this country have been so subordinated to educational administration that we regard it as perfectly natural that all the high honours and rewards of the teaching profession should be bestowed on those who desert it to become administrators or bureaucrats.

It is only by realizing the extent of this human tendency to extol our instruments, even to the neglect of the ends they should serve, that we can avoid attributing the narrowness of legalism and clericalism to purely economic class-interests. Why should the clergy as a body have opposed Copernican astronomy or Darwinian biology? Surely the training and the career of a priest do not make him an authority on physics and biology; and what harm to religion if we recognize that the Hebrews, like all other peoples, had cosmologic myths? We shall better understand the reason for this if we compare it with the outcry of the American legal profession when certain new points were made as to United States history and political theory. Thus when Professor Beard called attention to the financial interests of those who framed our Federal Constitution, the New York State Bar Association rushed to condemn him very much as the Church condemned the Copernican astronomy. Let us assume, for argument's sake, that some of Professor Beard's contentions are highly questionable. Why should lawyers rush in to meddle in historical questions that, as the report they adopted shows, are marvelously beyond their competence? When Theodore Roosevelt, in the days before the World War destroyed his progressivism, pointed out the inadequacies in the legal philosophy with which our courts were choking much-needed social legislation, he was attacked by almost all the leaders of the bar. The argument to which they all resorted, namely, that courts merely declare what the law is and have nothing to do with shaping its policy, was known to legal scholars since Austin as a childish fiction. It is surely a most childish fiction to pretend that our judges have had nothing to do with making our constitutional law what it is today. The leaders of the bar themselves do not make any such silly pretension when they praise John Marshall as the one who effectively moulded our federal constitutional law in the first third of the nineteenth century. What led distinguished lawyers to adopt such an absurd position, in which their hysterical vehemence could not hide the extreme senility of their learning? Economic interests alone will not explain this similarity of attitude of lawyers and clergy. Pure natural pride in the prestige of a high profession must be taken into account, just as it must be to explain why physicists and biologists nowadays rush to deliver the *ex cathedra* opinions of science on social issues on which they are most generously ignorant.

The clergy had been not only the educational directors but also the intellectual leaders of the community, and the discovery of new truths by outsiders was a blow at their prestige. Just so the spread of new insight as to American history and political theory was a blow to the lawyers who regarded themselves as the leaders of a learned profession though they were merely business men or client-caretakers. Of course, both the clericalist and the legalist are motivated by a deep fear of the genuine dangers that the new doctrines undoubtedly contain. But "if hopes are dupes, fears may be liars." The dangers of the Copernican astronomy were real only in the state of transition. They have no terrors for those who have grown up under it. So the dangers of limiting the powers of our courts in constitutional decisions are real only if we ignore the fact that the rights of life and property are just as safe (if not safer) in countries like England and France, where the courts have no such power as they have with us.

The case for the contention that only courts can protect our fundamental rights is in fact a house of cards that a healthy intellectual breath can scatter to the four corners of the earth. Its defenders are constantly arguing as if it were self-evident that the legislature (with the concurrence of the executive) is always bent on destroying our liberties, and that our courts are always defending them. This is a pious dogma, hallowed by repetition, but it is never supported with sufficient historical instances to make it worthy of really serious intellectual consideration. What great attack on the rights of the people has Congress made in the last thirty years from which only the courts have saved us? On the other hand, any one can name a whole host of decisions in which the rights of labour, of women and children, to some protection from grinding exploitation have been defeated by the courts. It is a remarkable indication of the power of dogmas over facts to note how intelligent lawyers who will condemn decision after decision for being based on inadequate knowledge, will still oppose any "tampering" with the powers of the courts. Their logic is like that of the old optimists who were willing to admit that everything in this world is a necessary evil and yet maintained this to be the best of all possible worlds. An empirical study of judicial decisions certainly shows that judges, like other mortals, are not free from the unconscious bias of class interests, and that in interpreting legislation like the Sherman Anti-Trust Law, the United States Supreme Court has fallen down and shown itself simply incompetent as a national organ. But though this could hardly have been denied if we were dealing with the question as historians or scientists, a pious tradition makes the sober truth sound blasphemous. This sanctification of the traditional instrument, the fear of using aught but the "Past's blood-rusted key" to open the portals of the future, is the common source of legalism and clericalism.

The clericalist and the legalist have an undue advantage in identifying their causes with those of religion and law, causes for which humanity is always willing to make extreme sacrifices. But that the identity is not complete is seen clearly in the career of Jesus of Nazareth. In the days of Jesus both clericalism and legalism were represented by the Pharisees, who carried the legalistic idea into religion, and wished to control all of life by minute regulations similar to those which governed the life of the high-priest. To make the life of every individual as holy as that of the high-priest was indeed a noble ideal. Yet it was also deadening through the mass of casuistry to which it gave rise. Jesus' protest that the Sabbath was made for man, not man for the Sabbath, cuts the foundations of all legalism and clericalism. It makes us see the profound foolishness of those who, like Cato, would adhere to the law even though the republic be thereby destroyed. Without a legal order and some ministry of religious insight, the path to anarchy and worldliness is indeed dangerously shortened. But without a realization of the essential limitations of legalism and clericalism there is no way of defending the free human or spiritual life from fanaticism and superstition.

BOOK THREE

LAW AND REASON

The Place of Logic in the Law [1]

I
T IS a curious fact that while critics and reformers of the law
formerly used to take their stand on self-evident truths and
eternal principles of justice and reason, their appeal now is
predominantly to vital needs, social welfare, the real or practical
need of the times, etc. Those who believe law to be not an isolated
island *in vacuo* but a province of the life we call civilization, occupying similar soil and subject to the same changes of intellectual season
as the other provinces, will see in the fact noted above nothing but
an indication of the general passing out of fashion of the old rationalism or intellectualism.

The seed of the protest against the overemphasis of the logical
element in the law was planted by Jhering and Justice Holmes over
a generation ago.[2] But legal science in this country was then so far
behind that of Germany that the logical elaboration and systematiza-
tion of the law embodied in the work of Langdell and Ames proved
the more pressing need and obtained the right of way. There are
many indications that the forces of anti-intellectualism are now rising
in American legal thought, and they are sure to find powerful support in the public impatience with legal technicalities.

Imitators or followers seldom possess the many-sided catholicity
of the pioneer or master. Thus Jhering and Justice Holmes, while
emphasizing other factors, by no means deny all importance to legal
logic. A large part of Jhering's *Geist* is devoted to a logical analysis
of the method and general ideas of the law;[3] Justice Holmes is
careful to emphasize the function of general ideas in the development of the law (e.g., the idea of identity in succession after death
and *inter vivos*), and his book abounds in illustrations of how diffi-

cult legal problems can be cleared up by just logical analyses.[4] But the new, more zealous crusaders against legal ideology are less cautious, and are inclined to deny all value to logic and general principles.[5] Now it is a rather simple task to show the inadequacies of the proposed substitutes for the traditional principles of legal science. Sound common sense, the lessons of experience, the unspoiled sense of justice, the teachings of the as-yet-to-be-established science of sociology, or the somewhat elusive and perhaps altogether mythical will of the dominant class, cannot, without the aid of a logical legal technique, help us elaborate the laws of gifts, sales, mortgages, or determine the precise liability of a railroad company to those who use its sleeping-car service. It is also easy enough to refute these new crusaders out of their own mouths and show that they themselves attach great value to a clear and logically consistent elaboration of the law.[6] But such easy refutations, while they may be just, are seldom illuminating, unless we examine the situation with some thoroughness. This may lead us into the supposedly foreign fields of logic and metaphysics. But at the time when the foundations of our legal system are questioned both inside and outside of the legal fraternity, it would be only the wisdom of the ostrich that would counsel us to refrain from entering into these fields because, forsooth, the old tradition says that law is law, and has nothing to do with any other field of human inquiry. It may be reassuring to orthodox legal scholarship to note that the foremost representatives of the exact and natural sciences have now outgrown the childish fear of metaphysics as the intellectual bogey—witness the writings of Russell, Poincaré, Duhem, Ostwald, and Driesch.

I

A suggestive parallel can be drawn between the functions of the law and of natural science. Both facilitate transactions by increasing our reliance on the future. We build our modern houses, bridges, and machinery because science makes us more certain that these structures will withstand the variations of pressure, etc. We enter into business because we expect that people will continue to desire certain commodities, and we count on the state to continue to protect us against robbery. We sell on credit not only because we expect that most people will be moved (by habit or conscience) to pay, but also because the law provides us with a machinery for collecting what is due. If our debtors also know that this machinery exists, they will pay more readily and the expense of using this legal machinery will be accordingly reduced. That the law should be readily knowable is, thus, essential to its usefulness. So far is this true that there are many inconveniences or injustices in the law that men would rather suffer than be paralyzed in their action by uncertainty. Primitive law, i.e., all legal systems uninfluenced by Greek science, tries to achieve this certainty by fixed rules or dooms enumerating specific actions and their consequences, just as they store up wisdom in isolated saws or proverbs. Clearly the multitudinous and complicated relations of modern life could not possibly be regulated by such a method. Like the classical Romans, we utilize instead that most wonderful dis-covery, or invention, of the Greeks—the rational deductive system. We try to reduce the law to the smallest number of general prin-ciples from which all possible cases can be reached, just as we try to reduce our knowledge of nature to a deductive mathematical system. This rational form also gives the law the appearance of complete freedom from arbitrary will and thus satisfies the modern demand for equality in the enforcement of law.[7]

The law, of course, never succeeds in becoming a completely de-ductive system. It does not even succeed in becoming completely consistent. But the effort to assume the form of a deductive system underlies all constructive legal scholarship. In our own day, for instance, Thayer's general views on evidence and Wigmore's classical treatise on the subject have transformed a conglomeration of discon-nected rules into something like a system. Ames's doctrine of unjust enrichment has brought together a number of artificially tacked-on appendages to the law of contract into the somewhat coherent body of law known as quasi-contract. Forty years ago we had so little of a general theory of torts that if any one had thought of writing a treatise on the subject he might simply have treated of a number of torts in alphabetic order. Today not only have we a general theory of liability, but also there is a marked tendency to make the law of torts and the law of contract branches of the law of obligations. This effort at generalization and system has always been the task of the jurist. We use the notions of property, contract, or obligation so often now that we are apt to think that they are "as old as the law itself." But legal history shows clearly enough that the notion of property came as a result of a long process of unification of diverse laws against robbery. A great deal of material had to be eliminated before the abstract idea of property could be extracted. The idea of contract is so late that even as developed a legal system as the Roman had no general law of contract, but merely laws of *stipulatio*, *depositum*, *pignus*, *locatio conductio*, etc. The notion of possession seems to the classical jurists simply one of fact. But the possessory remedies did not originate in the principle of possession but rather in a number of diverse situations.[8]

In thus endeavouring to make the law systematic, jurists are not merely pursuing their own purely theoretic or scientific interest. They are performing a duty to the community by thus transforming the law. A legal system that works with general principles has powerful instruments. Just as the generalized arithmetic that we call advanced mathematics has increased manyfold our power of solving physical problems, so a generalized jurisprudence enlarges the law's control over the diversity of legal situations. It is like fishing with large nets instead of with single lines.

As nature has other cares besides letting us paint her deductive charm, she constantly reveals aspects that hamper or complicate our beautiful analytic equations. So, also, the affairs of practical life generate situations that mock our well intentioned efforts to reduce the law to a rational system. In the presence of these, as of other seemingly insurmountable obstacles, human frailty is tempted to blink at the difficulties. So urgent is the need for assured first principles that most people resent the service that the sceptical-minded—the stray dogs of the intellectual world—render by showing the uninhabitableness of our hastily constructed legal or philosophic kennels. In the legal field, the blinking at the practical difficulties is facilitated by the ready assurance that if our principles are just it is none of our fault if any inconvenience results. *Fiat justitia, pereat mundus* is a very edifying excuse for refusing to reëxamine our principles in the light of the harsh results to which they lead.

According to the prevailing popular theory, facts are "out there" in nature and absolutely rigid, while principles are somewhere "in the mind" under our scalps and changeable at will. According to this view scientific theories are made to fit preëxisting facts somewhat as clothes are made to fit people. A single inconsistent fact, and the whole theory is abandoned. Actually, however, what we call facts are not so rigid and theories not so flexible; and when the two do not fit, the process of adaptation is a bilateral one. When new facts come up inconsistent with previous theories, we do not give up the latter, but modify both the theory and our view of the facts by the introduction of new distinctions or hypothetical elements. If the facts of radiation do not fit in with the theory of the conservation of energy, an ether is invented and endowed with just as many properties as are necessary to effect a reconciliation, though in the end this results in inordinate complexity. Similarly legal theories attempting to assimilate new facts by stretching old rules and introducing distinctions and fictions become so complex and full of arbitrary elements that the very end of legal system is thereby defeated. It is this artificial complexity that caused the abandonment of the Ptolemaic astronomy and is causing the abandonment of the physics of the ether today. The classical system of common-law pleading, based on a few self-evident principles, was just such a system. It fell precisely because, as the forms of actions expanded to comprehend the new industrial order, the system became so choked with artificial distinctions and fictions that a conservative and long-suffering people had to sweep it all away. Similarly has the law of employers' liability, based on a simple principle—no responsibility without fault—grown to such monstrous complexity (witness Labatt's voluminous book) [9] that legislation is sweeping it away.

The foregoing parallel between natural science and legal system should, of course, be corrected by noting the important differences between the two. Legal principles are not so simple or so readily applicable to single cases as are the principles of physics; nor are the facts of the legal order so definite and so rigid as those of the physical order. Crucial experiments are possible in science. Single experiments have sometimes caused such difficulties to reigning theories as to lead to their ultimate abandonment. The facts of physics admit of highly exact description in terms of number and can be indefinitely repeated, whereas the "facts" of the legal order, "practices," or decisions, can almost always be disputed and disregarded as entirely wrong in principle. Nevertheless, enough has been said above to indicate that the rôle of deduction is not an accidental incident in law and natural science but is rather an essential part of their life.

II

In modern times the widespread opinion has grown up that deduction is incapable of genuinely extending our knowledge and can serve at best only as an ornament of exposition. It is sometimes thought that the introduction of the "case method" in law-teaching marks the entrance of inductive scientific methods in law. The latter view is, however, obviously a misapprehension. Both Langdell and Ames regarded the case method as a sound pedagogical device, but in no way doubted the existence of legal principles according to which cases should be decided. Langdell even asserted that the number of such principles is very small. [10] It is from an entirely different quarter that the whole of traditional legal science has, because of this very belief in principles, been attacked as scholastic and out of harmony with the methods of modern science. [11] Whatever may be these critics' knowledge of modern science, they certainly have a very vague idea of scholasticism, and use the term as a locus for all that is intellectually undesirable, a sort of inferno for all ideas to which they are opposed. Now there is one virtue that no one who has ever read Aquinas or Duns Scotus denies them, and that is clarity and consistency—a virtue which, if not sufficient for admission into the modern juristic heaven, is at least not to be altogether despised. Moreover, every student of the history of thought knows that the contrast between modern science and medieval philosophy is not to be dismissed by the mere shibboleth of induction or deduction. The founders of modern science—Copernicus, Kepler, Galileo, Huygens, Descartes, and Newton—certainly did not despise deduction. The history of science completely belies the dogma as to the fruitlessness of deduction, and shows many important physical discoveries, such as Maxwell's discovery of the electromagnetic character of light, brought about by deductive or mathematical procedure. The great apostle of induction was Bacon—a good lawyer, trained in the handling of cases in the Inns of Court, but one who made no contribution at all to any natural science.[12] The present apotheosis of induction arose in the middle of the nineteenth century as a result of a violent reaction against the frenzied excesses brought about by the classical German philosophies of Fichte, Hegel, and Schelling. It became a dogma of popular philosophy through the popularity of Mill's *Logic*. Now Mill was not himself a scientist. He was an administrator—an official of the East India Company—and his acquaintance with natural science was gathered from such secondhand sources as Whewell's *History of the Inductive Sciences*. But so strong has become the hold of Mill's simple formulæ on popular thought that even men of science have accepted his account of scientific method—which is not surprising if we remember that healthy men or athletes are not necessarily good physiologists or trainers. The actual procedure, however, of natural as well as of legal science involves constant reliance on principles, and is incompatible with

Mill's nominalism, i.e., the assumption that only particulars exist in nature.

It may seem a bold and reckless statement to assert that an adequate discussion of cases like *Berry* v. *Donovan*,[13] *Adair* v. *United States*,[14] or *Commonwealth* v. *Boston and Maine R.*[15] involves the whole medieval controversy over the reality of universals. And yet, the confident assertion of "fundamental principles of justice that inhere in the very idea of free government" [16] made by the writers of these decisions, and the equally confident assertion of their critics that there are no such principles,[17] show how impossible it is to keep out of metaphysics. Can we dodge the question by saying that while legal principles are unchanging the law is a practical or a progressive science? [18] How can a principle or undisputed formula remain the same if all the cases to which it is to be applied are constantly changing? You may decide to enter the realm of metaphysics or not, just as you may decide to go to church or not; but you cannot deny that an intelligent decision in either case demands considerable thought.

The matter is not very difficult if we refuse to be browbeaten by a word like "reality," which often represents nothing definite except a certain emotional afflatus. It ought to be quite clear that abstractions and universals exist in every situation in which individual things can be said to exist, and by the same evidence. If any statement like "Smith is white and an honest man" is true, whiteness, honesty, and manhood must exist as truly as Smith. Similarly, if it is true that one body is equal to, greater than, or less than another, then the relations of equality, greater than, or less than, exist just as truly as the bodies between which they hold. If the results of logical and mathematical reasoning are observed to hold true of nature, it seems more proper to say that nature is logical and mathematical than to suppose that logical and mathematical principles are just words having no meaning in nature, or that they have a dubious existence "in the mind only" (the "mind" being conceived as outside of nature). The difficulty that most people have in conceiving of the existence of universals is due to the tendency to *reify* all relations, i.e., to think of these relations or universals as if they were themselves additional *things*, instead of what they are defined to be, viz., qualities or relations of things. This shows itself in the naïve question, "*Where* do these universals exist?"—as if universals were particular entities occupying space. In brief, it seems that the actual procedure of natural and legal science demands the doctrine that universals do exist, but that they exist as universals, not as additional individual things. Surely a barren if somewhat truistic doctrine, you may say. But the following may show that it offers us a clue whereby to distinguish the use from the abuse of logic in the law.

III

Every science must use logic to test whether certain conclusions do follow from given premises. But that which distinguishes one science from another, e.g., law from physical chemistry, is the subject-matter, the axioms and postulates from which conclusions are drawn. The subject-matter of the law is the regulation of the conduct of individuals living in those more or less permanent relations which we call society. Now, from the point of view of logic the existence of men in society or their desire to regulate their mutual relations is just as brute an empirical fact as that water expands when cooled just above the freezing point. All metaphysical philosophies of law (like Stammler's) that pretend to have no empirical elements at their basis, thus really attempt the logically impossible. You cannot construct a building merely out of the rules of architecture. As a matter of fact, all metaphysical philosophies of law do smuggle in, in more or less disguised form, the main material facts of the social order. In this they are assisted by a fact that empiricists —especially those intoxicated with the doctrine of evolution—do not fully realize, viz., the large fund of common humanity possessed by all peoples whose history we can study. Private law especially deals with those traits of human nature that have changed least in the comparatively short period that is covered by the whole of legal history. Our history "starts with man full grown. It may be assumed that the earliest barbarian whose practices are to be considered had a good many of the same feelings and passions as ourselves."[19] Thus is explained the paradoxical fact that metaphysical philosophers of law, who try to ignore or rise high above the factual order, are frequently more productive of genuine social insight than those who are lost in the multitudinous but unimportant details of historic or ethnologic jurisprudence.

The law, at any given time, is administered and expounded by men who cannot help taking for granted the prevalent ideas and attitudes of the community in which they live. Even if it were logically, it would certainly not be psychically, possible for any man to think out an absolutely new system of jural relations. The law-reformer who urges the most radical change can justify his proposal only by appealing to some actually prevailing idea as to what is desirable; and the history of the law shows how comparatively small is the addition or subtraction to the system of jural concepts and ideas that the most creative judges and jurists have been able to bring about. There are, therefore, first or fundamental principles of the law that may be regarded as practically or quasi *a priori*. But though we cannot avoid relying on principles, the complex and constantly changing subject-matter requires continuous caution and a mind humbly open to the dangers of the eternal tendency of all intellectual effort in the direction of oversimplification.

Among the first principles of the law there are at least two kinds: (1) axioms or fundamental assumptions (*a*) as to fact, e.g., that men desire their economic advantage, and are deterred from actions to which penalties are attached, and (*b*) as to the aim of the law, e.g., that property should be protected, that men should be equal before the law, etc.; and (2) postulates that are really ways of procedure or methods of analysis and construction, e.g., the distinction between rights and duties, or between law and equity, the principle that no man can be his own agent, or that no man can convey more or a greater estate than that which in law he has. The abuse of first prin-

THE PLACE OF LOGIC IN THE LAW

ciples of the first class consists in setting up economic or political
maxims of public policy that are at best applicable only to a given
period or historical economic system, as eternal principles for all
times. Examples of this may be found in the use of the principle that
the public interest always demands competition, a free market, and
an open shop, and the maxim that only by the separation of powers,
checks and balances, and judicial control over legislation can liberty
be maintained. The fallacy of regarding these as eternal first principles is readily detected and has been frequently pointed out in
recent times. The fallacy, however, of setting up what I have called
above postulates, as eternal necessities of all legal system, is less
easily detected. These postulates have the appearance of self-evident
truths. But physics has learned to regret accepting such seemingly
self-evident propositions as that a thing cannot act where it is not,
and modern mathematics has learned that such seemingly self-
evident assertions as that the whole is greater than a part, or Euclid's
parallel postulate, are not necessarily true. The theoretical sciences
now select their fundamental propositions not because of their immediate self-evidence, but because of the system of consequences that
follows from them. A practical science like the law ought not to
despise that procedure.

The abuse of self-evident principles is at the basis of what the
Germans call *Begriffsjurisprudenz,* which Professor Pound calls
mechanical jurisprudence,[20] and also of that which is unsatisfactory
in the old natural law. The analysis of a few additional examples
may perhaps make my point clearer.

In discussing creditors' bills in equity, Langdell says:[21] "Indeed,
when a debtor dies, his debts would all die with him, did not positive law *interpose* to keep them alive; for every debt is created by
means of an obligation imposed upon the debtor, and it is *impossible* that an obligation should continue to exist after the obligor
had ceased to exist." I have italicized the words "interpose" and
"impossible" because these and the later expression that the question is "as old as the law itself" bring into relief the underlying

view that the law itself is a logical system in which it is forever impossible for a debt to survive the debtor. But if that were so, how could positive law bring about the impossible? Could positive law change the rules of arithmetic, or make the diagonal and the side of a square commensurate? In point of fact the principle in question is not logically necessary at all. It arose at a time when the creditor could dispose of the actual body and life of the defaulting debtor, hence the relation between debtor and creditor could have been entered into only by people who personally trusted each other. If the law of the Twelve Tables had allowed an assignment of a debt, it would have been socially as serious as if our law allowed an assignment of marital rights. Later on, when the rigour of the old law was softened, the practical reason why the creditor might not be replaced by another person disappeared, and the debtor-creditor relation became depersonalized at one end. The difficulties in the way of depersonalization at the other end were not the logical ones but the practical ones of harmonizing the security of credit and the maintenance of family continuity on the basis of inheritance. But habits of legal thought in regard to the personal character of the debtor-creditor relation still produce the familiar difficulties of subrogation, etc.

Another illuminating instance of the confusion between actually existent and logically necessary rules of law is to be found in that most sagacious of the great practical Roman jurists, Papinian. The *postliminium*, as is well known, was instituted to the end that citizens might not have their civil rights diminished because of unavoidable absence due to state service. Now, if one, before acquiring title by *usus*, is captured by the enemy, should possession be restored to him? No, says Ulpian,[22] "for possession is for the most part a matter of fact, and matter of fact is not included in the scope of *postliminium*." The reasoning here seems conclusive. The law can restore old rights, it cannot restore past states of fact. Reflection, however, shows that while this limitation on the right of *postliminium* may have been practically wise, it was by no means logically necessary. An affirmative answer to the question would not have attempted to restore the past but would merely have terminated or wiped out rights acquired by others through the applicant's capture. "Nor ought the applicant," continues Papinian,[23] "to be allowed an *utilis actio,* as it is very unjust to take a thing away from an owner where there was no *usus* that took it away; a thing *cannot* be regarded as lost where it was not taken out of the hands of the party who is said to have lost it." This "cannot," however, is not at all convincing when we remember that in the same book it is laid down [24] that "soldiers being quartered in Rome are treated as being absent on state service."

Shall we, then, give up all reliance on principles? That would be as wise as giving up the use of our eyes because they are, as a matter of fact, poor optical instruments. Just as a scientific optics aims at correcting our vision through the determination of the natural error of myopia or astigmatism, so a scientific jurisprudence makes such natural principles as "One cannot convey more than in law he has," or "No rights can be acquired by the commission of wrong," more useful by showing their necessary limitations.

Closely connected with the use and abuse of first principles is the use of artificial concepts or abstractions in the law. Jhering has long ago pointed out [25] that juristic technique is able to reconstruct and simplify the law by a process of analysis similar to the process whereby, in the course of history, language becomes represented by a more or less phonetic alphabet. The natural unit of language is the sentence or the word, represented in primitive form by a picture. By a process of abstraction we pass from that stage in which thousands of signs are needed to the stage where a few simple phonetic elements suffice to reproduce all the possible combinations of language. Just so, scientific jurisprudence endeavours to analyze all laws as combinations of a few recurrent simple elements. From this point of view, the artificiality of legal concepts is not an objection to their employment. Indeed, there is an advantage in purely artificial symbols. They carry with them only the amount of meaning

contained in their definition, without the intellectual and emotional
penumbra that more familiar terms always drag with them. The
most dangerous concepts of the law are those like direct tax, republican form of government, interstate commerce, restraint of trade,
and the like. They seem to be definite in themselves, but when we
come to apply them, they prove most elusive. The law, for instance,
says, "No taxation except for public purposes." What are public purposes? The courts have ruled that municipalities may give bounties
to grist-mills and railroads, but not to factories. Communities may
sell gas and electricity, but not coal; may abate a dam for the relief
of privately owned meadows, but may not lend money for rebuilding
a burnt district.[26] This seems quite arbitrary. And when judges try
to rationalize their position by introducing such distinctions as that
between direct and incidental benefits to the community, a logician
cannot help feeling that while the decisions may be good, the reasons are certainly bad. It is the pernicious fiction that judges never
make the law but only declare "the will of the legislator" that makes
people blink at the essential indefiniteness of concepts like "due
process of law" or "interstate commerce," and pretend to believe
that all the constitutional law on these subjects is deduced from the
few words of the constitutional enactments. The real work of judicial interpretation is precisely that of *making* these concepts definite
by fixing their limits as questions about them come up.

Underlying the logical use of concepts are, of course, the logical
rules of division, such as the one which demands that subdivisions
shall be mutually exclusive. As the law has its excuse for being in
the need to regulate future conduct, it must express itself in terms
that will exclude the possibility of a case's falling in both or neither
of two classes which it may set up. Jurists, however, have not paid
attention to the difference between logical division and natural classification. The naturalist who studies vertebrates finds that the multitudinous and widely different species may be grouped into fishes,
reptiles, etc. If each of these groups has some important trait, the
classification will be satisfactory to the naturalist, even though it does

not rule out the possibility of species' being discovered on the borderland, betwixt and between the groups distinguished. The distinction between plants and animals is a useful one even though there are many species to which either term can be applied. The law oscillates between natural classification and logical division and readily throws the incautious jurist into confusion. In enforcing a constitutional provision for "the equal protection of the laws," courts soon realize that an abstract equality, regardless of all differences such as age, sex, occupation, mode of life, etc., would render the law absurd. The courts, then, are forced to recognize the existence of natural classes. But having recognized these natural classes, the prevailing attitude of our courts is to view them as if they were absolute logical divisions. The consequent difficulties are amply illustrated in the chapters of Professor Freund's book on the *Police Power*.

The difficulty of foisting an absolutely logical division upon the facts (or pretending to find them in nature) is illustrated in the usual classification of rights and wrongs. Let us take Langdell's as an illustration. His classification presupposes an absolute distinction between rights and duties. This distinction is not defended. It seems to be based simply on the idea of advantage and disadvantage. May there not be legal relations that can just as well be called rights as duties? Some of the very onerous rights of trustees come very near being of that type. Further Langdell says: [27] "Absolute rights are either personal rights or rights of property. Every personal right is born with the person to whom it belongs, and dies with him. Personal rights, therefore, can neither be acquired nor parted with, and hence they are never the subjects of commerce, nor have they any pecuniary value." But though "we can neither number them nor define them," there is one that is specifically mentioned, viz., "the equal right of all persons to use public highways, navigable waters, and the high seas." Shall we, however, say that an expressman or shipowner cannot sell his right to do business on a given route or river? How does the right to use a navigable river differ from the right to buy and sell liquor or to serve people as an innkeeper? I have no doubt that Langdell's classification of rights and wrongs is useful in helping us to analyze many actual situations, and the difficulties I am raising can probably be met by introducing additional subtle distinctions. But the foregoing considerations indicate that we are not dealing here with an absolutely accurate distinction. The difference between a useful approximation and an absolutely accurate distinction is of practical as well as of logical importance. If our classification is only approximate, we must apply it cautiously, expecting some day to come across actual cases that it will not fit, and where practical injustice will result from the attempt to *make* the facts fit our preconceived account.

The various instances of the abuse of legal logic adduced by writers like Jhering, Korkunov, Demogue, and Pound are all cases of an overhasty application of logic to a complex material and do not, of course, show the break-down of logic itself. Nevertheless, it is fair to add that a great many of the difficulties are due to the inadequacies of the popular accounts of logic. The Aristotelian logic, with its subject-predicate doctrine, is primarily a logic of subsumption and applies best to a system like the biology of which Aristotle was a master, viz., a system of fixed classes. Modern logic can deal more adequately with a changing system, since modern logic, like modern mathematics, operates with the invariant rules governing possible transformations.

The limitation that underlies the traditional logic shows itself in the familiar difficulty as to the presence of discretion in the law. The law is primarily directed toward certainty, which, according to the classical view, can be produced only by definite rules that leave no room for individual discretion. Individual discretion, whether of judge or of legislator acting under constitutionally limited powers, appears to this view synonymous with the absence of law. Thus in the criminal law the old maxim is, Fix the offense definitely and the definite penalty. To individualize punishment seems to the old view to abandon legal security and to open the flood-gates of judicial arbitrariness. This view, however, is based on an inadequate logic, which fails to appreciate the necessarily provisional character of all legal classification and the consequent necessity of discretion to make definite that which would otherwise be really indefinite. Logically the task of the law is similar to that of the wholesale manufacturer of shoes or any similar commodity. Human feet vary in size, and perhaps there is truth in the saying that no two are exactly alike. On the assumption that the shoe should fit the foot, the theoretical consequence would be that no two shoes should be made exactly alike. Experience, however, without contradicting these postulates of the perfect art of shoe-making, finds that a limited number of classes of "sizes" will satisfy all normal demands. How is the number of these "sizes" determined? Obviously by striking a balance between the (very slight) inconvenience of having a shoe that may be one sixteenth of an inch too long and the inconvenience of doubling or tripling the number of sizes. The same method is at the basis of the criminal law. The number of ways and circumstances, for instance, in which the life of one person can be destroyed by another is endless. What the law does is to group them into a small number of classes, viz., murder, manslaughter, etc., attempting to define the characteristics of each type in such a way that no one can take the life of a fellow being in a way that society disapproves without falling in one or other of these groups. There is, of course, no logical reason why the division into groups should be so rough, and it is abstractly possible to carry the classification to any degree of fineness and discrimination,—except that the difficulty of making juries understand the difference between murder in the first degree, murder in the second degree, and manslaughter is already sufficiently great. It is foolish to attempt results more delicate than the instruments at your disposal will permit. Would we attempt to carve a delicately featured wooden statue with an ax? Judicial discretion in the individualization of punishment is simply an attempt to bring into the penal machinery a greater degree of discrimination than is practically possible by the prescription of hard and fast general rules.

The same argument applies to legislative discretion. "If the legislature has power to fix the maximum number of hours in an industry to ten, then why not nine, etc.? Where are you going to draw the line?" The answer is that no such line can be drawn *a priori*, since we are dealing with a line that must necessarily vary in different industries and at different times.

Jurists, like other men, are in their attitude to the employment of logic either intellectualists or mystics. The intellectualist not only trusts implicitly all the results of reasoning, but believes that no safe result can be obtained in any other way. Hence in law he emphasizes the rule rather than the decision. This, however, leads to an ignoring of the absurd consequences to which the logical application of rules frequently leads. *Summa jus, summa injuria*. The mystics distrust reasoning. They have faith in intuition, sense, or feeling. "Men are wiser than they know," says Emerson, and the Autocrat of the Breakfast Table, who was not a stranger to the study of the law, adds, "You can hire logic, in the shape of a lawyer, to prove anything that you want to prove." But shall we subscribe to the primitive superstition that only the frenzied and the mentally beclouded are divinely inspired? Like other useful instruments, logic is very dangerous, and it requires great wisdom to use it properly. A logical science of law can help us digest our legal material, but we must get our food before we can digest it. The law draws its sap from feelings of justice and social need. It has grown and been improved by sensitively minded judges attending to the conflicting claims of the various interests before them, and leaving it to subsequent developments to demonstrate the full wisdom or unwisdom of the decision. The intellectualist would have the judge certain of everything before deciding, but this is impossible. Like other human efforts, the law must experiment, which always involves a leap into the dark future. But for that very reason the judge's *feelings* as to right and wrong must be logically and scientifically trained. The trained mind sees in a flash of intuition that which the untrained mind can succeed in seeing only after painfully treading many steps.

They who scorn the idea of the judge as a logical automaton are apt to fall into the opposite error of exaggerating as irresistible the force of bias or prejudice. But the judge who realizes before listening to a case that all men are biased is more likely to make a conscientious effort at impartiality than one who believes that elevation to the bench makes him at once an organ of infallible logical truth.

A good deal of the wisdom of life is apt to appear foolishness to a narrow logic. We urge our horse downhill and yet put the brake on the wheel—clearly a contradictory process to a logic too proud to learn from experience. But a genuinely scientific logic would see in this humble illustration a symbol of that measured straining in opposite directions which is the essence of the homely wisdom that makes life livable.

Law and Scientific Method [1]

I T WAS an English judge who once thanked God that the law of England was not a science. The sense of gratitude to God is often somewhat capricious; but there can be no doubt that the English bar has not only neglected the science of law but has felt a positive aversion for it. This was not overstated by one who said that the very word "jurisprudence" was offensive to the nostrils of the English lawyer. Nor is this merely the English preference for muddling through. We must take into account the historical facts as to the relation between the English universities and the Inns of Court. As the universities would not teach English law, the business of preparing men for the well organized profession of law fell into the hands of strictly professional corporations, whose traditions had little in common with the clerical and other-worldly traditions that prevailed in Oxford and Cambridge up to very recent days. And yet some part of the scientific spirit—something of the scholar's interest in history and respect for fact, and something of the spirit of detachment—did penetrate the English bar, partly through the separation of the barrister from the business of the solicitor and partly at least through the philologic studies that leaders of the bar pursued in the classical courses at the public schools and at Oxford and Cambridge. Certainly the old rules of pleading showed a highly refined logical technique.

Much more unfavourable for the development of any science of law have been the conditions in this country. Up to the last quarter of the nineteenth century, we had no real universities; and the practical demands on the service of lawyers were so great that any attempt to regulate their educational qualifications was resented by the public as an undue interference with the natural right of every enterprising citizen to choose and pursue his own calling. It is therefore not surprising that until very recently our law schools functioned practically as trade schools, and their connection with the colleges or universities was rather nominal. For men to make the teaching of law their major occupation is for us a new phenomenon, and I cannot help recalling the contemptuous references to the teachers of law that I heard at a meeting of a great state bar association not so long ago. To one who was neither a lawyer nor a teacher of law the vehemence of the contempt was rather amusing.

I venture to submit these trite observations in order to call attention to the fact that despite the rapid expansion of our law schools in the last decade, and despite the increase of scientific interest in the law as shown in our law reviews, we are still under tremendous pressure to prepare our students for practical success at the bar rather than to advance the science of the law. We may, when we view the situation abstractly, admit that ultimately the most practical thing that our law school can do for the community is to promote the science of law; but under pressure of immediate practicality we are loth to change the strictly professional curriculum. We fear to introduce theoretic studies as remote from immediately practical legal issues as are pathology in the school of medicine, physiological psychology in the school of education, or rational mechanics in the school of engineering. Men were undoubtedly successful physicians, teachers, and engineers before the introduction of such studies, but no one doubts today their necessity to give men a liberal insight into their work. So men have been and will continue to be successful at the bar without direct attention to the science of the law. Indeed, if we were to judge by purely and immediately practical results, our present law school curriculum might be viewed as already too theoretical. A knowledge of the existing law, let us courageously admit, is not the sole, nor perhaps even the most important, condition for practical success at the bar. The art of properly manipulating judges, juries, and clients is at least as important, and yet does not, and rightly should not, receive the attention of the law school. The public interest that the university ought to serve is no more intimately connected with the personal success of the lawyer than with that of the modiste, the shoe-maker, or the plumber. The primary object of the university as a public institution can only be the advancement of our legal institutions through the development of a liberal understanding or science of the law.

I

If scientific method be a way of avoiding certain human pitfalls in the search for truth, then the law surely compares favourably in this respect with other human occupations. Court procedure to determine whether A and B did make a contract, or whether C did commit a criminal act, shows a regard for orderly attainment of truth that compares very favourably with the procedure of a vestry board in determining the fitness of a minister, or of a college in selecting a professor.

When we come, however, to the appellate work of higher courts, in which new public policies are decided under the guise of their legality or constitutionality, we find courts making all sorts of factual generalizations without adequate information. The facilities of our courts for acquiring information as to actual conditions are very limited. Courts have to decide all sorts of complicated issues after a few hours of oral argument and briefs by lawyers. Are ten hours per day in the old-type bakery a strain on the baker's health? Will a workmen's compensation act or a minimum wage law take away the property of the employer or of the worker that receives less than the minimum of subsistence? It is not to the credit of any system that its chief exponents can put their amateurish opinions against those of physicians or economists who have given these questions careful scientific study. Yet the law cannot simply and uncritically accept all the opinions of economists or sociologists. After all, on many important points social scientists are not agreed among themselves; and certainly the social sciences do not demonstrate their results as rigorously as do the natural sciences. Much of what passes as social science is just exercise in technical vocabulary, or mere plausible impressionism, without any critical methods for testing data or accurately determining whether certain assumed results are really true. A good deal of psychology, normal and abnormal, is still in that condition. This, of course, is no argument for the law's ignoring what experts in these fields have to say. But it should impress upon us the necessity for the law itself—in the persons of jurists, judges, and advocates—to have a trained sense of scientific method.

It was the great Poincaré who once said that, while physical scientists were busy solving their problems, social scientists were busy discussing their methods. Making due allowance for Gallic wit, there is in this statement much to sober a too sanguine generation that expects heaven on earth as a result of a universal conversion to scientific method. A little critical reflection shows that the term "scientific method" is seldom used with a very definite meaning. If it denotes the art of teaching men how to make discoveries in the sciences, we may well say that such an art is as unknown as the art of training great poets. Certainly we should expect little in this respect from books of logic, the authors of which have seldom made any contributions to science, and indeed often write from mere hearsay about it. Nor can we expect much from scientific specialists who occasionally take time off from their own work to write on scientific method in general. With some honourable exceptions their utterances are naturally as naïve as that of the successful athlete or robust old man discussing general hygiene, or the successful man of affairs laying down the law as how to educate others to his level of attainment.

But where the uncritical expect too much, wise men will not despise the little illumination that they can get. After all, experience shows that those who have received no training in a given field seldom, if ever, make discoveries in it. Knowledge of past achievement

seems a most necessary condition for the advancement of any subject. But a creative capacity in any field is not developed by learning by rote all its specific rules. Even if all of the latter could be
acquired in a few years, at the end of the time there would be new
rules. Effective scientific training enables men to handle new situations precisely because science seeks to get at the constant elements
or laws that remain identical throughout the changes in a given
field. It is, at any rate, by the possession of certain modes of analysis
which reveal such constant or logical elements in the new situation
that a scientifically trained man differs from the one who has merely
routine knowledge. The latter, as habitual, may be more sure in
familiar situations, but it breaks down in novel situations.

II

Whatever services scientific method is to render, it is reasonable
to demand that it shall not hinder the growth of the science to which
it ministers. But this is precisely what the method known as positivism or behaviourism does when it denies that there can be any
normative branch of jurisprudence—that is, when it denies scientific
character to questions as to what the law ought to be.

A superficial conception of science at the basis of what used to
be called materialism, and is now called behaviourism, supposes that
science can deal only with what actually is. But this is just nonsense.
The actual has meaning for science only when judged in the light
of some ideal or possible alternative. Indeed all mathematical and
theoretic science deals with ideals and possibilities. Mankind at
large, to be sure, happens to be interested in those theoretic sciences
which find application in the actual world. But this does not deny
the normative character of theoretic science. Positivists like Duguit
and Ardigo, who insist that a science of the law should restrict itself
to the law that is, generally fall into a crypto-idealism, that is, they
set up some idealization of the actual law as the desirable state that
ought to be. In the early stage of the historical school in this country

many, like Langdell, Ames, and Gray, were inclined to set up the law of England at the end of the eighteenth century as the ideal of the common law. But no actual law is ever a complete system, as actual. It cannot be used to settle new issues without expanding along the lines that seem desirable to the jurist. The law cannot avoid taking sides and committing itself upon such questions as whether it favours freer divorce, or a strict or liberal interpretation of the power of the state over private property. We are constantly faced with the question whether certain desirable remedies should be granted under circumstances that would mean a tremendous increase in the amount of litigation. What is this but a question of public policy?

The positivists justify their position by the contention that it is up to the legislature to determine the policy of the law, and that judges and jurists must simply obey it. But even if we ignore the part that judges and jurists play in making the law, we cannot ignore the fact that intelligent obedience requires a painstaking understanding of the purpose of the law. Even in military affairs, General Foch has taught us, discipline requires intelligent initiative in order to bring about conformity to the purpose of the superior command. Unintelligent obedience is always dangerous, even when the rules are most excellent (see the lamented Christy Mathewson on Inside Baseball).

We can thus see the one-sidedness of those who, like Ehrlich, tend to confuse the sociologic with the juristic point of view. The study of "living law" is a study of custom—a very important condition of law, but not a sufficient determinant of it. For actual practices may be contrary to the policy of the law. The law cannot accept anything as legal merely because it is the practice of a large number of people. Custom must meet certain criteria before the law will sanction it. It is doubtless of the utmost importance to know the actual conditions under which a legal rule is to be applied. But it cannot be too strongly insisted that the knowledge of such social conditions belongs to economics, or to some branch of descriptive social science. Law is a method of regulating social action, and the science of law has a content over and above that met in the knowledge of actual conditions.

At this point we may also dispose of the myth that scientific method is inductive—a myth that was originated largely by a famous lawyer, Francis Bacon.[2] But it is well to remember that Langdell, the father of the "case system," like Bacon laboured under a thoroughly rationalistic conception that not only was the number of legal principles very small, but that also the number of cases was limited and could easily be manipulated to show all the possible principles. Few today profess this simple faith. The view that science can begin without ideas, hypotheses, or anticipations of nature and proceed first of all to gather the facts, is nothing less than silly. For what facts are we to gather as relevant for our inquiry? Indeed, to find out what are the facts is the very purpose of scientific investigation. It is an illusion to suppose that we can build up a legal system or science of the law by simply gathering all the cases together. For the very first question, What does the case stand for? involves a theoretic issue—namely, On what principle can the actual decision be supported, or from what principle can it be deduced? The notion that a single case or even a number of cases can by themselves prove a principle is of course the old fallacy of arguing from the affirmation of the consequent. If decisions in specific cases are either right or wrong, the question of principle is already involved.

This suggests certain considerations in regard to statistical methods in legal science. Theoretically, it might seem that every assumption of general fact that the law makes ought to be capable of being tested statistically. Thus, the assertion that the rigour of punishment acts as a deterrent of crime seems to involve the correlation of only two factors and ought to be tested statistically. The first difficulty, however, is one familiar to all students of social science— namely, the difficulty of isolating our factors. Groups of figures can show a correlation only on the assumption that all other factors balance each other or remain constant, an assumption which there is reason to believe is seldom perfectly true in social affairs. Other questions of fact involve unique elements not sufficiently numerous to be the subject of numerical methods. Thus, we cannot by statistical comparison of conditions in common and civil law countries really settle the question whether the principle of *stare decisis* does in fact make the law more certain. Our instances are too few, and the possible factors too many, to make the statistical results conclusive.

These difficulties are familiar enough, and while they do not prevent statistical work in the social sciences, they certainly militate against the conclusiveness of the results obtained by such methods. In general, our statistical work depends upon the initial hypothesis that guides us in selecting the relevant facts and assigning a meaning to the possible correlations.

This brings us to the second limitation as to statistical methods in legal science, and that is that they are not applicable to purely juristic questions, to questions as to the meaning or validity of legal principles. In general, theories of value in economics, ethics, and politics cannot be discovered or established by statistical methods, though the latter may be used in the verification of factual generalizations.

The fact that questions of value have to be dealt with by dialectical rather than statistical methods puts a limitation on the use of history for juristic purposes.[3] History is undoubtedly a method of extending our experience. It helps us to eliminate vicious rationalism, the tendency typified by Blackstone to find false reasons for actual legal rules. Yet, by itself, history cannot establish standards of value or of what is desirable in the law. In fact, the same sets of historical facts teach different lessons to those who have different biases as to what is desirable. It is customary to have historical introductions to all sorts of practical discussions; but generally they are like the chaplain's prayer that opens a political convention, graceful and altogether unexceptionable, but hardly determinative of subsequent proceedings.

Moreover, in the reaction against Blackstonian rationalism, legal history has recently fallen into the inverse fallacy. I refer to the method of explaining old rules as mere survivals. No one doubts that many rules continue their existence after they have outlived their original function. But it is also true that many rules formerly useful, and now no longer so, have died. Is it not likely then that those which have survived may have done so because of a greater social vitality in serving some actual social need? This seems to me to hold with regard to the unusual liability of the common carrier. The latter is not adequately explained as a mere survival. It survived because of its utility.

Finally, if history is not to be a blind enslavement of the living present to the dead past, we must always be on guard as to what past rules are no longer suitable, and this requires not only a knowledge of past facts, but also an understanding of the needs of the present as well as of the past. This involves a theory of social needs or ends that the law ought to serve.

III

If at this point I am accused of still believing in the old classical deductive methods—so discredited in the minds of modernistic illuminati—I must enter a plea of confession and avoidance. I admit faith in the hypothetico-deductive method, but I deny that it has ever been justly discredited. On the contrary, the method of beginning with hypotheses and deducing conclusions, and then comparing these conclusions with the factual world, seems to me still the essence of sound scientific method. The prejudice against deduction is inspired by the abuse of that method on the part of those deficient in knowledge. Such abuse, however, is inherent in all human methods.

Stated positively, deduction has three functions in scientific method that ought to be rather obvious in the field of law:

First, it enables us to develop the implications of propositions and thus find out their true meaning. Knowledge grows most rapidly when we can properly utilize previous knowledge. Those who know make the most discoveries.

In the second place, deduction helps to make our assumptions explicit and this makes possible a critical attitude towards them.

In the third place, deduction enables us to deal not only with the actual, but also with the possible. It thus liberates us to explore the field of possibility, where there are to be found many things better than the actual.

Let me say a word about the second of these services. I say we begin always with hypotheses or assumptions. For the most part, however, it never occurs to us that we are making assumptions. We think we are starting with obvious truths. But propositions seem to us self-evident simply because it has never occurred to us to doubt them. It is, however, the business of scientific method to doubt all that pretends to be self-evident—e.g., that all property must have an owner, that no one can acquire rights by committing wrongs, that the maxim *Caveat emptor* is necessary to encourage commerce, etc. Modern geometry has discovered new regions of investigation by learning to look at Euclid's axioms as questionable assumptions. The same is true as to the axioms of Newtonian mechanics. Recently a distinguished economist has shown that a rational economic science can be built up on assumptions contrary to those prevailing among orthodox economists.[4] It would not be difficult to show that most of the principles appealed to as self-evident in legal discussion might easily be denied and their contrary shown to be just as plausible.

This does not mean universal scepticism, but only the recognition of the fact that as human beings we start not with absolute certainties, but with hypotheses or guesses suggested generally by tradition and previous knowledge, but not on that account necessarily free from error. Scientific methodology has no objection to traditional views as such, except to warn us that as traditional views are fallible, the only way of getting at the truth is to treat them as among a number of possible views and compare them with others. This process may lead us in the end to maintain the established views as the best. We may even contend that that which has stood the test of long experience has much to commend it. But even when the traditional view is accepted, a critical, logical examination of it refines it and thus enables us to eliminate irrelevant and unfortunate excrescences on it.

A deductive system that enables us to derive many legal rules from a few principles makes the law more certain, so that people can better know their rights. You cannot pass from past decisions to future ones without making assumptions. From the statement that a court has ruled so and so in certain cases nothing follows except in so far as the new cases are assumed to be like the old ones. But this likeness depends upon our logical analysis of classes of cases.

The fact that, like other human institutions, the law does not always succeed in being consistent, is no argument against its trying to be so. The fact that we do not always succeed in attaining health is not an argument for being satisfied with disease. The admission that death will overtake us is no reason against seeking to prolong life.

The law cannot abandon the effort at consistency. We must remember that the law always defeats the expectation of at least one party in every lawsuit. To maintain its prestige, in spite of that, requires such persistent and conspicuous effort at impartiality that even the defeated party will be impressed. This is most effectively promoted by genuine devotion to scientific method.

Those who distrust logic commonly appeal to experience. But the fact is that experience without logical vision is stupid and brutish and supplies no guide for the good or civilized life.

What is experience? In its original sense, and the one which it still has to those uncorrupted by subjectivistic philosophy, experience denotes something personal that happens to us. Thus, we say we are fortunate in never having experienced the effects of ether or of certain diseases. In this sense, personal experience is obviously not an adequate basis on which to decide the policies of the law. But if we generalize the term "experience" to include all that which has happened to human beings in general, and is likely to happen in the future, experience is certainly not something that is given in itself, but the very thing to be discovered by logical methods. Certainly the experience of the past, or of the future, is not given to us, and it is by scientific study relying on the canons of logic that we reconstruct the past and predict the future.

Trust life rather than theory, say our modernists. But is it true that by mere living our problems are solved? Is not life full of illusions and frustrations? Life is the seat of all that is ugly as well as beautiful; of disease as well as health; of all that is vile and loathsome as well as of all that is inspiring. At all times it carries the seeds of death. The law, like other institutions of civilization, is organized to advance the good life, and what distinguishes that is not to be attained by abandoning our intelligence.

Law without concepts or rational ideas, law that is not logical, is like pre-scientific medicine—a hodge-podge of sense and superstition, as has indeed been most of the world's common sense as distinguished from science.

To urge that judges, for instance, should rely on their experience or intuition in disregard of logically formulated principles is to urge sentimental anarchy. Men will generalize in spite of themselves. If they do it consciously in accordance with logical principles, they will do it more carefully and will be liberally tolerant to other possible generalizations. But those who distrust all logic think that they deal with facts when they are occupied with the product of their own grotesque theories.

Science, to be sure, is abstract. It tends to emphasize abstract considerations and deals with the definable classes rather than with the particular cases. But in doing so it forces us to see things from a wider point of view, and this tends to make us more just to the diversity of human interests. The air of unreality that science presents to the uninitiated is like the unreality which modern machinery presents to the old-fashioned artisan or to those who cultivate the soil by hand.

Nor can we respect the metaphysical objection that life is changing but concepts are fixed. It is precisely because concepts are fixed in meaning that we can measure or determine the rate of change. Should the rules of arithmetic be changed whenever the volume of our business transactions is changed? Will even the change of our system of weights and measures require us to discard the multiplication table?

The real objection to conceptually mechanical jurisprudence is one against all human activity that is unintelligent. So-called strong judges, who decide to follow principles regardless of consequences, are simply too lazy to examine countervailing considerations and special circumstances which are relevant to the application of these principles. At best they are guilty of the fallacy of simplism, of supposing that the law always consists of theoretically simple cases, whereas the concrete cases actually before us are more complex because they generally involve many principles. This is the root of what is sound in the distinction between "law in books" and "law in action," and in the warning that the needs of life should not be sacrificed to the needs of the study.

From this point of view we can see reason for rejecting the extreme formalism of Stammler and of the school of Kelsen, which seems to dominate contemporary European legal thought. There is a downright logical absurdity in Stammler's efforts to derive substantive rules of law from purely formal or logical principles. Nor can Kelsen establish by quasi-mathematical methods positive rules of law that can be the rules of any actual jurisdiction. The force of the analogy of mathematical physics which he, Felix Kaufmann, and his other followers invoke is really against them, since mathematical physics differs from pure mathematics precisely by making assumptions as to what exists—something that can never be derived from formal or pure mathematics.

In general, law is a specific type of existence and its specific nature cannot be deduced from something else. Kelsen's argument for a pure or unitary method would be sound if the law were the object of a pure and unitary science. But this cannot be so long as the jurist has to deal with different kinds of problems, historical, psychological, logical, and ethical, as well as mixed questions such as when we ask: What is it that courts do when they interpret a statute?

The law, and especially present American law, is desperately in need of a scientific elaboration. The old way of dealing with the law as a body of empirical rules has definitely broken down. *Stare decisis* means little in a changing society when for every new case the number of possible precedents is practically unwieldy. Without principles as guides, the body of precedents becomes an uncharted sea; and reliance on principles is worse than useless unless these principles receive critical scientific attention.

But if law is a fit subject for university study, it deserves to be studied not merely for its practical consequences, but also for the insight that it offers as to human life. Civilized life would be sadly impoverished if literature were devoted entirely to advertising or propaganda, even for righteous causes, or if the fine arts were used only for practical purposes rather than as ends in themselves enriching the enjoyment of life.

The theoretic study of the law is one of the ways in which we can attain a deeper and wider view of human existence, and that is good, if anything is.

Justice Holmes and the Nature of Law [1]

ALTHOUGH Justice Holmes has for nearly fifty years been generally recognized as one of our most distinguished judges, and has since 1881 enjoyed an enviable international reputation as the author of the leading modern classic on the common law, he seems to have exerted remarkably little influence on the actual development of American law. It is only in recent years that our teachers and writers of law have begun to make his thoughts the basis of their work.

I. HOLMES AND THE JUDICIAL TRADITION

Is there any branch of law that can be said to have been moulded by Holmes as constitutional law was moulded by Marshall or the conflict of laws by Story? Carrying to the bench the soldierly spirit of loyal and disciplined acceptance of the task assigned to him, he has nevertheless suffered the ironic fate of becoming most popularly known as a writer of dissenting opinions.

Profound and eloquently expressed as are his views in *Vegelahn* v. *Guntner*, or in the Abrams case, and irrefutable as are his constant protests against the unconscionable stretching of the terms "liberty," "property," and "due process" in the Fourteenth Amendment, they seem nevertheless to have gone entirely unheeded in the actual march of our law. The various admirers of Justice Holmes—and they are fortunately an increasing number of the younger generation—and all those who wish to understand his real position in the history of American law will do well to face candidly the seemingly anomalous character of his judicial career.

Many explanations may be offered. But the one especially interesting to students is the fact that Holmes has been above all the great thinker on the bench, and the influence of the thinker is apt to appear merely critical to the practically-minded of his own day. For great thoughts cannot be attained without enduring loneliness.[2] It is only when integrated over a long period, *sub specie æternitatis,* that the positive influence of the thinker becomes generally visible. It is certainly true that no man, not Marshall, Kent, or Story, came to the bench with greater learning and power of philosophic reflection than that which the author of *The Common Law* brought with him as he left the professor's chair at the Harvard Law School to enter the Supreme Court of Massachusetts. Now the relatively recent expansion of our university law schools, resulting in increased opportunity for legal scholarship, makes it clear to us that the American bar of the past half-century has not been predominantly a scholarly profession. Our lawyers have been too busy serving the practical needs of our expanding industrial and commercial economy, as well as supplying the vast majority of our legislative and administrative officials. And while the body of our judges has contained its just proportion of men of practical insight and intellectual power, it has necessarily shared the characteristics of the bar from which it has been chosen. These characteristics are only intensified by the greater age of our judges, due to our method of choosing them from among those who have already been successful at the bar (instead of training men for the judicial career directly, as is the Continental custom). "Judges commonly are elderly men and are more likely to hate at sight any analysis to which they are not accustomed and which disturbs repose of mind."[3]

It is not, therefore, surprising that the American judiciary as well as the American bar should have clung so long to the old eighteenth century conception of law—especially constitutional law—as a body of absolutely fixed principles hovering over and above human affairs, and so constituted that the judge need only know these principles to deduce just decisions in all possible cases that can come before him. Logically this is connected with the old naïvely rationalistic dogma that from certain intuitive self-evident principles as to geometry, nature, or morals, all sorts of material conclusions could be deduced, independently of any empirical knowledge. Of course, in practice, judges cannot entirely ignore the factual situation before them. But all too often, alas, has the old rationalistic theory of the law been invoked by courts as an excuse for evading a thorough or scientific analysis of the actual state of affairs.

This comes out perhaps most clearly in the attitude of our courts towards the modern factory owner's liability to his working people for the inevitable accidents of the industry. Courts long persisted in thinking in terms of the old quasi-ethical maxim, "no liability without fault," and used it as a sort of protection against the duty of examining the economists' claim that the question should be dealt with as one of insurance, the cost of which could be added to the price of the product and shifted to the consumer. Had courts seen that, they might not have found it difficult to agree with Justice Holmes who, as far back as 1897, pointed out that it was not at all unreasonable to ask whether "the public should insure the safety of those whose work it uses." [4]

Why should not the public pay for the actual human cost of the products that it consumes? If it will not do it through the price of the commodity, it will do it in the form of charity to the victims of these accidents, and the latter form of payment has many obvious social disadvantages.

The same remotely abstract conception of law that makes courts take refuge in phrases about liberty of contract or deprivation of liberty and property, to the detriment of any thorough-going analysis of the actual social situation, shows itself in the opposition to minimum wage legislation. If an industry pays a man less than the cost of the minimum of subsistence, it is either starving him or else getting a subsidy by making some one else (probably some charitable agency) pay part of the cost of its labour. The former is a most inhuman way not only of killing people, but also of preparing the

soil for physical and social diseases; and the latter is a socially uneconomic way of running any industry, for it hides the real cost of
production. In the light of such considerations, how inept to talk of
taking away the labourer's property when he is deprived of the
"liberty" to work under conditions of starvation! [5]

There are those who explain this attitude of our courts to labour
legislation as traceable to class bias. Judges are selected from the
most successful lawyers, and success at the bar generally means
wealthy clients. It is natural for one who has looked after the interests of such clients to continue to have an open ear to their just
claims, and he cannot be expected to have as much sympathetic
understanding of the claims of factory workers with whom he has
not had such educative relation. On this point Justice Holmes's view
may well be quoted and requoted: [6]

"When socialism first began to be talked about, the comfortable
classes of the community were a good deal frightened. I suspect that
this fear has influenced judicial action both here and in England, yet
it is certain that it is not a conscious factor. . . . I think that something similar has led people who no longer hope to control the legislatures to look to the courts as expounders of the constitutions, and
that in some courts new principles have been discovered outside the
bodies of those instruments, which may be generalized into acceptance of the economic doctrines which prevailed fifty years ago, and
a wholesale prohibition of what a tribunal of lawyers does not think
about right."

When judges and conservative lawyers speak, as they have, of
being bound by law rather than economic theory, they assume their
antiquated economic theories to be self-evident facts and, as such,
part of the fixed legal order.

Justice Holmes, despite the popular impression to the contrary,
likewise begins with the old classical individualistic economics, which
assumes that the profit motive necessarily leads to a maximum productivity of desirable goods, that men render the greatest service
when under the illusion of self-seeking. [7] But as a disciplined thinker,
or to use his own term, as a civilized man, he has learned to doubt

his own first principles and to realize the necessity for further knowledge. As the responsibility for investigating the facts and framing desirable policies is the task of the legislatures, he does not think it the judge's business to interpose the judicial veto on what he thinks very unwise legislation.

This disciplined and thought-provoking scepticism extends to all fields of law. Do we really know how law operates? "What have we better than a blind guess to show that the criminal law in its present form does more good than harm?" [8] No wonder that at a time when the legal profession generally had little doubt that John Marshall and the authors of the *Federalist* were beyond human limitations, it was shocked to hear the Chief Justice of Massachusetts, in answer to a motion that the court adjourn upon the centenary of Marshall's assumption of office, confess to "some little revolt from our purely local or national estimates. . . . A man is bound to be parochial in his practice. . . . But his thinking should be cosmopolitan and detached." [9]

Men live by symbols and symbols acquire their prestige through age. And in a country of moving populations, with often conflicting backgrounds and temptation to violence, the law, especially the Constitution, has been a symbol of national unity as well as of social order. But, "My keenest interest is excited, not by what are called great questions and great cases, but by little decisions which the common run of selectors would pass by because they did not deal with the Constitution or a telephone company, yet which have in them the germ of some wider theory, and therefore of some profound interstitial change in the very tissue of the law. The men whom I should be tempted to commemorate would be the originators of transforming thought." [10]

II. HOLMES AND RECENT JURISTIC THEORY

If the scholar or intellectual pioneer in Holmes has prevented him from floating in the current of traditional judicial dogma, the same

sceptical distrust of one-sided simplicity, the same bent to do justice
to the many conflicting considerations in the complex reality of the
law, has prevented him from committing himself to those simple
sweeping denials or assertions which, as slogans, are dear to those
who like to run in schools or sects.

While since its publication in 1881 his *Common Law* has been
extensively quoted and highly acclaimed, I know of no American attempt, previous to Gray's *Nature and Sources of the Law,* to state
Holmes's view of the nature of the law as a system or social institution. I mention Gray not as a disciple of Holmes, but as a sufficiently
kindred spirit. While the unpretentious manner in which Gray put
his homely wisdom has prevented his book from receiving as much
attention as it deserves, it, together with Pound's earlier essays,
opened the present era of American juristic thought. In the course
of the last two decades of discussion, the solid merits of Holmes's
realistic views of the law as "an anthropologic document" have become more and more obvious. The danger today is not that they
will be ignored, but that their rich content will be impoverished by
being harnessed to some "ism" such as functionalism, behaviourism,
institutionalism, or the like. Thus contemporary irrationalists frequently support their case by his dictum, "Experience, not logic, is
the life of the law." This, however, is to tear a passage out of its
qualifying context. Holmes does characterize as a fallacy the notion
that "the only force at work in the development of the law is logic."
But "in the broadest sense, indeed, that notion would be true. The
condition of our thinking about the universe is that it is capable of
being thought about rationally." The fallacy is rather in supposing
that some actual system of law, ours, for instance, is logical in the
sense that "it can be worked out like mathematics from some general
axioms of conduct." [11] In any case Holmes's work is full of the
keenest sort of logical analyses of legal doctrines.[12]

Thus Mr. Frank, in his interesting book *Law and the Modern
Mind,* can well quote Holmes as to the illusory character of the pretension to absolute certainty in the law. It would have been better,

however, if he had added Holmes's insistence that the efforts of the law must always be directed to narrow the zone of uncertainty as far as possible. One can well quote Holmes to the effect that the force and content of legal rules change with time. But Holmes has been wise enough to realize the historical truth that certain phases of human life have remained relatively constant for long periods and that elements of the law may be the same today as in ancient Rome.

As I have referred to this in a previous essay,[13] I may restrict myself for the present to pointing out the danger to Holmes's legal realism by identifying it with current behaviourism.

1. *Uniformities of Conduct and Legal Norms*

The traditional American conception of natural rights so confused law and morals that Holmes has rendered a great service to clarity by recalling us to the fact that a bad man may be perfectly within the law, that terms like "rights," "duties," "fault," "negligence," and the like have a definite legal, as distinct from moral, meaning, and that, whatever our moral standards, we must recognize the law as that which has back of it the organized force of the state.

Many, however, of those who, like Holmes, reject the old confusion between law and morality, ignore his cautious qualifications and profess to do away altogether with the normative point of view in law. They make law synonymous with what people actually do, i.e., with social behaviour.

Those who do this are largely influenced by the positivistic conception of scientific method, according to which the latter consists exclusively in observing facts and extracting from them laws and uniformities. They therefore think that if we restrict ourselves to the study of certain uniformities of behaviour, we can build up a fruitful science of law. It would take us far afield to show the superficial one-sidedness and the inadequacies of this conception of scientific method. Here I can only point to such works as Poincaré's *Sci-*

ence and Hypothesis to call attention to the much more active rôle that ideas as hypotheses play in selecting what "facts" shall be considered relevant to our inquiry. It is well also to note that every well developed science like mechanics or thermodynamics considers what would happen if actually unattainable or incompletely attainable ideal conditions were realized. But for our present purpose it is sufficient to note that if the behaviourists succeeded in compiling a list of uniformities of social or economic conduct, they would have a descriptive sociology, not a juristic science. For just as the laws of organic behaviour constitute physiology, not hygiene or medicine, so uniformities of social behaviour may constitute a social physiology, not a social hygiene (of which juristic science must be a phase). This is not to deny that knowledge of the ways of actual social conduct is an indispensable part of any science of law. But we must not let hazy ideas of science make us forget that law is essentially concerned with norms that regulate, rather than with uniformities that describe, human conduct. The laws that natural science seeks to discover, such as the laws of mechanical motion or the conservation of energy, are uniformities which if valid at all cannot be violated. Despite the popular confused talk about violating the laws of nature, we cannot go counter to the law of gravitation, whether we fall or fly. If any one could in the least depart from such a law, it would then be proved false as a scientific or universal law. But it is of the very essence of legal rules that they are violable and that penalties or sanctions are provided for their various violations. They do not state what always is, but attempt to decide what ought to be. It is precisely when there is no desirable uniformity in the way vehicles use the road that a law is made to regulate traffic. Whether men do or do not endorse certain papers, or whether they do or do not brew intoxicating liquors, is a physical fact of sensory observation. But the legal consequences of such facts are not determined when these facts are. The former depend upon the legal rules that we regard as binding norms in these given cases.

A great many efforts have been made to avoid this categorical distinction between the existential or descriptive and the regulative or normative. One of these attempts is to deny the imperative character of the legal rules by pointing to legal definitions, permissive laws, and other seemingly declarative propositions. But this is decidedly a near-sighted view of the matter. Definitions are not laws in themselves, but they are binding elements in the law, being in effect rules of interpretation that decide which of a number of possibly conflicting meanings shall be enforced. An order does not cease to be a command because it contains an explanation of what it is that is commanded. Nor is a law permitting a man to do something at his option, e.g., to dispose of his property by testament, any less a part of the system of imperatives, in this case of what we call the law of property. It is certainly an imperative to the children or other heirs, who, when the will is properly made, must yield certain goods to legatees or devisees.

By far the most extensive effort to eliminate the normative aspect of law is to make law identical with custom, with the ways that in fact prevail in social life. Among recent writers, a great array of distinguished names, Kornfeld and Ehrlich, Rolin and Duguit, J. C. Carter and Underhill Moore, may be cited as supporting this view more or less consistently. Nevertheless there is a rather obvious confusion back of it. Clearly there is a difference between social custom and rules of statutory or judicial origin, such as the requirement of writing in certain contracts, or the rule in Shelley's case. Many almost universal customs, such as the ways we eat our food, build our houses, engage in social intercourse, and the like, can in no way be said to be legal rules.

The confusion between law and custom is, however, difficult to avoid because human inertia and imitativeness give custom itself a regulative and normative force, compelling uniformity where the individual might otherwise diverge from the common way of doing things. And it might well be argued that not only is custom the sole law in some primitive communities where there are no official courts, but that the obedience of modern men to the decision of judges and state officials grows out of, and rests upon, customary deference to or acceptance of authority. We do apply the term "law" to the marriage and inheritance customs of peoples like the American Indians, who have no courts or legislatures. And is not this the more fundamental law from which modern state law develops? In the light of the foregoing it has struck many acute minds [14] as absurd to contend that courts make the law. Is not the conduct of people necessarily governed by some law before the courts are ever invoked? And do not courts themselves operate under law?

This objection, however, involves a failure to discriminate between two different things called by the name "law," to wit, rules as uniformities that human conduct actually embodies, and rules as norms according to which justiciable issues should be decided. These two things are of course intimately related. Legal norms are the historical outcome of social behaviour, and in turn they help to determine many customs in a modern community, since men's conduct is governed by their expectations of how the courts will rule. But the fact that legal norms are conditioned by historical situations, and depend for their very existence on certain social habits of obedience, does not make such norms identical with the uniformities of social behaviour.

In a modern state we often have conflicting usages and customs, so that specific rules are enacted by the legislatures; and these rules as well as others are elaborated by courts and enforced by the state. This is the kind of law about which we consult a lawyer whenever we are uncertain or in conflict with others, and this is the kind of law about which the jurist is engaged when he tries to develop legal doctrines. Questions in it are settled by judicial procedure and not by sociologists or experts on custom, though the latter may be advantageously heard by the court. The study of what people actually do in a given situation is, indeed, indispensable to a proper solution of any legal problem. But it is a necessary, not a sufficient, condition for such a solution. We need also to determine whether any given practice should or should not receive legal protection. This question involves consideration of the aim of the law, without which it is indeed unintelligible. This aim is ideal, and actual conduct conforms to it more or less.

Justice Holmes's constant insistence on the aim that the law serves helps us to understand not only the logical nature of the law, but also the condition of its growth and of its proper functioning. "A system of law at any time is the resultant of present notions of what is wise and right on the one hand, and, on the other, of rules handed down from earlier states of society and embodying needs and notions which more or less have passed away." [15] The mere fact, therefore, that we have been in the habit of doing things in a certain way tends to make us continue in that course. But it is not always the best way.[16] The scientific or reflective jurist must therefore be constantly questioning the worth of prevailing practices, just as the judge must consider the diverse social advantages and disadvantages that should determine his decision.

It is the essence of positivism to view the law exclusively as uniformities of existing behaviour, in total disregard of any ideals as to what should be. This, however, cannot but result in an unavowed natural law in which habit and inertia become the absolute norm or rule. Behaviouristic theories are thus bound, if consistently carried out, to end where our old conservative natural-law theories did. Without deciding as to whether or when such conservatism is desirable or undesirable, it is well to insist with Justice Holmes [17] that "A body of law is more rational and more civilized when every rule it contains is referred articulately and definitely to an end which it subserves."

2. *Nominalism and the Reality of Rules*

The decisive rôle of judicial decisions in modern law leads some behaviourists to substitute the behaviour of the judge for that of the people, as the substance of the law. The most direct expression of this is the view of Professor Bingham that the law consists of the actual individual decisions and that rules are no part of the law, but are mere subjective ideas in the minds of those who think about the law.[18]

If we are to have a rational science of law, we must realize the untenability of this position, which is not at all involved in Holmes's dictum that "the prophecies of what the courts will do in fact and nothing more pretentious are what I mean by law."

Bingham's position is explicitly based on a dualistic metaphysics that assumes a mind and a world external to it. Judges, cases, and decisions presumably exist in the external world. But "Principles and rules cannot exist outside of the mind. . . . The external expression of them does . . . the meaning then exists only in the mind of the speaker or writer as he makes it." This is an old popular metaphysics going back to medieval times, and still regnant, but quite untenable on reflection.

Let us in the first place distinguish between the meaning of things, and what exists in our minds when we apprehend this meaning. The former belongs to or follows from the nature of the things considered, while the latter depends not only on there being such objective meaning but also on our willingness and ability to apprehend. Consider, for instance, the meaning of entropy or of the chemical law of multiple proportion. It consists, as Peirce has shown, of all the possible consequences that follow from it. We may, by study, learn more or less of this meaning, and it may then in a metaphorical sense be said to have entered into, and to be in, our mind. But the condition of this happening is that there should be such meanings in the nature of the things studied. If the law of entropy or that of multiple proportion is true, its objective meaning or set of consequences held true before they entered the mind of any speaker or writer—indeed before our planetary system was formed. The meanings of things do not, then, depend on the mind of the individual thinker, speaker, or writer. Rather does the fate of the individual depend on his seeing what there is to be seen of the principles or rules which enter into these meanings.

Far from its being absurd, as Bingham asserts, to suppose that principles and rules can exist independently of the comprehension of the individual observer, that is exactly what we all assume whenever we undertake to teach any science or systematic truth. And the law is no exception. Certainly when the lawyer argues any case or tries to expound any legal doctrine, he tries to make his hearer or reader comprehend the meaning of certain rules or general principles previously not in the mind of the hearer or reader. And it is a sheer fallacy to suppose that because meanings may in a sense be said to enter into or exist in our minds when we apprehend them, they cannot therefore be genuine parts or features of the objective world apprehended.

Back, however, of the subjectivist's failure to realize the objectivity of meaning is the nominalist's difficulty in seeing the reality of the universals that enter into all meaning. This difficulty, as has been intimated before, arises from the fallacy of reification, that is, of regarding universals as if they were additional particular things, so that it seems reasonable to ask, Where are they? But the question shows a confusion, since everything localized in time and space is by definition particular. As all, however, that we can ever say about anything involves abstract traits, relations, or universals, no one can well dismiss them as mere meaningless sounds or words on paper, and the nominalist tries to meet the difficulty by locating all universals or abstractions in the mind. But if there is any difficulty about conceiving them in objective nature, that difficulty is not cured by putting them in the mind. For if the nominalistic logic is good it should lead us, as it led Berkeley, to deny that there can be any universal ideas in the mind. My idea of a triangle (in the sense of an image existing in the mind) must be of a particular size, scalene or isosceles, etc. Indeed, Professor Bingham does argue that there is no real identity between a rule in the mind of A and a rule in the mind of B that in common speech would be called the same rule.[19]

But why stop here? If the same rule cannot exist in two different minds, can it exist in the same mind at different times? Indeed, how can any existing mind or anything whatsoever be the same if there is no identity in nature? And if there is no identity in nature, all references to any object as the same are false or meaningless. If, per contra, abstract identity and diversity are real traits of things in nature, there is no difficulty in recognizing them as universal principles that are part of the objective meaning of things. Things and their meanings do not exist in absolutely separate worlds "external" to each other, if these meanings follow from or express the nature of things. Rules, we are told, help us to analyze the facts. They could not do so if the facts were unrelated to them and had nothing in common with them.

The root difficulty of the nominalist is that he confuses the existence of particular images in individual minds with the objective meaning of principles or rules in our common world. In considering a rule, such as the rule in Shelley's case, different thinkers may look at it from different points of view and see different phases of it. They will have different images in their minds and will express themselves in different words, perhaps in different languages. Yet it is possible for them to mean or refer to the same object. Otherwise, there could be no possibility of argument or communication. Communication presupposes a common world.

If the reader finds the foregoing paragraphs too abstruse, he may consider the reality of rules and principles independently of the metaphysical quagmire on which Bingham chooses to rest it. The gist of the question is, Do or do not legal decisions that form the law necessarily involve rules and principles? The issue may perhaps be made somewhat clearer if we ask whether a given judge is acting in an official or a purely personal capacity. Obviously, if we make any such distinction it is because there are rules that give legal effect to the judge's decision only when he acts in conformity with them. Moreover, within the scope of the judge's legal power we may distinguish between the rulings that are taken as precedents in similar cases and the exercise of discretionary power that issues binding orders which do not serve as rules for the future. Thus a judge may legally deny the plea of counsel for an adjournment; but so long as it does not serve as a precedent the denial cannot be said to make law, though it is within the law. The same is true of any discretionary administrative act, e.g., when a postmaster refuses to listen to my suggestions as to the improvement of the service.

The *mediatore* in the Spanish market who terminates the haggling by making the two parties close the bargain can hardly be called a judge. Neither is an arbitrator a judge, unless his decisions are supposed to follow or embody some rule or principle of social authority. Consider on the other hand a court of appeal deciding that the trial judge erred in admitting certain evidence, that replacement value rather than original cost is the proper basis on which to compute railway rates, or that the law of the domicile should govern the validity of a divorce. In these cases, the decisions are clearly meaningless apart from the rule that they explicitly embody. But every decision of a court is nowadays taken by the community as a norm or rule for all similar cases because of the community's faith that the courts will consistently enforce that rule. Mr. X sues Bank Y for a specific amount of money computed on the basis of the value of the Russian rouble at a specific time. We can say that the court decides only the case before it. But in fact all who deal in foreign exchange are affected and adjust their practices accordingly. For they expect that the courts will rule similarly in all similar cases. The element of identity that makes different cases similar is what we formulate as the rule of the case.

Bingham admits that courts are and should be governed by constitutional provisions and statutes enacted by legislatures. Are not these formulated in general rules? And are not parts of the common law as definite as that?

The present wave of nominalism in juristic science is a reaction by younger men against the *abuse* of abstract principles by an older generation that neglected the adequate factual analysis necessary to make principles properly applicable. It is natural, therefore, for the rebels to claim as their own one who for more than the time of one generation has valiantly stood for the need of more factual knowledge in the law. But no group can claim Justice Holmes as its own unless it shares his respect for the complexity of the legal situation and exercises the same caution against hastily jumping from one extreme error to the opposite. Holmes's position is, I judge, in perfect agreement with that of a logical pragmatist like Peirce: Legal principles have no meaning apart from the judicial decisions in concrete cases that can be deduced from them, and principles alone (i.e., without knowledge or assumption as to the facts) cannot logically decide cases. But Holmes has always insisted that the man of science in the law must not only possess an eye for detail but also "insight which tells him what details are significant." [20] And significance involves general principles that determine which facts are relevant and which may be neglected as irrelevant. The law consists of prophecies as to how the public force (as directed by courts) will act. But the judge whom Holmes [21] most respects is the one who, like Shaw, not only has technical knowledge, but also understands "the ground of public policy to which all laws must ultimately be referred." Indeed, no modern state appoints judges at random or backs up their arbitrary whims. Judges are generally required to have some legal knowledge, so that their decisions, despite the element of discretion,[22] should conform to the general pattern of the legal system. Such conformity would be impossible if the judicial decisions were entirely capricious. If the decision of each case were independent of any principle explicitly stated by some authority or implicitly contained in previous cases, there could be no point in judge, counsel, or any one else studying or knowing any law. No case can serve as a clue to any other except to the extent that they both contain some common elements to which a common principle is applicable.

The fact that the judge has a large element of discretion need not prevent us from expecting of him, as of any other official—perhaps even more than of others—conformity to the law. "Sittest thou to judge me after the law and commandest me to be smitten contrary to the law?" Justice involves conformity to some rule, not anarchy.

The difficulty of seeing what rule a given case involves is partly due to the traditional way of talking about the *ratio decidendi* as if a single case by itself could logically determine a rule. Since every individual case can be subsumed under any number of rules of varying generality, it clearly cannot establish any of them. It is only because every case is related more or less to previous cases—no human situation can be altogether unrelated to all previous situations—that a decision on it tends to fix the immediate direction of the stream of legal decision. The relation between decisions and rules may thus be viewed as analogous to that between points and a line. No single point nor, in strict accuracy, any finite number of points can by themselves completely determine the nature of the line or curve that passes through them. For every curve is the locus of an infinite number of points that conform to its rule or formula. We have to know the nature of the curve before we can determine whether any given point is on it or not. The practice of physicists in drawing continuous curves through a number of points that are near to each other (the latter representing accurate observations or measurements), and then using this curve for purposes of interpolation and extrapolation, suggests that a number of points may determine a line. This has led inductively minded jurists to view particular decisions as the primary realities and to look on rules as secondary and entirely derivative. But this is an inadequate view. In the physical as in the legal field, neither specific observations or decisions nor the law or rule is absolutely certain. Error may enter all of these, and to banish the inquiry whether any particular observation or decision is in any way erroneous is to rule out the possibility of rational or scientific inquiry.

Actual scientific procedure uses what are regarded as established laws or rules to determine the correctness of particular observations or decisions, and uses large numbers of reliable observations or decisions to test the correctness of proposed laws or rules. The logical circularity of this procedure shows that in this way we cannot attain absolute material truth. But we can by ever enlarging our circle obtain the best that is available. Thus Kepler tests the proposed Ptolemaic, Tychonian, and Copernican lines or laws of planetary motion by their relative accuracy in meeting the well authenticated tables of astronomical observations. But the question, which observations are the best and most reliable, can be answered only on theoretic grounds. So in the law we test rules by the closeness with which they fit what we regard as the right decisions in particular cases; but if the question is raised as to whether any particular decision is right or not, we test it by rules that we regard as operating in analogous cases, i.e., in cases that embody the same principle.

3. Behaviourism and the Need of Critical Thought

After many years at the bar and on the bench Justice Holmes declared, in 1897, that "we have too little theory in the law rather than too much." [23] But legal theory, if it is to be worth while, must be closely reasoned and thoroughly tested. Will the new efforts at a legal philosophy now arising in this country meet this requirement? The hurried rhythm of our life and our too eager desire to make theory bear on practice are serious difficulties in the way. But the gravest peril perhaps is that in reacting violently against our former isolation of law we shall neglect the results of centuries of legal scholarship and slavishly imitate other social sciences or borrow from them methods and results that are not suitable to our subject. Let us not forget that some of the social sciences are very young, and are as yet in large part only vocabularies of generous aspiration. Scientific sobriety certainly demands a more critical attitude to the results of current social psychology than some recent writers on law have shown. One trained in the law should have a better sense for what constitutes demonstrative evidence.

It would obviously carry us beyond the proper limits of this essay to try to substantiate the last contention. But I may point rather dogmatically (for the sake of brevity) to the dangers of introducing the language of behaviourism into legal theory. We may be told that there can be nothing dangerous in calling a judicial decision sub-vocal behaviour, and the reasons that a court gives for its decisions, vocal behaviour. But just as our economy may suffer from bad currency, science may be confused by a terminology that fails to make proper distinctions.

To call a decision the behaviour of the judge is to confuse physically organic with social-teleologic categories. We usually mean by the behaviour of the judge those physical acts which are connected with his organism. Doubtless the judge's organism functions when he speaks or writes; and we believe that it conditions his individual thinking, though precisely how, we do not know. But the legal effect of a judicial decision is altogether different from the physical effects of what is properly the judge's behaviour. The latter is something in the physical world and operates continuously in time and space. But a legal decision relates situations remote in time and space through a purely logical connection. The logical relation involved in the question whether a given state of affairs can be subsumed under a rule laid down in a given decision, is a non-temporal one. As a social event, also, a legal decision does not operate on the pattern of physical causation. Whether, for instance, one on whom a decision is legally binding will actually obey it or not depends on an independent judgment and will. The decision orders me to pay, but I may decide not to, and it is not at all certain that the order of the court will be physically enforced.

These distinctions may seem too obvious and rudimentary. Yet their neglect produces regrettable confusion in the otherwise admirable presidential address, in 1927, of Professor Oliphant before the Association of American Law Schools. Using the behaviourist formula of stimulus-response to denote the relation between the facts of a case and the judge's decision, he naturally jumps to the conclusion that the latter relation is as constant and predictable as that between physical stimulus and organic response. And Professor Oliphant bases the hopes and program of legal science on this assumption. But this is to beg the whole question. It is not at all certain that a similar state of facts in two cases will always produce a similar decision. It seems rather obvious that the decision will depend not on facts all as objective as physical stimuli, but rather on what the judge thinks are the facts and what law he thinks applicable. When the judge is mistaken (and at least one learned counsel almost always thinks so), it is clearly not the objective facts but the judge's subjective impressions and reflections that operate. Because of human insensibility to many facts before us and the tendency to believe in "facts" that do not really exist, "the response of [the judge's] intuition of experience to the stimulus of human situations" has not, so far as we can tell, that ascertainable constancy and objectivity characteristic of physiologic behaviour.[24]

This over-sanguine ignoring of a real difficulty in the behaviouristic analogies leads Professor Oliphant to belittle an important source of knowledge, namely, the court's written opinion. It has become a fashion nowadays to belittle the reasons people give for their conduct. Admittedly men may be mistaken as to their reasons and motives, and judges are no exception. But can we say that the judge's intuition of the facts before him is free from the possibility of similar error? It may be urged that the language of judicial decision is often determined by pious platitudes. But do not pious platitudes likewise determine actual decisions? It seems rather strange to suppose that the language habitual to people will throw no light on their thought and the motives of their conduct. The contrary seems more probable.

But what is even more serious is the fact that the behaviouristic stimulus-response formula leads Professor Oliphant to speak *as if* he held the mystic and pernicious doctrine that judges' actual decisions are always wise, or at least always wiser than their reasons: "We may more freely criticize what courts have said, but we shall more cautiously criticize what they have done, realizing, as we shall, that they were exposed to the impact of more of the facts than we."[25] But obviously a court may have been unwise precisely because, like a jury, it allowed itself to be influenced by the impact of present but irrelevant facts which on subsequent reflection we can see should not have been decisive. If the judge's decision be more important than his reason, it should need more criticism.

This need for criticizing actual decisions on the basis of the ends that they should serve is a necessary consequence of Holmes's conception of law. It is, fortunate that the prestige of his position supports the inherent wisdom of his teaching.

We are living in a period when hasty impressionism is in the air. Men are impatient with mere theory that does not lead at once to "practically constructive" results, and there is perhaps even more popular impatience with theory that seems merely critical. But the honest thinker must be ready to say "We do not know" when the evidence is not all in and what we have is inconclusive. This need not dampen our ardour in whatever venture solicits our efforts, but it is well to have the example of the soldier, lawyer, and judge who, preëminently loyal to his practical duties, has always recognized the supreme importance of theory in law as elsewhere.

Philosophy and Legal Science [1]

IN A scholarly and suggestive article on "The Rational Basis of Legal Science" [2] Professor Yntema has subjected my views upon the nature of law to an extended criticism, and thought to discover a number of fallacies in the arguments that I have used in their defence. Despite eminent courtesy and unusual persistence in hunting out and reading the scattered fragments of my writings, Professor Yntema's critique appears to me to be a remarkable achievement in misunderstanding. The misunderstandings that run through this article seem to me to have a common root in the assumption that because I am a philosopher by profession I hold certain popular and traditional views as to the nature of philosophy. These popular and traditional views have made of philosophy a sort of bogeyman that is used to frighten legal science into swallowing half-baked and thoroughly indigestible canons of procedure. According to the nurse-maid's tale, legal science can avoid the clutches of philosophy only by subsisting on nominalism, a metaphysic from which the juice of life evaporated in the Middle Ages. I am sufficiently apprehensive of the infant's digestive powers and sufficiently concerned with its welfare to think that the elimination of some traditional beliefs as to the shape and colour of philosophy may be pertinent and useful.

Philosophy to Professor Yntema, as to many others, appears to be a peculiar method of thought that sets itself up as a short cut to knowledge and thus seduces travellers from the arduous road of science. Indeed there seem to be three short cuts to legal knowledge offered by philosophy, and these are the paths of Mind, of Logic, and of Ought. It seems therefore incumbent upon the defenders of legal science to mark the quicksands that underlie these paths, so that men may continue to walk on the firm highways of science.

Now I do not wish to deny that some men who have been called philosophers have thought to derive answers to all sorts of empirical questions by some metaphysical, logical, or ethical manipulation of their inner consciousness. My own conception of the matter—and, I think, the conception of any one who has followed the modern development of logic—is quite different. Professor Yntema's defence of science seems to me, therefore, to proceed from a quixotic misapprehension of the nature of philosophy. A sober analysis of the relevance of metaphysics, logic, and ethics to legal science may demonstrate the futility of the fear that philosophy seeks either to destroy or to supplant scientific research in law.

I. METAPHYSICS AND LEGAL SCIENCE

There is no doubt that a prevailing tendency in philosophy since Locke and Kant has regarded epistemology, or the theory of knowledge, as a presupposition of metaphysics and of all rational inquiry. We are unable, according to this doctrine, to understand the nature of the world until we understand the nature of mind. Even a professed follower of Hegel (who opposed this view) has deemed it necessary to begin a systematic exposition of legal and economic philosophy by devoting a first volume entirely to epistemology;[3] Dean Pound has been criticized by Continental jurists for not doing likewise.

Professor Yntema feels that fruitful legal science need not begin that way. I believe that this feeling is justified. Mind is a part of the world, and all the difficulties that we meet in investigating the nature of the physical world reappear, often in more virulent form, when we seek to investigate the nature of the mind. There is thus no *a priori* ground for believing that truth in psychology must be attained before we can attain truth in other sciences. Nor is that belief supported by empirical evidence from the history of science.

The view that we must settle the problems of epistemology before we can deal with any other question is a view against which I have persistently protested, at least since 1910.[4] I can therefore see no justification whatever for Professor Yntema's suggestion that a professional interest in epistemology has led me to invite students of law "into the 'metaphysical quagmire' in which nominalism is involved."[5]

Professor Yntema, however, is primarily concerned not with the epistemological question of the nature of knowledge, but with the metaphysical question of the nature of particulars and universals. It would be captious, perhaps, to criticize his use of the term "epistemology" to cover the latter question. It is important only to note that his failure to distinguish between the problem of knowledge and the problem of being is paralleled by his failure to distinguish between psychology and logic, between the avowed assumptions of scientists and the implied assumptions of science, between the moral beliefs of a community and its moral needs. Throughout these confusions runs the central doctrine of the metaphysics that he defends, namely, that we can talk sensibly only of things that exist in space and time, so that abstractions or rules can be real only while they exist in a particular skull at a particular time. The validity of this metaphysical doctrine, variously known as conceptualism, nominalism, terminism, and subjective idealism, may well be examined in the light of the foregoing confusions.

Students of law, like all other intellectual workers, are likely, sooner or later, to make assumptions that involve one or another answer to the basic problems of metaphysics. When one of these answers happens to be untenable it does not help the situation to urge that we are lawyers and not metaphysicians. The untenable assumption remains untenable no matter what the professional occupation of the one who makes it.

A generation ago it was the fashion of judges and eminent lawyers to claim that law was law and had nothing to do with "theoretic" economics and other social sciences. This did not prevent them

from making all sorts of unavowed assumptions in these realms—
and these assumptions did not become true in fact by being called
legal rather than economic.

Similarly it was the fashion a generation ago for students of natural science to announce rather loudly their utter independence of
metaphysics: "We make no metaphysical assumption or presupposition." This was perhaps useful in view of the illegitimate claims
of some of the old metaphysicians, who tried to dictate as to what
science might or might not undertake (though none of them went,
in this respect, to the extremes that the anti-metaphysical positivist
Comte did). But the growth of science soon showed that this pretended absolute independence of the natural sciences was a snare.
Workers in natural science are bound to involve themselves in assumptions as to the ultimate nature of things (which is metaphysics)
and the soundness of these assumptions, as distinguished scientists
soon began to recognize,[6] is not guaranteed by the fact that the
makers of these assumptions are not fully aware of what they are
doing. In the long run the only safe way to avoid absurd metaphysical assumptions is to pay some attention to such inquiries.
Metaphysics is a bogeyman only to infantile minds. It is, after all,
as James said, but an obstinate effort to think clearly. If mutual
interdependence, rather than absolute sovereignty or independence,
be the rule in the republic of the sciences, there is no reason to
believe that the question of nominalism can be absolutely excluded
from legal science. In any case if it is raised, even by lawyers, it
must be dealt with on its merits.

Now it is not in fact true, as Professor Yntema asserts, that Professor Adler and myself are the ones who are trying to introduce
the serpent of metaphysics into the Eden of jurisprudence. The
question of nominalism has been widely raised by those jurists who,
in the name of "realism," deny reality to rules, principles, and ideals.
The question of how much weight a judge ought to give to the
immediate facts of the case before him, and how much to the varied
situations in which parties not before him will rely upon his deci-

sion, is not, to be sure, a metaphysical question. But when Mr. Frank, for instance, takes the position that "the business of the judge is to decide particular cases," [7] and supports this position not by an empirical analysis of the relative importance of litigated cases in the whole field of legally controlled conduct, but by the *a priori* principle that "rules are merely words," [8] he is basing an empirical judgment upon a metaphysical dogma. Philosophical analysis of that dogma may compel a more critical attitude towards the practical judgment that is inferred from it. So, too, Professor Bingham's conclusions as to the amount of uniformity in judicial decisions may be true or false regardless of his metaphysical assumptions. But if he defends his view with the argument that rules exist only in the mind,[9] rather than on the basis of a statistical survey of actual decisions, one can only accept his conclusions as a matter of juristic faith or else examine the metaphysical assumptions from which he derives them. In attempting such an examination in my article on "Justice Holmes and the Nature of Law," I suggested that the question of the reality of legal rules might be considered "independently of the metaphysical quagmire on which Bingham chooses to rest it." [10] Professor Yntema, however, has chosen to argue the question in terms of metaphysics, and since this argument throws some light on the origins of the contempt that current legal thought exhibits towards rules and principles, it deserves to be answered on its own level.

As nearly as I can understand his argument, Professor Yntema contends (1) that Bingham is not a nominalist; (2) that nominalism is defensible; and (3) that the subject ought not to be discussed.

(1) Any one who believes, as Professor Bingham does, that rules, laws, or universal relations exist not in external nature but "in the mind only," is by all the canons of historical usage a nominalist.[11] To prove that I have "falsified" Bingham's point of view, Professor Yntema cites the latter's assertion that generalizations "are only mental implements manufactured by the mind." But this is the very essence of nominalism. It is true that this has also often been called

conceptualism—but the latter is only another name for nominalism, since it involves the same denial of the objectivity of universals or abstract relations.[12] The logical basis of nominalism is the denial that different things can be identical in some respect or phase, and Professor Bingham follows this so far as to deny that two different speakers can have the same idea. If he were consistent (which no nominalist is) he would have to deny that any one individual can have the same idea at different times, or that any individual can in any sense be one and the same despite change. But this would render all consistent or intelligible discourse impossible.

Apparently Professor Yntema argues that since mind exists, one who locates universals in the mind does not really deny the existence of universals. This is strictly true. Clearly one who admits the existence of mind is, to that extent, not a nominalist. For mind, as distinguished from any particular mind, is itself a universal, an abstraction. But surely the same objections can be brought against the existence of the abstraction "mind" as can be brought against the existence of any other universal. I see no philosophical merit in the position that mind is the only universal. This does, however, seem to me to be a possible position, and if Professors Bingham and Yntema choose to accept it, they may avoid nominalism at the price of accepting ontological idealism. I cannot think, however, that they mean to assert that mind is the only universal. What they really mean to assert, I think, is that universals exist only when they are apprehended by a particular mind at a particular time. And the difficulty in which this position lands them is that if only particular minds exist with no universal characteristics in common, it becomes meaningless to say that universals do have even a mental existence. The universals "triangle," "contract," and "table" cannot be said to exist as universals if every mind that apprehends them apprehends something different from what is apprehended by other minds. Neither Professor Bingham, therefore, nor Professor Yntema avoids nominalism when he asserts that universals exist in the minds that apprehend them. They are in fact confusing mental images, which are always particular (if they exist), and true universals, which are objective relations. This distinction has become a commonplace in philosophy since Berkeley.[13]

That Mr. Frank does not avoid nominalism by ascribing a *verbal* existence to rules is too obvious to call for argument. No nominalist has ever denied that rules exist *as words*. The question is whether they exist in any other sense. Mr. Frank says that they do not.[14] Of course he is not a consistent nominalist, and is almost as vivid in his denunciation of nominalism as he is in his denunciation of my critique of nominalism.[15] But this lapse from nominalism on the part of Mr. Frank is verbal and temporary. He returns forthwith to the position that law must be viewed as a formless mass of isolated decisions, from which he infers, quite logically, that legal rights and duties are unknowable.[16] Far from regarding this as a *reductio ad absurdum* of his nominalistic premise, he insists that if Professors Adler and Cohen would only become practising lawyers they would agree with this curious conclusion. There are, however, many practising lawyers other than Mr. Frank who do not allow the specialized experience of trial practice to blind them to the large degree of certainty as to the lawfulness or unlawfulness of conduct that attends men's everyday lives outside of courts and law-offices.

(2) The objections against nominalism raised in my article on "Justice Holmes and the Nature of Law"[17] do not seem to me to be logically met by any of Professor Yntema's miscellaneous remarks. I do not, for instance, see how his distrust of metaphysics in general because of the absence of a consensus can justify a dogmatic position in it as to the relation of the mind, ideas, and the external world.

Professors Bingham and Yntema are in an old and hopeless difficulty when they assume as they do that rules are in the mind only and yet that they are in some way the rules of things or events in a world external to that mind. Ideas that are in the mind only cannot, *ex hypothesi*, extend beyond the mind into an external world and there grasp the true nature of things. And if rules, principles, or laws do truly express the nature of things, then these things are truly, objectively, or in fact so related. In other words, abstract rules of relation are to be found in the very objective world in which are located the things related.

Attempts to avoid this logical realism and to adopt a sharp metaphysical dualism between the mind and the objective world (so that rules are in the first, and the things ruled in the latter) have historically failed. Some have tried to solve the difficulty by assuming a preëstablished harmony (as did the Leibnizians) and some assumed (as did the Occasionalists) that God creates objects every time we think of them. Professors Bingham and Yntema will either have to adopt some such transcendental explanation or else give up their metaphysical dogma that rules are exclusively in a mind to which nature is external.

(3) As nominalism has been introduced into the discussion of legal science to defend the view that law consists exclusively of the distinct and separate decisions of individual cases; and as the latter view is highly questionable, it is of some importance to remove an untenable support to a dubious position. Moreover, while I cannot subscribe to the atomistic conception of the law as consisting exclusively of individual decisions, and while I regard it even as in some forms dangerous to the progress of legal science, it seems to rest on a sound motive, and its partial truth can be made clearer if it is divested of its nominalistic setting. Professor Bingham has expressed with commendable boldness the general dissatisfaction of all logical realists with the traditional view of the law as an ethereal or ghostly set of rules or principles that judges may apprehend and apply to specific cases but may never change or modify.

Whatever is true about the law, it is certainly rooted in human experience and it is moulded by actual judicial decisions.

But truth is not generally attained by jumping from one extreme to another. If rules without actual embodiment cannot constitute a real system of law, neither can an indefinite number of inherently distinct decisions that are connected only in some external mind. The connection between different cases that makes the study of some throw light on others—and there would be no legal science without such connection—must be in the nature of the facts studied and not arbitrarily manufactured by the mind that apprehends them.

This is not to deny that the influence which a decision exerts upon society and upon later courts is a product of human beliefs and attitudes.[18] The relations between cases are infinite, and our human perspectives choose some as important and disregard others. Thus cases have a different significance in different ages, in different places, and in different classes of society. A recognition of this fact, however, does not require the conclusion that a decision is merely the sum of people's actual opinions as to what happened in a particular court on a particular day. These actual opinions do not exhaust the possible interpretations of the legal event, and they are, moreover, opinions about something that happened, and not inventions of history. In so far as Bingham seeks to attack the absolutism that imposes a single pattern upon every event and ignores alternative patterns as "incorrect," he is attacking a point of view with which I have no intellectual sympathy, and I can only wish that he exhibited a more discriminating marksmanship in the attack.

Cases can be subsumed under different rules, just as points can appear in different curves. Rules apply to diverse cases, just as lines include diverse points. To paraphrase a famous remark of Kant, rules without cases are empty and cases without rules are blind. A case is significant if it is really connected with others according to some relevant rule. It is therefore not enough to know how Judge X decided a given case. If it involves a rule of evidence, a rule of conflict of laws, or the like, the rule is an essential part of the decision, without which the decision would not be of any scientific significance.

In this respect, again, the analogy of physical science is suggestive. In revolt against the romantic view of nature as governed by occult forces, nineteenth century physics developed the view that analyzed everything into independent atoms. Come what might, each atom was independent of every other and remained the same, in the language of Maxwell, as when it emerged fresh from the hand of the Creator. This view proved unsatisfactory. It could not deal with action at a distance and the attempt to introduce continuity by means of an ether only complicated matters. Modern physics has banished occult forces and independent atoms or particles, and has replaced them by "fields" in which particles and their influence are inseparable. In the same way legal science, it seems to me, should operate not with occult principles or independent atomic decisions, but with fields or contexts in which different elements can be distinguished and related. And this is largely a task of logic.

It may be contended, and I imagine that some of the younger Viennese philosophers like Carnap would contend, that the issue as to nominalism is a verbal one—that if we critically examine the issue in the light of the different definitions of the terms "mind," "external world," and "existence," both realists and nominalists will, if they are consistent, be found to assert that rules exist as rules and do not have the kind of existence that only particulars have.[19] I am perfectly willing to grant this as a theoretic possibility. But the usual implicit assumption, that verbal differences or differences of definition are of no importance, must be rejected as superficial and as belied by the facts of history.

Nominalism has, in fact, always been associated with individualism in the practical or social sciences as well as with atomism in logic and theoretic physics.[20] Professor Yntema takes it for granted that nominalism tends to make us emphasize the need of empirically verifying generalizations or assumed laws. That is, I think, true to a limited extent. But it is also true that the process of verification often fails because, having exhausted our critical scepticism on general ideas, we uncritically assume as facts that which sound logic shows to be only the result of old metaphysical assumptions. Facts do not always lie around loose, ready to be picked up at will; nor are they given us as data. True facts are rather what we find as a result of scientific inquiry, in which general principles are used to correct faulty observation as well as inadequate reasoning. Ideophobia thus often serves as an excuse for romantic impatience with or distrust of critical reason, rather than as an aid in making us submit to the painful rules of scientific method in the search for objective truth. In any case we need to be on our guard lest the nominalistic tendency impoverish legal science by unduly cutting it off from helpful coöperation with the not altogether unrelated sciences of logic and ethics.

II. LOGIC AND LEGAL SCIENCE

The effort to formulate the law as a rational system of rules has encountered distrust on the part of some scholars who have a genuine interest in the scientific study of legal problems, but who have been misled by misconception as to the nature of logic. Logic, it is widely asserted, is dangerous. Now we may admit that logic is dangerous, just as a sharp knife is dangerous. It can be used in bad as well as in good causes, depending on our final ends. But in any case the process of drawing out the logical consequences of a premise reveals its meaning and thus makes our choices more intelligent.

There are those who go further and, in the manner of romantic philosophers of the type of Rousseau or Fourier, regard logic and preoccupation with intellectual formulation as a restraint and interference with our more reliable natural sentiments, God-given instincts, or intuitions. I cannot here argue this issue. We may all grant that a judge unlearned in the law and distrustful of fine-spun arguments may sometimes, on the basis of a "hunch," decide a case justly where more scholarly judges might falter, just as a country doctor or even a quack may sometimes help a patient when more scientifically trained physicians fail. The margin of error in human affairs is, even under the most favourable conditions, very large. But success in a lottery is no argument for lotteries; and the fact that some judges muddle through on bare "hunches" is no argument against training in legal science.

There is a third attitude, which views logic as dangerous because it is entirely useless and only distracts our attention from the real factors in a legal situation. This attitude most often expresses itself in the contempt for the Aristotelian syllogism on the ground that men seldom, if ever, actually think that way. This, however, involves an unpardonable confusion between psychology and logic, between the question of how men do in fact think (when they do), and the altogether different question of the adequacy of the evidence for any asserted proposition.[21] Thus the question as to what actually goes on in a judge's mind which determines him to issue an injunction in a given case, is a question of psychology. In the distant future, perhaps, we may settle such questions on the basis of demonstrable knowledge. At present we resort to shrewd but disputable guess-work. Logic is concerned with the simpler, less exciting, but more definitely determinable issue concerning the adequacy of proof. Thus in the case mentioned before, viz., the issuance of an injunction, the principle of the syllogism means that the granting of the request will be completely justified legally if two propositions are established as premises: (1) The factual premise, that the conduct of the given defendant is of a certain character, and (2) the jural premise that conduct of this character is of the class against which a judge is legally authorized to issue an injunction. That the two premises completely prove the conclusion no rational being can well dispute.

Those who distrust formal logic are not as absurd as they pretend to be. They are expressing in a confused way a distrust not of logic but of what I have called the jural premise.

Back of the hunt for jural premises in every decision is the general juristic postulate of lawfulness, that the judge should decide every case according to the law and not according to his own arbitrary will. It involves the juristic assumption that for every case which can possibly come before a court, the law has a completely determining or governing principle. If you wish, you may call this the dogma of the self-sufficiency, the complete adequacy, or the closed character of the law as a system of principles.

From the point of view of scientific procedure, the postulate that for every case there is a legal principle may be viewed as similar to the postulate that for every physical event there is a cause. We do not, of course, know the actual causes of all physical events. The principle of causality cannot, therefore, be said to have been logically proved by experience. But it has justified itself precisely because it makes men look for causes and this search, when well organized in what we call scientific method, has proved the most fruitful organon for the extension of reliable knowledge. Can the same be said for the juristic postulate? Has the search for a legal reason for every decision been a fruitful instrument for understanding and perfecting the law?

Two objections are currently urged against this juristic postulate. The first is that the reasons judges give are seldom the real grounds of their decisions; and the second objection is that new cases cannot be decided by the old established principles.

That the real ground, or psychologic motive, of a judge's decision is apt to be more subtle and complicated than the premise which he finds in the law, no one need dispute. For our motives are generally the resultants of a number of factors, few of which come up to the level of clear consciousness. But the psychologic question is irrelevant to the logical one as to whether the legal principle given by the judge, or some other principle not so given, is adequate to prove the legality of the decision. Moreover we may grant that in looking for reasons, judges frequently find bad ones, and announce them with undue certainty. Good causes are apt to generate bad reasons. For confidence in the goodness of our cause makes us careless in accepting arguments that seem to support it. But this is a matter that can be corrected only by sound logic.

The second objection to the postulate that for every legal decision there must be a given ground strikes a deeper note. Life is developing new and unexpected situations. New cases, cases of novel impression, are bound to appear. Indeed, it may be urged that as no case is exactly like any other, there must be more or less novelty in every case that can draw the serious attention of a learned court or can cause differences of opinion among experienced lawyers and judges. Leaving supernatural claims aside, the legal system, as a human product, cannot possibly be endowed with omniscience or the power of foreseeing all contingencies. For courts, then, to assume that for every case there is a preëxisting (substantive) rule, is a false and vain pretension that can only work intellectual havoc, because it leads to the stretching of old terms so that they become ambiguous or meaningless. While formal logic can show the unsatisfactory character of the resulting arguments, we need something more. We need to recognize the fact that a judge's decision is, and should be, based not on existing rules, which are frequently inadequate, but rather on a sensitive perception of the actual factors in the case and a mind inventive in finding just solutions that will meet the diverse needs of life. Decisions embodying such solutions bring new rules into the law and thus make it possible for the law to grow and to meet changing conditions adequately.

In so far as the foregoing argument emphasizes that no set of existing rules can be adequate for all time, and that the judge and the jurist must be inventive, it seems to me not only sound, but of vital importance. But to draw anti-logical conclusions from it seems to me to involve regrettable confusion. There is no justification for restricting the scope of logic to deduction from rules already established or recognized.[22] Surely logic is applicable to any proposed rule, to the contrary of those prevailing as well as an infinitude of others that might have prevailed in the past or which may prevail in the future. The wide-spread misconception on this point is not due only to the conservative bias that identifies the logical or reasonable with the familiar and which prevents us from seeing any consistency in that which is new and untried. The misconception is reënforced by the positivistic prejudice which supposes that true science is only of that which actually exists rather than of the whole field of possibility. But any attention to the process of experimental verification shows the necessity of considering the logical consequences of rival hypotheses, only one of which can represent the existing state of affairs. This is likewise the condition of any significant social experimentation. We must use logic to draw the consequences not only of existing institutions but also of possible alternatives that have not yet been tried.

If we get rid of the bias in favour of the positivistic or narrow conception of logic and existence, we may discriminate between the sense in which the attack upon the jural postulate is valid and the sense in which this attack is invalid. The attack upon the postulate that a legal ground exists for every legal decision is well made only if that postulate is taken to assert the *historical* existence of such ground. The attack is not well founded, however, if that postulate is properly understood as ascribing only logical existence, i.e., validity or significance, to the legal ground of a decision. We may recognize that while no body of rules ever actually enunciated will do justice to the multifarious peculiarities of new cases, each of these new cases *can* be subsumed under general rules. The jural postulate asserts, not that the rule of every case is known and understood before the case arises (which leads to what I have called the phonograph theory of the judicial function),[23] but simply that the decision of every case is logically subsumed under general legal rules, which may not be thought of until after the decision, and which may, in fact, never be thought of at all. A postulate that asserts no more than this cannot be refuted. As a methodologic principle it may serve the same function that the postulate of causality serves in the natural sciences. As the latter principle cautions us against accepting any fact as independent of all other facts, i.e., as miraculous, so the former principle cautions us against accepting any decision as independent of all other decisions. If a decision strikes us as just, we will explore the lines of similarity to find other situations in which a corresponding decision will be justified. If a decision strikes us as unjust we will explore the same lines of similarity to learn the extent to which the decision is token of a wider injustice. In either case, our knowledge of the law and of the decision in question is enriched.

The existence of similarity between new and old social situations points to a certain continuity of social life in which the law must share. The introduction of new rules of law, no matter how wide in extent and revolutionary in character, cannot exclude all continuity of pattern in the legal system. No matter how wide-spread our dissatisfaction with existing institutions and no matter how radical the desired transformation of our legal system, we do not in fact and cannot in theory wipe out *all* our past desires and habits. Changes can be effected only by existing machinery. Legal change, like all other change, involves, then, some persistent elements. If I make an artistically desirable alteration in a work of art, e.g., a drama, the new element introduced must fit in better with the remaining or unaltered parts than that which has been cut out. Similarly, if any new scientific principle is proposed to take the place of an old one, e.g., Einstein's principle of relativity to replace the classical one, the new principle can be justified only if it fits in better with the general body of established laws and accepted facts. It is not sufficient that the new principle of relativity predicts new observable phenomena. It must also explain all the more numerous phenomena explained by the classical mechanics. And even the new facts or phenomena, such as the bending of light rays near the sun or the shift in certain spectra, have their meaning only on the basis of previously established laws of optics, astronomy, etc. For the meaning of scientific facts always depends on the interpreting principles or assumptions. Now if we can thus view science as a continuously self-corrective system, we may, in a limited way, apply the same conception to the legal system.

There can be no objection to the view that the law is a closed system if this is taken in a purely formal sense, namely, that all legal changes are legal only if authorized by the general principle of legality, i.e., by the jural system. This is indeed a purely formal or tautologous statement. But it is none the less useful as a principle of analysis. Thus, the American constitutional system is a closed one so long as all amendments of it are in the manner authorized by it. But there is nothing in logic to prevent a constitutional convention or some other agency from abrogating it, just as the Constitutional Convention of 1787 abrogated the Articles of Confederation in a manner not authorized by the latter. Revolutions, however, cannot be matters of daily occurrence in anything like an orderly legal system. And the social need for continuity must find expression in the legal system as in other human affairs. Even the most ardent revolutionist generally admits that his proposed revolution is not an end in itself but a means for the establishment of a new or better order. But if a new order is to be established the new principle must be consistently carried out and this will generally involve taking into account old as well as new legal rules—assuming that no human revolution can completely wipe out all our past habits.

If the foregoing argument is sound, the effort to formulate the law as a system of rules must be an integral part of a comprehensive legal science, as well as a condition of the legal order itself.

III. ETHICS AND LEGAL SCIENCE

Professor Yntema's critique of my views on the nature of law is primarily directed against the conception of a normative legal science. In defending the validity of the normative or ethical approach to legal problems, I am not anxious to appropriate the honorific connotations of the word "science" for this mode of approach. Every one today can, and often does, call his occupation scientific; and thus we hear of scientific management, of the science of Egyptian archæology, numismatics, heraldry, and the like. There can be no legitimate objection to this use of the word "science" in its original sense as a synonym of true knowledge. But whether any investigation in such a field as law is scientific in the sense that it makes significant and reliable additions to our knowledge, can be judged better by its achievement than by its program. The great

Poincaré once remarked that while in the physical sciences men are concerned about their results, in the social sciences they are always disputing about their methods. This is, I think, true but perhaps unavoidable. When men are distracted in a maze such as that which social life offers us, what is more natural than that they should disagree as to where to turn?

To this genuinely pathetic phase of our intellectual life there is added the sad illusion current at least since the days of Raymond Lull or Francis Bacon, and perhaps since Aristotle, viz., that there is a science, variously called Logic, Scientific Method, or Universal Organon, that can teach us the art of discovery by telling us the right road to the unknown. True logic does not make that illusory promise. Logical reflection, to be sure, aids us to learn from experience by analyzing the causes of past failure, and it is even more positively helpful in exploring the fields of possibility and opening the roads to research by undermining the powerful walls of "Impossible!" which ignorance sets up against unfamiliar ideas. But while great discoveries in science depend upon previous study and reflection, inexplicable genius and unpredictable good fortune enter to an incalculable extent.

In urging, therefore, the need of studying what the law should be I am merely calling attention to the fundamental craving for justice that men have felt throughout the ages and suggesting that concentrated effort and study along certain lines may be helpful to some extent. It has never entered my mind to oppose any other type of investigation in the legal field. But when any one in the name of Legal Science sets up his own type of investigation as the *only* legitimate one, I must humbly but firmly protest. Some of the "empirical" or "realistic" investigations in the field of law may succeed in bringing fruitful results. I ardently hope that they will. But a hopeful program does not justify arrogance or intolerance towards those who are not convinced of its perfect sufficiency. My own program may be a puny one but it has a right to live.

Professor Yntema prejudices the cause of normative legal science by two devices that are readily disposed of: (1) By capitalizing the word "ought" Professor Yntema gives colour to the charge that it involves some kind of transcendentalism or perhaps even supernaturalism. That is entirely baseless. The category of "ought" or "should," of logical or ethical validity, is no more transcendental than Professor Yntema's contention that legal science *should* follow certain directions rather than others. Nor does he really help his case by quoting my statement that not life but the good life should be the object of our human endeavour.[24] That dictum is obviously a defence of the virtue of discrimination and a recognition of the sad fact that life can become unbearable so that a free man, unafraid of superstitious taboos, will leave it as one leaves a smoky or ill-smelling chamber. What possible transcendentalism is there in that? Professor Yntema is particularly unfortunate in selecting as a representative of transcendentalism one whose chief written effort is a book in defence of naturalism and who has repeatedly announced that he is not afraid of being called a materialist.[25]

(2) Professor Yntema further prejudices the cause of normative legal science by asserting that it has behind it the "tremendous inertia of the literary and speculative tradition." [26] This claim rests on a history of "the tradition of the law" that is mythical, at least as far as England and America are concerned. Anglo-American legal thinking has been from the beginning, and up to very recently, predominantly practical, professional, and independent of the universities. Owing to the fact that the medieval universities taught only the (then) universal canon and civil law and not anything local like English law, legal education and legal thought were fashioned by the strictly professional groups organized in the Inns of Court. And the main current of American legal thinking and writing has been, up to our own day, even more independent of the cultural influences of literature and philosophy. We must remember that the requirement of a law school education as a prerequisite for admission to the bar is an almost contemporary achievement. We still have with us those who became lawyers by the ap-

prentice method, i.e., by clerking in some practitioner's office. And even our law schools have in their organization and curricula been dominated not by literary and speculative, but by the narrowly practical, tradition from the time that they were in effect trade schools. Those that were connected with universities were so only nominally or administratively, not culturally. It is not, then, accurate to say, as Professor Yntema does, that in the United States "the university tradition in law was for a time partially interrupted." [27] It is only in our own day that it is beginning. Our universities are just beginning to annex the law schools and to make law teaching an independent profession, instead of a supplement to a busy lawyer's occupation.

Practical lawyers, we know, do not hesitate to condemn particular decisions or statutes as "bad" law. But the general fashion among the orthodox has surely been to profess exclusive preoccupation with the law that *is* and to boast of freedom from any speculative interest in the law that ought to be. This general attitude of the bar influences even its most enlightened members. Thus Pollock relegates all considerations of what the law ought to be to the field of legislation or politics, with which lawyers are not concerned.[28] Even Dean Pound, always intensely interested in the question as to how satisfactorily the law works in actual life, sometimes accepts Pollock's distinction.[29]

I do not wish to maintain that normative jurisprudence is opposed only by a narrowly practical tradition. Other factors enter. In Europe the hostility to the consideration of what the law should be dates back to the romantic reaction against the revolutionary and rationalistic legal theories of the eighteenth century, a reaction which in the form of historicism set up the dogma that it is vain to propose to change the law which results from the necessary evolution of the folk-spirit. Spencerian evolutionism and deterministic positivism have on their own grounds repeated this dogma of the futility of human effort to remake the law nearer to our heart's desire.

In thus repelling the attempt to discredit normative legal science by assigning it an improper historical ancestry, my aim is only to clear the ground for a discussion of the case on its own merits. I do not believe that the truth of a proposition can be adequately established by showing the bad reasons or inadequate motives of the opposition. Moreover in this case I have always sympathized with one of the motives of the opposition to normative social science. As I have elsewhere remarked, "This effort to look upon human actions with the same ethical impartiality with which we view geometric figures is admirable." [30] The positivist's determination to study the facts as they truly exist, and his opposition to the introduction of value judgments into the social sciences, are sound in so far as they are based on the perception of the fact that science requires the investigator to keep his own bias out of the subject matter he studies. The scientist must stand outside of his material and be ethically neutral even in the study of ethics. When the investigator begins to take sides his reasoning generally becomes as corrupt as that of any other partisan or sectarian.

I share, for instance, Professor Underhill Moore's low opinion of attempts to prescribe for the body politic without an adequate knowledge of the relevant social facts.[31] But surely this does not mean that we must close our eyes to the social policy that more or less controls these facts, or refrain from asking how well or ill it works. Shall we study the facts of marriage and divorce, of competition and tariffs, or of war between nations, without asking whether these things are good or bad for the people or communities involved, for their descendants, and for humanity at large?

My position, as indicated in "Justice Holmes and the Nature of Law," was surely not of opposition to the scientific study of the social facts that the law must take into account (though whether any study is actually worthy of being called scientific can be answered only after critically examining it when it is finished). But while such factual study is necessary, it is not sufficient for a complete legal science.

A seemingly serious criticism against my argument in favour of the normative point of view is Professor Yntema's long list of various senses in which I use the word "normative." I do not think, however, that there is any valid objection to using the same word with different shades of meaning. Indeed, any one who opens a large dictionary can see how unavoidable this is so long as we use common words. The important thing is to avoid ambiguity by making the context show an unequivocal meaning, and Professor Yntema has not pointed out any instances of equivocation in the passages to which he alludes.[32] Nor do I think that he can. For in all these cases I was dealing with variants of only one meaning, namely, considerations of what is valid or obligatory under certain assumptions.

Let us, however, proceed to our main problem. Professor Yntema attacks the view that law itself is normative as well as the view that there can be a normative science of law. Let us consider these propositions in order.

Legal science is normative, in the first place, in the sense that it deals with norms. Legal rules, whether embodied in statutes, accepted legal doctrines, or judicial decisions, are normative, in that they contain imperatives or orders regulating what men should do. This is so rudimentary and obvious that it seems impossible that any one should dispute it.

We may arbitrarily define the word "law" in any sense we please, but the law studied in law schools, and that about which men consult lawyers, is the law laid down by courts in the form of orders or commands. These commands are usually addressed in the first instance to certain officials, to the clerk of the court, to the sheriff, etc., and direct what the latter should do. Because the resulting or anticipated actions of the clerk and sheriff affect one or both parties in the suit and others who may be in a similar position, these court orders are in fact also imperatives to an indefinitely large number of people.

I can see no merit in Professor Yntema's argument that the judgment of a court is "a judgment and not essentially a command." [33]

If the court's judgment sets in motion the sheriff who will attach my goods, then how in the name of the empirical science of law can any one claim that it is not a command? One may as well argue that if a man with a gun to enforce his "judgment" declares, in my hearing, that I shall be filled with lead if I do not give him my watch, I have not received any order or command, but have only heard a judgment or prediction.[34]

The fact that many legal propositions can be stated in the declarative rather than in the imperative mood is beside the point. For these propositions become law only when they are necessary parts of the legal order that is recognized as imperative. A judge's definition of contract is part of the law if it determines one rather than another decision in specific cases. On the other hand, any assertion on his part of a proposition in legal history or human psychology that is not a necessary element or condition of a legal order, is merely the judge's opinion. Surely many of the private opinions of judges are not the law of the land. But the very question as to who is properly a judge and when his order ought to be regarded as an official one depends for its answer on what legal or constitutional principle we assume as the one that ought to govern the situation. When a Chicago judge, for instance, orders one charged with burglary to leave the state, to go to church regularly, or to make a reasonable contribution to some charitable or political organization, is his command a legal order? The answer depends upon our assumed principles prescribing the scope of the judicial office.

From a logical point of view, then, there can be no question that the law can be viewed as setting up rules that serve as norms, in the sense that they command obedience and control conduct. What sort of science of such norms is possible? There are at least three approaches to such a science, which we may characterize as legal history, legal sociology, and normative jurisprudence.

One who wishes to study law can begin by describing what was actually decided at any given time in a determinate place. Such description constitutes legal history.

We can, however, go further and describe not the facts that are made unique by their position in time and place but rather uniformities or abstract patterns that repeat themselves, e.g., that masses of men always engage in certain activities which produce food, that women behave in certain ways to their young children, or that under certain conditions population will increase. Such abstract uniformities or "laws of the social nature of man" form the subject matter of sociology.

It seems clear that many of those who invoke Justice Holmes's dictum that the law is the prediction of what the courts will decide, conceive of legal science in some such manner. For any prediction that is not an arbitrary guess must be based on the hypothesis of some recurrent pattern or relatively constant configuration of repeatable elements that make one case like another. Otherwise we should get no help from studying the previous decisions of any judge or court. But legal decisions are not merely physical acts of the judge in question. They are related to each other in accordance with the generally prevailing rules of interpretation, precedents, procedure, and the like. Descriptive legal science, or legal sociology, must take account of such rules.

One may, however, take a still different point of view, to wit, the teleologic one, which is related to that of descriptive sociology as is hygiene to physiology. One may ask not only how the organic bodily processes work, but also how some of them, such as the hardening of the arteries or the oxygenation of the blood, can be decreased or increased. Similarly, one may ask not merely what men actually do under certain conditions, but also what they should do to attain certain ends that they either profess to accept or would accept if they saw the whole situation clearly. Now, in a completely determinate or mathematical system, where there is an exact identity between what is and what should or must be, there is little substantial difference between the theoretic or mechanistic and the teleologic points of view. There is no difference of content between the proposition, "If $2ab$ is added to $a^2 + b^2$ the result will be a perfect square," and the proposition, "In order to obtain a perfect square we ought to add $2ab$ to $a^2 + b^2$." If our knowledge of nature, then, revealed a completely determinate system, there would be no difference between normative and descriptive science. But while certain regions of our most advanced sciences, such as mathematical physics, approximate to such an ideal of knowledge, social phenomena are certainly not known in their complete determination. In any case there is an actual difference between asking what men generally do in fact and asking what they ought to do—between asking what the courts have actually decided or predicting what they will decide, and asking what they ought to have decided or should decide in the future.

In all the arts where human purposes enter it is always relevant to ask whether or to what extent these purposes have been attained. All such investigations may be said to be normative in that the investigator himself employs for the purpose of the investigation an ideal standard or norm according to which he measures the efficiency, the beauty, or any other quality under investigation.

Such norms may be called technical or conditional, since they are limited to particular fields. Thus the standard of economic efficiency applies to enterprises with a pecuniary aspect, but not necessarily to friendship or the enjoyment of nature. The standards or norms of literary craftsmanship do not apply to engineering. Certain standards, however, such as happiness and human dignity, seem to enter into all phases of human life, and ethics employs these most pervasive elements to organize all technical norms of human interest into a rational system. Such organization may be said to be an evaluation of these individual technical norms, since it reveals their significance in a wider human perspective.

Just as the economist may refuse to go into the general field of ethics or human welfare, and limit himself to judging human transactions by the standard of economic efficiency or productivity, so may the jurist confine his inquiry to issues that can be dealt with by reference to such standards as legality, constitutionality, etc. But if the economist or the jurist wishes to extend his vision to include the relation of his technical standards to human life and welfare he is necessarily involved in ethics.

Those who try to rule out from science all questions as to what ought to be are never consistent. They bring in their own ideal of what ought to be in a disguised or unavowed form. Duguit, for instance, while opposing all considerations of what ought to be, blandly assumes that all that is conducive to social solidarity is good and ought to prevail. Many others refuse to consider what the law ought to be because of the assumption that what exists ought to prevail. But that is clearly a debatable proposition of normative jurisprudence.

We need not, however, rest our case entirely on this *argumentum ad hominem*. The opponents of normative jurisprudence may admit that legal rules can be criticized from the point of view of the desirability of their social results, and yet they may contend that such critical normative considerations are the subject of art, or of technique, and not of science. But this distinction between art and science is superficial and does not go to the root of the matter. If normative jurisprudence is an art, it is certainly not an art that deals directly with the organization of physical things. Rather does it seek to organize judgments into a rational or harmonious system. And in this sense all science may be viewed as a rational art. Physics may thus be regarded as the art of transforming all our judgments of natural existence into a coherent system that will not be in conflict with any possible physical observation. Similarly, ethics or the general theory of value is an attempt to organize all our judgments of approval or preference into a coherent system, so that every one of them will be determinate, rather than purely arbitrary, and in the long run best express our emotional and volitional nature. From this point of view ethics includes not only judgments as to the traditional issues of individual morals but also all questions as to the ultimate values of all human activities in the arts and in institutional life.

In thus viewing normative jurisprudence as depending on, or even as a part of, ethics, we are in no way confusing legal science and ethics. On the contrary, to insist that laws may be ethically bad is to insist that that which is contrary to good ethics may still be law. The law that Justice Holmes's "bad man" uses to work ethical iniquity may undoubtedly be the law of the land. If that were not the case, the whole of human striving for the abolition of unjust laws would be meaningless.

The seeming paradox in urging that normative jurisprudence thus ultimately depends on ethics and yet is relatively distinguishable from it, ought not to puzzle us if we use the federal rather than the imperialistic analogy as to the relation of the various sciences, that is, if we recognize the element of pluralism and relative independence of different domains within the unity of knowledge. A science like general physics formulates laws applicable to all branches only because these laws have been observed to be in fact true in all these branches. But when we advance in generality, differences are not wiped out. In any case various uniformities are observed to prevail in distinct realms, and in respect to laws peculiar to a given field that field is relatively independent.

The way in which jurisprudence can be said to be both dependent on and yet relatively independent of ethics may be illustrated by a reference to the nature of justice.

Law is frequently spoken of as the administration of justice and this provokes "hard-boiled" jurists or judges to say that they are concerned with expounding the law that is and have no speculative opinions as to what it ought to be.[35] There is a great deal of value in this attitude. It is a good thing for the community that a judge should not put his arbitrary opinion against the expressed will of the community, expressed perhaps in a statute that it took years of hard fighting to enact. The hard-boiled judge is therefore defending the virtue of fidelity to the legal system that he is sworn to administer.

The judge who favours one party because of a bribe, or because of any other consideration that does not grow out of the merits of the case before the court, is said to pervert justice. Legal justice, then, means the faithful administration of the law as it is. To ensure this the judge should study the case and the general historic purposes of the existing law so that his decision may be in harmony with the general demand of the community rather than the expression of his own arbitrary will or personal bias. In this respect it seems that jurisprudence is independent of ethics. The assumption that it is better to have courts decide according to some law rather than according to the whim or caprice of the judge may be discussed by the ethical philosopher. The legalist may well say, "This is my fundamental assumption and the ethical philosopher may do with it what he likes."

And yet the issue cannot be settled so simply. For if the existing rules of law do not foresee all possible contingencies, and if the judge must decide all cases, then he must legislate or make new law, and then the question of material justice obviously enters. The conscientious judge must ask which of the various possible decisions that he can see best suits the interests of the community which he serves. Now it may be contended that cases of novel impression are relatively rare. Yet elements of discretion are present in most cases, and in asking whether an existing rule should be extended or restricted, the judge's opinion as to its justice is bound to be influential. And the more carefully he studies the question of the justice of the existing law, whether it is or is not oppressive and detrimental to the best interests of the community, the better will be the character of the decision.

In general we may say that those who oppose the normative point of view in legal science and insist on the study of empirical facts confuse the necessary with the sufficient conditions of a complete legal science. There can be no normative or critical legal science without a thorough knowledge of the actual facts of human conduct. But such a knowledge of actual conditions is not sufficient for all purposes. We must consider the question of the goal or value of legal rules, and keep on asking whether certain practices should be repressed or strengthened. The study of what is desirable may be as scientific as any branch of logic or mathematics—so far as our study is dialectical. To the extent that normative jurisprudence must make factual assumptions, it suffers from the same frailty as all other social sciences, and that is the pitiful inadequacy of our actual knowledge. But scientific method, while it cannot eliminate this result of our mortal human finitude, can train us not to attach more confidence to our factual judgments than a critical study of their probability would warrant. If we cannot be like the gods, knowing the absolute difference between good and evil, we can at least have the knowledge of our limitations; and if this does not guarantee salvation, it at least helps us to avoid the vanity that needlessly adds to the heavy load of human suffering.

"Real" and "Ideal" Forces in Civil Law [1]

JURISTS, like philosophers and artists, have always divided themselves into idealists and realists. Idealists are those who are so impressed with the ideal order, which visible things only partly embody, that they are charged with neglecting the poor brute facts. The realists are so impressed with the hard actual facts, especially the unpleasant ones, that they are charged with neglecting the possibilities of change or improvement inherent in things.

These differences seem to be primarily differences of emphasis, due to differences of temperament, but external conditions make one or the other tendency predominate for a time. Up to a few years ago idealism held almost complete sway among teachers of philosophy in American universities, and our legal thought was dominated exclusively by a naïve idealism that saw nothing in the common law but justice and the accumulated reason of mankind. It has been suggested that the Hegelian idealistic philosophy was peculiarly fitted for an academic class,[2] and this is all the more probable when we remember the strength of the theologic or genteel tradition in American academic life.[3] Thus we find beneath the idealism of both lawyers and philosophers the realistic motive of defending the established order—witness the writings of William T. Harris, Ladd, and the followers of Caird, as well as the numerous books and articles in our law reviews written by men whose lives have been spent defending the interests of property. It would be interesting to trace the similarity of motives that led to the rise of a juristic realism in the writings of publicists like Brooks Adams or Bentley, and the various forms of protesting realism among the younger American philosophers. But that would carry us beyond the point I wish to make, which is that in actual men the idealistic and realistic motives so interpenetrate that a sharp classification is apt to be superficial and misleading. Nevertheless, for purposes of understanding, such distinctions are indispensable, at least as starting points.

If, thus warned, we look for the realistic and idealistic motives in legal thought we find them in the conflicting views that law is reason or justice, and that law is force, the will of the sovereign, or the interest of the stronger or dominant class. The controversy between these two views has raged since Plato to his own satisfaction refuted the view of Thrasymachus that justice is the interest of the stronger, and it may seem hopeless to try to add anything. Nevertheless I believe progress can be made, not by the easy refutation of one side or other, but by a careful analysis of the factors in the situation on which the opposing claims are based. This is certainly not so interesting as the method of sweeping refutation, but its results, though meagre, may be more substantial.

In nearly all modern jural and political discussion that styles itself scientific, law is defined as the will of the sovereign. Now if the sovereign, whoever or whatever that may be, is not the Omnipotent Himself but some human being or group, it is clear that there are limitations upon that will. Not even in autocratic Russia did everything happen in accordance with the will of the sovereign. Not only were many laws not enforced or obeyed, but the sovereign found it impossible to express his will in the law itself. The Russian sovereign undoubtedly wanted all his subjects to be patriotic and Greek Orthodox; he would have given a great deal to get rid of his troublesome Jewish and Mohammedan subjects. But while he could restrict them, he could not make a law to get rid of them altogether—any more than he could make the Russian church Protestant or make its language French. Legally, of course, there was nothing to prevent him from doing any of these things. But that merely shows the limitation of the purely legal standpoint; for obviously in making the law, the sovereign, if he has any intelligence, will avoid enacting rules that cannot be enforced and which can only serve to show his impotence. Thus all intelligent law-making rests on the knowledge or estimate of what will be obeyed. The perception of this fact has led to the theory that all law rests on the consent, acknowledgment, or obedience of the subjects.[4] This, however, overlooks the fact that in the freest commonwealth laws are obeyed that many people bitterly and emphatically resent. It is true that when I obey a law because of fear or external compulsion, I may still be said to exercise my sovereign prerogative of choice, since I may choose not to obey and take the unpleasent consequences. Nevertheless there is a real difference here—the difference between contributing to a relief fund and contributing to a highwayman or to a hostile invader. There is thus an empirical basis for the distinction between the part of the law founded on force (or external compulsion)[5] and the part that appeals to us as inherently just or natural.

Though realists and idealists have long disputed as to the relative importance of these external and internal factors in the law, it ought to be obvious that the proportion between them varies according to time and place; and it would be vain to try to settle it *a priori*. It is a historical question to be settled by empirical, statistical information. Few thoughtful jurists would today accept the extreme realistic position of Lassalle, and of those idealistic anarchists who believe that the law rests exclusively on the police and the militia. While it is true that a small organized minority can overawe and compel obedience from a large unorganized majority, it is not a fact that the majority of people in any existent community under a civil law feel themselves in the position of a crowd of unarmed men held up by a lone bandit. The amount of awe and veneration for those in authority is too wide-spread even among the most oppressed classes.[6] Contrary to the anarchistic analysis, also, most people prefer to obey rather than take the initiative and responsibility of commanding. The police and militia cannot possibly explain why the bulk of the civil law is obeyed; because the very existence of a modern military or police force depends upon a general habit of obedience and respect for law in the community. If most men preferred to settle their disputes with axes or pistols instead of by means of an expensive legal duel, a modern police force would be utterly futile. Moreover, there is some show of truth in the contention that the state or sovereign does not order any one to obey the rules of the civil law. The state does not *directly* order any one to keep his contracts, to register his deed, to attest his will, or to refrain from slandering his neighbour. The rules of the civil law may be viewed as judicial rules for settling private disputes. They affect general conduct only because suits can be brought and the state will support the judgment of the judge by disposing of *some* of the goods (if there are any) of the one against whom judgment has been rendered. This distinction is formal and not substantial; but it calls our attention to the important fact that where private interests of individuals do not demand it there will be no enforcement of the civil law. Private interests (which include matters of honour, the desire for revenge, or satisfaction of outraged justice) thus supply the motive force. The sanctions of the civil law take this force for granted and regulate it just as river works regulate the current but presuppose gravity as the motive force.

These considerations seem obvious enough. Yet all the controversies between those who hold the imperative theory and those who hold the declarative theory of the law may be traced to an overemphasis of what we have called the regulative and motive forces.

When we come to consider the law as a regulative force and the factors that make it what it is, realistic jurists rely on political or economic power—the idealists on reason and justice. Now it ought to be clear that these factors cannot be mutually exclusive, since they move on different levels. Moreover, in the absence of a quantitive social science enabling us to measure in some definite way the relative weights of different factors, it seems as futile to discuss which is more potent, economics or ethics, as it would have been to discuss the question which is more powerful, heat or electricity, before the discovery of the correlation of energies. Nevertheless, these one-sided views, that law is determined exclusively by political, economic, logical, or ethical forces, are with us and the task of criticizing these theories cannot be dispensed with.

The political interpretation of law need not detain us long, since it is clearly in the field of legislation that political forces find their primary expression, and legislation is a subordinate factor in civil law. I do not mean to deny the important place of legislation in the development of our property law, nor the way the legislation of our day is transforming the law of industrial and commercial relations. But legislation becomes effective in the body politic only after it has been digested by the process of juristic interpretation and judicial decision. And while it would be folly to maintain that the political convictions of judges never find expression in the related branches of the law, it seems a fact that jurists and judges do not for more than a limited period represent a sufficiently homogeneous political interest to make the influence of their unconscious political bias the predominant one in the whole law.

The economic interpretation of law takes its starting-point from the perception of the fact that the great bulk of the law deals with economic interests or interests having an economic value. When this is combined with the imperative theory of law and a very simple division of society into the dominant class and what may be called the subject class, we have the views of Loria and Brooks Adams,[7] according to whom law is the expression of the economic interests of the dominant class. In the orthodox Marxian system this is attached to a system of Hegelian dialectics, in which the system of economic production acquires all the potency of the Hegelian absolute idea in generating all social institutions. The adherents of this view have been able to bring forward relatively few instances from legal history or from the actual law of today that are indisputably examples of class interests expressing themselves in the law. This argument, however, is not conclusive. Legal history is a biased wit-

ness, since most existing legal histories have been written by ideol-
ogists who, ignoring all non-legal factors, have written the history
of the law as if it were a continuous exercise in which juristic logic
was the sole determining factor. A concrete example will make this
clear. Professor Burdick has written a learned article [8] attacking the
validity of several illustrations of Brooks Adams's that the law is
determined by the interests of the dominant class. Professor Burdick's procedure consists in showing that there were plenty of precedents and logical reasons for the judges' deciding as they did.
Obviously, however, this utterly fails to disprove Mr. Adams's contention, since the existence of a good logical reason does not pre-
clude the coexistence of a real economic one. To disprove the existence of unconscious economic bias as a determining factor, Professor
Burdick would have to show that equally good reasons and precedents could not possibly have been adduced on the other side; and
that is out of the question. The law is not a closed logical system
like pure mathematics, in which every proposition is absolutely
necessitated. Was there ever a case carried up to a higher court
where the losing side did not have some reasons and precedents on
its side? Legal reasoning depends on multitudes of assumptions,
based on experience and judgments as to public policy. The fellow-
servant rule, which Professor Burdick defends, was decided by Lord
Abinger and Chief Justice Shaw expressly on the ground of public
policy. If the delegate of a butcher boys' union or a brakemen's
association were the judge, would he have had the same view of
public policy? It would be foolish to maintain this, in view of the
criticisms which the rule in question has received from the ablest
and best-trained legal minds.[9]

When lawyers speak of a decision as being necessitated by logic,
and say that the judges could not have helped making the particular decision that they did, it is because they accept all the premises on which the decision is based. But it is absurd to say that juristic
logic has no influence at all in making decisions what they are. Only
a fanatic devotion to the logical consequence of a preconceived the-

ory could induce people so to ignore human experience as to deny that men generally, and legislators and judges in particular, are ever influenced by reasons and arguments. If economic interests, as Mr. Adams tells law students, are bound to express themselves in the law as much as the earth is bound to pursue its path around the sun, why teach law at all? Obviously, the legally trained mind decides differently from one not so trained.

Indeed, the whole theory of economic determinism applied to the law illustrates the powerful influence of popular *theories* as to what science is. It is popularly supposed that there is a physical force, gravity, which does something to keep all the planets in their proper places. This conception of force, however, is an anthropomorphic survival of primitive animism. Careful modern physicists do not use "force" in any such sense. Indeed, there is a very marked agreement to give up the notion of force altogether.[10] At any rate, actual physics offers no analogy for a system dominated by a single force; and, as Aristotle pointed out, it is a sign of lack of scientific culture to try to carry over the exactness of mathematics and physics into fields where they do not apply (because of absence of exact measurements). Certainly, no one surveying the facts of our complicated social system without a preconceived theory would see in it a single dominant class. Social and economic conflicts take place along many different lines, and these lines, like those between employer and employee, native and foreign-born, Catholics and Protestants, agriculturists and manufacturers, North and South, cross and recross each other. The law is designed to be the means of regulating these conflicts. As a matter of fact, the bulk of the civil law does not deal with any special class interests at all, but rather with private arrangements in which the members of the dominant class, whatever that may be, may sometimes be more interested than others. The laws of contract, mortgages, sales, and wills, laws against fraud, seduction, assault and slander, marriage laws, divorce laws, and the like are certainly not imposed upon an unwilling population by a dominant class. Professor Pound has actually shown [11] how considerations of juristic logic and consistency have led, as in the case of the law of partnerships, to results directly contrary to the interests of the commercial class, which is supposed to be the dominant one.

Similar considerations are true with regard to ethics. It must be granted that ethical ideas as to right and wrong are somewhat plastic, that men readily convince themselves that what is to their interest is just. This is facilitated by the way in which given groups habitually identify their interests with those of the whole community. Thus, the working classes habitually speak of themselves as the people; the middle classes think of their interests as the interests of the public; while the commercial classes always refer to their interests as those of the country. Yet for all that, it is absurd to deny the fact that ethical ideals have been powerful factors in making the law. Indeed, when we survey the history of the law, it would seem that religion has moulded the greatest part of the law under which mankind lives. Religious conceptions, for instance, have had more to do with making our marriage laws than has anything else. It is a religious conception that prevents euthanasia. The changed attitude of the law as to the relation between husband and wife, which marks the nineteenth century, is part of the general movement of humanization, which shows itself also in our attitude to the criminal, the insane, and the helpless. Whether we take the pretorian law, English equity, or the influence of seventeenth and eighteenth century natural law on international law, constitutional law, and criminal law, we everywhere find ethical ideals exercising profound influence, apart from, and often contrary to, the interest of the class that the jurists represent.

All this, of course, does not impugn the great importance of economics in law, as determining both the social interests to be safeguarded and the incidence of judicial decision. But the true relation of juristic technique to economics is, I apprehend, similar to the relation of the technique of the engineer to economics. Bridges are built and their location and material determined by economic reasons, but the technique of the engineer is independent of economics. The modern tendency to belittle the importance of logic, known as anti-intellectualism, is part of the reaction against the old liberalism, which rested on a rationalistic basis. Legal liberalism, as represented by a man like Coke, viewed the law as the dictate of reason, just as the adherents of the Enlightenment tried to prove all things. But we know that all things cannot be proved, since proof rests on assumptions; and reason cannot determine the whole law because reason has to do with judgments (determining the appropriateness of means to end) and cannot determine the ultimate ends that are a matter of ultimate choice. Hobbes is, therefore, right in putting will above reason in the law. But when we have said that reason determines the means appropriate to a given end, we have by no means belittled the importance of reason; for the means at our disposal, as I have tried to show elsewhere,[12] very frequently determine the ends that we are to choose. A study of juristic logic, therefore, would be of the greatest assistance in clarifying the relative places of the imperative and the rational elements in the law. Logicians have neglected this task because the logic of imperatives has not been developed.[13] It must be noted, however, that legal imperatives are in some respects like the directions in a guide-book. "Take the car going to the north" is grammatically an imperative, and logicians have generally excluded such sentences from the category of propositions. In point of fact, however, this imperative is an expression of the judgment that the taking of such a car is necessary to reach the desired end. That is, if you want to get there, you must take the car. The subjunctive clause, being understood, is not expressed. Similarly, the law says, if you want your title or right secured, you must register your deed, give notice, etc. The law is, of course, imperative in a wider sense than a guide-book, for it not only tells men what will happen under specified conditions, but also by its orders to its servants brings those conditions into being. But the legislator also, in his enactments, makes judgments that certain situations will arise and that if certain arrangements or provisions are made, certain consequences will follow. It may be urged that the logical question whether these conclusions do or do not follow is immaterial to the enforcement of the law, that if the legislator is mistaken in his judgment, those charged with the enforcement of the law are not responsible for the results; but the situation is not so simple. We cannot altogether eliminate the legislator's judgment from the law, because those who have to enforce the law must be guided by this judgment in order to determine the actual contents of the law. The process of judicial interpretation, which is necessary for making all legislation effective, cannot be worked out by mere fiats. It must use a developed logical machinery. It must act under rules of justice (whose content is dependent upon social science). It must also invent modes of adjustment on the basis of logical, or consistently developed, distinctions. The abuse of logical distinctions frequently leads to the vicious results of *Begriffsjurisprudenz*.[14] But this does not mean that the use of logical distinctions can be dispensed with.

Without attempting to deal with the technique of ethical judgments in the development of the law, I may barely mention one objection against the fruitfulness of the principles of ethics or natural law in jurisprudence suggested by Planiol.[15] He enumerates several principles of natural law or justice, and then intimates that such principles will not carry us far in the development of the concrete law, e.g., of mortgages. Now, it is perfectly true that if you look at these principles by themselves, very little of the law of mortgages can be deduced from them. But so also if you look at the axioms of geometry in their abstract form. Few concrete geometric propositions could be deduced from them immediately. This, however, does not mean that these principles are not operative. Principles of justice are assumed in almost all branches of the law, but they are applied to the concrete material of social life, and the conclusion is based, therefore, not merely upon ethics, but also on the factual judgments and the juristic technique that operates with them.

The moral of my meagre tale is not only that the enforcement of the law, which Professor Pound rightly calls the life of the law, depends upon the maximum satisfaction of all the conflicting interests that enter into social life, but also that this, in turn, depends to some extent upon the scientific development of jurisprudence and ethics. This moral also has applications to the realms of public law and international affairs. Our constitutional law will become effective only so long as it recognizes itself as a means for bringing about social adjustment between conflicting claims, not by mere fiat, but by a scientific determination of interests in accordance with prevalent feelings of right and justice. Our labour troubles, and the rebellion and civil war in Ireland have shown the break-down of a constitutionalism that does not take account of the actual demands and aspirations of different classes. Similarly with regard to international affairs. It has become the fashion to laugh at international law and we can consistently deny that it is law, because of the absence of an international police. But if it is true that there are other forces besides the police that make the law operative in human life, there is no reason why considerations deduced above from private law may not apply to international law.

Rule Versus Discretion [1]

AMONG the diverse attitudes that people take to our courts of law, nothing is more usual than the remark of educated people: "If our judges would only occasionally forget their legal technicalities and rely more often on common sense and justice, we would have less reason to be dissatisfied with their work." This remark is based on the belief that the end of courts of law is to render justice, and that the technical rules are at best only means towards this end and ought not, therefore, ever to stand in the way of the end itself. To which the lawyer answers that if the judge is to feel free to disregard a law in the interest of what he thinks justice, then the law becomes a dead letter and we are given over to the arbitrary sway of caprice, which is equivalent to anarchy or tyranny. The classical expression of this point of view occurs in Maine's *Ancient Law*. Commenting on the fact that the Greeks "disembarrassed themselves with astonishing facility from cumbrous forms of procedure and needless terms of art and soon ceased to attach any superstitious value to rigid rules and prescriptions," Maine says that it was not for the ultimate advantage of mankind that they did so, for "no durable system of jurisprudence could be produced in this way. A community which never hesitated to relax rules of written law whenever they stood in the way of an ideally perfect decision on the facts of particular cases, would only, if it bequeathed any body of judicial principles to posterity, bequeath one consisting of the ideas of right and wrong which happened to be prevalent at the time. Such a jurisprudence would contain no framework to which the more advanced conceptions of subsequent ages could be fitted. It would amount at best to a philosophy, marked with the imperfections of the civilization under which it grew up." [2]

The attitude of the legalist to a system of law that merely achieves justice is similar to the attitude of a properly trained physician to an empiric medicine that merely cures people. To be worthy of respect, both justice and medicine must work not empirically from hand to mouth, but according to a scientific system of rules. The predominant reason for this rationalistic attitude in law is a practical one, the need of certainty in human transactions and security against unforeseen changes. Justice has been, and is still in several fields, administered according to the sense of justice of the judge. But the judge decides a controversy only after it has arisen. In entering, however, on any transaction that involves reliance on future conditions, people must in some measure know beforehand what they may and what they may not do. Hence the need of definite rules to govern human transactions and according to which controversies shall be decided. The other advantages of justice administered according to rules or laws, viz., that it provides a check against partiality, ignorance, etc., are really subordinate to this great desideratum of certainty.

The non-legal philosopher may be inclined to question the assumption at the basis of the foregoing view, to wit, that the popular sense of justice is more variable and less certain than the popular knowledge and understanding of the law. But whatever may be said on the two sides of this question, it is certain that wherever we meet a non-homogeneous population such as characterizes our urban life, there we find actual differences of moral standard, and laws, like treaties of peace, are necessary to establish uniform standards.

Legal philosophers, especially those of the English school, make a great deal of the need of certainty in matters that are morally indifferent. The familiar illustration of this is the rule of the road. [3] It makes no difference whether the rule of the road is to turn to the left or to turn to the right. The important thing is that there should be a rule so that people may know how to avoid collision. The legal or conventional part of justice, Aristotle tells us, "is what originally was indifferent, but having been enacted, is no longer so." [4] The assertion is also frequently made that "it is often more important that a rule should be definite, certain, known, and permanent, than that it should be ideally just." [5] Though this may be somewhat questionable from a rigorous ethical point of view, there can be no doubt that most people would rather stand a small loss than remain long in a condition of doubt as to their rights.

For these reasons the legalist regards discretion on the part of the magistrates as anarchy and the appeal from law to justice as shallow and vicious. But now the plot thickens. Having banished the layman or the empiric, the legalist meets his Nemesis in his own household. The requirement of certainty and the effort to eliminate all discretion on the part of the magistrate make legal rules rigid, formal, and inimical to progress. And when the law (in its effort to keep up somewhat with the progress of life) develops, it becomes tremendously complex, so that it becomes in practice unworkable and even uncertain. Hence, legal history shows, if not alternating periods of justice according to law and justice without law, at least periodic waves of reform during which the sense of justice, natural law, or equity introduces life and flexibility into the law and makes it adjustable to its work. In course of time, however, under the social demand for certainty, equity gets hardened and reduced to rigid rules, so that, after a while, a new reform wave is necessary.

It would thus seem that life demands of law two seemingly contradictory qualities, certainty or fixity and flexibility; the former is needed that human enterprise be not paralyzed by doubt and uncertainty, and the latter that it be not strangled by the hand of the dead past.

A detailed analysis of the factors which enter into this problem and make it so significant today is not necessary for our present purpose. It may be useful, however, to consider here the logical aspect of the dialectic immanent in this field of human endeavour.

That the dilemma between framing hard and fast rules or else allowing room for discretion is a real one, can be seen in other fields of human endeavour as well as in the law. It is felt by every one who has to give orders to a human subordinate. You attempt to guard yourself against his mistakes or departures from your settled policy by laying down fixed rules. But when your subordinate rigorously follows these rules, you are vexed that he does so mechanically without using common sense or "judgment." In the ancient and honourable art of war the tendency has been to emphasize mechanical obedience. Yet military history abundantly shows how initiative on the part of subordinate officers or even privates has carried the day. A distinguished authority in our national game has said that the too-scientific players "follow the rules even when the rules are bad—which is worse than no rules at all," and every one recalls the case of the British pickets at Balaklava who were so highly trained that the camp was surprised before they knew it, when common sense might have saved the day.

The most general form of this difficulty in the field of practice is to be found in the political philosophy of Plato and Aristotle.[6] Shall the law or the just man rule? Plato, as is well known, decides on the latter alternative, using the analogy of the physician who, though he writes out a prescription, ought to be free to change it when he finds that conditions have changed. As a rule, however, he tells us, it is better that the law should be obeyed. Aristotle, perhaps influenced by the polemic motive, decides in favour of government by law rather than by men; but when we consider his admission that laws are frequently the result of party bias, and his continued insistence that equity exercised by magistrates is necessary as a corrective to the abstract generality of laws that cannot possibly take all circumstances into account, we see that our American publicists are not really genuine disciples of the Stagyrite when they deify the one-sided dogma about "government by law" as the final revelation of political truth for all times to come. In the intellectual realm

this difficulty shows itself in the form of the familiar dilemma between rationalism and empiricism. Should we put our faith in rules
or in concrete cases? In his address before the International Congress
of Physicists, the great Poincaré began, "Experience is the only
source of truth: it alone can teach us anything new; it alone can
give us certainty. These are two points which no one can contest."
But a moment later he tells us that "there are good experiments
and poor ones," and then, again, that "the physicist *cannot restrict
himself to generalizing his experiments, he must correct them.*" [7]
Thus we keep on appealing from principle to fact and then back
again from fact to principle. This is especially noticeable in ethics.
How are we to settle disagreements as to ethical matters? By appeal
to principle! But if the principles are questioned, we appeal to
particular instances.

It is the essence of traditional rationalism—the naïve faith in the
adequacy of all intellectual distinctions—to declare that certain
things cannot be or certain tasks cannot be performed because they
involve contradictions. The history of human thought ought to
warn us against this easy assumption. All human difficulties seem
contradictions before they are solved. For a man to cross a river
and not get wet seemed a patent contradiction before the invention
of boats. At any rate, a distrust of the classical forms of rationalism
leads to a wise scepticism about sharp antitheses. Certainty and
flexibility may be difficult qualities to bring together, but they are
really not logical contradictions. In the past we have tried to create
certainty exclusively through hard and fast rules, and this has admittedly broken down in practice. The legalist's dilemma, either a
rigid rule without discretion on the part of the judge or else arbitrary caprice, does not, however, exhaust all possibilities. If it were
true, there would be no middle course between absolutism and anarchy. (In the American theory of government, "the Law" takes
the place of the absolute monarch or sovereign.) As a matter of fact,
discretion is not necessarily lawless. When we praise any one for

showing fine discretion on any occasion, we certainly do not mean
that he has acted in an anarchic manner. Discretion, in general, represents more or less instinctive evaluation or appreciation of the diverse
elements that enter into a complex; and such instinctive evaluation
must precede conscious rule-making.[8] Rules are the limits that the
continued exercise of discretion establishes. It is this which enables
us to understand the present tendency in American public life to
take away administrative duties from courts that exercise them according to fixed rules, and transfer them to commissions clothed with
large discretionary power. Doubtless these commissions will, sooner
or later, formulate their discretion into rules (as did the courts of
chancery), but observe that such commissions have means of studying the effect of their decisions, and of modifying their attitude in
accordance with the results of enlarged experience, while our regular courts can only guess at the social effects of the rules that they
work out, and have no guide except reliance on *a priori* maxims.

In European countries the emancipation from legalistic rationalism has taken the form of a revolt against the ancient dogma that a
judge can decide controversies growing out of modern conditions
by finding the will of a legislator who could not possibly have
foreseen the complicated changes that time has brought about. The
adherents of this school of *Freie Rechtsfindung* (*libre recherche
scientifique*) insist, however, that they are not contending for a lawless jurisprudence. On the contrary, they insist that if judges avail
themselves of the material offered by the social sciences, the interests of social security will be all the better protected.[9]

In the legalist's references to discretion we always find a sharp
antithesis between rules of reason and arbitrary will. It is easy to
dismiss all this as based on an antiquated faculty psychology, but
such verbal refutations, though popular, are not very illuminating.

What is reason?

When the defenders of the classical theory of law tell us that law
is reason, they mean that law is deduced from legal first principles
that are as eternal, self-evident, and binding as the axioms of

Euclid.[10] Hence the consistent adherents of this view, like Christian Wolf, do not hesitate to deduce the most detailed regulations of life, table manners, etc., from natural law.

Against this view we have, besides the refutation of the self-evident character of Euclid's axioms and consequent distrust of self-evident propositions generally, a whole mass of evidence that the self-evident principles to which legal philosophers have appealed are vague, frequently in contradiction with other equally self-evident principles, and always really dependent on a fundamental choice or preference. Principles like "equality before the law" are clear only so long as we do not apply them to actual problems where all sorts of distinctions between people have to be made; the "right of each man to what he produces" comes into flat contradiction, in the case of invalids, etc., with the equally self-evident "right to life." Even the supposedly definite principle that "the whole is always greater than the part" becomes somewhat vague when applied to moral issues by such a clear thinker as St. Thomas, when, for instance, he says, "As the part and the whole are in a certain sense identical, the part may in a certain sense claim what belongs to the whole." [11]

As a matter of fact, when people approve a proposal as reasonable or condemn it as unreasonable, they mean in the first case either (1) that the proposal agrees with their own usual assumptions, (2) that the proposal forms an intellectually coherent or consistent body, or (3) that ulterior as opposed to immediate interests are safeguarded by it. A system of justice according to law (which involves trained jurists) is eminently reasonable in all these three senses; i.e., (1) it is conservative, (2) it emphasizes coherency, system, or, if you please, intellectual symmetry, and (3) it safeguards fundamental interests.

Those, however, who insist that reason or logic does not determine the ends of the law, that it is merely a tool to bring about ends that we have on other grounds consciously or unconsciously adopted, are misled by too simple an analysis of the relation of means or instrument to its end in supposing that the end determines the means and never vice versa. Reflection on actual situations shows that this is not true. Give a boy a hatchet and he will want to do things for which he had no desire before; or, if this illustration is not sufficiently dignified, consider how the invention of rapid means of travel and communication has introduced Speed (alias Efficiency) as the supreme deity of our civilization and final arbiter of our personal as well as social ends.

Philosophy has for some time been engaged in deciding the relative claims of rationalism and empiricism, and has tried to do so, in the main, on the basis of an analysis of the procedure of the mathematical or physical sciences. A thorough study of the seesaw between rule and discretion in law suggests the inadequacy of the current antithesis between these two points of view. The rationalistic and empirical motives cannot be fully understood unless they are seen in their application to the whole life that we call civilization. Thus the fundamental motive of all radical empiricism comes out most clearly, I venture to think, in James's essay on the "Moral Equivalent of War," [12] with its expressed preference for all the horrors of war rather than "a world of clerks and teachers, of coeducation and zoophily, of consumers' leagues, and associated charities." Empiricism is the motive that makes us all impatient of restraint and disdainful of the world of rules and regulations with its ceremonies and red tape. It makes us tired of routine and anxious for the thrill of novelty. It glorifies immediacy, and is essentially an attitude of trusting "nature." [13] On the other hand, rationalism, the love of order and certainty, sets greatest value on what the temperamentalist calls the artificialities of life; it makes us build houses to protect us against winds, rain, and the variations of temperature, and likewise set up theories to protect us against the flood of new and unexpected experiences. Its essence is thus the setting-up of bounds or limits to minimize the bewildering variations of nature and to eliminate some of the shock of novelty. Just as it builds dams and dikes to control the great rivers, so it sets up laws and ceremonies to provide channels through which the fitful floods of human passion and impulse may run more or less smoothly.

To recognize the inseparability of these two motives in the life of civilization is an aid to any adequate appreciation of the purely logical problem of rationalism versus empiricism.

BOOK FOUR
CONTEMPORARY LEGAL PHILOSOPHY

Tourtoulon[1]

FOR the last century, legal history has been predominantly a stronghold of ideophobia and distrust of philosophy. Imbued with the principle of induction, as preached by empirical philosophers, men supposed it simpler to find out the facts of the past and arrange them in historic order than to face the complicated contemporary situation and interpret present facts in the light of underlying principles. But while a certain uncontemplative digging for facts buried in old documents or year-books, or a semi-mechanical arrangement of them in chronologic order, is easy enough, it does not constitute significant history. The true historian must know the meaning of the facts he wishes to get at; and the interpretation or meaning of past facts is at least as complicated as that of present-day facts.

Legal history cannot therefore be intelligently pursued without general ideas as to human purposes, causation, and historic laws, as well as ideas as to the meaning of laws and legal institutions. For law is one of the means by which man tries to control his fate; and a careful historian, one as little addicted to *a priori* considerations as Vinogradoff,[2] cannot but be impressed with this aspect of his material.

Of course the legal historian may not be conscious of the general or philosophic ideas at the basis of his assumptions and procedure. One can walk well without giving much attention to the laws of mechanics and physiology. But in the higher reaches of thought, when we come to more complicated situations, conscious resort to principles becomes necessary. To hide from ourselves the general principles that we do in fact follow, and to delude ourselves into the belief that we have no philosophy, is certainly not conducive to clear thinking. In any case, it is highly desirable for one engaged in the history of law to make the leading ideas of his science the object of careful study. This is what Professor Tourtoulon has done in his *Principes philosophiques de l'histoire du droit*.[3] The teaching of the history of law at the University of Lausanne has, by long tradition, some features that rather mark it off from the courses usually conducted in Continental schools. It seeks to deal with universal history, not confining itself to national boundaries. Moreover, it does not draw any sharp line of distinction between the history of law and the philosophy of law on one side, and the technique of law on the other side. This is illustrated by the chain of personalities who were the predecessors of Tourtoulon in that chair—Hornung, eminent as a legal philosopher; Secrétan, father of the distinguished philosopher of that name; Roguin, a legal technician and logician of the first rank, author of *The Rule of Law* and of the standard modern treatise on *Comparative Law of Succession;* and Brocher de la Fléchère, his immediate predecessor, a scholar whose profound contributions in comparative law and other fields deserve to be better known.

The traditions of this chair have thus inspired Tourtoulon to give to his researches and lectures that free range of thought which would liberate the history of law from any conventional limitations, and would enable it to seek universal bases for its explanations and conclusions.

The result is a philosophy of law somewhat different from the usual treatises on the subject. It does not deal directly with the usual problems as to the fundamental principles or elements of the law, or of its leading institutions, such as personality, property, or family. It starts rather with the law as an active entity, and considers the logical and psychological aspects of its life and growth.

Tourtoulon is not an avowed disciple of any particular philosophic school. Indeed, he seems to eschew the method peculiar to technical philosophers, viz., the dialectic development of first principles. He is too wise to try to fit the complicated legal world within the hard and narrow confines of abstract formulæ. He relies rather on the rich intuitive insights of a keen and well-informed mind, which constantly carry him to the heart of things. With extraordinary good sense he turns the lancet of judicious scepticism on the commonly accepted first principles, and reveals the diverse confused thoughts that the accepted phrases serve to cover. This he does in the interest not of negative dogmatism, but of intellectual prudence, kindly, scrupulous, and searching.

This good sense shows itself characteristically in his attitude to the doctrine of social evolution. He refuses to swallow the popular, but altogether unscientific, dogma that there is a "single determinate direction along which all social institutions are forever bound to go." Against evolutionary and other teleologies he wisely cautions us that men are too prone to look for a single purpose in that which is the resultant of many causes. He distrusts the type of legal history in which the law develops dialectically out of its own concepts—the dialectic evolution made fashionable by Hegel. Law develops largely because of conditions under which it is administered, and to which it must be applied; and this truth he well illustrates by the variation of the law as to servitudes and easements of light in Mohammedan and Byzantine countries.

But precisely because he is too full of the sense of the complexity of the causes of human events, he also avoids the too simple doctrinaire form of the economic interpretation of legal history, though he rightly recognizes the fact that people generally rebel against wrongs more energetically when their own interests are affected.

Tourtoulon is also on guard against the popular Spencerian myth of a universal law of evolution from the simple to the complex—for it is popular, doubtless because it enables us to construct history *a priori* without the arduous labour of critical historical research. He puts his finger on the essential weakness of this formula as a key to history when he points out that what is simple to us may not have been so in previous times.

Equally judicious are his remarks on the relation of law to natural selection. He is courageously honest in recognizing that in all forms of society the weaker are pushed to the wall and eliminated, even when they are least aware of it. "The scythe of death has the most attractive ribbons attached to it." He is as pitiless as Huxley in showing up the pious humbug that obscurantists read into the phrase "survival of the fittest." Survival is a physical fact, and the fitness is determined by physical factors. The moral qualities associated with such physical fitness are certainly not always desirable. Good men often do not survive precisely because they devote themselves to causes other than their own survival. And the social qualities that make men associate for mutual aid only serve to make them more effective exterminators of the non-associated. But law is not directly a biologic fact and it is a mistake to stress the analogies between the biologic struggle, decided by such factors as fertility and immunity, and the social struggles that the law regulates.

Tourtoulon's method of beginning each chapter with abstract considerations may sometimes produce the appearance of a fondness for abstract and oversubtle distinctions. But the ensuing treatment in the chapter generally shows these distinctions to be weighty and important. This is especially true in the psychologic chapters. A good example is his distinction between collective and social thought —a distinction that puts us on guard against the usual uncritical assumption that the laws or resolutions of a group necessarily represent the thought of the individual members in isolation.

Against the older rationalism, which started with the idea of man as a rational being and regarded all legal institutions as adapted to their end, there has recently arisen an irrationalism, which finds the rational adaptation of means to ends only in the realm of the subconscious or unconscious. Here Tourtoulon treads his way with circumspection, drawing nice distinctions between desire and will, and not disdaining to notice the features of the law that make it a sport or social recreation. Man is an emotional being in his legal as well as in his other relations. Emotions as such are neither logical nor illogical, but alogical. Hence it is a fallacy to assume that all laws enacted under the influence of strong feeling, or passion, are necessarily bad. For no laws are ever made without the influence of feeling, and it is not wise to ignore this fact. The law has its roots in the affections that men have for the institutions under which they grow up.

The practical consequences that Tourtoulon draws, such as the need of liberal institutions for peoples of mixed races, seem of unusual worth for American jurists. Democracies are apt to be impatient and intolerant of natural diversity, and are perhaps less likely to exercise the fine wisdom of inactivity that made the leaders of the Church of England declare (Art. 34), "It is not necessary that Traditions and Ceremonies be in all places one or utterly alike." Against unreflecting haste in seeking uniformity, and against those who regard mere "mixing" or sociability as the fount of all virtues, Tourtoulon does well to point out the necessity for protecting within proper limits the rights of natural aversion—the right to ignore those to whose ways we are not drawn. Only by ignoring each other sufficiently, as we learn to do in large cities, can we peacefully live side by side in large numbers and still coöperate in case of need.

Against the recent tendency to replace all individual psychology by social psychology, and to seek in the latter (as does the school of Durkheim) the basis of all law, Tourtoulon has some very pertinent criticism. His conclusions judiciously indicate the truth between the social or national emphasis of Savigny and the individualism of Jhering. Lawyers may find the chapter on social psychology difficult reading; but if it does nothing else it will save them from being overawed by the pretended "science" of social psychology. The devotees of the latter are full of pious programs and hopes, but as yet offer little substantial scientific achievement, resorting as they do to the most uncritical elaboration of material derived at second hand from unreliable sources. It would be well if the lawyer's training in sifting evidence could be applied to the evidence of folk-lore and popular anthropology at the basis of our popular social psychology.

The chapter on the maladies of thought, with its references to mythologies in law, is a new and substantial contribution to legal philosophy. It shows that many phenomena which have been the subject of elaborate rival explanations can be more readily understood in the light of the well-known weaknesses of the human mind, such as credulity, aversion to face unpleasant or rigorous truth, and so on.

Students of law will find in the chapters on the Simple Rational one of the best available treatises on juristic technique.[4] Definition, analysis, maxims, analogy, fiction, juristic "construction," are all treated with a wealth of learning and suggestive insight. Especially valuable is the treatment of the function of analysis in controlling legal procedure and isolating the point at issue. Students of the old forms of action and of the Anglo-American common law pleading will readily be able to extend these observations. In the treatment of fictions, also, the remark that many fictions are due to an aversion for saying unpleasant things suggests how closely the fictions that are the courtesies of the law are related to other forms of social ceremonies. The reference to the rowers in Mistral's *La reine Jeanne*,[5] who, not certain of their objective, decide to row *as if* the fairy castle were there, contains a wisdom wider than the law.

Tourtoulon's account of fictions, however, leads us to a query as to the adequacy of his classification. Does it sufficiently discriminate the different types of fictions included under one head? In his exposition, numerous varieties—linguistic short cuts for purposes of exposition, artificial concepts or devices for purposes of simplifying the subject, verbal conventions, euphemisms, metaphors, hypothetical reasoning, and reasoning about types—are all treated under the same rubric. Furthermore, can we accept his inference that logic is not applicable to fictions, to juridical constructions, and to juridical science generally (so far as the latter is not merely a study of existing facts)? This untenable inference (in which Tourtoulon partly accords with Geny's *Science et technique en droit privé positif*)[6] is due to the fact that his conception of logic does not extend beyond the traditional school logic.[7]

The traditional logic, from Aristotle to Mill, is essentially the logic of classificatory zoölogy and botany—the only natural sciences that these great men knew at first hand. While it is undoubtedly capable of extension, it is best fitted only for the *classification* of existing things and their inhering qualities. Tourtoulon, therefore, naturally feels that this logic is not directly applicable to fictions and legal constructions; for there we are dealing with the non-existing, and with questions not of truth but of fitness.

But the term "logic" also denotes the *correctness of the conclusions* drawn from premises. And it is not true that we cannot draw valid inferences when our premises relate to questions of fitness or the adaptation of means to ends. If juristic procedure were to be excluded from science on that ground, we should also have to rule out a most perfect physical science like mechanics, which (as Hertz has shown in the introduction to his *Mechanics*) decides questions ultimately in terms of the fitness of a system of propositions. There are doubtless differences of degree, in the vagueness of the data, between jurisprudence and mechanics; but there is no fundamental difference in logic. Perhaps Tourtoulon is also carried too far by his definition of fictions as "falsehoods which deceive no one." It may be maintained that in reality the law does not assert, e.g., that an adopted son is a natural son, or that the high seas *are* in a given parish in London. What is essential is that the law grants to certain persons the same rights which it grants to natural sons, and that it applies the same rule to events at sea which it applies to events on land. It is certainly confusing if the law, after it has decided to make such extensions of its rules, gives up the effort to carry them out logically.

It is matter for regret that this wider conception of logic as dealing with the correctness of inferences from all sorts of assumptions, whose subject matter may be conventions (as in mathematics), resolutions (as in the moral sciences), or idealizations (as in the exact physical sciences), is not yet generally available to the educated public. Some material on this theme will be found vivaciously presented in Vaihinger's recent work, *Philosophie des Als Ob* (a work that receives careful and illuminating comment in Professor Tourtoulon's Appendix). Unfortunately, however, that book is, as its author admits, a work of immature youth. By trying to explain everything as fiction, making the "make-believe" or "as if" cover everything, the distinctive characteristic of legal fictions and constructions is lost. But the essential unity of logic in the physical and social sciences is there brought out, despite a lamentable amount of misinformation.

As one who deals honestly with fundamentals, Tourtoulon cannot avoid touching on the metaphysical aspects of the law (for metaphysics, it is well to be reminded, is but the obstinate effort to think clearly as far as the human mind can go). This he does more specifically in the chapters on "pure" law and on metaphysical law.

In these chapters Tourtoulon shows himself profoundly influenced not only by Geny and by his own colleague Roguin, but even more so by the Neo-Kantian metaphysics of Stammler, as expounded by Djuvara and Reinach. But while our author thus persistently asserts the existence of *a priori* elements in the law, he also keeps to the old positivistic assumption that logic and scientific demonstration can deal only with empirical facts of existence. This places his metaphysical doctrines of "pure" law and justice in the anomalous position of being logically indemonstrable, and yet categorically necessary.

It is Professor Tourtoulon's respect for Kant and for the transcendental philosophy that here leads him to support a good deal of genuine and profound insight by arguments that students of modern logic and mathematics regard as obsolete and untenable. A careful analysis is necessary to disengage what is sound from what is unsound in his position.

Kant wrote at a time when people thought they knew with absolute certainty that space must follow the laws of three-dimensional Euclidean geometry. This certainty (as Kant clearly saw) could rest only on *a priori* intuition. The later development of non-Euclidean geometry, however, has clearly shown that this absolute certainty, or *a priori* intuition, is a delusion—that in fact we have no means of asserting in advance of experience what system of geometry nature will actually follow. The realization that the axioms of our most perfect science, Euclidean geometry, are not (if interpreted as asserting the existence of natural objects) categorically certain, but are rather only convenient hypotheses, inevitably makes us distrust all propositions claimed to be categorically true, intuitively certain, or self-evident. This distrust is naturally more justified in the variable realm of law. Tourtoulon frequently argues that just as all the facts of arithmetic presuppose the category of quantity as *a priori,* so do the facts of law presuppose certain categories. This argument breaks down when we see modern arithmetic developed without presupposing the category of quantity at all. Indeed all the Kantian epistemologic arguments from facts to the certainty of their presuppositions simply illustrate the logical fallacy of arguing from the affirmation of the consequences. All our presuppositions are really only hypotheses to explain the facts, and the certainty of the facts (if they are certain) may confirm but cannot prove the hypothesis that explains them.

There is truth in the assertion that there *are* certain elements of the law logically prior to, or independent of, the empirical existence of human life. This truth can readily be recognized if we clearly distinguish between principles of procedure and substantive principles. That which substantially exists in natural time and space is essentially changeable, and one can never have any absolute knowledge of what is past or future. But when we examine the principles of procedure of all sciences, we find certain invariant relations between all premises and their consequences. These principles of logic we do not create. We find them. But without them no valid argument as to anything actual or possible can be constructed. Now the principles according to which all conclusions follow from their assumed premises do not change with time, for the simple reason that it is meaningless to speak of abstract relations existing in time. (Abstract relations can only be said to exist logically, if we mean by this simply to assert their universal validity for all possible arguments.) To the extent, then, that law necessarily depends on logic for its elaboration, Professor Tourtoulon is perfectly correct in insisting that the logical element of law is independent of any human institution. For it would be absurd to try to derive or prove the principles of logic from the instances in which they are embodied. To claim validity, every such demonstration would have to assume the very principles it tried to prove. But these logical principles are negative and regulative; they do not determine the matter of particular premises of any one science, precisely because they are the regulating principles of all sciences.

Tourtoulon's position may perhaps be rendered a little plainer by considering the two stages of his argument, which we may refer to as (a) the stage of Roguin, and (b) the stage of Reinach.

(a) Roguin has insisted that some elements are necessarily found in all legal systems actual or possible. This is obviously a matter of definition. If by "legal system" we mean anything at all, we mean some set of relations. It follows, then, that every legal system will be subject to the logical rules according to which these elements can possibly be combined. If you encounter a system in which these elements do not exist, it will *by definition* not be a legal system at all. Such an abstract development of legal logic possesses (as Roguin and Tourtoulon have indicated) great usefulness as an auxiliary science.[8] It opens up the field of possible solutions to concrete legal problems, and thus saves us from falling into the natural dogmatic assumption that any particular solution which happens to occur to us is the only possible one. When, however, this abstract or "pure" law is used by itself apart from a full appreciation of the complex actual or historical facts, it is apt to produce the very opposite effect of closing our minds to the concrete possibilities before us. This is amply illustrated by judges or jurists who in their anxiety to be rigorously logical fall into the vice of false simplicity, which von

Jhering has called *Begriffsjurisprudenz*, and Pound, mechanical jurisprudence.

(b) Reinach's "Die apriorische Grundlagen des bürgerlichen Rechts" appeared originally in Husserl's *Jahrbuch*.⁹ As Tourtoulon's reference to Husserl's philosophy is very brief, a few remarks about it may be in order. The philosophy of Husserl, following that of Meinong, is rooted in an insight of the inadequacy of the old positivistic logic which assumed that logical demonstration is concerned only with what actually exists. As the life of all mathematical or theoretic sciences consists in the development of the consequences of rival hypotheses (which development is necessary before we can conceive of crucial experiments to decide between them), and as contrary hypotheses cannot all be true, it follows that a great deal of the life of science consists in developing the consequences of hypotheses, irrespective of whether these hypotheses are true or not. Moreover, in sciences like mechanics or thermodynamics, our reasoning proceeds from assumptions as to free bodies or frictionless engines, though such bodies cannot possibly exist in nature. This means that there is a scientific point of view from which hypotheses or assumptions have logical characteristics, apart from the question whether their subject-matter has actual existence.

This enlargement of the conception of valid logic has many important applications to juristic study. For one thing, it renders nugatory the positivistic ideal of juristic science as dealing only with *what is*. It shows us that a science of what ought to be, of desirable or just law, may be logically as rigorous as mathematics. It also enables us to dispense with Geny's artificial and misleading distinction between "science" and "technique" in law, since it shows that science is itself a technique, and that no technique can dispense with logic in its elaboration.

Unfortunately, however, Reinach's own study seems far more influenced by the traditional Kantian conception of the *a priori* than by the newer logical philosophies. He is not satisfied to maintain merely that law must be subject to the regulative principles of logic, but seeks to establish substantive legal principles, *a priori,* going as far as to maintain, e.g., that the obligation to keep promises is *a priori* necessary for all legal systems—a proposition that is not only far from necessary, but actually false. No known legal system makes all promises legally obligatory. The distinction between those which are and those which are not so obligatory clearly depends on empirical elements. Similar considerations hold with regard to Professor Tourtoulon's attempt to establish as *a priori* the distinction between private and public law, or the distinction between rights over animate and rights over inanimate objects. We can no more deduce material generalizations or distinctions from the formulæ or regulative principles of logic alone than we can get a house by merely manipulating the rules of architecture.

These abstract considerations will also assist us to pronounce in what respect our author's theory of justice is tenable and in what respect untenable.

To define justice as "the according to each that which is his own or his due" ("*suum cuique tribuere*"), might seem at first perfectly futile. Tourtoulon's example of Talmudic casuistry in reference to the ownership of a house shows how slippery is the question, What *is* a man's own? Indeed, it is the very object of a theory of justice to define what is justly a man's own. To assert that every one is justly entitled to keep whatever he actually possesses would be a monstrous perversion of what has generally been meant by justice. A number of attempts have been made to avoid this difficulty, but they have not succeeded. Thus it is urged that in virtue of being the first occupant, Robinson Crusoe is justly the owner of his island. It is "his." But it is by no means self-evident that it is just for him to exclude other persons subsequently shipwrecked upon the island, even if all the available food on the island were the result of his own labour. If the poor, weak, or helpless have a just right to life, others cannot have a just right to exclude them from the means of maintaining life. The doctrine that each is entitled to the full produce of his labour is, as an absolute proposition, untenable. Another example is the claim that a man's personality is his by nature, and that no one has a right to interfere with it; whence it is concluded that slavery is always and absolutely unjust. But here again we are apt to be misled by words. If slavery denotes an unjustifiable interference with personality, it is obviously unjust *by definition*. But to say that all interference with personality is unjust, even for the purpose of correction, or of preventing harm, is to make justice absolutely useless for the legal regulation of society, since all law involves some interference.

Professor Tourtoulon has the courage of his convictions and recognizes that the justice which he defines as the *suum cuique* may not be desirable or good. But if so, why should we ever follow justice at all? He answers that justice is not a principle of action, but one of evaluation. Yet is not this still clearly inconsistent with the sharp distinction between justice and the good or desirable? How can we evaluate except in terms of the good and the better?

Nevertheless, our author's doctrine of justice covers a great deal of shrewd wisdom having fundamental validity and importance. Whatever characteristics a legal system may have, it must (so long as legality means what it actually does mean to all people) include lawfulness, or the regulation of conduct by general rules or principles. Legal justice, then, means that laws should be kept—that we cannot have a law and yet avoid it by exceptions in special cases. Equality before the law, or the impartiality of the judge, amounts to just this faithfulness or respect for the law that is. *Suum cuique* means that if the proper legal authority has awarded a disputed property to my neighbour, I should obey that decision even if I consider it unjust. This principle to be sure cannot be absolute. There are times when the actual legal order is so monstrously unjust that patriotic citizens must rebel. This, however, in no way denies that, other things being equal, lawfulness or legal order is a great human good, and for the maintenance of it men at all times are willing to endure a great deal of material injustice.

In order to maintain his metaphysical conception of justice, Professor Tourtoulon argues that men could not pursue the ideal of justice if it were empirical or arose in our own nature. To this the answer might be made that only the ideals that arise in our own nature can be pursued at all. Certainly bread, or the welfare of our children, is no less desirable because hunger or parental affection arises in our own nature.

In thus submitting our author's metaphysical doctrines of "pure" law and justice to a critical scrutiny, we only follow and apply the candid, critical spirit that he himself so admirably illustrates throughout this book, and more especially in his criticism of the positivist's attempts to derive rules as to what *ought to be* either from the accumulation of past facts, or from the "social nature" of man. The attempt to derive concrete or particular consequences from metaphysical assumptions alone is an impracticable one, since modern logic has shown that from universal premises alone no particular conclusion can be drawn. For true universals are hypotheses, and from no accumulation of assumptions alone can we derive a fact.

If the reader ask, Why labour at this arid topic?, the answer is that only by refuting, or at least mitigating, the claim of metaphysical absoluteness put forth in the theory of "pure" law and justice, can we fully justify the profound and mature wisdom that Professor Tourtoulon elsewhere shows throughout this volume,—the wisdom of moderation. This spirit of moderation is what lawyers are apt to have developed in them by the very practice of their profession; but they are apt to forget it when they come to formulate their views theoretically. The religious reformer can aim to make men perfect. Having the absolute truth revealed to him, he knows both the absolute goal and the necessary means. Not so those who deal with laws, which are always based on more or less rough estimates as to the general future effects of measures designed to meet, not the needs of every one, but only those of the generality. Logical rigour in juridical thinking is, doubtless, a great good. As our author acutely remarks, those (especially theorists) who vaguely appeal to life or practice generally show that they have not the stamina to follow arguments rigorously to their logical conclusions. But the principles of law cannot extend beyond the law which is their field of application.

For we must remember that not the whole of life can be legally regulated, and that the supreme virtue of the law, justice, must frequently yield to the more humane virtue of charity. Those who care for pompous rhetoric may repeat that law is nothing but justice, reason, and so on. They may even find satisfaction in such banal cant as that law protects liberty but not license. But an honest jurist like Tourtoulon knows that to define liberty as the power to do only what is right is like defining a sou as a piece of money to be given to the poor.

The lawyer, like the physician, sees the shadows as well as the lights of human life; and, if wise, he learns not to expect too much of the law, and to be tolerant of human imperfection. Such a sense of imperfection together with a spirit of tolerance is one of the best safeguards against the spirit of fanaticism that uses rigorous principles to shut the gates of mercy on mankind. No single aphorism so well sums up this viable attitude of the lawyer as our author's dictum: "There is no need to throw to the dogs all that is not fit for the altar of the gods."

ON CONTINENTAL LEGAL PHILOSOPHY [1]

I

Philosophical-Legal Literature in French, German, and Italian: 1912–1914 [2]

WHILE professional philosophers have been withdrawing from the field of jurisprudence, jurists, like other intellectual workers, have been driven more and more by the exigencies of their own work to a philosophical consideration of their own fundamental problems. Besides the general breakdown of the ideophobia that was so fashionable in the latter part of the nineteenth century, special circumstances have brought issues involving the fundamental principles of jurisprudence to the foreground. The adoption of the German Civil Code, which throws upon jurists the task of determining what is "good faith" and "morals," the adoption of the Swiss Civil Code with its explicit recognition of the judges' power of supplementary legislation, and the rise in France and other countries of social legislation involving new forms of responsibility and consequent new methods of interpretation [3] have all led to the breakdown of the classical theory according to which the law springs complete and fully armed from the brow of a somewhat mythical being called the will of the sovereign. German historicism as well as French and English positivism had all kept the eighteenth century faculty psychology, with its air-tight division of the mind into reason and will, and consequent sharp *a priori* distinction between the functions of the legislator and the judge. As there are many demands of practical life that call for just such a sharp distinction between the function of the legislature and that of the courts, the classical theory managed until recently to hold its sway despite occasional mutterings of intellectual discontent.

The general intellectual and practical circumstances referred to above have, however, led to an organized revolt against the traditional view. This may be dated from Geny's *Méthode d'interprétation et sources en droit privé positif* (1899). With massive learning and an overwhelming wealth of illustrative material, Geny pointed out that the legislator cannot foresee all and foreordain everything, and that the interpreter of the law must, therefore, engage in a free scientific inquiry into the social principles applicable to given cases, if the law is to be developed along lines satisfying the needs of modern life. So long as the duty of the judge was conceived as that of a faithful but passive mouthpiece of a preëxisting law, questions of social policy were no part of legal science. With the recognition, however, of the law-creating function of judges and jurists, questions as to the end or the policy of the law have become unavoidable. This has led to a reconsideration of the views as to the relation of law to ethics, logic, and social science, and has thus raised in significant form philosophical questions as to legal methodology. Towards the latter part of the nineteenth century, the view generally prevailed—witness the works of Windscheid and Laurent—that the main outlines of legal doctrine had received a definitive form and that only various details remained to be determined.[4] Our age, however, delights to question fundamentals in all realms. But it is not sceptical. It has found a simple way of establishing new fundamentals by means of the principle of historical evolution. If we can show that any legal or ethical principle is the result of or expresses a tendency of evolution, the principle of universal progress will at once make it as canonical as the older ways of Providence.

This procedure is well illustrated in Duguit's *Les transformations générales du droit privé* (1912), in which, under cover of a survey of the transformations of private civil law since the adoption of the Napoleonic Code, Professor Duguit attacks the whole classical theory of law, root and branch. Professor Duguit regards the notion of subjective rights as too metaphysical for any positive legal science, and endeavours to show that legal progress is away from a metaphysical, subjective, and individualistic conception (as embodied in the Declaration of the Rights of Man, and the Code Napoléon), to a positive, objective, and social system of rules. Thus the rapid growth of our corporation law shows that no actual will is necessary in order to have subjects of legal rights—unless we take refuge in the mystic doctrine that business corporations have wills or souls of their own. Thus also the notion of responsibility as based on "fault" (twin sister of theologic "sin") is giving way to the conception of responsibility based on the objective determination of the risk involved in a transaction or undertaking. The notion of property as the absolute right of individual dominion, he shows, has given place to the notion of property as a social arrangement for the conservation of wealth and therefore essentially subject to constant social regulation or restriction. With the abandonment of the notion of subjective rights, there goes, of course, the whole classical theory of juristic acts, transactions, etc. Hence positivists as well as Catholics have rushed to the defence of the doctrine of subjective rights.[5]

The most effective answer, however, to Duguit's book comes from legal history itself, which, like nature, does not run for the convenience of our generalization but has an irritating way of showing progress in opposite directions. Thus property has, in the period covered by M. Duguit, not only become more subject to social regulation but also (as in the case of copyright, or in the abolition of communal property) become more individualistic.[6] This is well illustrated in an excellent survey of the actual legal changes of the nineteenth century by Charmont, *Les transformations du droit civil* (1912). It treats more in detail the changes in family law, the legal position of women and children, as well as the increasing restrictions on private property; and in the last three chapters gives one of the best discussions we have of the theory of risk, fault, and responsibility, in the light of modern industrial conditions and legislation.

Modern industrial conditions have not only scandalized classical jurisprudence by developing the notion of an objective responsibility independent of all personal fault but even more so by the new notion of *abuse of rights*. As a legal right has always been held to define the limits within which one may legally act, it seems that an abuse within one's rights is a logical impossibility. Legal abuse can only begin, it would seem, where rights end. But the exigencies of life sometimes overcome even the difficulties of juristic logic, and French courts have, in passing on strikes, lock-outs, and boycotts, been forced more and more to resort to this notion of abuse of rights. Here, as elsewhere, the seeming defiance of logic turns out on closer examination to be the successful assertion of practical needs over against an inadequate theory. The classical jurisprudence regarded the law as a body of definite *existing* principles, which courts were merely to apply. Now, however, transformism has invaded also the realm of legal thought, and it is beginning to be recognized that as new situations are coming up, courts must in fact make law, or at least modify old rules by stretching or restricting them. The law gives the employer the general right to engage or discharge any one he pleases, and to the workman the corresponding right of entering or leaving the employment. But does the employers' right include the right to discharge men because they belong to a union, and does the workmen's right to leave include the right to do so in order to compel a fellow employee to enter the union? Logically it seems we must answer in the affirmative. But courts feel that social order or the interest of the public demands a more qualified answer. And this is accomplished by the general principle that rights are bestowed for social purposes, and therefore any exercise of one's rights that leads to anti-social results is to be regarded as abusive. The doctrine is thus a general principle whereby the social end of a right is made to determine its varying limits in different cases. It thus seems a clear instance of legal pragmatism.

The whole doctrine is critically examined in Roussel's *L'abus du droit* (1914). Roussel makes some telling points against that softheartedness which would banish all strife from this world and in his insistence on the value of clear thinking. In the main, however, his objections rest on the assumption that law, as distinct from morality, must be absolutely definite, and therefore judges must not let their sense of humanity blur the clear outlines of the rights fixed by the law. But this assumption that the whole law is a logically closed system, which no longer has to draw its nourishment from the breasts of its mother Justice, is precisely what the newer jurists are disputing. In harmony with the anti-intellectualism now prevalent in popular philosophy, and characteristic of other forms of modernism, they no longer regard judges and jurists as automata for unfolding the logical content of fixed legal concepts, but as the living organs of society for re-creating the law in harmony with daily needs—the theory of the division of power to the contrary notwithstanding.

It is natural for reformers or protestants to divide themselves into sects. Some emphasize the opposition to logic and juridical construction, as contrasted with common sense, humane sentiments, and the teachings of sociology (Fuchs,[7] Wüstendörfer [8]); while others insist simply on more adequate concepts to enable the law to *develop* (Stampe [9]). Some insist that the judge is to legislate only *præter legem*, to fill up the blanks in the legal system (Danz [10]). But others claim that a unitary method requires judicial legislation even *contra legem* (Wüstendörfer [11]). Some contend for the claims of the living law of today and its needs, determined by social science, in contrast to the will of the legislator, determined by history (Kohler,[12] Ehrlich,[13] Kantorowicz [14]); while others insist on social interests in harmony with the historically ascertained ends of the legislator (Heck [15]). Some isolate the culture or ideal of the age so that they suppose definite juridical deductions can be made from it (Berolzheimer [16] and Kohler [17]); while others insist on a more inductive procedure based on a trained sense of what is required in individual cases (Jung [18]). In their common insistence, however, that the legal system is not eternally self-sufficient but must always continue, through judge and jurist, to draw on social science, ethical sentiments, or the culture of the age, these writers defy the historicist and positivist condemnation of all rational or non-positive law. Hence they are accused by their opponents (Bartolemei,[19] Gareis [20]) of undermining the value of the law by opening the door to arbitrary decisions that would be subversive of all the social interests which depend on the certainty and impartiality of the law.

The one who might fitly be called either the stormy petrel or the *enfant terrible* of this *Freirechtsschule*, Kantorowicz, has not hesitated to ascend to the source of the modern historical school and lay hands on Savigny himself, showing the limitations of the latter's conception of jurisprudence and the inadequacy of his criticism of the old natural law (*Was ist uns Savigny?* 1912).

This has brought forth a carefully elaborated apologia for Savigny by Manigk, *Savigny und der Modernismus im Recht* (1914), in which the attempt is made to show that it is these modernists who have the wrong conception of jurisprudence, and that when they are right, they have already been anticipated by Savigny himself. As is usual in such work, texts are frequently tortured to make them confess the desired meaning. Nevertheless there is here enough genuine criticism of the modernists' attack on the historical school to warn us that all sharp contrasts are but pedagogic devices to make our intention clear. They may express a tendency but cannot pretend to strict historical accuracy in point of fact. Manigk's book leaves one with a very sober sense of the complexity of legal method and the vanity of monistic attempts to claim everything for a single method or panacea, no matter how new.

When law is viewed in the process of being made, rather than as a completed, sanctioned system, the state or sovereign can no longer be regarded as the exclusive source of all law. This is vigorously brought out in Jung's *Problem des natürlichen Rechts* (1912) and Ehrlich's *Grundlegung der Soziologie des Rechts* (1913). Jung, who in previous books had attacked the notion of positive law as a closed logical system, here takes the growing character of the law in the process of interpretation for granted. What, however, is the method according to which this is done? In spite of a too liberal reliance on the principle of social eudemonism based on popular Darwinian evolutionism, Jung, more than any other modern jurist, emphasizes the primacy of the individual case. Law grows out of the effort of man to protect himself against wrong, which, following Schopenhauer, Jung regards as the primary positive idea of the law. Jung carefully examines the relation between the feeling of right and wrong in a given case and the principles that jurists assert as the justification or basis of the decision, and thus gives us something of actual juristic logic.[20a] But his acceptance of the popular inadequate conception of induction (which makes principles somewhat gratuitous afterthoughts) and a pseudo-scientific belief that the determination of what is, is superior to the determination of what ought to be, prevent the successful carrying out of this admirable attempt to give us a theory of natural law or justice as an actual source of the law.

Ehrlich's primary interest is in what he calls living law, the law that is actually operative and controlling in the affairs of men. From this point of view he is compelled to join the protest against the exaggerated importance hitherto attributed to the state in the field of law. The state, according to him, is a latecomer in this field and does not even today exhaust the life of the law. Most people obey the law because of custom and not because of direct coercion by the state. The main work of the state in the realm of law is rather educational, to see that the citizens are brought up in habits of obedience. The state and its juristic organs are responsible only for adjective law, i.e., the law that regulates the remedies which protect the living law. The norms for deciding cases become operative only in litigated disputes that, from the social point of view, represent the pathology of the law. The family that goes to court is pretty much broken up, as a family. To the jurist, litigation is the primary matter, but in the mind of the community, the concrete legal institution is. Like Kantorowicz, Ehrlich sharply opposes the historical school, which, as in Savigny's treatise on possession, emphasizes the past at the expense of the present. History cannot be the basis of law any more than paleontology can be the basis of physiology. Our knowledge of the past of the law is more dependent on our knowledge of the present than the latter is on the former. The vital part of the law, then, must be sought not in the past, but in present day arrangements, not in a mythical folk mind but in the actual social arrangements of today. Hence a new program of legal studies. The actual system of property holding of Austrian peasants will not be found in the code, which is based on Roman law and not on actual practice. The actual law must be sought in archives, notarial records, acts of incorporation, notices of the formation and dissolution of partnerships, etc.

Ehrlich's book suffers from the fact that he draws no clear account of what he means by law and how he distinguishes it from customs and morals.[20b] The lines between law and morals, he tells us, are shifting. This, however, is all the more reason for demanding clear ideas. Thus it may be urged that what Ehrlich calls living law is simply custom, which, as such, is not law at all, though it may become so under certain conditions. Moreover, his assumption that state law merely regulates procedure, and that the latter is subsequent to the substantive law, is not easily borne out by historic fact.

An energetic though laborious protest against the over-emphasis of custom or social practice as a source of law is found in Oertmann's *Rechtsordnung und Verkehrsitte* (1914). In opposing the claims of social science in the interpretation of law, he asserts that all law is either the work of the state, or becomes law because recognized by the state; and he even goes far to deny the old claim of the historical school that law does arise in custom. Not social practice, but the continual application of a rule by the courts, makes it law. In thus emphasizing the law-making function of the courts he comes very near the position of the *Freirechtler*, that judges must put the breath of life into the dead sentences of the statute book.

While those engaged in civil law have been thus engaged in trying to make civil law more flexible, those engaged in public law (which is popularly supposed to be an indeterminate branch of politics) have been trying to elaborate a rigorous logical technique. An unusually able book representing the latter movement—showing familiarity with Kant and Sigwart as well as with the police laws of the various German communities—is Walter Jellinek's *Gesetz, Gesetzesanwendung und Zweckmässigkeitserwägung* (1913). Starting from the fact that courts have to pass on the legality of administrative acts but have no authority to inquire into the appropriateness or necessity of such acts, Jellinek tries to determine the meaning and limits of this administrative freedom or discretion. In the course of this inquiry he examines carefully the logical morphology of the law in the process of its application. He has some pertinent remarks on the imperative theory of the law, though like his distinguished father he holds that all law is, as such, of state origin. While he holds tenaciously to the view that the interpreter of the law is engaged in a process of determining a historically objective fact, a meaning actually intended by the legislator, his treatment of what he calls the undetermined concept is very suggestive in showing the large share of freedom in the process of interpreting the law.

A similar attempt for French law, though more narrowly legal, is Michoud's *Etude sur le pouvoir discrétionnaire de l'administration* (1913).

More revolutionary in its attitude toward established ideas in public law is Duguit's *Transformations du droit public* (1913). Attacking vigorously the notion of sovereignty as appropriate only to Byzantine and medieval conditions, M. Duguit suggests the notion of public service as the fitter basis for public law, the responsibility of public officials to be determined accordingly. Laws are binding not because they are willed by the state, but because they are the conditions under which human beings can live in society. Thus on the basis of extreme positivism M. Duguit comes to a position very near that of the old natural law with its insistence on the judge's veto over unconstitutional legislation and the strict responsibility of public officials.

An American lawyer reading for the first time Stammler's introductory article to the *Zeitschrift für Rechtsphilosophie in Lehre und Praxis* (1914-21) or the concluding article in the collection *Systematische Rechtswissenschaft* (*Kultur der Gegenwart*, 2nd ed., 1913) is sure to suppose that he is in the presence of the traditional German philosopher trying to deduce everything from *a priori* principles but remaining in the cloudy region of abstruse abstractions.[21] Yet Stammler is primarily a jurist who, taking the distinction between just and unjust law seriously, and finding no light on the essence of that distinction in the writings of the historical school, has been led to an adaptation of the Kantian philosophy as supplying the needed criterion. Starting with the Kantian distinction between the changing and conditioned *content* and the unconditioned unchanging *form* of the law, Stammler tries to determine on the basis of the Kantian epistemology the eternal form of all just law. He naturally rejects as empirical all ends such as material comforts, national integrity, or the cultivation of the arts and science, and sets up the pure form of a community of free-willing men as the absolute end valid for all times and places. On the basis of this absolute end Stammler and his followers try to determine the limits of freedom of contract, the proper interpretation of the German Civil Code provisions for good faith (Sec. 242) and good morals (Sec. 826) and the proper application of the Code of Civil Procedure in the case of goods sold at auction (Sec. 825).

In the high and rarefied air in which the argument starts it is hard to see how Stammler can effect a transition from such formal concepts as the transcendental unity of apperception to any actual content of the law. No more than Kant does he succeed in showing how a pure logical form can, apart from material premises, determine the actual content of a law; nor can he disprove the fact that all sorts of opposing claims in controverted questions are equally compatible with the essentially vague ideal of a community of free wills. Stammler, like other Neo-Kantians, seems to me to confuse the logical form of consistency, indispensable to all rational effort in law and ethics, with the ultimate end or ideal, which must necessarily involve a matter of choice. Just as reason cannot prove all propositions, but presupposes certain premises as accepted, so reason cannot determine the ultimate end but can only show the fitness of means to ends.

The rich content of this *Zeitschrift* as well as Stammler's *Theorie der Rechtswissenschaft* (1911) serves to show the justice of Simmel's remark that in works of this kind it is not impossible for solid superstructures to rest on very flimsy foundations. But perhaps it would be more just to say that Stammler's legal results form a solid building which rests on earthly experience, but to its indweller seems supported by logical threads from the epistemologic heaven.

A very clear exposition of Stammler's point of view (though not avowedly designed as such) is Djuvara's *Le fondement du phénomène juridique* (1913). The elaborate technical epistemologic machinery is lost in the passage across the Rhine and the angular logical rigidity softened in the French garb. But the two fundamental characteristics of Stammler's viewpoint, the emphasis on the categories of pure reason as the source of the specifically juristic element in social facts, and the attempt to derive all rights and obligations from the free meeting of minds, emerge very clearly. On an independent basis, but leading to the same result is Del Vecchio's *Il concetto del diritto* (1912), now translated into English as Part II of his *Formal Basis of Law*. Neither Djuvara nor Del Vecchio, however, seem to take notice of the insuperable difficulties that the facts of the legal order, such as employers' liability or the laws of inheritance, offer to the theory that makes all obligation rest on consent. If the state needs my land, justice may be said to demand that I be given the fair market price. But does that mean that I necessarily do consent to part with the house, the treasured emotional associations of which nothing else in the world can replace?

A similar result, from a professed Neo-Hegelian starting-point, is found in Kohler's general survey of the legal situation, *Recht und Persönlichkeit in der Kultur der Gegenwart* (1914), and in his more technical book on the law of competition, *Der unlautere Wettbewerb* (1914). Both attempt to derive all legal obligations from the rights of personality. Kohler was one of the pioneers of the sociologic interpretation of law, but his attempt to derive the rights of competing business corporations from the rights of personality leads to the weirdest kind of *Begriffsjurisprudenz*. Does personality for legal purposes mean anything more than a point that is the focus of rights and obligations? If we once see that rights and obligations are the primary objects of legal science, and that associations represent groups of rights and obligations in some respects like and in some respects different from those possessed by single individuals in similar legal situations, we shall be spared a great deal of absurd metaphysics. In no field does the baneful and fruitless word "reality" cause so much confusion as in the field of jurisprudence and more especially in the question as to the reality of legal personality.

Kohler's *Recht und Persönlichkeit* was written before the World War and ended with a very inspiring survey of the position of international law; but after the war broke out he saw fit to recant his noble vision.[99] It is a great pity that a scholar of his standing should have descended from the heights where the search for impartial and international truth reigns supreme into the arena where rage the temporary conflicts of hatred and economic interests. In his recantation Kohler restricts humanity to Germany, Turkey, and Italy (this was before May, 1915); and his intemperate denunciation of England will certainly not add to his reputation for scientific sobriety.

One of the few avowedly philosophical attempts of the *Freirechtsschule* is Radbruch's *Grundzüge der Rechtsphilosophie* (1914), and for a book of this title it sticks rather close to juridical matters. Radbruch does not attempt, like Stammler or Kohler, to storm the empyrean; but gives us a careful analysis of what is meant by the validity of law, and a fresh account of the relation of law to politics. Radbruch is not taken in by the over-hasty monism that refuses to take note of the distinction between the normative and the existential standpoints. But his reliance on the Windelband-Rickert philosophy leads him to overemphasize the pathos of legal thought, which must move in both the theoretical and the practical realm. "Youthful idealism and hunger for reality will always seek to construct bridges leading from jurisprudence to ideals and life; the resignation of manhood will insist on isolation and self-sufficiency."

Written along the traditional Hegelian lines of the Italian school are Petrone's *Il diritto nel mondo dell spirito* (1912) and Rensi's *Il fondamento del diritto* (1912). The second volume of Barillari's *Diritto e filosofia* (1912) is a synthesis of Kantian and Hegelian elements to produce a juridical epistemology based on the conception of absolute knowledge. Biavaschi's *La crise attuale della filosofia del diritto* (1913) is written from the religiously orthodox standpoint, but, beyond some suggestive criticisms, does not offer anything new.

As the Italian universities require a separate course on the philosophy of law in the law faculties, books on what the Germans call the general theory of law are called philosophy of law in Italy. This is certainly the case with Miceli's *Principii di filosofia del diritto* (1914), an admirably gotten up volume which, in spite of nine hundred pages, is of small pocket size and altogether in substance as well as in outer form one of the most satisfactory text-books on the subject. In spite of the title of this book, and of his larger four-volume book bearing a similar title, Miceli insists that a philosophy of law is impossible, and that what passes as such is a mixture of ethics and of the general theory of the law. But why may not both ethics and the general theory of the law be philosophical? Miceli's objection is based on the traditional conception of philosophy and the gratuitous assumption that reflection on empirical material cannot rise to "high speculative concepts." Somewhat similar in scope to Miceli's book—though the very antithesis in external make-up—

is Cosentini's *Filòsofia del diritto* (1914) which embodies a great deal of the material of his earlier book, *La réforme de la législation civile* (1913). Cosentini belongs to the school of liberal positivism, and conceives of the philosophy of law as a handmaid to the sociology of law. Philosophy must not be too critical, but must restrict itself to an examination of the logical and phenomenologic essence of juridical facts and their relation to other social facts. Social ideals, however, he admits, are actual facts of the utmost importance in legislation and in judicial law-making, through the filling up of the lacunæ of the law. Hence the philosophy of law must not restrict itself to a study of the law as it is, but must help in its transformation.

Belonging in the main to what might be called the school of idealistic positivism is A. Levi's *Contributi ad una teoria filosofica dell' ordine giuridico* (1914), a development of his earlier book, *La société et l'ordre juridique* (1911). Levi is a devoted follower of the venerable Italian philosopher Ardigó. He insists on the possibility of a philosophy of law that is not merely a historic or ethnographic jurisprudence or simply the general part of legal science. But he rejects all attempts at deontology. He seeks to base his philosophy of law on psychology and gnoseology, a positivistic adaptation of epistemology. He sees an analogy between the reaction of modern jurisprudence against the theory of innate rights prior to the existence of society, and the reaction of soulless psychology to the existence of a substantial self. The problems of the philosophy of law thus include: (1) the presuppositions of juridical experience and the criticism of the common consciousness of legal thought; (2) the concept of law and the nature of the juridical order leading to a critique of the technique of laws; and (3) the indications of the tendencies of juridical evolution and the criticism of the historical consciousness of right. It is thus seen that while the deontologic standpoint is rejected and we are repeatedly warned that we must not give norms to experience, it is nevertheless kept in a powdered form in the treatment of the separate questions.

While jurists dealing with their own subject matter have thus been raising vital philosophic issues from new points of view, their results when they consciously turn to general philosophy do not seem to me to be of much value, for when they leave their own field they are inclined to accept inadequate traditional principles that were framed without regard to the specific subject matter of the jurist. This seems to me to be well illustrated in the introductory volume of Geny's *Science et technique en droit privé positif* (1914). Geny, indeed, attempts to avoid this difficulty by choosing freely elements from scholastic common sense, Bergsonian intuition, and the psychology and sociology of positivism; but very little of his *approfondisement* of legal method moves outside of the traditional and somewhat antiquated logic and psychology embodied in such books as Ribot's *Evolution of General Ideas* and the ordinary text-book of formal logic. The footnotes, indeed, contain an astonishing number of references to modern classical treatises on the methodology of the natural and social sciences, yet the substance of the book impresses one as nothing more than a collection of the commonplaces of familiar epistemology illustrated with legal material. The fundamental distinction of the book between science and technique (the former dealing with what is given and the latter with what is constructed) is certainly not clearly thought out. (Witness, for example, the reference to technique as "the work of artificial if not arbitrary will." [22a]) There are, of course, many valuable observations in the book, but these, like the remarks on analogy,[23] are independent of the main thesis and were, indeed, substantially embodied in his earlier book.

While Geny's philosophic eclecticism reminds one of Cousin, the elaborate bibliographic footnotes, the formal long-winded introductions and divisions of the subject, and other ceremonious delay in getting down to the subject matter, and, above all, the naïve faith in epistemology show the tremendous influence that Germany has been exercising lately on intellectual France. Geny is impressed by the fact that Berolzheimer's five volume treatise on legal philosophy [24] devotes the first volume to epistemology. But is there a single problem in the four subsequent volumes of Berolzheimer's book that is decided by reference to the first? I can see no more connection there than between the saying of grace before meals and the composition of the dishes.

The large volume of M. Fabreguettes, entitled *La logique judiciaire et l'art de juger* (1914), contains some interesting remarks on evidence and other matters, but bears little on juristic logic. Much more of the last topic will be found in an unpretentious contribution to the Wach *Festschrift* (1912) by Wehli, "Beiträge zur Analyse der Urteilsfindung." [24a]

I have restricted this survey to philosophic efforts on the part of professional jurists. I ought to mention, in conclusion, several noteworthy attempts to enlarge philosophic technique to enable it to cope more adequately with legal as well as other material. The philosophy of Husserl, like that of Meinong, with its attempt to free the consideration of the essence or character of things from the question of their existence, seems to me of great promise for jurisprudence in the direction of simplifying needlessly complicated problems like that of legal personality, animus and corpus in possession, etc. Unfortunately, however, the study in Husserl's *Jahrbuch* (1913) devoted to this topic, "Die apriorischen Grundlagen des bürgerlichen Rechts," by Reinach, is too much dominated by an unclear conception as to what is *a priori* and by the common weakness of those unacquainted with legal history, namely, that of regarding certain arrangements as logically necessary when they are merely the results of historical accident.

Another effort to develop a Kantian *Kulturphilosophie*, along lines suggested by Hermann Cohen's *Ethik des reinen Willens*, is Münch's *Erlebnis und Geltung* (Supplement No. 30 to the *Kantstudien*). Münch tries to show how the regulative function of ideas determines the content of practical judgments and how ethics as a transcendental philosophy of history can enable us to determine which system of value represents concrete reason for the present state of civilization. Münch makes out a very clear case against philosophies of the type of those of Carlyle, Hegel, or the popular evolutionists who think that everything that triumphs is necessarily in the right. But he has not as yet offered us any satisfactory criterion to enable us to choose which of the historical systems of value are the preferable ones. Indeed he himself seems very close to the Hegelian point of view.

On an entirely independent basis, philosophically and juristically, is Walter Pollak's *Perspektive und Symbol in Philosophie und Rechtswissenschaft* (1913). Every science is, as a creative activity and vital effort, historically determined by certain volitions and interests, and in turn modifies these. The question then may be raised not of the absolute correctness of a science but of the extent to which it satisfies the vital demands that brought it forth. In the elaboration of perspectives or points of view, symbols or picturesque expressions appeal to the scientific imagination so as not only to give it satisfaction but also to suggest further research and the discovery of new relations. This is applied in a very suggestive way to the field of law and to the way in which juristic conceptions are determined by laws, customs, and the world-view of the time, but in turn modify all these. Juristic method thus has to use history, sociology, and even theology as heuristic principles.

II

Modern French Legal Philosophy [25]

There are two ways in which one can try to induce an American student of law to become familiar with foreign thought on the subject. One may thrust at him a systematic treatise like Jhering's or Kohler's, which begins with fundamentals, and say to him: "Go to it. Master this book and you will be able to reflect on your own work all the better." This may be the way of thoroughness, but it is certainly forbidding, and if the testimony of personal experience be worth anything, also barren. The other way is to bring the student into contact with judiciously chosen representative essays or extracts that pick up the thread of the argument nearer the concrete material where the student's daily thoughts leave him. If one can thus manage to strike fire and arouse genuine interest, the way for more thorough study is opened. The selections from the works of Charmont, Duguit, and Demogue published under the title *Modern French Legal Philosophy* are well calculated to arouse such interest.

It is a penchant for systematic completeness that has misled the editor of this volume to include so much from Fouillée. Fouillée was a prolific writer and a man of fine character, but his facile characterization of the French, German, and English "spirit" and his peculiar doctrine of *idée-force* have been neither influential nor representative of French legal-philosophical thought. In a history of French culture, Fouillée might very well be used as an illustration of the national liberalism that established the Third Republic and led to the breaking of the Concordat. But there are certainly many portions of the works of Saleilles, Tarde, Tanon, or Hauriou —not to mention Durkheim—that would have been far more appropriate for the present purpose.

The selection from Charmont includes the greater portion of his book, *La renaissance du droit naturel* (1910). Charmont draws no distinction between natural law, juristic idealism, and juristic individualism. Hence he finds a revival of natural law not only in the work of Stammler and Geny, but also, in the juristic recognition of social solidarity, in the work of Duguit, and even in pragmatism. But while this inevitably involves a radical vagueness in Charmont's own constructive suggestions, his book is one of the most effective exposés of the practical bankruptcy of the historical and positivistic schools of jurisprudence. In the search for a satisfactory basis for the distinction between just and unjust law, the historical and positivistic schools have been able to offer us little help, and their boasted refutation of the normative standpoint of the old natural law is an illusion. They have unconsciously set up a tyrannical natural law of their own, inimical to the freedom of the individual and to legal progress. Charmont is at his best in pointing out how the ultra-positivist Duguit gets back, in spite of himself, to the normative natural-law attitude in his theory of an objective law based on social solidarity. Duguit's recent work, in spite of his professed hostility to the standpoint of "the rights of man," bears out this point of Charmont. For does not Duguit's limitation of the sovereignty of the state, and his doctrine of unconstitutional legislation, carry us far into the old natural law?

Duguit is represented in this volume by nearly one hundred and ten pages of translation from the first volume of his *Etudes de droit public* (1901). These selections give a fairly good idea of Duguit's vigorous and unconventional method of attacking the problem of the law and the state; and his criticisms of the great German publicists like Gierke or Jellinek are certainly lively and suggestive. But on some points his more recent books show a new departure, and it is a pity that they are not in any way represented in this volume. Mr. Spencer's own comments on Duguit seem to me very illuminating.

The last part of this volume consists of a translation of Book I of Demogue's *Les notions fondamentales du droit privé* (1911). This seems to me by far the most valuable work on the philosophy of law published within the last few generations. Its value consists not only in the extraordinary wealth of ideas that fill almost every page, but even more in the wonderful way in which it steers between the Scylla of dogmatism and the Charybdis of scepticism. A contrast between this book and any of the works of the great German jurist Stammler is very instructive. Stammler has undoubtedly brought forth several important fruitful ideas. But he seems to take it for granted that they will be valueless unless they are spun out in all directions with excessive formalism. Demogue is satisfied merely to present his ideas in a suggestive way, leaving it to the reader to make the obvious applications. Stammler works in black and white; everything is rigid and absolutely certain; there is no room in his world for any "perhaps." Demogue realizes the complexity of human affairs and the limitations of all the first principles that have been suggested as solutions for all possible legal problems. Instead of offering a new first principle of his own, he is satisfied to render the more useful service of indicating the scope and possible applications of many of the first principles that do play a rôle in the life of the law. His discussion of the conflict between the need for security of possession and the need for security in transaction carries philosophic ideas very near men's "business and bosoms." Equally pertinent is his discussion of the various interests served by the law and the proper place in it of the principles of justice, equality, and liberty. To one who regrets that the whole of Demogue's volume was not here translated, it is some consolation to reflect how difficult it is to render into English his terse and beautiful French.

May this volume help to destroy that widespread but foolish notion that in legal thought this country must forever remain a British colony! Perhaps it may remind us that in the creative period of American law men like Kent and Story drew heavily on French civilians like Domat, and that those framers of our Constitution who wrote the *Federalist* drew their inspiration not only from Montesquieu but also (as regards their ideas on federalism) from Mably, with whom they were more familiar than with Polybius.

III

Rudolf von Jhering [26]

Despite its great influence upon Continental law and jurisprudence, Jhering's *Zweck im Recht* is a work of antiquated psychology and mediocre philosophic power. In view, however, of recent discussions of pragmatism, its theme, if not the execution, is of timely interest. In the course of a long and energetic career, as a writer and professor of law, Jhering became dissatisfied with the method of the historical school of jurisprudence, which since the day of Savigny had held undisputed sway. Contrary to its view that law is always the result of deterministic, unconscious evolution of a *Volksgeist*, Jhering became convinced that law is the result of a conscious effort and struggle on the part of individuals; and that instead of the prevailing method of deducing the content of law by conceptual analysis of its necessary nature, its end or purpose was rather to be sought for.

As the philosophy of the historical school had, with the aid of ideas taken over from Schelling and Hegel, been worked out with the appearance of great thoroughness, Jhering felt obliged to work out a contrary philosophy of his own. Unfortunately, however, Jhering had no philosophic training or native ability in that direction. His mind was broad rather than deep, fruitful in shrewd insight (sometimes bordering on the commonplace), but so mastered by his material as to be unable to affect a stable organization of the large ideas that his material suggested. Thus, accepting the popular mechanical psychology and sociology of his day (1877), he assumes conscious egoism as the sole motive power of human life, and tries to show how, by means of a system of levers (reward and coercion), the social institutions of commerce and law are built up. In the course of this process, society, or the more enlightened portion of the community, steps in like a *deus ex machina*. But the nearer Jhering comes to the legal material with which he is more familiar, the more he forgets his peculiar intellectual ritual and lets the situation speak for itself. Thus his condemnation of legal egoism,[27] his critique of the laissez-faire policy of Humboldt and Mill, his distinction between the point of view of sacrifice and the one in which the individual identifies his end with that of the community,[28] are not only independent of his fundamental assumptions, but will be found to be inconsistent with them.

The idea of purpose in law is undoubtedly a far-reaching and fruitful one, but divorced from a comprehensive philosophy of life and human values it becomes futile, offering no test or method of deciding between conflicting purposes. Thus Jhering finds the problem of the proper limitation of state activity insoluble and concludes that "legislatures will, in the future as in the past, measure restrictions of personal liberty not according to an abstract academic formula, but according to practical need." [29] But what *is* the *greater* practical need in any given situation largely depends on our implicit philosophy of life. Here as elsewhere, Jhering fails because empty rationalism and blind empiricism exhaust for him (as for others) the possibilities of scientific method. The study of Kant might at least have cured him of that limitation.

For some reason or other utilitarianism (and may we not say pragmatism?) has generally been supposed to be necessarily associated with empiricism or positivism, and it is well to note with Professor Geldart [30] that there is no inconsistency between utilitarianism and idealism, certainly not if utilitarianism is defined as "nothing but the refusal to isolate any part of human action and to consider it apart from its consequences." [31] A close examination of any field of practice like law shows it is always some union of utilitarianism with idealism, like the Platonic, Kantian, or Hegelian, that proves the most effective.

In spite of Jhering's philosophic limitations the translation of the first volume of his *Zweck im Recht* will be useful to the legal profession of this country, which is still predominantly under the influence of legal scholasticism or, as Professor Pound calls it, the mechanical jurisprudence of concepts. American jurists as a body also need the keen criticisms of the individualistic maxims of our law, and need to be reminded that "it is not true that property involves in its 'idea' the absolute power of disposition," and that "the principle of the inviolability of property means the delivery of society into the hands of ignorance, obstinacy, and spite." [32]

Geldart's very meaty introduction to the English translation of Jhering's work calls attention to the great differences between the English common law and German civil law due to the fact that the latter has been taught in the universities while the former has been taught in unacademic professional guilds, the Inns of Court. What Geldart says of England is, in spite of the more or less close connection between our law schools and universities, still true of the United States. For our law schools, much older than our real universities, have up to this day been entirely dominated by practical professional aims; and until the last generation their graduates formed but a small part of the legal profession. The recent expansion, however, of our universities has brought about the rise of a class of law teachers who look upon law teaching as their profession (instead of an addition to their practice), and this is bound to bring about a scientific study of the law such as prevails in civil law countries. Indeed the publication of the Modern Legal Philosophy Series and other similar ventures are fair indications of it.

A second introduction by Chief Justice Lamm, of the Supreme Court of Missouri, is fairly typical of the old and established order of juristic thought in this country. Finding that Jhering's views rest on a Darwinian theory of natural evolution (against which, however, see Jhering's preface), the Justice feels it his duty to call attention to this dangerous novelty. Thus: "Is the 'fall' of man an unthinkable hypothesis? Are the concepts of justice, right . . . and all the noble precepts of natural law and natural equity, and moral law, the result of a slow evolution through the ages, the result of mere cause and effect? Or, are they of divine origin, implanted by his Maker in the breast of the just man, as some of us old-fashioned folks were taught to believe? . . . Is it not the instinctive deference to and reliance on those natural equities, as implanted by Heaven in the human breast, that causes constitutional limitations to be put on the power of the legislature to abrogate them by law?" [33] Thus we learn that the fall of man and constitutional limitations on our legislatures are part of the same orthodoxy. Judge Lamm, I suppose, represents the liberal spirit among our American judges and older practitioners. There are certainly many who do not speak of the new heresies in so kindly and urbane a fashion.

IV

Joseph Kohler [34]

A succinct account of Kohler's general philosophy and its relation to law will be found in the first chapter of his *Moderne Rechtsprobleme*. Law is a part of human culture (i.e., of the process of human development), and can be understood fully only in a philosophy that grasps the character and aim of this development. In spite of an obviously eclectic tendency, which shows itself in a predilection for such diverse modes of thought as Hindu mysticism, Hegel, and Nietzsche, Kohler's temperament will not allow any other alternatives than extreme positivism and his own pantheism. The arguments by which he establishes his position are vehement and suggestive, but not always logically convincing. Certainly the fact that positivism happens to be of French and English origin is not a scientific argument against it even in Germany. Moreover when one considers Kohler's use of history and the actual content of his legal system, one has reason to suspect that his differences with the positivists are more formal than substantial. This is particularly true of his treatment of criminal law and procedure, which occupies more than half of his *Moderne Rechtsprobleme*.

Kohler begins his discussion of criminal law in the approved German manner, with a series of elaborate arguments for free will against determinism. In spite, however, of his protestation that this is the basic problem of criminology, he does not make out a real difference between the empirical consequences of his position and those of determinism. Not only are the influences of heredity and environment admitted, as well as the possibility of making valid inferences from the past to the future conduct of an individual, but also the whole tendency of Kohler's penologic policy is to minimize the importance of personal punishment (e.g., in the case of those we euphemistically call "cadets"), and to emphasize the preventive and meliorative functions of the state, not merely in the education of the young, but by state regulation of industry, the liquor traffic, the activity of the press, etc. His favourite penal device is such deportation as will enable the deported to begin life again under the proper conditions. (His statement that the results of the Russian system of deportation to Siberia and Sakhalien are most favourable is certainly not borne out by the best statistical information.) To be sure, Kohler sharply distinguishes between the right to *punish*, based on corrective or retributive justice, and the merely utilitarian idea of *prevention*, or even of ethical help. But no necessity for this metaphysical idea of retribution is established. If we give up all utilitarian ideas of social welfare, what necessity is there that the universe should be organized like a penitentiary, on the basis of rewards and punishments?

The argument that the notion of sin is the distinctive basis of Christianity and of our whole cultural system is not well founded. The concept of sin is also found among the ancient Babylonians, and among some very primitive peoples. Moreover, the notion of sin has no inherent connection with that of free will. Familiarity with penitential hymns, from the days of the Babylonians and the Old Testament down to the days of Thomas à Kempis or of Calvinism, shows that sin is not always regarded as a voluntary affair. The whole institution of sacrifice is based on the idea that sin is a more or less contagious body, with which people may come in contact and be contaminated in spite of themselves.

As observed above, the homage that Kohler pays to the metaphysical idea of retribution or atonement does not seriously interfere with his detailed views on penologic problems. Imprisonment to protect us against those who threaten our possessions is justified when these possessions are sufficiently important. The closest connection between Kohler's metaphysics and his criminology is perhaps to be found in his complacent belief that increase of crime does not hinder the progress of civilization.

In matters of criminal procedure, Kohler is an ardent admirer of English methods. His knowledge, however, of the history of English criminal procedure is not very accurate; witness his denial that torture ever formed part of English procedure. (Even as late as the eighteenth century, torture was legally used to compel the accused to plead.)

Though Kohler's attitude toward Continental criminal procedure is rather critical, he believes that more important than legislative changes is the adoption in spirit of two maxims: (1) No one is to be compelled to testify against himself, and (2) the defence is as sacred as the accusation or investigation. Kohler is inclined to view the former as an eternal self-evident principle, as a corollary to the principle of freedom of will. But if the maxim is taken thus rigorously, there can be no justification for compelling any one whose welfare is in any way bound up with the accused to testify, or for the state to examine the private books, papers, etc., of the accused. Our own experience in this country has amply demonstrated that this principle is useful only when properly qualified. Carried beyond its proper limitations, this principle has caused infinite mischief in the form of "immunity baths" etc.

Kohler's regard for the right of the accused leads him to urge that the person found innocent should not only have his actual costs repaid by the state, but should also be reimbursed for the trouble and loss sustained by the arrest and trial. He thinks it is due to the influence of capitalism that people get excited at the prospect of the state taking away the private property of an individual, but make no protest at the state taking away from an innocent person the personal right of freedom (and all that it carries with it) without any remuneration. But capitalism is hardly the root of this anomaly. It is rather to be found in the preoccupation of all our Western legal systems with the idea of property; witness the common law of torts as regards seduction and injury to feelings.

Kohler also uses the recent discoveries of psychology in regard to the fallibility or aberrations of perception and memory, to point out the danger of pressing witnesses or parties so as to extract a full story, or of supposing that the agreement of two independent witnesses is necessarily conclusive as to the facts of the case or as to the falsity of one who tells a somewhat different story.

On the question of the jury system, as in the other matters of criminal procedure, Kohler is an enthusiastic admirer of the English. Because of the difficulty of framing questions that a jury can readily and unambiguously answer by yes or no, he would seem to be in favour of general rather than special verdicts. The peculiar modifications of the jury system in states like New York, which make it a fit instrument to delay or defeat justice, are apparently unknown to Kohler. He favours the active participation of laymen in criminal as well as in trade and commercial courts, (1) to offset the one-sidedness resulting from technical preoccupations, and (2) to bring into the administration of justice the knowledge of the usual modes of thought and conduct, how people are affected by various transactions, etc. Kohler's classical philosophy will, of course, not allow him to say that the advantage of the jury system is that it makes our criminal procedure conformable not to abstract justice, but to the sense of justice of the community.

To the main objection to the jury system that it represents untrained intelligence, which therefore is unable to understand the psychology of evidence, Kohler answers that jurists are likely to overemphasize their own material (i.e., records), while jurymen may use the same caution that they employ in their daily business. Still, Kohler would have one jurist on the jury to explain legal questions, and would take certain purely technical questions, like those of psychiatry, entirely away from the jury.

v

Hugo Krabbe [35]

Professor Krabbe's volume on *The Modern Idea of the State* is a book that utterly fails to make any serious contribution to the subject, and would not be worth the attention of philosophers or jurists if it were not for the fact that its irresponsible sentimentalism is rather significantly characteristic of the prevailing wave of anti-intellectualism. "Irresponsible sentimentalism" may be an unusually severe judgment on a supposedly scientific work, but I cannot see that any other characterization fits the position of one who believes in abandoning the intellect and letting political life be guided by instincts or feelings of what is right and wrong.[36]

Professor Krabbe's thesis, which he supports with more iteration than evidence, is that the modern state is based on law and that law is nothing but the feeling of right and wrong. With proper restrictions and qualifications this is obviously a part of the truth, which has been maintained by numerous writers from Aristotle to Schlossman and Jellinek. But restriction and qualification, even in such complex subjects as law and politics, are foreign to the temper of anti-intellectualists, who care more for the wide sweep of their theses and are willing to ignore the absurd consequences that follow from them. Now it is quite obvious that a large part of the law today is concerned with technical matters that are morally indifferent, in the narrower sense of the term, and on which the vast majority of the laymen in the community have no ideas or feelings of any kind; they do not even know of their existence. Moreover, a great deal of the law is, for many reasons, directly contrary to the prevailing sense of right. Powerful and unscrupulous minorities frequently write their will into the statute books. Even laws that originally represented the popular conception of right may cease to do so under changed conditions and yet be maintained through the organized selfish insistence of the few or the inertia of the many.

These obvious considerations are passed over by Professor Krabbe without any serious attention. The part that the intellect, in the form of legal science and technique, plays and must play in the development of any rational legal system he passes over with one contemptuous reference;[37] and the glaring fact of the frequent conflicts between law and the popular sense of right and wrong he dismisses with the facile assertion that any statute contrary to what the majority feels to be right, is not law at all, even though it be actually enforced and obeyed. The motive of such an arbitrary limitation of the word "law" (to denote law felt to be just by the majority) would be comprehensible (though not justified) if Krabbe were an adherent of the doctrine of men like Lorimer, that only just or natural law is law at all. But as he claims to be a positivist and aims to describe the positive law that actually prevails,[38] his position seems to me hopelessly confusing. It would certainly be regarded as the height of absurdity for any one to maintain that the Federal Constitution under which the people of the United States have been living for over one hundred and fifty years is not the law of the land, in that it provides that it cannot be amended by a bare majority vote. Yet so enamoured is Professor Krabbe with his thesis, and so disdainful of the realm of facts, that he calmly maintains this patent absurdity in principle.[39]

These considerations are so obvious that it seems highly instructive to consider why a professor of public law at a great historic university should so flagrantly overlook them and yet his book be deemed worthy of translation into English. The answer seems to me to be found in the fact that this book, like others that have appeared recently, represents an intense reaction against the highly unsatisfactory character of our dominant political theories. These theories are not only offensive by virtue of their dry pedantry and futile scholastic refinement, but even more so by their ignoring of the aspirations of man for a better state of human society. But the limitations of pedantry and scholasticism can be overcome only by more adequate learning and more persistent thought, just as the human craving for a more satisfactory emotional life can be better satisfied by rational organization than by relying on the feelings of the moment. But whatever may be said of the effects on art and conduct of the present wave of impatience with, and contempt for, organized intellectual deliberation, it can certainly never accomplish anything in the field of science. The fact, therefore, that at the basis of Professor Krabbe's effort there is sympathy for the spiritual nature of man only makes his failure more pathetic.

The dangers of a purely sentimental sympathy with the spiritual nature of man, i.e., a sympathy without careful analysis either of what that spiritual nature is or of the conditions under which it can best express itself, are well illustrated in the practical conclusion to which Professor Krabbe arrives on the subject of international law.

Completely ignoring the tragic events of recent decades, with their recrudescence of all forms of brute violence, the author complacently asserts that "we no longer live under the dominion of persons, either natural or fictitious legal persons, but under the dominion of norms of spiritual forces," [40] and that international law is one of these norms.[41] But as the author cannot altogether escape the patent fact that actual international law, based on common consent, is very frail and undeveloped, his concluding solution is a brute tyranny in international affairs like that of the early modern kings when "a self-constituted sovereign, standing above the patch-work of legal communities and superior to an unorganized judiciary, was able by means of an instrument of power dependent upon itself alone to imbue the entire people with the idea of authority." [42] German world-imperialism at its worst never went as far as this.

The long introduction that the translators have added to this book seems to me to move on a far higher intellectual plane than the book itself. It is a pity, however, that they did not apply to their author the same keen criticism that they have directed against others. Thus, when they show that amorphous concepts like "the people" cannot supply a basis for sovereignty, one feels they should have gone on to show how impossible it is for "the people's" sense of right to produce of itself an actual body of definite law. The sense of right cannot by itself produce a legal system, any more than the sense of comfort can by itself produce suspension bridges or irrigation canals. Without the conceptual work of intelligence, feelings remain blind, as the sage of Königsberg long ago pointed out.

There are a number of subsidiary but not unimportant points on which the assertions of the translators seem to me open to question. One of these is that Locke has been more influential politically than

Hobbes. This seems true if we judge by the number of times Locke is still quoted. But Hobbes's great contribution to politics, the legal supremacy of civil over ecclesiastical authority, was so effectively done that few outside of the late Mr. Figgis have questioned it.

The facts of the case do not seem to me to justify the translators' denial of the proposition that corporations have no legal rights except what the state accords them. If the state should declare any corporation illegal, the corporation may continue to exist, but illegal it will be, no matter how justified it may be morally in refusing to obey the law. With all due admiration for Gierke's prodigious learning, we must decide he has not yet overthrown the fiction theory of corporations.

As others have done in recent attacks against the theory of sovereignty, the translators rely on a confusion between jural and politico-moral considerations. Thus they argue that the rule of the British constitution which makes a cabinet resign upon an adverse vote is law even though the courts cannot enforce it. To which the answer is that nothing is to be gained by confusing the custom with the law of the constitution. The custom is enforced by the demands of parliamentary life (but it has at times been broken). The law is enforced by the courts. The circumstances of parliamentary life make it now impossible for a man with a divorce record to hold a cabinet position, just as it would be impossible for him to be a college president. You may call it metaphorically an unwritten law, but it is intellectually clearer to call it what it is, custom or convention. The distinction between law and custom is jurally clear and useful. Why abandon it?

Finally, I must respectfully protest against the too facile reduction of both altruism and egoism to patently foolish propositions. Altruism and egoism, like other "isms," are doubtless one-sided, and the whole truth is certainly not included in either. But no influential altruist or egoist in the history of philosophy has maintained the foolishness imputed to him by the translators of this book.[43]

VI

Giorgio del Vecchio [44]

Professor del Vecchio is today one of the most distinguished European teachers of the philosophy of law. He has a thorough command of the literature of his subject, and his criticism of the regnant Continental positivism is acute and penetrating. But specializing in the philosophy of law exposes one to objections from both philosophers and lawyers. It is true that the essence of law is not grasped by a purely historical treatment, but from this it does not follow that an *a priori* handling of the concept of law is a safe method of getting insight in this field. It is true that conceptual analysis plays a greater part in law than in almost any other science, but Del Vecchio does not take account of the formidable movement of protest among jurists against the mischief of this formalism or *Begriffsjurisprudenz*. This movement deserves all the more respect because it is in line with the tendency of all modern science, including mathematics.

Indeed, our author's own analysis of the concept of law shows how many things can escape the deductive net. Thus he holds it as self-evident that law must deal with will-acts, but the laws of a civilized country hold me responsible for the acts of my servant done contrary to my orders, or entitle me to inherit the goods of my uncle, though the latter's living and dying as my uncle was not due to any act of mine. According to Del Vecchio's analysis, law is always determined by some ethical principle. But not only does the consciousness of mankind testify to the existence of iniquitous laws but also a great deal of law, like the rule of the road, is not directly concerned with ethics at all. In the development of the law of a subject like mortgages, the jurist finds that consideration of justice will not carry him very far. Much law depends on technical rules, the logic of analogy, etc. The real danger in the method of conceptual analysis consists in temptation to separate law from the context of life and to treat it as if it had a separate existence. In point of fact, however, law always presupposes that people are moved by certain motives, and endeavours to control or modify these results by artificial weights or sanctions in the form of civil or criminal liability. The conceptual treatment of legal rules is thus likely to miss the fact that these rules take their meaning from the social mores which they attempt to strengthen or deflect. The unintelligible character of law apart from the conditions of life to which it applies is seen clearly when we study a foreign system like the Roman or Hindu law.

The confusion between law as it is and law as it ought to be is facilitated in Europe by the fact that the word for "right" and "law" is the same (*diritto, droit, Recht*). Del Vecchio is also influenced in this respect by his adherence to Kant, who habitually confused existence and validity. This is seen in such statements as that historical progress is a dictate of reason.[45] The question whether there has actually been more progress than degeneration is one of the weight of factual evidence and is not to be settled by dictates of reason.[46]

All of the advanced sciences are today outgrowing the juvenile fear of metaphysics, and Del Vecchio renders a real service in pointing out that formal study only renders clear what otherwise we would only assume unconsciously.[47] This, however, does not necessitate the assumption of the whole Kantian metaphysical machinery. The principle that no human being should be treated merely as a means is, within certain limits, valuable, but does not really depend on the notion of the absolute ego or freedom. The only use Del Vecchio makes of this principle of absolute freedom is to condemn slavery absolutely. But this, as Kohler has shown, is not at all a closed question. It certainly is not when we ask what slavery is.

If books like Del Vecchio's are to aid us in getting rid of the old eighteenth century natural law and in finding some tenable rational criterion for the evaluation of our law, the limitation of the Kantian formalism must be recognized.

ON THREE POLITICAL SCIENTISTS[1]

I T IS one of the ironies of fate that concentrated study, so essential to real achievement in any field, tends also to make us lose the right perspective as to the relation of our chosen field to life as a whole. We readily recognize this irony in the old-time humanists who, to open up the treasures of ancient literature, had to devote their lives to the intricacies of Latin syntax, so that they naturally came to regard Latin prose composition as the centre of all human education. Can it be that the modern humanist engaged in the study of politics is entirely free from this irony of fate? Food for reflection in this regard is afforded by three recent contributions to political science, Herbert Fisher's *Studies in History and Politics*, Léon Duguit's *Law in the Modern State*, and Harold Laski's *Foundations of Sovereignty*.

The first book is by the distinguished historian of the republican tradition in Europe. As historian, essayist, and statesman, Mr. Fisher continues the great tradition of Macaulay, Bryce, and Morley—a tradition of wide and accurate learning, cautious and sound judgment, mildly liberal aspirations, and a gentlemanly silence about the grimy soil of human nature and selfish interests, wherein questions of public policy have their roots if not their justification. Thus Mr. Fisher explains carefully and frankly why British administration in India is the costliest in the world. But the economic and social effects of this government of India, on Great Britain as well as on India itself, are ignored.

Mr. Fisher knows too much history and actual politics to fall into the view of amateurs that our fragmentary knowledge of the past can directly solve for us the perplexing problems of the present.

History is rather a field in which to apply and thus develop our political judgment and imagination. For the soul of history is not so much the acquisition and arrangement of material as the exercise of insight and appreciation. Mr. Fisher's own insight thus manifests itself in his reflections on particular events or issues. Typical of the best of these is the observation that while arbitration cannot banish war, it can diminish the accumulation of minor grievances. At other times, however, we have comments like the following: "Military conscription is an honourable duty to the state, a school of patriotic virtue," etc. But though it unified Prussia it has "given a military direction to the thoughts, feelings, and aspirations of a vigorous people." [2]

In the main, Mr. Fisher represents the school that views history as predominantly a matter of politics. The weakness of this in concrete cases shows itself in the essay on Lord Acton, which leaves us without any explanation of the relative barrenness of that prodigiously learned man. One wonders what Mr. Fisher himself thinks of Lord Acton's amazing judgment that George Eliot is the greatest figure in literature since the death of Goethe.

Mr. Fisher shows eminent good sense in explaining why Rousseau prevailed so decidedly despite his obvious limitations. Instead of wasting excessive ingenuity on this point, as do most writers on Rousseau nowadays, Fisher relies rather on the obvious fact that Rousseau was right, that he was attacking an unjust and corrupt order which richly deserved to be overthrown. It is a pity, however, that a historian should repeat the popular myth that Rousseau's *Social Contract* was "founded on imaginary history." The second sentence of that book—so often referred to but so seldom read—amply refutes that charge.

No one can read through Mr. Fisher's book without a feeling that it deserves the honorific epithets which the author himself is so fond of applying, viz., thorough, solid, robust, and masculine. The latter term occurs so often as to suggest by contrast why this and other admirable books on politics by Bryce, Morley, etc. are after all somewhat dull—they lack what Goethe calls the eternally feminine that ever draws or lures us on.

Professor Duguit's book is more unified not only because it has a single theme but even more so by the fact that it has a definite thesis to maintain. In his predilection for general ideas, Duguit is as typically French as Fisher is English in his cautious avoidance of them. This is all the more significant in that Duguit restricts himself to the field of law and professes adherence to strict scientific methods and a positivistic abhorrence for metaphysics. His positivism, however, like most positivisms, turns out to be not a greater respect for facts, but rather a zeal for dogmas that are sharply antithetic to the old dogmas. If the older theories of law are individualistic, subjective, and moralistic, the new theory must be collectivistic, objective, and realistic. Of course, a trained and accomplished scholar can readily find many facts to show that this is the trend of history. Doubtless also the new dogmas explain some facts better than did the old ones. But what Duguit naïvely ignores is that history cares little for the comfort of theorists, even of the positivistic kind, and brings forth plenty of facts to comfort and confound both sides.

Thus the individualist can point to various forms of property that used to be communal but which are now individual, to family obligations which have been modified in the interests of greater individual freedom, and many similar considerations. Duguit can readily show that the will of the state or people, which is the alleged basis of legal sovereignty, is a metaphysical fiction. But he states more than he can prove when he asserts in opposition that all law originates not in any human will but in the objective conditions that are necessary for the public service. The obvious fact is that many laws are passed because some people want them although these laws may not aid the public service in the least and may in fact hinder it. The citizen who would disregard these laws because Duguit says that such enactments have no legal force, will find himself in serious trouble with the law.

Duguit's antimoralistic bias, based on a superficial theory that

science can deal only with what is and never with what ought to be,
cuts him off from any consistent argument as to what ought to be
the law. His assertion that the objective conditions of social coöperation themselves dictate all the law is as mythical as the social will
which he rejects. Laws are in fact made by definite human beings
and in accordance with their desires, prejudices, perceptions, etc.,
and wilful or unwilful ignorance of the objective conditions of good
laws is certainly a patent fact in actual law-making. So long as
human beings, devoid of omniscience, have to guess as to what will
be the effect of their enactments, the adaptation of laws to the public
service will always remain something to be desired rather than
something completely achieved.

Duguit tries to save his doctrine of the legal nullity of statutes
that do not promote the public service by arguing that courts should
have the power to declare certain statutes unconstitutional. As a
positivist he cannot say they ought to do so, nor that in France they
actually do so; he can only affirm his own guess that they will do so
in the future. It is interesting, however, to note that Duguit, like the
defenders of the judicial power in this country, argues on *a priori*
logic, and not on the basis of the actual results that have ensued from
the American practice of having the opinion of courts prevail over
the combined opinion of legislature and executive as to the meaning
of the Constitution. Certainly no one has as yet shown that where
courts have overruled the legislature and executive their decisions
have always rested on sounder views and more thorough knowledge
as to the actual needs of the situation.

Duguit's book is undoubtedly keen, learned, lively, and instructive. He is especially illuminating in showing how people are actually governed by the rules of private corporations, etc. In the main
he has sound moral views and stands strongly for the rights of minorities and other rights of man. But his doctrinaire positivism compels him ostentatiously to chase all rights and moral considerations
through the front door only to let them in surreptitiously through
a back door. The futility of this unedifying proceeding becomes ob-

vious when we realize that by no hocus-pocus can we extract a description of what ought to be from a mere description of the facts that are. If "what should be" is not contained in our premises, it cannot be logically found in our conclusions.

Mr. Laski combines the English historical with the French theoretical method of approach to political discussion, and he writes with a learning and vivacious enthusiasm all his own. Mr. Laski burst upon the American scene in 1916, a dashing young Lochinvar who soon made us feel that our official custodians of political science were somewhat passé. Nevertheless, though it is impossible to read this book of Mr. Laski's without admiration for many telling points, his main ideas as to the nature of sovereignty are by no means clear or convincing. In his zeal to overthrow old views he does not stop to analyze them carefully. He does not always discriminate between sovereignty as a legal concept and the historical fact of actual political power. No one has maintained that any actual human government is in fact omnipotent and can achieve anything at all that it wishes to. The essence of the traditional doctrine of sovereignty is that in applying the law, a judge or administrative official must not allow the rules of any church, trade union, or any other body to prevail over the law of the state, which he is sworn to enforce. Obviously, if the law of the state could at any time be set aside by private groups within it, there would be no use in having any common system of law and courts. I do not know whether Mr. Laski now disputes the necessity for this sovereignty of the state law in its own courts, though in his first two books [3] he seemed to argue that the courts might set aside a law when it conflicts with conscience or the doctrines of some church—a proposal that if accepted would lead to legal anarchy. When Mr. Laski now argues for plural sovereignty, he seems to have in mind a political scheme by which the central political authority will give up the attempt to legislate on all matters and leave a great many things to be determined by private corporations and syndicates. On this point he makes many telling arguments, especially in the admirable essay on "Administrative Areas."

But to my understanding, few modern writers deny that our legislatures are overloaded and are incompetent to pass on the bewildering variety of all the phases of modern life. If Mr. Laski were to content himself with urging such delegation of legislative power to the extent that it proves feasible, few would disagree with him. Such devolution of legislative power is in no way inconsistent with the sovereignty of the law. For any arrangement by which it would be effected would itself become part of the organic law of the state. But Mr. Laski does not seem to be willing to urge his program as a working hypothesis, to be tried wherever it serves vital needs. He must needs defend it with the dogma of pluralistic sovereignty, and that of the real personality of corporations. Thereby he gets himself into gratuitous trouble. You cannot cure the evils of monistic absolutism by multiplying the number of absolute sovereigns, and the belief in the actual personality of every corporation subjects him to the taunt of turning what is a legal fiction into a communal ghost.

Common fairness compels us to add that Mr. Laski's good sense frequently makes him arrive at sound conclusions despite his inadequate dogmas. Thus in his valuable essay on "Vicarious Liability" he has no hesitation in speaking of the "impersonality" of large corporations employing thousands of men. But Mr. Laski ignores entirely the grave dangers to the freedom of the individual involved in his pluralistic régime, though it is a notorious fact that local tyrants can, if not interfered with from without, oppress us far more effectively than a tyrannous central government. Modern monarchies did not arise, as one might suppose from certain unguarded statements of Mr. Laski,[4] because people at the time of the counter-reformation fell in love with the concept of unity. Modern monarchies arose because the tyranny of one king was the effective means whereby modern enterprise was liberated from the more oppressive tyrannies of local barons and guilds. This is a capital fact which all those who preach a return to medievalism should not ignore.

The limitations of Mr. Laski's contributions to politics, despite their brilliance and soundness in many details, are in a measure due to the English guides whom he follows with too uncritical an enthusiasm. Maitland, for instance, was undoubtedly a rare genius in the exercise of historical imagination, in re-creating out of apparently insignificant details the whole living situation as it must have occurred in the past. But he had no particular aptitude in political analysis, and even less can be said of his venture in the metaphysics of corporations. Mr. Laski's enthusiasm for Acton and Figgis leads him to attach undue importance to the present political significance of obscure figures in the Conciliar movement and similar incidents in the history of the Catholic Church. Mr. Laski would have done better to study actual political federalism in Canada, Australia, Germany, and Switzerland. The steady growth of nationalism in the United States and the progressive loss of prestige of our state governments, is certainly of greater significance for Mr. Laski's thesis than the writings of Withrington or James I. I venture to think that Mr. Laski might not so readily have overlooked fundamental distinctions if he had been somewhat more familiar with German political science and discussion, e.g., the work of Gumplowicz and Simmel. Even Mr. Laski's references to Gierke are to views filtered through Maitland and Figgis. He certainly gets nothing of Gierke's reverence for the state, nothing of Gierke's intense nationalism, which is the basis of his championing German as against Roman law. Clearly, sentimental attachment to country or national state that has its basis in literature and tradition gives the state power which other groups do not have.

In the main, however, I think the limitations of both Mr. Laski's and M. Duguit's books are due to an unavowed craving for absolute distinctions, which is apt to be strongest in those not devoted to technical philosophy. The public demands it of those engaged in political discussion. People generally cannot get enthusiastic about tentative policies and reserved statements. They crave absolute certainty from the statesman as well as from the physician and the priest. That is why the most influential factors in the world's political discussion have been absolutistic theologians like Calvin, doctrinaire Hegelians like Karl Marx, or classificatory zoölogists like Aristotle—not to mention certain non-political but disturbing remarks in a famous Sermon on the Mount. But in justice to Mr. Laski it should be mentioned that he recognizes that "man is no less a solitary than a social creature."

Roscoe Pound [1]

IT IS fortunate that the first American to dare to put "philosophy of law" into the title of a book is one who has not only been our foremost legal scholar but has also had experience at the bar and on the bench. The prestige of the latter is needed to overcome the deep prejudice of the "practically" minded against any avowedly theoretical treatment of the law. This prejudice is not altogether baseless. The vagaries of transcendental philosophers have been as inept in the law as in the natural sciences. But bad metaphysics cannot be avoided by ignoring philosophy and burying our heads in the sands after the alleged manner of the ostrich—witness the "practical" lawyers who involve themselves in metaphysical quagmires by speaking of *mens rea*, or the "meeting of minds" in contract, or "the will of the legislator" in circumstances that no legislator could have foreseen. These confusions are not of merely intellectual interest—they are decisive of the way in which the law is to meet the human needs that it ought to serve. Thus the metaphysical theories of natural rights and free will have led courts to nullify legislative efforts to protect otherwise helpless workmen against the economic oppression of company stores, payment in truck, etc.

It might perhaps be more correct to say that Dean Pound has sought to build up a philosophical jurisprudence rather than a philosophy of law—i.e., he has sought to make the science of law as philosophical or reflectively rational as possible rather than to answer the questions that one primarily interested in philosophy would ask concerning the rôle of the law in a unified theory of human life and natural existence. But the endeavour to define the spirit of the common law as a method of thinking is of importance to all those interested in the methods actually pursued in one of the major adventures of the human spirit.

Although Dean Pound has been a prolific writer, many of his essays and addresses expound from different angles the same fundamental ideas. We may get their essence by following three of his books, *The Spirit of the Common Law, An Introduction to the Philosophy of Law,* and *Law and Morals.*

I

The Spirit of the Common Law is, in the main, an analytical-historical survey of the leading ideas that have moulded the common law in America, concluding with two chapters illustrative of the essentials of the process of judicial empiricism and legal reason. According to this survey, six factors have tended to make the common law in America unusually individualistic. Two of these—the old seventeenth and eighteenth century theory of natural rights, and the philosophy of free will and laissez faire of the nineteenth century—have been operative in all modern civilized countries. Two others—the character of primitive Germanic law and the struggle of the English courts against the Stuart kings—have influenced English as well as American law; while two others—Puritanism and the condition of people living in a sparsely settled country with an open frontier—have given a peculiar turn to the individualism of American law.[2] At the same time the social or integrating principle represented by feudalism has never ceased to operate, and the tendency to think of rights and duties not as inhering in the separate individual, but as attached to a given relation,[3] has never departed from the common law and has even distinguished it from the modern Roman law of Europe.

The extent of this survey shows Dean Pound to be remarkably free from the currently fashionable but logically despicable habit of trying to refute doctrines by their chronology. Instead of dismissing doctrines as medieval or eighteenth century, he analyzes their actual operation and seeks to extricate their permanently valuable elements while vigorously pointing out those effects which have been actually baneful. This same scientific sanity also shows itself in the refusal to be stampeded for or against the term "individualism;" it seeks a just estimate of the extent to which free individual initiative is essential to social welfare.

Dean Pound has himself at times characterized his philosophic position as pragmatic. This is certainly true in the field of ethics, to the extent that pragmatism is a continuation of social utilitarianism represented in law by Jhering. However, as a logician and especially as a legal historian, Dean Pound is decidedly Neo-Hegelian, showing markedly the influence of Kohler in emphasizing the ideologic factor. Though he is remarkably liberal in his conception of the variety of the factors that determine legal development, and though he believes that the sociologic jurist should seek the conditions and motives back of legal ideas, he nevertheless insists that the chief factor in legal development is to be found in the logical force of the analogy or analogies that chance to be at hand. This tends to minimize the importance of political, economic, and other social factors and to characterize different periods of legal development almost exclusively in terms of single dominant ideas. Thus he speaks abstractly of the triumph of the common law in the twelfth century where others might see the masterful personality of Henry II fighting Thomas à Becket, or of its triumph in Tudor times over Roman law where others would see the triumph of organized corporations of lawyers in the Inns of Court. Similarly, he refers to the views of the Spanish jurist-theologians without any intimation that we are dealing with the utterances of Jesuits in the struggle of the Papacy against the Protestant princes.

No one can well dispute Dean Pound's contention that social phenomena are complex and may be viewed from different angles. At times, however, he seems to argue as if the presence of ethical motives and logical reasons proves that economic forces were not influential. This is clearly an inadequate view, since logical, ethical, and economic considerations are not mutually exclusive. There is a large mass of evidence to show that our honest convictions are largely moulded by the interests of the class to which we belong. We see justice clearer in cases where our sympathy has been developed by our particular experience. In large measure men act first and justify their acts afterwards. Slave-owners fervently believed slavery to be right, but not because they first reasoned it out on abstract grounds and then became slave-owners. Also as men's material environment differs, the analogies that seem to them most cogent differ. I have heard of an estimable judge who came from a small rural community and talked of the employment contract as analogous to swapping two cows for a horse. Such an analogy would not occur to, or would not have much force with, one in contact with the realities of modern factory employment. Would the fellow servant rule and the doctrine of assumption of risk, which Dean Pound regards as intrusions into the common law, have been invented if Lord Abinger and Chief Justice Shaw had been labourers? Might they not have found some analogy in the feudal element of our law for putting the burden on the master rather than on the servant?

Dean Pound seems to me to have been unduly influenced against the economic interpretation of legal history by superficial arguments used in its defence by men like Brooks Adams. There is certainly no reason for denying the elementary fact that economic factors influence the law as they mould other human institutions. The law of fixtures, the limited rights of combinations of labourers, the duties of employers to employees, the limited liability of ship-owners, as well as the greater penalties for crimes against property than for most crimes against the person, readily occur as illustrations of where the law protects the interest of one class against that of others. Indeed, the whole law of property may be viewed from this point of view. For the law does not merely protect possessions acquired in a prelegal stage. It largely determines how the future social product shall be distributed. Hence the struggle for economic advantages cannot be kept out of the law.

Not only as a student of logic but as one who believes that no greater calamity could happen to human life than the complete triumph of anti-intellectualism, I can only express my personal delight at the great importance Dean Pound assigns to the ideologic element in the making of the law. Nevertheless, the method of ideologic history has its marked logical danger. For the ideas emitted in the course of any human struggle are never meant to be actually carried to their full logical consequences, as if they were the premises of some geometric system. The reasons we give to justify our practical aims always take the form of premises much wider than the demands of these immediate aims. (This is, I suppose, what is meant by the current term "rationalization.") Hence the meaning of dominant ideas in the historical realm is always in fact limited in ways incomprehensible without a knowledge of the actual conditions and motives under which they arise. Ample historical learning and good sense generally enable Dean Pound to avoid this logical danger of the ideologic method. In the last chapter he lessens the emphasis on purely jural analogies and explicitly maintains that legal changes are not always caused by legal phenomena,[4] and that the function of the legal historian is to illustrate how rules and principles have met concrete social conditions rather than to furnish self-sufficient legal premises.

In the chapter on "The Pioneers and the Law" he has also given us a model treatment of concrete social-economic interpretation of legal development. Nevertheless, it seems to me necessary, in view of Dean Pound's obvious enthusiasm for Kohler, to repeat the old warning against identifying historical epochs with certain ideas that develop from each other by an immanent Hegelian dialectic. To seek for the leading idea dominating a given country and period may be a useful way of organizing our material. But when it is reified or hypostatized it makes us ignore or minimize the actual diversity of conflicting ideals that in any time or place actually prevail. A good illustration of this is Dean Pound's assertion that the nineteenth century demanded that the law should stand still. In fact, however, the demand for change was vocal enough in certain classes of the population. It was only the resistance of very definite and more powerful interests that prevented any change. Nor are the practical conclusions of Neo-Hegelian ideology always safe—witness Kohler's defence of the retributive theory of punishment.

In a book like this, intended for a general audience, certain undefined general terms like "individualism" are necessary or at least unavoidable; and I think that the context generally indicates Dean Pound's meaning clearly enough. Nevertheless, the unwary reader is likely to be somewhat misled by the use of a term like "individualism" in connection with things as diverse as primitive Germanic law, Puritanism, the philosophy of natural rights and free will, and the character of life on a frontier. A good deal of the "individualism" of primitive law is but apathy and fear of interfering with what the gods have brought about—something altogether different from the reformist passion to liberate the energies of human personality. One is also apt to be somewhat confused when told that the strict Germanic law, unlike the more mature Roman law, was individualistic,[5] and yet that Roman law is individualistic when compared with the essentially Germanic feudal law.[6] Indeed feudalism, which regarded sovereignty as a matter of contract and public office as private property (a view that prevailed in some of our Southern States up to the Civil War) may in this respect be regarded as extreme individualism.

The identification of Puritanism with individualism offers several historical difficulties. I cannot see that distrust of magistrates was ever characteristic of the Puritans in this country. The remarks of Pastor Robinson about "consociation" may be challenged in this connection on the ground that Robinson was a Pilgrim, i.e., a Separatist and a believer in toleration, which was certainly not the position of the Puritans. The latter, as followers of Calvin, did not believe in toleration, any more than in free will; and in their constant emphasis on "the discipline" they certainly magnified the power of magistrates to regulate the personal life in minute ways. Moreover, when the common law came to be moulded in America at the end of the eighteenth century, Puritanism had been definitely checked by Deism and other liberal movements; witness the life of Benjamin Franklin. Of the men who may be said to have laid the foundations of the American common law—Coke, Blackstone, James Wilson, Marshall, Gibson, Kent, and Story—only one, or at most two, can be characterized as Puritans. A reference, also, to the Puritans who settled in the West Indies (Barbados, etc.) tends to indicate that the individualistic features of our common law which Dean Pound attributes to Puritanism may be rather due to the sparsely settled conditions of the country. To this day the demand for excessive regulation of the moral life of our fellow beings is more characteristic of rural than of urban communities, though sumptuary legislation is found under the most diverse conditions.

The last two chapters of *The Spirit of the Common Law* are more particularly devoted to the illustration of the process according to which law grows. This process is in the highest degree instructive to those who wish to see the interplay of variable and relatively constant elements in actual operation. The substantive rules of the common law are constantly changing, not only through the introduction of new premises by the legislature, but even more so by the gradual and persistent modifications effected by jurists and judges in the guise of finding, interpreting, and applying the law. In this flux continuity is assured both by intellectual habit, which makes it easier for the judge to decide all similar cases in the same way, and by the social need for certainty, which demands of the judge that he shall decide according to some definite principle on which people can rely in their conduct. The permanent or perduring element of the common law is to be found, therefore, not in any of its substantive rules, but in its character as a method of legal thinking. (By "permanent" we obviously mean constant throughout a relatively long span of time.) Dean Pound puts the permanent features of the common law in (1) the system of judicial empiricism by precedents; (2) trial by jury; and (3) the supremacy of the law. From this list we may omit trial by jury, of which little is said in this volume and which does not prevail in equity procedure, by which a great many of the fundamental rights of labour and capital are actually determined today. Let us consider the other two features.

(1) The wide-spread assertion that common law judges are absolutely bound by precedent can certainly not be maintained in an unqualified form. If it were true, the law could never be changed, as it constantly is, by judicial decision. When lawyers speak of the principle or *ratio decidendi* established by a case, the logician rightly objects that a particular case can never uniquely determine the principle from which it is deduced. (The neglect of this is the familiar fallacy of affirming the consequence.) Dean Pound, therefore, more correctly speaks of precedents as analogies. Since in a developed legal system we generally have more than one analogy in a given case, the judge's decision is not necessitated entirely by logical deduction, but is largely influenced by judicial tact and sense for the weight of competing analogies. Judicial decision, then, is an art not entirely necessitated by strict logic. As in other arts, certain modes or habits are generally viewed as binding. But the maxim that judges must consider themselves as absolutely bound by precedents is obviously a fiction that tends to limit the judge's personal opinion of right and wrong and thus to ensure greater stability by forcing on his attention the analogies of previously adjudicated cases. As a fiction it thus compels a certain amount of enlightenment or intellectual consideration. But as no two cases are absolutely alike, the process of distinguishing any case from preceding ones enables the law to retain its fluidity. Dean Pound can thus maintain that our common law system, in which the judge is ruled by precedents, is more fluid than the Continental system, in which the law is fixed largely by theoretical jurists who systematically elaborate the provisions of written codes. *A priori* this seems plausible. (The com-

pactness of this volume doubtless prevents Dean Pound from bringing in the detailed evidence for this contention.) The jurist, like
other theorists, is apt to ignore many practical considerations in his
proud zeal for consistency. On the other hand a great American
lawyer has likened the common law judge to an experimenter in
chemistry who must rely on records of previous experiments but
who is not ready enough to admit that the record of former experiments may be wrong. Judging by the amount of litigation in this
country as compared with that which prevails in countries governed
by Roman law, there is reason to believe that where the jurist plays
a greater part, the law receives a more logical development and is
therefore more certain, and litigation is less frequent. Many have
held that the doctrine of precedents is an expression of the empirical
temper of the Anglo-Saxons, who prefer muddling along rather
than relying on preconceived principles and orderly plans made in
advance—a distinction strikingly illustrated when we compare English with French books on mathematics. But, whatever truth there
may be in this, the main distinction is the one laid down by Pound,
viz., that the common law puts the judge while the others put the
jurist in supreme control of legal development. This distinction,
however, must not be made too hard and fast. For jurists and especially text-book writers have had a tremendous influence on the
actual growth of our common law; witness Wigmore's *Treatise on
Evidence* [7] or Bishop on *Marriage and Divorce*.[8] On the other hand,
as the decisions of French and German courts are being reported
and commented on, they are bound to be influential, even though
formally their authority may be disputed. The greater dignity of
the judge in common law countries is due to the fact that England
became an organized central monarchy long before other European
countries, and the King's courts therefore acquired predominance
earlier.

This brings us to the second point, the supremacy of the common law.

(2) The phrase "supremacy" or "sovereignty of the law" is often

used to denote the supremacy within the state's courts of the laws
sanctioned by the state over any other laws such as those of private
corporations, churches, etc. Obviously, if the judge were free to set
aside the law of the state whenever in the judgment of one of the
parties it conflicted with religion, morality, or public policy, we
should cease to have any legal system at all. The supremacy of the
law in this sense is thus a jural ideal or postulate. The courts may,
in fact, unintentionally or even intentionally exceed the large element of discretion accorded to them; and the unwieldy machinery
of impeachment may or may not be brought into play. But the decision will stand in any case by virtue of the moral-political maxim of
the supremacy of the law, i.e., that it is the duty of every citizen
or government official to obey the final decision of the court, whatever that may be. As a political maxim this is of great general force
because the most crying abuses brought about by legal authority
generally involve less danger to the state than would reversion to
anarchic or lawless justice. Nevertheless, we have no right to make
this maxim absolute. For the actual law, as administered by human
beings of limited intelligence and limited goodwill, always involves
more or less injustice and immorality. Hence at critical times it becomes the ethical duty of individuals or of communities to disregard
the law in the interests of justice and human welfare. To refuse to
do so is to disregard the maxim that the Sabbath is made for man
and not man for the Sabbath—a dangerous saying, but one necessary
to save us from the deadly blight of Pharisaic legalism.

When Dean Pound uses the phrase "the supremacy of the law,"
he seems in the main to insist that in making and administering the
law judges must be independent of the political sovereign, king,
parliament, or the voters. This again is a political proposition of
great expediency. For judges are experts like engineers and physicians, and it is generally undesirable for the lay sovereign to interfere in professional matters. Dean Pound, however, does not seem
to be satisfied to treat this merely as a matter of *general* expediency.
Some of the arguments he uses in its defence border close on abso-

lutism, as when he justifies Coke's dictum that judges rule under God and the law. Whatever ancient peoples may have believed, there is no rational ground today for the view that the work of judges is more divine than the work of other men. (Coke himself was an outrageously vile character.) Nor is there any reason why the community should not have the right to reject the work of judges, just as it has the right to reject the work of engineers or educators. Of course it can do so only at its peril. But there is also peril in complacent acceptance of irresponsible rule by a judicial or any other aristocracy of experts.

At times, Dean Pound indicates clearly enough that judges are engaged in a task of social engineering imposed upon them by the community; from which it would seem to follow that, like other social functionaries, they should be responsible or answerable to the community for the results of their work. This responsibility, however, tends to disappear practically (i.e., it becomes a responsibility to God only) when we insist, as Dean Pound does, that the work of courts is reason and that all political interference with them is caprice. Doubtless if we use "reason" in the sense made familiar by Santayana, as the organization of human life and expression so that our impulses will tend to fulfil themselves in harmonious rather than in discordant ways, then law with its orderly procedure for hearing both sides and critically examining the relevant evidence certainly deserves to be called organized reason. But we must not forget that actual law is a human product—made and administered by judges who are not free from human limitations in intelligence and goodwill. To make, therefore, a categoric identification of law with reason tends to ignore these limitations and to encourage the kind of legal optimism that Blackstone made famous or infamous. Indeed, to identify the actual with the ideal is the essence of all fanatism, of idolatry in religion, bigotry in morals, and absolutism in politics. Dean Pound himself has sufficiently pointed out the actual specific evils into which the law has fallen by virtue of this claim to absolute supremacy. It has, for instance, enabled fortified monopolies to prey upon society and has hindered the development of the personality of the labourer. Indeed, he has also pointed out a serious defect in the fundamental structure of our legal system which prevents its work from being as rational as that of some other of our political agencies. Thus, courts have very limited sources of knowledge. They cannot possibly give the time that many important measures before them really demand, and they cannot delegate their power. They must decide between the two parties before them and have no means of studying the full effect of their decision on third parties. Above all, they have no power of initiating investigation and framing rules in advance. In view of these limitations I cannot see how one can justify the view that any movement away from judicial to executive or legislative justice is necessarily arbitrary and irrational.

Dean Pound's unqualified opposition to all political interference with the work of the courts seems to me especially unfortunate in a country like the United States, where every political issue except the tariff sooner or later comes up before the courts. In no other advanced civilized country are purely political questions like taxation, labour legislation, etc., rendered so uncertain because of the difficulty of knowing how the courts, the final authorities, will decide. Dean Pound makes a great point of the fact that some British dominions are beginning to follow our method of giving the courts power to declare certain statutes unconstitutional. This, however, seems a minor matter so long as these constitutions do not contain our bills of rights and essentially vague terms like "due process," "equal protection of law," "liberty," "direct taxation," "republican form of government," etc.—terms whose essential vagueness gives the courts as much power as they wish to take over all political issues.

If our actual system, whereby the welfare of millions is controlled by a chance majority of a very small number of elderly judges, is to be defended at all, it should be by an enumeration of the instances where judicial opinion has actually turned out to be wiser than that of legislatures and voters. Dean Pound puts forward no such mass of empirical evidence to justify his stand against the recall of judicial decisions. Despite an *a priori* distinction between judicial reason and legislative caprice, Dean Pound would scarcely identify the judicial nullification of the federal income tax or of the New York Workmen's Compensation Law with reason, nor would he identify the nullified statutes or their constitutional reincarnations with arbitrary will. Lincoln, in his effort to preserve the Union, flatly disregarded orders from the courts—even from the Supreme Court—and patriotic citizens were with him, as they were in recalling the Dred Scott decision by force of arms. Nor did the British people lose the benefits of civilization when their Parliament recalled the decision of their highest court in the Scottish Church case.[9] No one, indeed, has pointed out with greater justness than Dean Pound this very necessity for occasional relapses to "justice without law," or the limitations of judicial law-making arising from the fact that courts have no adequate machinery for getting at the facts required.

In opposing all popular or political review of the work of the courts, Dean Pound relies heavily on the fact that judges are members of a learned profession, and that the criticism of their decision by their fellow members can be relied on to cure the shortcomings of their work. No one can doubt that criticism from one's fellow professionals is much more powerful than criticism from the public at large (though the latter is never completely negligible). In these days of rampant irrationalism it is well to meet Dean Pound's courageous faith in the power of science, which makes him believe that improved legal training will cure the radical evils of our legal system. But it is not necessary to reject this faith to see its obvious limitations. Professional legal opinion is class opinion, and every class of experts has its special limitations. (This is altogether apart from the fact that the leaders of the bar are as a rule in the service of clients of those propertied classes which can afford to pay the highest fees.) History is full of instances of opposition to needed reforms on the part of the legal profession. Substantial improvements in legal justice have generally required pressure from outside the legal profession. This is true even in the realm of procedure. The old common law forms of pleading, for instance, long continued to defeat the ends of justice because of their attractiveness from the point of view of technical finesse. The danger of absolutistic ideas is precisely in that they limit us to only one way (usually the traditional one), whereas life demands many ways. Here again I must add that no one has shown more carefully than Dean Pound himself the necessity of vivifying the law by new premises drawn from legislation. Indeed, the doctrine of the efficacy of human effort is the very essence of his philosophy.

II

Dean Pound's views on the great substantive branches of the law, viz., liability, property, and contract, are most adequately stated in the last three chapters of *An Introduction to the Philosophy of Law*.

The chapter on liability is in the main devoted to the historical and analytic motives of the theory that the law does and should put liability only where there is fault—a dogma that led the New York Court of Appeals into an unfortunate conflict with enlightened public opinion in the famous Ives case.[10] Dean Pound has no difficulty in showing that this dogma does not agree and never has agreed with all the facts of our legal system, that actually we hold men liable who have committed no fault whatsoever and have in fact used every possible precaution. Thus we hold the master of a ship, an innkeeper, or a common carrier absolutely liable for certain goods, no matter how much care he has taken. In many cases of legal "negligence," the culpability is clearly fictional. Men are "deemed" or "presumed" to be culpable because the law holds them liable, not because they are in fact, or in any real sense of the word, at fault. Hence those who try to maintain the consistency of the established theory tread on the tail of their own argument.[11] The notion of "fault" is, indeed, ethical in its origin, and comes into the law, according to Pound, only in the stage of equity or natural law, with the metaphysical idea of free will. As a generalization it did great service in systematizing the law of torts, and thus improved and humanized the administration of justice. But it can never altogether replace the older standard of acting at one's peril where others must be protected from the harmful results of one's ignorance and awkwardness as well as from insufficient care and downright aggression. Dean Pound thinks that all the facts of legal liability can be deduced from what he calls the four postulates of civilized life. Civilized man must assume (1) that he will not be interfered with by wilful aggression, (2) that others will act with due care, (3) that others will restrain potentially dangerous things or agencies in their control or employ, and (4) that those with whom he deals in the general course of society will act in good faith. From these postulates follow not only the law of tort but also the law of contract and the large number of obligations that can be viewed as either, or are in fact neither.

The hitherto current ethical-metaphysical theory of liability based on fault, is, no doubt, inadequate; and Dean Pound's theory has all the analogies of science and engineering in its favour. But I regret that he has left out of account the insurance theory of liability, i.e., that in the imperfect state of human knowledge and capacity there are bound to occur mistakes, accidents, and other unpreventable losses, and that those losses should be borne in the first instance by the party in the better position to insure against them. Thus with regard to industrial accidents the employer is held liable because he is in a better position to figure the cost of insurance in advance and can add it to the legitimate cost of production. I venture to think that without the principle of insurance as a method of social distribution of inevitable losses, Dean Pound's theory will be found incomplete. Moreover the insurance theory of liability is clearly supplementary rather than antithetic to an objective theory of fault. Where the losses are in any way avoidable, an objective standard of fault is applicable to the extent that it makes for the utmost possible care, but where experience has shown that no amount of care will eliminate certain losses, the cost of these necessary incidents of the social process should not be borne by the accidental victim.

In the chapter on contract, Dean Pound traces, with his usual rich and varied learning, the history of the fundamental ideas of contract both in the civil and in the common law. He thus shows how it comes about that the civil law is superior in protecting promises by making specific performance rather than money reparation the rule. On the other hand he rejects the civil-law theory (which has exerted so much influence on the common law through the followers of Austin and Maine) that the law gives effect only to the free agreement of two wills. The law actually protects an objectively evinced promise and pays little attention to subjective intentions as such. Dean Pound rejects with equal emphasis the equivalent and the bargain theories of contract and the doctrine of consideration that they involve.

Against the doctrine of consideration it is urged that our textbooks have not agreed on any formula for it, nor our courts on any consistent scheme of what it does and what it does not include. In any case consideration need not be real and its inadequacy is always immaterial. An imposing catalogue of situations is given in which our courts are enforcing promises that are not bargains [12] or do not involve even technical consideration. [13]

The doctrine of consideration has persisted, according to Pound, partly through the too naïve belief that the common law represents an eternal legal order, and partly through the wide-spread belief that "talk is cheap" and not always to be taken at its face value. This, however, should not be pushed so far as to interfere with the ordinary course of business, which depends on the reliability of promises. At this point, remembering the previous emphasis on the need of being able to rely on the acts of others as the basis of all obligation, the reader may expect Dean Pound's adherence to the injurious-reliance theory of contracts, i.e., that promises are enforceable because they have been relied on by the promisee to his injury.

Actually, however, he expressly rejects this view without giving direct reasons. He is intent on establishing a positive basis for the law of contract in the fact that expectations based on promises are the very substance of wealth in a commercial age, "that a man's word in the course of business should be as good as his bond and that his fellow men must be able to rely on the one equally with the other if our economic order is to function efficiently." [14]

While the last proposition is in general true, a certain distinction may well be added. It is not true that all business demands such a standard with equal urgency. Contrast the case of a stock-broker with that of a real-estate broker. The former could do very little business on the floor of the stock exchange without the strictest reliance on the spoken word. But if a benevolent jurist were to offer real-estate brokers a law making every oral promise enforceable, they would certainly not rush to accept it, perhaps not more than professional diplomats. The reason is that most people do not like to be in a position where a hasty word or one uttered in a weak moment may involve very heavy obligations. In this fact, it seems to me, we have a psychologic reason why people generally want the law to bind promises only when they are accompanied with some formality or solemnity.

The chapter on property is also in the form of a historical and analytic sketch of the main theories that have prevailed, and Dean Pound pertinently remarks that hitherto "philosophical theories of property . . . have not shown how to build but have sought to satisfy men with what they had built already." [15] Philosophically this is expressed by saying that they have taken the existing order as a picture of the necessary and universal. In doing this they have frequently relied on arguments that appeal more to goodwill than to facts and logic. Thus the identification of private property with liberty or personality generally presupposes that property consists of goods that are objects of purely individual or personal enjoyment. But as modern property is for the most part in the instrumentalities of production, the rights of property are also rights to limit the liberty and personality of others who are dependent on these tools to be productive. Juristically, however, the great argument against metaphysical theories of absolute rights of property is not merely that they all import into their premises that which they wish to prove, but that they are futile in that they fail to give us any light as to what *is* private property under given circumstances. Thus they do not tell us, e.g., when an inheritance tax is confiscatory, nor even to what extent the right of controlling things after one's death is essential to private property. The actual variations in the power of disposing goods by will, and the fact that no civilized country is without restrictions on the *jus disponendi*, are matters inadequately dealt with by such absolutistic theories.

Dean Pound's own view is that the law of property is the attempt to realize the postulate of civilized life that men may control "what they have discovered and appropriated to their own use, what they have created by their own labour and what they have acquired under the existing social and economic order." [16] With regard to these three sources of property it may be noted that they are not coördinate, that while the first two have been emphasized in the history of the subject, the third is really the most inclusive category. The right to appropriate what one has discovered is obviously of very limited application in modern life; and the right to the full produce of one's labour is practically meaningless in a society where the division of labour is so complex that no one is ever in a position to tell what part of any object or process a single individual could have produced or invented by his own unaided labour. The actual relative monetary value of the different services that enter into the creation of any economic object is obviously itself the result of the existing social economic order (including the legal rules that it employs). Hence, Dean Pound's postulate is simply the general postulate of legal order, that every one should be protected in the possession of that which he has acquired under the existing legal rules, whatever they be. That this is not mere tautology can be seen in the large and almost central rôle which it assigns to rights by prescription. Prolonged possession creates expectations and it is the essence of the legal order of civilized society to make reliable expectations possible.

There is, however, a serious misunderstanding involved in the popular view that the law of property merely protects what a man has already acquired. Modern property law, in fact, not only regulates conflicting claims to possession of goods already in existence, but by protecting such rights as that of drawing interest, profits, etc., determines the future distribution of the social product. The right to enjoy individual possessions would be of relatively little importance without the right of acquisition. The average life-period of modern capital goods, such as tools, machines, ships, etc., is so short that a law which merely protected possession or even the exploitation of existing goods would leave the door open to the most radical transformation of society. We must remember that while mankind · as a whole acquires its goods by working on external nature, individual man in socialized industry acquires his goods mainly by social coöperation, and his share is fixed not by nature but by social rules. Hence, while the postulate of legality indicates that it is generally preferable to conform to the existing rules, whatever they are, rather than to take the chance of the "waste and friction involved in going to any other basis," [17] it is, of course, not true that any set of property laws is as good as another. The choice between them must involve political as well as social-economic considerations. For property law is not merely a method of protecting the "instinct" of acquisitiveness and the individual claims grounded therein, but is also a system of distributing power over the means of production; and in the last analysis the justification of any particular system of distributing economic power is whether such a distribution will tend to further a greater production of that which is deemed good for human life.

Dean Pound's learning on all related subjects is so accurate and up to date that it is surprising to see him bring in the antiquated notion of an "instinct of acquisitiveness." [18] Men's actual desires for acquisition and exclusive possession are certainly not congenital but depend on all sorts of social conditions. The Eskimos cannot understand the idea of private property in food that any individual has acquired, and many civilized people find it difficult to understand the Indian's idea of private property in his personal song. It may be well to note in passing that modern anthropology also indicates that the progress from collective to private property is by no means a universal rule, that development in the contrary direction also occurs frequently.

III

Though none of our great courts ever claimed to be merely courts of law and not courts of justice, it has been fashionable for professors of law to boast of being concerned only with definite positive law altogether apart from morality or what the law should be. If there has been a marked change in this attitude in recent years it has been largely due to the tireless work of Dean Pound himself; and his volume on *Law and Morals* reiterates his fundamental contention that while morality and law must not be confused, they cannot be sharply divorced without detriment to the law. For the life of the law, its enforcement, depends upon the moral feeling of the community. Moreover the actual content of legal rules cannot be intelligently developed without a knowledge of the human aims that they are designed to serve.

It has become customary with Dean Pound to approach his problems through the analysis and criticism of what the diverse schools of jurisprudence have taught on the points at issue. Students of the history of jurisprudence will naturally be very grateful for the pithy and luminous way in which the significance of many figures and movements in legal thought is thus indicated. But for one who wishes to understand the problem in itself the historical approach has obvious limitations. That we cannot understand the present without a knowledge of the past is true enough; but the proposition is no whit less true if the words "past" and "present" are interchanged. The different stages of development, from the primitive and the strict law to the maturity and socialization of the law, are not strictly chronologic but, as elsewhere indicated, "stages in the historian's discourse." Likewise, the distinction between the various schools of jurisprudence is only an idealization of dominant but abstract tendencies. No great individual jurist ever belonged exclusively to the analytic, historical, or philosophical school; and there are many lines of cleavage, e.g., that between organicists like Gierke and individualists like Maine or Jhering, which cut athwart Dean Pound's classification and are of primary importance in studying the relation between law and morality.

Had Dean Pound brought together directly his own views as to the relation between law and morals, separated from historical references, his views would certainly have had the advantage of greater clarity and persuasiveness. The method he has followed has not, for instance, given him the opportunity to discriminate carefully the different ideas that are generally lumped together and vaguely covered by the word "morals." We may illustrate this by considering Dean Pound's reply to the argument that to allow judges to proceed largely on personal feelings or intuitions as to what is right, is at best "a law of tyrants." His reply is "that here we are in the domain of ethics, and that ethics, too, is a science and not without principles." [19] Now if we distinguish ethics as a science from the actual body of prevailing moral judgments (Austin's "positive morality") it will be generally recognized that the science of ethics has even less influence on actual moral judgments than jurisprudence or the science of law has on actual legal judgments. For legal judgments are generally decided by a body of men who have more or less studied legal theory, while moral judgments are made by every one, and even ethical theorists cannot always carry their theories into their daily judgments so as to overcome habitual ways of thought that held sway before the theories began. Thus the situation as regards workmen's compensation laws [20] can be accurately put only by saying that first the moral sense of the community demanded liability even where there was no fault, that this then brought about a change in the law, and that jurists followed the law and formulated the insurance or objective theory of liability without fault. The science of ethics has yet to incorporate this and recognize the necessary limitation of the idea of fault, which is after all but the offspring of theologic "sin," closely related to irrational taboos.

Possibly also we need a greater emphasis on the distinction between morals as personal habits, customs, etc. (mores, *mœurs*, etc.) and morality as the normative aspect of all human enterprise, the aspect that makes judgments of right and wrong logically possible.

Personal morals, e.g., in matters of sex and dress, come into the law as part of the police power, though the enforcement of contracts, the power of disinheritance, the revocation of a gift, the loss of the right of guardianship, and other matters may often be affected by the question as to what is contrary to "good morals." Now with regard to such standards of personal morality it seems clear that the law will not, and perhaps ought not to, be directly ruled by the science of ethics. Should the judgment of a professor of ethics decide what plays are obscene or immoral? German, French, and Italian jurists who find in their codes provisions about *gute Sitten* [21] *bonnes mœurs*,[22] *buoni costumi*,[23] are generally agreed that the standard which the law should enforce is the one prevailing in the community as a whole and not that which prevails in some one class, no matter how enlightened it considers itself. But this means a good deal in modern urban communities, where there is much variation of moral judgments. It serves as a warning to the judge not to impose the standards of his own group on the community generally. Thus enlightened judges may find themselves compelled to enforce prevailing moral standards that they do not themselves approve on reflective or scientific reasons.

On the other hand, if we use "morality" in the wider sense as governing all human relations, it must include the whole law, even its technical rules, which control matters otherwise morally indifferent. For if the law is to be judged in the end by the way it serves human purposes—by the way it meets the supreme demands of what Dean Pound calls enlightened social engineering—it must appeal to moral principles. Unfortunately, however, the difficulties that prevent social science from giving us reliable conclusions are pervasive. An enlightened court, for instance, may take an unfavourable attitude to the rules of a trade-union that restrict output. It may feel itself justified by the economic principle that such rules are uneconomic in effect. Others, however, reason that a restriction of output may save the life of the workers from wasteful competition in speeding up, and that this human gain far outweighs the loss of commodities of which society may have too much anyway. As a professor of ethics I freely confess my failure to see how a science of ethics can at the present time definitely settle such issues. Where you cannot eliminate the variable element of individual estimate you are bound to have differences of opinion. A great deal of private law, like public law, is the result of treaties that the ambassadors of diverse conflicting social interests, represented in legislatures, agree to as a result of bargains and compromises. A recognition of this need not prevent judges and jurists from trying to take the point of view of interests of the community as a whole; but it weakens the usual criticism of the work of commissions as merely work of arbitration devoid of principles.

We do not, in fact, have a ready supply of principles for all human situations. We need to discover them by the methods of trial and error that characterize human experience in new situations. This is not to deny the practical importance to the jurist of reflective or scientific study of ethical principles. Such study helps us to true impartiality and liberalizes judicial decisions by making judges realize that what seems to them obviously just may be due to class prejudice. Such moral scepticism may seem the very denial of ethics to those who are temperamentally dogmatic. But it is an indispensable wisdom making for viable tolerance and restraining the use of uniform law to crush the diversity or variability that is the condition of free life and progress. Thus a liberal view of ethical principles would make us see that while the principle of *respondeat superior* has not absolute universality, it has as much justification as the principle of individual responsibility. The latter has, in fact, always been more or less limited.

In this connection it is well to note as against Dean Pound's interpretation of Kant that in a very definite sense Kant no more overthrew the old natural law than he tried to overthrow the old ethics or the old physics. What he did try to do in this and in other fields, like theology, was to remove the old metaphysical bases in order to make room for epistemologic and transcendental-ethical foundations. This is important because if the essence of the old dogmatic natural law is the confident appeal to substantive ethical principles as eternally self-evident, Kant remained a dogmatic adherent of natural law, leaving no room in his system for new ethical truth to be discovered by experience in time. But despite Kant's own timidities his critical attitude toward the old metaphysics (following Hume) was undoubtedly a great solvent, and Dean Pound is to this extent justified in regarding modern philosophic jurisprudence as beginning with him.

The fact that Kant clearly distinguished between the *Tugendlehre* and the *Rechtslehre* as parts of a theory of morals should prevent us from subscribing unqualifiedly to the statement that the historical school banished ethical considerations from jurisprudence.[24] What it did was to subordinate individual morality (*Moralität*) to social ethics (*Sittlichkeit*), which includes the norms of politics. This is rather important because a popular misunderstanding of it has led countrymen of Hobbes to accuse the Germans of subordinating morality to politics.

As my own interest in the law differs in some respects from Dean Pound's, I cannot flatter myself that my critical exposition of his views has always rendered them perfect justice. Philosophy demands a closer articulation of ideas than most jurists, sensitive to the immediate claims of practical life, think worth pursuing. We must certainly grant that legal philosophy, in its haste to achieve systematic theories, has often done violence to human actualities and needs. But no one has insisted more clearly than Pound himself that this search for system is not only necessary for a rational grasp of the law, but indispensable for a humane and effective administration of justice. It helps us to harmonize conflicting rules and to decide which of competing tendencies or analogies in the law is to be favoured in new cases. Even purely negative criticism of prevailing doctrines tends to keep such doctrines more fluid, so that the law that they mould becomes better adapted to its practical ends.

Dean Pound's work is not only a great credit to American scholarship, but heartening to all those who still believe that human affairs need the light of reason.

John Chipman Gray [1]

A KEEN French jurist, Duguit, who visited this country in 1921, is reported to have expressed astonishment at the pedagogic excellence of some of our law schools and the complete absence of any attention to the philosophy of law. Like other foreign visitors, Professor Duguit was not altogether fortunate in his guides. He certainly would not have made the latter part of his statement if he were acquainted with the spreading influence of Justice Holmes and of Professor Gray, and with the work that the present dean of the Harvard Law School has been carrying on since 1901. But taking the country as a whole, there can be no doubt that our law schools are still regrettably backward in the philosophic or scientific study of law as a social institution. This is because our law schools are, owing to their historical origin, still on the whole more under the influence of the professional spirit of the bar than under the scientific influence of the university. Thus when Theodore Roosevelt in his Progressive days gave expression to the wide-spread dissatisfaction with the antiquated social philosophy back of the trend of our judicial decisions, the American Bar Association embarked on a campaign of "education" to convince the public that judges merely declared the law and had no part at all in making it. And from our law schools came no protest against this view, which had long before been characterized by a scientific jurist as a childish fiction.

Genuine thinkers, however, will be found in all walks of life. The Massachusetts Bar and the Harvard Law School, which gave us Justice Holmes, can also boast of Professor Gray, who has done more than any one else to undermine what I have ventured to call the phonograph theory, according to which the judge only gives out to the public that which the law speaks into him. Gray was in many respects an old-fashioned lawyer unduly preoccupied with property law. But unlike the vast majority of his profession, he was a thorough and liberal scholar who did not despise foreign learning and experience, and did not allow respect for the conventions to interfere with the perception of fact. Thus he does not hesitate to admit that, in our system, law may be "the opinion of half a dozen old gentlemen, some of them conceivably of very limited intelligence." The argument that law is the will of the people because, if it were not, the people would overthrow it, is met by the grim analogy of the power of the horses of a regiment to overthrow the riders. His remarks on Judge Story, one of the tin gods of the legal profession, are illuminating and liberating. Above all, this book seems to be marked by the mature wisdom that comes from grappling with difficulties rather than from clever devices for avoiding them. This shows itself in the variety of concrete homely illustrations with which the author always confronts high principles, as when the supreme principle of morality, the greatest good of the greatest number, etc., is confronted with the question of the liability of a Pullman Car Company for samples of hat-pins left by a travelling salesman. The incautious reader may be misled by the humour of the illustration and see in it the fashionable contempt for general principles. In fact, however, Professor Gray does believe that the judge's general philosophy will influence his particular decisions. But if principles will not directly or indirectly throw light on these daily cases they are of no value to the philosophy of law.

By close reasoning Gray establishes the position that law may be viewed as the body of rules laid down and followed by courts in their judgments and decisions. This view has been gradually finding recognition in our more liberal law schools. But some who in the main accept Gray's position, and indeed build upon it, are a little frightened by the robust consistency with which Gray maintains his thesis. For if law be nothing but what the courts will recognize as such, then it follows that rules according to which people actually regulate their conduct do not constitute law unless judges put their stamp upon them. Many, Justice Cardozo among them, regard this as obviously absurd. To me it seems rather the beginning of logical sanity to start with this very distinction between the social rules that prevail in popular opinion or practice and the jural rules that prevail in judicial decision. Though these two sets of rules obviously influence each other, they are certainly not identical; and sociologists have fallen into inextricable confusion by indiscriminately applying the term "law" to these different sets of rules. Gray does not contend that in making the law judges are entirely untrammelled—no human being is ever completely untrammelled. The body of judicial decision is in fact limited by the same forces that rule the state, though who the real rulers are it is hard to say. In any case Gray's position is much more in accordance with the fact that on a great many questions that come up before the courts there is no popular opinion at all. Indeed, it is precisely because in modern society it is as impossible for people at large to make laws as to build suspension-bridges that experts are employed to do both. Hence, more or less organized professional traditions and opinion are probably what judges care for most, and are in certain fields the strongest single factor in making the law what it is. Intelligent laymen can pass judgment only on the results and pronounce them good or defective.

He who enunciates an important truth against the current of his time and place is almost inevitably bound to give it an undue sharpness of outline. Perhaps also the practical lawyer, preoccupied with issues that must be settled by a yes or no, is more inclined to paint his truth in black and white where those not so pressed can resort to intermediate shades. In any case Gray has emphasized a hard and fast distinction between law and the sources of law where Continental jurists like Demogue and Kantorowicz see transitions from one to the other. By the sources of the law Gray means materials out of which it is fashioned. But as Aristotle pointed out long ago, the distinction between material and formed or finished product is a relative one. Cloth is a finished product for the weaver, but only material for the tailor.

Who then is the maker of clothes? Imagine some one to arise and soberly suggest to a distracted multitude the tailor theory as to the making of clothes. Imagine also a resultant hue and cry of protest from the adherents of the social theory who insist that clothes are made not by tailors but by society. The tailor theory, they insist, is woefully superficial. Society makes clothes through innumerable interconnecting agencies such as the farmers who raise sheep and shear their wool, the weavers who make the cloth, the designers who determine their pattern, and finally the people who, by buying and wearing them, determine what clothes shall be made.

This picture fairly represents the controversy over Gray's position. His critics insist that what judges make should not be called law but judicial decisions; that the latter become law only when adopted by society, just as they might insist that tailors do not make clothes, but garments that become clothes only when they clothe people.

It is tempting to dismiss all this as a merely verbal controversy arising out of the different uses of the words "law" and "make." But there is more to it. We have here also a real difference of interests. One party is interested primarily in what goes on in the court and in the lawyer's study. And the other party is concerned with what is happening in the social milieu. And the intensity of our interests inclines us all to view the interests of others as pale and insignificant. But when all is said, the fact remains that Gray is substantially right, that judges make law as surely as tailors make clothes. This does not deny the truth and importance of the more general or social point of view. But the specific truth of Gray is not to be lost sight of if we are to view it as a part of a larger complex.

One of the inconsistencies charged against Gray is that he asserts both that judges make law and that judicial decisions as precedents are one of the sources of the law. This again is, from one point of view, a purely verbal matter. Gray might just as well have said that the past law made by judges is one of the sources or materials out of which judges at any time make new law. But the real point is that Gray distinguished between the law and the judicial decision in itself, and on this point the difference between him and some of his critics is fundamental. There are those whose picture of everything is punctiform, always made up of separate and distinct atoms or instances. Relations are external to the things they relate. We may call this the heap theory. Others see everything as made up of lines whose intersections give us the visible points. We may call this the reticular theory. Gray's critics are atomists who see the courts producing heaps of decisions and that, they insist, is all there is to law. Rules are figments that exist not in the "external world" but only in the minds of speakers or writers. Gray, however, sees that the significance of every decision is the line or rule that runs through it and connects it with other decisions, past or future. This line may or may not be in the clear consciousness of the judge who makes the decision, but the chances generally are that the abler judges at least are not mere automata but men of some vision, who see more or less of the general lines of social policy and the demands of social sentiment. A great judge like Holmes may even be aware of his own bias. In any case, to the scientific student of law, the significance of any decision is the rule that it embodies. When judges decide cases they are not mere arbitrators. Their decisions (not always their written opinions) lay down the rules that jurists have always called positive or prevailing law. Modern organized communities are governed by these rules.

Gray's *The Nature and Sources of the Law* is a classic in the sense that it stands up in the shifting currents of the years. For it was written by a wise man who was willing to wait until his thoughts matured.

Jerome Frank[1]

DISCUSSION of our political life cannot have much reality while we talk of democracy and the will of the people, and our actual government remains an irresponsible judicial aristocracy. A small number of judges can, under the guise of interpreting the law, settle for a long time any vital issue in accordance with their own class bias or antiquated opinion as to social and economic needs. In the progressive *ante bellum* days, proposals were discussed for the recall of judicial decisions and for other ways of making the law more responsive to the present-day interests of the majority of the people. But the leaders of the American Bar, either because they feared the removal of issues from the field of their professional power to the political forum where the wishes of *hoi polloi* might count, or else because they really did not know any better, began a campaign of "education" and "sold" to the public the idea that the courts have nothing to do with making and changing the law. This theory of a complete Law that speaks into the mind of the judge, who like a phonograph does nothing but repeat it, had frequently been shown by intelligent jurists since the days of Austin to be a fiction. But the prestige of the leaders of our bar, the desertion of the Progressive cause by Theodore Roosevelt, and the general shadow of the oncoming World War made this fiction prevail, and it still holds the fort as our orthodox national myth.

Mr. Frank's book is, therefore, of importance as a valiant attack on the orthodox position, by a keen lawyer who knows the ropes and brings to his aid an unusually varied learning, including the fashionable form of psychoanalysis.

Having in my own way for over eighteen years fought against this citadel of legal unreason, my inclinations are naturally to hail Mr. Frank as an ally in a righteous cause. Also because Mr. Frank is a highly esteemed friend, it would be pleasant to dwell on the great merits of this book and its timeliness. But others have already done so, and the public has so approved its readable quality as to put it already into a second printing. It seems to me, therefore, more useful to point out why, though the author's heart is in the right place and his courage most admirable, he is not likely to disturb the enemy very seriously. The book is not well organized; the shots are often carelessly fired and wide of the mark, many of the shells are duds and some may act like boomerangs. This friendly criticism of an ally is all the more necessary because these defects are characteristic of our young liberals who, though they talk much about science and the methods of science, woefully neglect the art of close reasoning and seldom trouble to produce logically conclusive evidence for their contentions.

Mr. Frank's book is not well organized. The various chapters are rather loosely strung together, and the subject-matter is distributed without any careful plan among them, as well as among sixty-two pages of miscellaneous appendices, and thirty pages more of notes in addition to footnotes. Mr. Frank confuses his references, fails to do justice to the authorities he quotes, and in moments of illumination makes wise qualifications in footnotes that he subsequently ignores in the text. These are in themselves minor matters. Mr. Frank is a busy lawyer, and we should be grateful for the labour, often useful and illuminating, that he has from time to time devoted to this book. But unfortunately the outer lack of order is correlated with a failure to think through what he ultimately wants to say.

His central aim is to deny the complete certainty of the law. Does Mr. Frank, however, wish to rush to the other extreme and, substituting one childish simplicity for another, maintain that there is no certainty in the law at all? Here we have a regrettable lack of clarity. An affirmative answer to the last question is logically involved in his extreme nominalism or denial of rules, which he develops in his unfortunate polemics against Pound, Jhering, and Dickinson.[2] Thus he quotes with approval Dean Green's categoric assertion that "the control of judges is not to be found in rules," [3]—a recklessly anarchic statement that ignores the daily experienced necessity for rules as checks not only on judges but on the ignorance and bias of all private as well as public agents.[4] It ignores also the ever pressing need of uniformity in various phases of modern life.

Mr. Frank, however, has no clear idea as to what he is thus committing himself to; and elsewhere, especially in footnotes, he explicitly recognizes the existence and need of some rules and certainty in the law. This admission, however, still leaves his fundamental thesis rather vague and inconsequential, and his polemics pointless, if not unfair. For obviously, if the law contains both rules and discretion, both certainty and uncertainty, the significant issue is precisely the one that Dean Pound faces and that Mr. Frank dodges, viz., where to draw the line between legal rule and judicial discretion. Without such a line there cannot be much definite meaning in Mr. Frank's contention that he is arguing only against the conventional *exaggeration* of the importance of rule and certainty. We cannot tell that any one has exaggerated unless we have measured or at least estimated the *correct* amount. But such a task seems so uncongenial to Mr. Frank that he is most unfair in his attack on Pound's effort in that direction. To grant that Pound has not adequately solved that most difficult problem would not justify Mr. Frank's argument here. The latter, if generalized, would deny the distinction between day and night, by asking where in the twilight zone we are to draw the line where one ends and the other begins. No one can well deny Pound's contention that the field of property and contract is full of exact rules, such as the legal rate of interest, the age of contractual responsibility, the number of witnesses necessary for a will, and thousands of similar rules.

Again, Mr. Frank has not faced clearly the essential question as to whether the central phenomenon that he is examining, viz., the craving for certainty, is found only in the law or whether it exists also in other fields, e.g., in medicine. He begins his book as if he were dealing with something peculiar to the law, something that explains the anomalous position of the lawyer in the community. His explanation, however, is in terms of a supposed general fact of human nature—the reliance of the child on the authority of the father. This is certainly contrary to all canons of scientific procedure. For if the cause is general, it ought to manifest itself in all fields of human life, and if the effect is special to the law, there must be special causes that Mr. Frank has not faced.

There can be no doubt that the desire for complete certainty— the craving for absolute truth—is a trait of all creatures born of woman. Does not Mr. Frank himself believe that his formula, that the law is a *growing* or changing affair, is the real or absolute truth? Or does he grant that tomorrow it *may* be proved once for all that the law *is* a fixed and eternally unchanging system? Mr. Frank does not really face the theoretical and practical conditions of this craving for, and assumption of, absolute knowledge, because of his preoccupation with his pet theory that in the legal field this craving is due to a transference of father-authority to the Law personified. This theory is neither plausible in itself nor is there anything like scientific evidence offered for its adequacy. In every community there are a number of people who for some reason or other have never had a chance to rely on paternal authority. Is there any evidence that they demand less certainty of the law than do the others? Again, when youth ceases to respect paternal authority and relegates it to the realm of Victorianism or old-fogeyism, *does* it transfer its old awe to the law? Or is not the law also apt to be viewed as absurd by rebellious youth? And if men begin to rely more on routine as they grow older and have less zest for adventure, why drag in the notion of a father-substitute?

Mr. Frank protests—perhaps too much—that his psychoanalytic explanation is only a partial one, and at times he calls it a fiction. It is hard in view of the confidence he shows in this explanation to make out exactly what he means by its partiality or its fictional character. His complacent assumption that psychoanalytic concepts like father-substitute are "the best instruments now available for the study of human nature" [5] begs more than he or any one else has as yet proved. Psychoanalysis has doubtless led to some therapeutic results. But so have Christian Science and other faith-cures, and a logician must contend that therapeutic efficiency does not prove the truth of all the different faiths that produce it. Psychoanalysis will become scientific only when, like biology, it becomes really critical of its own evidence, instead of resenting—as all sectarian faiths do—the demand for such evidence. In any case a little more scientific modesty as to the adequacy of his psychology would have saved Mr. Frank from the ridiculous procedure of trying to dispose of Jhering's effort to determine the certain element in the law by calling it "childish." [6] Mr. Frank's categoric denial of the postulate of "a universe completely governed by discoverable unchanging law" [7] involves an absolute knowledge for all future time. Would it be fair to call *him* childish for that? Despite the fashionable modernistic logicians whom Mr. Frank follows too blindly, the attempt to refute a man's views by inventing pejorative psychogenetic accounts of them remains the fallacy recognized and named by the old text-books. It is especially bad grace to apply a quasi-abusive epithet like "childish" to Jhering, who in his famous essay *"Im juristischen Begriffshimmel"* [8] has anticipated all that is sound in Mr. Frank's argument against undue certainty in the law. Jhering, however, was too sound a jurist to forget that the real problem is to find the precise relation between the certain and the uncertain elements in the law.

It may perhaps be unfair to judge Mr. Frank's book by a standard of logical rigour not generally applied to books written for the general public. But as Mr. Frank is engaged in a serious and important task, it must in the interest of the public be pointed out that the myth of a completely certain legal system, apart from the work of judges—a myth that has its roots in legal experience from time immemorial—cannot be overthrown by an admitted fiction from the mushroom science of psychoanalysis. The myth is in fact, like other persistent human beliefs, a half-truth, and its error cannot be overthrown unless we recognize the part of it that is based on the impregnable rock of logical truth.

In the interest of general sanity, which liberals ought not to ignore, we should note that the desire for undue simplicity is not restricted to Platonists and scholastics (epithets never used in a derogatory sense except by those who are woefully ignorant of the writings of Plato and of Thomas Aquinas). It characterizes all those who glibly assume that a world of change must exclude all constancy, and that the reality of particulars is inconsistent with the reality of universals. In this respect Mr. Frank, like others, has been misled by the theologico-philosophic vagaries of Eddington as to the meaning of Heisenberg's principle of indeterminacy. This principle is an empirical application to the electron of old truths as to the nature of measurement. But neither Heisenberg's principle nor the statistical view of nature can deny that different things have universal or common natures (that things come in *kinds*) and that science is a search for constant laws governing the changes of things.

If the natural human craving for certainty be childish, the complete denial of it would be complete madness. If I actually doubt that stones will continue to lie on the ground if undisturbed, that my body is material, and that my fellow beings continue to exist, the last-named will for their and my protection have to lock me up in some asylum. Mr. Frank is impressed with some of the harm of the pretended certainty of the law. He should reflect that modern life would be completely paralyzed without the constant effort to make the law more certain, so that people can know on what to rely in their enterprise. Uncontrolled discretion of judges would make modern complex life unbearable. Rightly does Mr. Frank hold up Justice Holmes as a mature mind on the bench. But that great jurist believes not only that there is certainty in the law but also that it can and ought to be increased. At any rate his greatness as a judge lies precisely in the preëminent way in which he distinguishes between the legal rule that limits the scope of his function and his own personal opinions.

Oliver Wendell Holmes [1]

UNDER the forbiddingly colourless title of *Collected Legal Papers* Justice Holmes has given us an extraordinary book of thoroughly matured human wisdom. The bulk of this volume is, indeed, devoted to technical legal essays—some of which have been epoch-making in the history of legal scholarship—but the law interests Justice Holmes mainly as a window looking out on life and destiny. And in the last few essays, especially, the rich insight into the ever recurrent issues of life is clothed in rare nobility of language.

That the law offers advantageous ground from which to view the whole of human life, its historic developments, actual motives, and ideal aims, is a statement that ought to be obvious to all. That it is seldom actually realized is probably due to the fact that the din of the market place and the "cash nexus" generally make the best-trained lawyers lifelong advocates for certain partisan interests, to the great detriment of their own larger vision. Be that as it may, this book shows "that a man may live greatly in the law as elsewhere; that there, as well as elsewhere, his thought may find its unity in an infinite perspective; that there, as elsewhere, he may wreak himself upon life, may drink the bitter cup of heroism, may wear his heart out after the unattainable." [2] After all, what does the world offer as a starting-point for the true philosopher except a maze of facts? And if he is sustained by a passionate curiosity as to the meaning of things and by a resolute determination to follow the interrelation of facts to the very framework of the universe, he can arrive at true fundamentals through the mazes of the law as by any other way. Indeed in pursuing this way, Justice Holmes has gained marked advantages over the professional philosopher. One who, as a creative scholar, has grappled closely with divergent facts in the effort to make them reveal hitherto hidden connections learns a wholesome respect for the complexity and toughness of the factual world and does not so readily attempt to put it into the corner of a formula. "To rest upon a formula is a slumber that, prolonged, means death." [3] Having also, unlike most professional philosophers, devoted a lifetime to the handling of actual issues that come up in the law, Justice Holmes does not succumb to the fashionable but foolish glorification of the practical over the theoretic or contemplative life. The increase of wine and oil is not the justification of art, nor is the sole justification of philosophy to be found in improved machinery and conduct. Art, science, and philosophy are themselves deep necessities as well as the finest fruit of the specifically human life that we call civilization.

A genuine philosophy is always the expression of a unique personality, and as such can never be fully explained by the accidents of birthplace, time, or the professional occupation of the author. But it may help us to get the drift of this book if we remember that our author is not only a lawyer, but also a son of Puritan New England, a soldier who fought under Lincoln, and above all a cultivated humanist who came to man's estate at a time when the work of Lyell, Darwin, and Huxley was shaking the human intellect out of dogmatic slumbers. The justice and delicacy with which these different elements are combined make this book a most significant expression of a vision of life that is truly American as well as profoundly human.

To associate Justice Holmes's views with Puritanism may be misleading at a time when Puritanism has become synonymous with "blue laws" and the disparagement of natural human desires. But it is well to be reminded that those to whom Calvinism came as a great redeeming vision of life were impressed not so much by the despisal of the flesh as by the glory of God, and that at all times men have been profoundly strengthened by being liberated from

petty personal aims and made to feel the glory of being instruments
of higher powers. Justice Holmes believes fully in "the joy of life
become an end in itself," [4] and that the main line of intellectual advance has been through men like Descartes and Galileo rather than
Calvin and Milton. But he insists as much as any Puritan that the
key to happiness is "to be not merely a necessary but a willing instrument in working out ends which are to us inscrutable." [5] If he does
not, as did the older Puritans, insist upon an anthropomorphic God,
it is because as a son of modern science he has a deeper intellectual
humility and a more genuine conviction of the limitations of man's
knowledge in the face of the unimaginable whole. Against modern
idealists who flatter our vanity by speaking as if the world were all
contained in our consciousness, he insists on the obvious truth that
we must recognize the existence of our neighbours, and that none
of us can make the world what he wills. Here, as elsewhere, "the
rudiments need eternal repetition." [6] When a man begins to reflect,
his inborn faculties and desires as well as the conditions under which
they operate are already formed. Justice Holmes insists on the
nobility as well as on the necessity of fighting for our ideals and
maintaining them against hunger and cold, even at the expense of
our lives. But after all, effort is only one of the ways through
which the inevitable comes to pass.[7] Our most fundamental beliefs
are the expression of our inborn character and limited experience.
Some of these, like the principles of morality, may have tremendous
emotional sanctions; but intellectual honesty compels us to admit
that such first principles must in the nature of the case be literally
prejudices, i.e., judgments in advance of experience. The fact that
we have to live by them before we can begin to determine their
truth, and, indeed, that only by fighting for them can we hope to
prove their truth, need not prevent the honest man from seeing
that his neighbour has to stake his life on *his* convictions or prejudices. When our fundamental preferences conflict sufficiently it may
be my life against yours. But it is only the easy-going stay-at-homes
who indulge in cheap vituperation and fail to respect the enemy.

He who has resolutely faced the enemy and has actually felt the weight of the opposing resolution, is wiser. It is thus that Justice Holmes, while glorifying the soldier's courage and the zest of struggle for our convictions to the extent of our life, can still recognize that the essential mark of the civilized man is to have doubted one's own first principles.[8]

This urbane or civilized scepticism supplies the wisdom to resist dogmatic absolutism. "It is not enough for the knight of romance that you agree that his lady is a very nice girl—if you do not admit that she is the best that God ever made or will make, you must fight. There is in all men a demand for the superlative, so much so that the poor devil who has no other way of reaching it attains it by getting drunk." [9] Scientific or rational man must learn to live without constantly demanding the final and absolute superlative. "We may leave to the unknown the supposed final valuation of that which in any event has value to us." [10]

The serene wisdom that comes with wide surveys of existence frees men from the idols of the cave, the tribe, and the forum; and it is refreshing to see Justice Holmes's complete freedom from all the current cant phrases about liberty and equality, democracy and progress. The only liberty that adds to the value of life is the liberty to do the work for which chance or fate has fitted us. Democracy is a useful word in calling attention to our common limitations and common needs, but no useful end is served by ignoring or minimizing fundamental natural inequalities. As to the notion of progress, of an ever "upward and onward" toward the Golden Age of the Future, Justice Holmes also shows a wise scepticism. Sooner or later the race of man, like countless other stately species that have lorded over this globe, may pass away. But this by no means justifies despair. The harvest of despair is only for those who needlessly sow vain hopes. The wise men of all generations live not so much for the future as in the eternal present, trusting that whatever we do is woven forever into the great vibrating web of the world.

Justice Holmes's long and honourable record of dissenting opinions in cases where the courts have ignored the human rights of labour, and have unduly extended the rights of property and "freedom of contract," has given people the impression that he is something of a radical. This, however, is not the case. He is a firm believer in the régime of private property and the traditional economics. His dissenting opinions thus manifest a rare intellectual integrity that enables him to distinguish between his own opinions and that which the Constitution leaves to the legislature to determine. This lends unusual force to his charge that our courts, unduly influenced by the fear of socialism, have taken sides on debatable questions and have unconsciously read into the Constitution economic doctrines that prevailed fifty years ago.[11] "Judges commonly are elderly men and are more likely to hate at sight any analysis to which they are not accustomed."[12]

Justice Holmes's own belief in the traditional economics according to which "ownership means investment and investment means the direction of labour towards the production of the greatest returns"[13] leaves him with scant sympathy for those who complain against the injustice of our unequal distribution of wealth. The possession of great wealth, according to his view, means not increased consumption but increased power, and this leads to a greater production of goods consumed by the many. Now quite apart from the very questionable truth of this doctrine, and apart from the many facts that show actual conflicts between private profit and public good, one cannot lightly brush away the deep and widely felt feeling expressed by Burns.

> It's hardly in a body's power,
> To keep, at times, frae being sour,
>   To see how things are shared;
> How best o' chiels are whyles in want,
> While coofs on countless thousands rant,
>   And ken na how to ware't.

To the conventional moralist envy and jealousy are mean and ungenteel emotions, to be eradicated. But to one who, like Justice Holmes himself, believes that the fundamental traits of human nature need to be cultivated and humanized rather than snubbed, envy and jealousy are as worthy of attention as hunger, sex, and the desire for personal recognition. Just as sex humanized becomes potent and beautiful love, so envy or jealousy humanized and rationalized becomes the sublime sentiment of justice. It is also significant that the community generally does not feel proud of those who win prizes in the economic struggle as it takes pride and vicariously shares in the glory of those who win prizes in athletics, statesmanship, art, and science.

There is one other doctrine that men of the younger generation view with greater scepticism than does our genial author, and that is the belief that "everything is connected with everything else." [14] Many parts of the world that we know are but loosely connected, and beyond there may be more discordant diversity than unity. In any case we hesitate to follow Justice Holmes when he speaks as if the cosmos had purposes to which we must subordinate ourselves. It may be vain to resist the inevitable. But to worship all that inevitably happens is a desolating idolatry, subversive of our integrity. Man's dignity and inner worth demand a rejection and a defiance of those elements in the universe which are inimical to our human aims. Humanity has rightly admired god-defying Prometheus, and even the pious editors of the Bible could not omit the old story of Jacob winning blessings through struggling with God by the river Jabbok.

Few of us, however, will quarrel with Justice Holmes's practical application of his creed. "The rule of joy and the law of duty seem to me all one . . . With all humility I think 'Whatsoever thy hand findeth to do, do with all thy might,' infinitely more important than the vain attempt to love one's neighbor as one's self. If you want to hit a bird on the wing, you must not be thinking about yourself and equally you must not be thinking about your neighbor; you must be living in your eye on that bird. Every achievement is a bird on the wing." [15] Whether you call it the primal curse or a sacrament that brings forth human worth, conscientious and sustained toil is the only way through which the objects of human desire can be really attained.

No one in recent times has emphasized as fully as Justice Holmes the necessary isolation of the one who wishes to achieve any real advance in the realm of thought. "Only when you have worked alone—when you have felt around you a black gulf of solitude more isolating than that which surrounds the dying man, and in hope and in despair have trusted to your own unshaken will—then only will you have achieved." [16] But we cannot achieve all our dreams. "We are lucky enough if we can give a sample of our best and if in our hearts we can feel that it has been nobly done." [17]

"The law is not the place for the artist or the poet. The law is the calling of thinkers." [18] It is easy for a professional philosopher to take Justice Holmes at his word and to discuss his book in the pale medium of abstract thought. But the wise reader will turn to the book itself for a concrete realization of the author's contention that to think great thoughts one must have a heroic soul.

Notes

JUDGE PARRY ON THE LAW AND THE POOR

[1] This essay is a review of Edward A. Parry, *The Law and the Poor* (Dutton, 1914), first published in *New Republic*, Vol. IV (1915), p. 25.

[2] Imprisonment for debt has been nominally abolished in several States, by statute or constitutional provision, but the courts have regularly construed such provisions as allowing imprisonment for failure to pay "claims" that are not legally debts (e.g., those arising out of bailment, assessments, fraud, and torts generally).

[3] Parry, *op. cit.*, p. 201.

[4] *Ibid.*, p. 201.

[5] *Ibid.*, p. 204.

[6] *Ibid.*, p. 100.

[7] *Ibid.*, p. 18.

[8] *Ibid.*, p. 262.

[9] *Idem.*

[10] *Ibid.*, p. 256.

[11] *Ibid.*, p. 306.

[12] *Ibid.*, p. 110.

[13] *Ibid.*, p. 153.

[14] *Ibid.*, p. x.

HERBERT HOOVER'S MYTH OF INDIVIDUALISM

[1] This essay is a review of Herbert Hoover, *American Individualism* (Doubleday, Page, 1922), reprinted, with slight verbal changes, from *New Republic*, Vol. XXXIII (1923), p. 352.

[2] Hoover, *op. cit.*, pp. 6, 25.

[3] *Ibid.*, p. 25.

[4] *Ibid.*, p. 17.

[5] *Ibid.*, pp. 63-67.

[6] *Ibid.*, p. 14.

[7] *Ibid.*, p. 70.

[8] *Ibid.*, p. 71.

[9] *Ibid.*, p. 33.

[10] *Ibid.*, p. 51.

[11] *Ibid.*, p. 11.

[12] *Ibid.*, p. 39.

[13] *Ibid.*, p. 40.

[14] *Ibid.*, p. 46.

[15] *Ibid.*, p. 1.

[16] *Ibid.*, p. 36.

THE LEGAL CALVINISM OF ELIHU ROOT

[1] This essay is a review of Elihu Root, *Addresses on Government and Citizenship* (Harvard University Press, 1916), reprinted, with slight verbal changes, from *New Republic*, Vol. X (1917), p. 109.

[2] Root, *op. cit.*, p. 406.

[3] *Ibid.*, p. 85.

[4] *Ibid.*, p. 514.

[5] *Ibid.*, pp. 261, 500.

[6] *Ibid.*, pp. 116, 117.

[7] *Ibid.*, p. 273.

[8] *Ibid.*, p. 102.

[9] *Ibid.*, p. 113.

[10] *Ibid.*, p. 450.

[11] *Ibid.*, p. 43.

[12] *Ibid.*, p. 524.

[13] *Ibid.*, pp. 201-02.

[14] *Ibid.*, p. 202.

THE CONSERVATIVE LAWYER'S LEGEND OF MAGNA CARTA

[1] This essay is, in substance, a review of William D. Guthrie, *Magna Carta and Other Addresses* (Columbia University Press, 1916), first published in *New Republic*, Vol. IX (Nov. 18, 1916), Literary Review, p. 18.

[2] At the time of the Domesday survey the number of freemen (including yeomen and clergy) was one-seventh of the total population of England.

³ Guthrie, *op. cit.*, p. 1.
⁴ Ives v. South Buffalo Ry. Co., 201 N. Y. 271, 94 N. E. 431 (1911).
⁵ Guthrie, *op. cit.*, p. 65.

AN AMERICAN JUDGE ON THE NATURE OF JUSTICE

¹ This essay is, in substance, a review of Lucilius A. Emery, *Concerning Justice* (Yale University Press, 1914), first published in *New Republic*, Vol. II (1915), p. 107.

² Emery, *op. cit.*, p. 8.	⁶ *Idem.*	¹⁰ *Ibid.*, pp. 43 ff.
³ *Ibid.*, p. 11.	⁷ *Ibid.*, p. 39.	¹¹ *Ibid.*, p. 55.
⁴ *Idem.*	⁸ *Ibid.*, p. 40.	¹² *Idem.*
⁵ *Ibid.*, p. 31.	⁹ *Ibid.*, p. 55.	¹³ *Ibid.*, p. 14.

THE BIRTHRIGHT OF ESAU

¹ This essay is, in part, a book review of Harlan Eugene Read, *The Abolition of Inheritance* (Macmillan, 1919), published in *New Republic*, Vol. XX (1919), p. 129.
² I follow the author in using the word "inheritance" in its popular sense as including the acquisition of goods through testamentary disposition.

NEW LEADERSHIP IN THE LAW

¹ Reprinted, with slight verbal changes, from *New Republic*, Vol. VI (1916), p. 148.
² "The Causes of Popular Dissatisfaction with the Administration of Justice," *American Law Review*, Vol. XL (1906), pp. 729, 737.
³ "The Administration of Justice in the Modern City," *Harvard Law Review*, Vol. XXVI (1913), pp. 302, 320.
⁴ "Do We Need a Philosophy of Law?" *Columbia Law Review*, Vol. V (1905), pp. 339, 347.

⁵ *Ibid.*, p. 348.	⁸ *Ibid.*, p. 325.
⁶ *Ibid.*, p. 344.	⁹ *Op. cit.* (note 4), p. 345.

⁷ *Op. cit.* (note 3), pp. 326-27.
¹⁰ "The Decadence of Equity," *Columbia Law Review*, Vol. V (1905), pp. 20-21.
¹¹ *Op. cit.* (note 3), p. 318.   ¹² *Op. cit.* (note 4), p. 353.
¹³ "The Need of a Sociological Jurisprudence," *Green Bag*, Vol. XIX (1907), pp. 607, 611.
¹⁴ *Ibid.*, p. 612.

PROPERTY AND SOVEREIGNTY

¹ This lecture, originally delivered at the Cornell Law School as the Irvine Lecture for 1927, is reprinted here, with slight changes, from *Cornell Law Quarterly*, Vol. XIII (1927), p. 8.
² *L'Esprit des lois*, Book XXVI, Chap. 15, 1748.
³ Austin, *Lectures on Jurisprudence*, 5th ed., 1911, Vol. I, p. 457.
⁴ Holtzendorff-Kohler, *Enzyklopädie*, 1913-15, Vol. I, pp. 179-80. Continental jurists generally regard Roman law as more individualistic than Germanic law. Gierke, "Der Entwurf eines bürgerlichen Gesetzbuches und das deutsche Recht," *Schmollers Jahrbuch für Gesetzgebung*, Vol. XII (1888), pp. 843, 875; Menger, *Archiv für Soziale Gesetzgebung*, Vol. II (1889), p. 429; Rambaud, *Civilisation française*, Vol. I, p. 13; D'Arbois de Jubainville, *Académie d'Inscriptions*, February, 1887. This seems also the view of Maine, *Ancient Law*, p. 228. Maitland's remark that the whole constitutional history of England seems at times to be but an appendix to the laws of real property

(*Constitutional History of England,* 1908, p. 538) only echoes the prevailing French attitude that their Civil Code is their real constitution.

[5] Adkins v. Children's Hospital, U. S. 261, 525; Supr. Ct. 43, 394 (1923).

[6] "Liberty of Contract," *Yale Law Journal,* Vol. XVIII (1909), pp. 454, 482.

[7] In granting patents, copyrights, etc., the principle of reward for useful work or encouragement of productivity seems so much more relevant that the principle of discovery and first occupancy seems to have little force.

[8] Economists often claim that unearned increment is the greatest source of wealth. See H. J. Davenport, "Extent and Significance of Unearned Increment," *Bulletin of the American Economic Association,* Series 4, No. 2 (1911), pp. 322, 324-25.

[9] Demogue, *Les notions fondamentales du droit privé,* 1911.

[10] *Cours de droit naturel,* 6th ed., 1868, p. 108.

[11] Thus the leading brewers doubtless foresaw the coming of prohibition and could have saved millions in losses by separating their interests from that of the saloon. But the large temporary loss involved in such an operation was something to which stockholders could never have agreed.

[12] Thus our courts are reluctant to admit that rules against unfair competition may be in the interest of the general public and not merely for those whose immediate property interests are directly affected. Levy v. Walker, 10 Ch. D. 436 (1878); American Washboard Co. v. Saginaw Mfg. Co., 103 Fed. 281, 285 (C.C.A. 6th, 1900); Dickenson v. N. R. Co., 76 W. Va. 148, 151, 85 S. E. 71 (1915).

[13] French Civil Code, § 544; Prussian Landrecht I, 8, § 1; Austrian General Civil Code, § 354; German Civil Code, § 903; Italian Civil Code, § 436. Cf. Markby, *Elements of Law,* 6th ed., 1905, § 310; Aubry & Rau, *Cours de droit civil française,* 5th ed., 1897-1922, § 190.

[14] The great Jhering is an honorable exception. The distinction between property for use and property for power was developed by the Austrian jurist A. Menger, and made current by the German economist Adolf Wagner.

[15] Holdsworth, *History of English Law,* 1916, Vol. VIII, Chap. IV, p. 100.

[16] Roussel, *L'Abus du droit,* 1913; German Civil Code, § 226; Walton, "Motive as an Element in Torts," *Harvard Law Review,* Vol. XXII (1909), p. 501.

[17] Laski, *Studies in the Problem of Sovereignty,* 1917, Chap. II.

[18] Malcolm, *Sketches of Persia,* 1861, pp. 215 et seq.

[19] It used to be thought that there could be no credit transactions if the creditor could not acquire dominion over the body of the debtor in default. Yet credit transactions have not decreased with the development of homestead laws and the limitation of imprisonment for debt.

THE BASIS OF CONTRACT

[1] Reprinted from *Harvard Law Review,* February, 1933.

[2] Maine, *Ancient Law,* 6th ed., pp. 170, 305. In referring to the feudal centuries as the golden days of "free" if formal contract, Pollock and Maitland (*History of English Law,* Vol. II, p. 233) assert that in that period "the law of contract threatened to swallow up all public law. The idea that men can fix their rights and duties by agreement is in its early days an unruly anarchical idea. If there is to be any law at all, contract must be taught its place."

[3] See Dr. Greenstone's article on "Prosbul" in the *Jewish Encyclopedia,* and Schürer's *History of the Jewish People in the Time of Jesus Christ,* 1898, Div. II, Vol. I, p. 362.

[4] See the tractate *Baba Metzia,* 94a, in which the prevailing opinion allows some stipulations as to money matters even contrary to the Torah.

[5] II Sam. 21, 24; Josh. 7.   [6] Ezek. 18:20.   [7] II Sam. 6:6-7.

[8] Cf. Esmein, *Le serment promissoire dans le droit canonique*, 1888, pp. 1 *et seq.*; 37 *et seq.*

[9] Maitland, *English Law and the Renaissance*, 1901.

[10] Holdsworth, *History of English Law*, 1926, Vol. VIII, pp. 100 *et seq.*

[11] Santayana, *Reason in Society*, 1905, p. 71.

[12] *Collected Legal Papers*, 1920, pp. 279 *et seq.* and 293 *et seq.*

[13] M. Weber, *Religionssoziologie*, 1920, Vol. I, pp. 30 *et seq.* Thorold Rogers, *Economic Interpretation of History*, 1888, pp. 84 *et seq.* Karl Marx, *Das Kapital*, 2nd ed., 1872, p. 750, and *Kritik der politischen Oekonomie*, 1859, p. 128. Similar views had been expressed by E. Le Lavelaye, De Tocqueville, and Guizot. See the article on "Christianity and Economics" in Palgrave's *Dictionary of Political Economy*.

[14] L. Brentano, *Die Angänge des Modernen Kapitalismus*, 1916, pp. 142 *et seq.*

[15] Quoted by Ashley, *English Economic History and Theory*, 4th ed., 1906, Vol. I, Part II, p. 391. Cf. Thomas Aquinas, *Summa Theologica*, 2a, 2ae, Q. 77, Art. 4, and Schreiber, *Die Volkswirtschaftlichen Anschauungen der Scholastik*, pp. 89, 105, 145, 158, 193, 200, 230.

[16] For Melancthon's views see Ashley, *op. cit.*, pp. 457 *et seq.* and Schmoller's *Ansichten*, p. 120. Calvin's celebrated letter to Œcolampadius is printed in his *Epistola et Responsa* (ed. Beza, 1575, p. 355), and is discussed by Böhm-Bawerk, *Capital and Interest* (trans. by Smart), p. 28, and by Ashley, *op. cit.*, pp. 458-60. Jewell, "Exposition upon the Epistle to the Thessalonians," in *Works*, Parker Society, Vol. II, pp. 851 *et seq.* Cf. Tawney's edition of Thomas Wilson's *Discourse on Usury*. For a general view of the question of usury see Brissaud, *History of French Private Law*, 1912 (Continental Legal History Series), pp. 385-388, 390; and Holdsworth, *op. cit.*, pp. 100 *et seq.*

[16a] See Plato's *Republic*, I, 331 B; and Cicero, *De Officiis*, I, c. 10; III, cc. 24-25. The canon law did not regard all promises, even under oath, as binding. See the *Decretales* of Gregory IX, Lib. II, tit. 24, cc. 1, 2, 3, 15, 23, 27 and 33; *Sexti Decretalium*, Lib. V, reg. 58.

[17] Reinach, *Die apriorischen Grundlagen des bürgerlichen Rechts*, 1922, ss. 2-4. Kant himself derives the obligation of contract not from promises but from the union of free-wills to transfer rights.

[18] Pound, *Introduction to the Philosophy of Law*, 1922, pp. 276, 236.

[19] Prov. 6: 1-5; 17: 18; 22: 26. Psalms 15: 4. Job 17: 3. See article "Covenant" in *Encyclopædia Biblica*; and Nowack, *Lehrbuch der hebräischen Archäologie*, 1894, Vol. I, pp. 341 *et seq.* and 354 *et seq.*

[20] On Greek Contracts see Plato, *Republic*, I, 555; *Laws*, V, 729 E, 847 B; XI, 917-18, 920-21; *Crito*, 51; Aristotle, *Politics*, I, 9, 1-11; *Rhetoric*, I, c. 15, § 22; *Ethica N.*, v. 2, 1131, a2. Theophrastos in Stobæus, *Florilegium*, 44, c. 22. Cf. Vinogradoff, *Historical Jurisprudence*, 1922, Vol. II, Chap. 9; Mitteis, *Reichsrecht und Volksrecht*, 1891, pp. 479 *et seq.* and Beauchet, *Histoire du droit privé de la république athénienne*, 1897, pp. 19 *et seq.*

[21] Tacitus, *Germania*, c. 24; Grotius, *The Jurisprudence of Holland*, ed. by Lee, 1926, Book III, sec. 52; Gierke, *Deutches Privatrecht*, Vol. I, p. 284; Vol. III, p. 2, note 2; p. 283; and *Schuld und Haftung*, 1910, p. 168.

[22] Brunner, "*Der Schuldvertrag bedarfte einer bestimmten hörbaren und sichtbaren Form*," in Holtzendorff-Kohler, *Enzyklopedie*, 7th ed., 1915, Vol. I, p. 137. Similarly: Brissaud, *op. cit.*, sec. 362, p. 451; Pollock and Maitland, *History of English Law*, Vol. II, p. 185; Esmein, *Etudes sur les contrats*, p. 69; Heussler, *Institutionen des deutschen Privatrecht*, Vol. II, p. 225; Von Amira, *Grundriss der germanischen Rechts*, sec. 70 (in Paul's *Grundriss der germanischen Philologie*, Vol. III).

[23] Brissaud, *op. cit.*, sec. 375.

[24] References to the enormous literature on the controversy as to whether there must

be a real will or intention to be bound as well as a declaration of the will, will be found in Windscheid's *Pandekten*, 8th ed., 1900, Vol. I, sec. 75; Enneccerus, *Lehrbuch des bürgerlichen Rechts*, 1913, Vol. I, secs. 136 and 155; Staudinger, *Kommentar zum bürgerlichen Gesetzbuch*, 1912, Vol. I, p. 434. See also Manigk, *Willenserklärung und Willensgeschäft*, 1907, pp. 27-150, and Binder, *Wille und Willenserklärung im Tatbestand des Rechtsgeschäftes*, reprinted from Vols. V-VI of the *Archiv für Rechts- und Wirtschaftsphilosophie*. In France this was taken up by Saleilles, *Déclaration de la volonté*, 1901, for criticisms of which see Lerebours-Pigeonnière in *L'Œuvre juridique de Raymond Saleilles*, 1914, pp. 399 *et seq.*, and Bonnecase, *Science du droit et romantisme*, 1928, pp. 229 *et seq.*

[25] Planiol, *Traité elémentaire du droit civil*, 1912, Vol. II, sec. 944.

[26] The old doctrine of *læsio enormis*, which used a plausible standard as to when a disparity of value made a contract unfair, has been abandoned because of the growth of the doctrine that we must let the parties completely determine the values involved. This is a great convenience in the process of adjudication, for it rules out all sorts of material inquiries. But it introduces a certain literal rigidity into the law characteristic of that which Dean Pound calls "the stage of the strict law."

[27] Hauriou, *Droit public*, 2nd ed., 1916, pp. 196-219. I am also indebted for stimulating reflections along this line to Demogue's *Les notions fondamentales du droit privé*, 1911, Book I, Chap. 4; and to his great treatise on obligations. Also to Karl Lewellyn, "What Price Contract?" *Yale Law Journal*, Vol. XL, pp. 704 *et seq.*

THE PROCESS OF JUDICIAL LEGISLATION

[1] The major part of the present essay was read at the first meeting of the Conference on Legal and Social Philosophy, April 26, 1913, and published under this title in *American Law Review*, Vol. XLVIII (1914), p. 161. Portions of the present essay are taken from a paper presented at the thirty-eighth annual meeting of the New York State Bar Association, January 22-23, 1915, and published under the title "Legal Theories and Social Science" in *International Journal of Ethics*, Vol. XXV (1915), p. 469.

[2] "The Importance of an Independent Judiciary," *Independent*, Vol. LXXII (1912), p. 704.

[3] American Bar Association, *Reports*, Vol. III (1907), pp. 45 *et seq.*

[4] Gray, *Nature and Sources of the Law*, 1909, sec. 275-76.

[5] Hornblower, "A Century of 'Judge-Made' Law," *Columbia Law Review*, Vol. VII (1907), pp. 453-57. In historical and biographical estimates of various judges it is quite usual to find them praised for developing or creating certain branches of law, e.g., nearly all accounts of Story praise him for having created our admiralty law, which, in truth, he did.

[6] "He [Marshall] was not the commentator upon American Constitutional Law; he was not the expounder of it; he was the author, the creator of it." Phelps, "Annual Address," *Annual Report* American Bar Association, 1879, pp. 173, 176.

[7] When our courts of appeal overrule our trial courts in almost a majority of cases and when the judgments of our federal Supreme Court are in so many important cases given by divided votes with strong dissenting opinions, it surely requires more than the mere lesson of daily experience to make one believe that the law on every subject is inherently fixed and certain and that all the judge has to do is to declare what it says.

[8] "A Government of Law, or a Government of Men?" *North American Review*, Vol. CXCIII (1911), p. 13.

[9] *L'Esprit des lois*, Book XI, Chap. VI.

[10] *Politics*, Book II, Chap. XIV.

[11] *Federalist*, 1818 ed., No. 47, p. 301.

[12] Baldwin, *The American Judiciary*, 1905, p. 22.

[13] See Wayman v. Sutherland, 23 U. S. (10 Wheat.) 1 (1825).

[14] *Commentaries on the Constitution*, 3d ed., 1858, Vol. I, pp. 364-65.

[15] Brown v. Turner, 70 N. C. 93, 102 (1874).

[16] French publicists frequently use the maxim of the division of power, but only to confine the judiciary to purely private litigation and prevent the civil courts from interfering with administrative matters, which are dealt with by special administrative courts. They do not profess to separate the executive from the legislative power. The doctrine of a complete and distinct separation of judicial from legislative power, like the related overdrawn antithesis between determinism and freedom, or reason and will, is typical of a certain naïve rationalism (regnant in the eighteenth century) which shows itself in an uncritical belief in the adequacy of rigid divisions, as of the faculties of the mind, the powers of the state, etc. The contrast between Aristotle's guarded statement (*op. cit.* in note 10) and Montesquieu's sweeping and unhistorical dogma (*op. cit.* in note 9) is instructive in this respect. See Bagehot, *The English Constitution*, 1867, Chap. 8; Bryce, *The American Commonwealth*, 1888, Chap. 26; Wilson, *Congressional Government*, 1886, Chap. 5.

[17] The prevailing usage in this country, since Calder v. Bull, is to restrict the term *ex post facto* to penal statutes, but in using the term in its general or literal meaning (as a synonym for retroactive) I follow the usage of Austin, *Jurisprudence*, 3rd ed., 1875, pp. 502-03; Markby, *Elements of Law*, 3rd ed., 1885, sec. 98; and Gray, *op. cit.* (note 4), sec. 224. That our constitutional prohibition against *ex post facto* laws as commonly understood has intensified the distrust of retroactive legislation is seen in the fact that unlike the courts of England and of the Continent, ours refuse to give a retroactive force to declaratory laws. See note 48 below.

[18] Hornblower, *op. cit.* (note 5), p. 458. This argument is a variant of the late Mr. Carter's theory that law is nothing but custom, which I regard as having been disposed of by Gray, *op. cit.* (note 4), sec. 599-620.

[19] "Puritanism and the Common Law," *American Law Review*, Vol. XLV (1911), p. 811; reprinted in Pound, *The Spirit of the Common Law*, 1921, Chap. II.

[20] Marshall, *Life of Washington*, 2d ed., Vol. II, p. 127.

[21] Jenks, *Law and Politics in the Middle Ages*, 1898, p. 7.

[22] Carter, *The Province of the Written and Unwritten Law*, 1889, p. 9.

[23] Bentham's view that all the law can be reduced to a simple code, by reading which every one can learn and on each occasion know what are his rights and what his duties, follows logically from the theory that the law antedates all judicial decisions. In this respect Bentham is certainly more consistent than his American critics who share his presupposition but think that for some curious reason the law preëxistent in the breast of the judge loses its magic potency when once written down, except, indeed, in the case of a written constitution.

[24] Geldart, "Legal Personality," *Law Quarterly Review*, Vol. XXVII (1911), pp. 90-91.

[25] The flimsy fiction that judicial decisions do not make the law, but are only the evidence of it, is really inconsistent with the doctrine of *stare decisis*. If decisions were only evidence of the law, why could not courts of coördinate or even inferior jurisdiction entertain evidence that any previous decision or judgment was wrong? Obviously, to the extent that such evidence is excluded, the past decision has made law.

There is no space here to indicate fully the logical confusion in the classical theory that each particular decision embodies a general rule as its *ratio decidendi*. A particular proposition can never uniquely determine a general one, and as a matter of fact any case, no matter how simple, can be cited in our system as an authority for various propositions of law of different degrees of generality. The true relation between decisions or judgments and rules of law is analogous to that between given points and the curves that can be drawn through them.

Professor Geldart and others seem to think it absurd to suppose that when a new case is decided "the facts of the case were previously governed by no law" (*Elements of English Law*, 1911, p. 23). This objection is based on a confusion between potential and actual existence, but we may here meet it by simply calling attention to the undoubted fact that vast regions of human relations, such as informal agreements, formerly not governed by the common law have by judicial decision been brought within its sway.

[26] See Sneddeker v. Waring, 12 N. Y. 170, 174 (1854).

[27] For modern instances or illustrations see Lefroy, "The Basis of Case Law," *Law Quarterly Review*, Vol. XXII (1906), p. 293 *et seq*. From the Continental and comparative point of view this has been significantly treated by Kohler, "Die Menschenhülfe in Privatrecht," *Jherings Jahrbücher für die Dogmatik*, Vol. XXV (1887), pp. 1-141.

[28] For the classical common-law conception of public policy see Co. Litt. 66 a. (1st Amer. ed., 1853) and Sheppard's *Touchstone*, Chap. 6. The attempt of Baron Parke to narrow the meaning of the term "public policy" to mean simply the policy already established in the law was, as Lefroy has pointed out, rejected by the House of Lords in Egerton v. Earl of Brownlow, 4 H. L. C. 1 (1853).

[29] See Willcox v. The Consolidated Gas Co., 212 U. S. 19, 29 Sup. Ct. 192 (1919). "Reasonablenesse in these cases belongeth to the knowledge of the law, and therefore to be decided by the justices." (Co. Litt. 56, b.)

[30] E. R. Thayer, "Judicial Legislation," *Harvard Law Review*, Vol. V (1891), pp. 170, 180.

[31] People ex rel. Hotchkiss v. Smith, 206 N. Y. 231, 99 N. E. 568 (1912). The court condemns certain things because "unnecessary" and others pass as "not sufficiently onerous." But "requirements which shock the sense of justice" (p. 242) are not always unconstitutional.

[32] Wigmore, *Evidence*, 2d ed., 1923, Vol. I, p. xv. Judge Baldwin cites with approval the statement of an English judge that "nine-tenths of the cases which had ever gone to judgment in the highest court of England might have been decided the other way without any violence to the principles of the common law." Baldwin, *The American Judiciary*, 1905, p. 54.

[33] This process is examined in detail by Thayer, *op. cit*. (note 30), pp. 181 *et seq*.

[34] Cf. the influence of the French Code on the German Civil Code, e.g., the doctrine of possession (B G B, sec. 932 *et seq*.) and the influence of the latter on the Swiss Civil Code in regard to common property, abuse of right, and mortgages.

[35] Cf. Forbes v. Cochrane, 2 B. & C. 448 (1824); Simpson v. Fogo, 32 L. J. Rep. Ch. 249 (1863); Liverpool Marine Credit v. Hunter, L. R., 4 Eq. 62 (1867).

[36] The abolition of the legal power of the husband to administer what Blackstone calls moderate correction, the abolition of the view that public office is a kind of private property (cf. Mial v. Ellington, 134 N. C. 131, 46 S. E. 961 [1903]), and the abolition of the view that a strike is inherently illegal, afford ready instances of modern judicial changes in the law.

[37] Note, for instance, the way in which, by stretching the law of conspiracy to include all sorts of combinations, it was changed from a statutory to a common law offense, and its form of pleading changed thereby. See Rex v. Journeymen Tailors, 8 Mod. 10 (1721); Rex v. Eccles, 1 Leach 274 (1783); Wright, *The Law of Criminal Conspiracy*, 1887, p. 42; and Bryan, *Development of English Law of Conspiracy*, 1908, pp. 126-30.

[38] For a vigorous defense of fictions, see Forti, *Il realismo nel diritto pubblico*, 1903, pp. 68-81.

[39] Holmes, *The Common Law*, 1881, p. 120.

[40] 1898, pp. 259, 327-33. For a similar view of presumptions from the Continental point of view see Fitting, "Die Grundlagen der Beweislast," *Zeitschrift für deutschen Civilprozess*, Vol. XIII (1879), pp. 1-79, especially the distinction between *Erfahrungsvermuthungen* and *Rechtsvermuthungen*, pp. 75-76. Cf. Bernhoft, "Zur Lehre von den Fiktionen," in the *Festschrift* in honour of Bekker, 1907. Cf. Planiol, *Traité élémentaire du droit civil*, 1908, Vol. II, p. 17; and Levi, *La societé et l'ordre juridique*, 1910, Chap. 3.

[41] Ives v. South Buffalo Ry. Co., 201 N. Y. 271, 94 N. E. 431 (1911).

[42] Fitzwater v. Warren, 206 N. Y. 35, 99 N. E. 1042 (1912), overruling Knisley v. Pratt, 148 N. Y. 372, 42 N. E. 986 (1896). Perhaps the future historian may find this change in the law not unconnected with the storm of disapproval that greeted the announcement of the Ives decision.

[43] *Negligence*, 3d ed., 1908, Vol. I, p. 608. That the fellow-servant rule and the doctrine of the assumption of risk were not necessary has been recognized by Pollock (cf. *The Genius of the Common Law*, 1912, pp. 104-05); Holmes (cf. "Law in Science and Science in Law," *Harvard Law Review*, Vol. XII [1899], pp. 443, 456); and Dicey (cf. *Law and Public Opinion*, 1905, p. 280). That the law might have developed along different lines can be seen in the history of the Scotch law (see Sword v. Cameron, 1 Dunlop 493 [1838]) until the Scotch courts were overruled in the Bartonshill case by the English House of Lords (6 W. R. 664 H. L. [1858]) and later again in Merry v. Wilson.

[44] A distinction between interpretation and construction is sometimes drawn, the latter being necessary only when the meaning is doubtful. But when parties are interested in finding different meanings, "constructions will be found." (This phrase was used by such a pillar of the orthodox theory as Elihu Root.)

[45] Thayer, *Preliminary Treatise on Evidence*, 1898, p. 204.

[46] Maitland, *Equity*, 1910, p. 66.

[47] Thus Lord Halsbury distinctly asserts that the worst person to construe a statute is the person who drafted it, because he tends to confuse what he intended to say with what he actually said. (Hilder v. Dexter [1902] A. C. 474, 477.) A judge who drafted a bill must thus divest his mind of all past impressions of it. In re Mew and Thorne, 31 L. J. Bcy (1862) 87.

[48] Ogden, Administrator v. Blackedge, Executor, 2 Cranch 272 (1804); Dash v. Van Kleeck, 7 Johns. R. 477, Kent, J., at p. 512 (1811); Smith v. Syracuse Ins. Co., 161 N. Y. 484, 55 N. E. 1077 (1900). This rule, however, is not followed in England (Attorney General v. Theobald, 24 Q. B. D. 557 [1890] and cases therein cited). This has been carried to the extent of collecting duties even though property has meanwhile passed to others.

[49] Wahl, *Les successions*, 1902, Vol. I, p. 513. For criticism of the classical theory of retroactivity and vested or acquired rights, see Vareilles-Sommières in *Nouvelle revue de l'histoire du droit*, 1893, p. 241 *et seq.* Cf. Aubry et Rau, *Cours de droit*, 3d ed., 1856, Vol. I, p. 30; and Planiol, *op. cit.* (note 40), Vol. I, pp. 250 *et seq.*

[50] A striking instance of this is to be found in Art. 757, French Civil Code. It was voted by the Assembly on the assurance by Treilhard, the reporter of the commission that edited it, that it provided for the wife a high rank among the heirs of the husband. As a matter of fact it puts the wife after all relatives, and even after natural children. See Mallieux, *L'exégèse des codes*, 1908, p. 16.

[51] Regina v. Hartford College, 3 Q. B. D. 693, 707.

[52] *Scire leges non hoc est verba earum tenere sed vim ac potestatem* (Celsus, Dig. I, 3, 17). On the Continent the movement for "free" creative or sociological interpretation has now met with general acceptance. It was elaborated with unusual keenness by Kohler in articles in *Grünhuts Zeitschrift*, Vol. XIII (1886), pp. 1-61, and *Jherings*

Jahrbücher, Vol. XXV (1887), pp. 262-97, but received little attention until the adoption of the German and Swiss civil codes made the topic a pressing one. Since the publication of Geny's *Méthode d'interprétation*, 1899, a whole literature on the subject has grown up, references to which will be found in Sternberg, *Einführung in die Rechtswissenschaft*, 1912, Vol. I, pp. 141-42; Cosentine, *La réforme de la législation civile*, 1913, pp. 268-78; and On Continental Legal Philosophy, pp. 286-318 of this volume. The logical and historical parallel between the rules and methods of legal interpretation and those of Biblical exegesis offers a theme that has not been developed.

[53] It also decides, incidentally, what the public should have understood or have taken the statute to mean.

[54] Rowan v. Runnels, 5 How. 134, 139 (1847).

[55] Douglass v. County of Pike, 101 U. S. 677, 687 (1879).

[56] Thayer, *Legal Essays*, 1908, p. 150.

[57] One of the most usual ways in which courts supplement a statute is by supplying definitions, for instance, defining "person" in the Fourteenth Amendment to include corporations. Again, if the legislature in an income-tax law defines "income" to include the unearned increment of land value, there is no doubt that this is substantial legislation. Would it be less so if, in the absence of legislative expression, the courts would so define it?

[58] For example, see Thayer, *op. cit.* (note 45), pp. 195-96.

[59] It is interesting to note that, in spite of the wide power of supplementary legislation given to administrative officers on the Continent, modern Continental codes recognize the need of judicial legislation, the German Civil Code implicitly (e.g., sec. 626) and the Swiss Code explicitly (Civil Code, Art. 1, 2). Cf. the Italian Civil Code, Art. 3, and the Austrian Civil Code, Art. 7. Even the framers of the Napoleonic Code recognized this. "A host of things are necessarily left to the rule of usage, to the discipline of learned men, and to the decision of judges." Portalis, "Discours préliminaire" (1836), Fenet, *Rescueil complet des travaux préparatoires du Code Civil*, p. 476.

[60] Malloy v. Chicago & N. W. R. Co., 109 Wis. 29, 85 N. W. 130 (1901).

[61] Silver v. Ladd, 7 Wall. 219 (1868).

[62] R. v. Harrald, L. R. 7 Q. B. 361 (1872).

[63] See cases quoted by Maxwell, *Statutory Interpretation*, 1884, pp. 115, 118, 163-68; and W. H. Loyd, "The Equity of a Statute," *University of Pennsylvania Law Review*, Vol. LVIII (1909), p. 76.

[64] Attorney General v. Edison Tel. Co., 6 Q. B. D. 244 (1880).

[65] The gist of Marshall's argument in Marbury v. Madison is that judges are sworn to obey the law, and, as the Constitution is the supreme law, the judges must disregard congressional interpretation of the Constitution when it conflicts with their own. But the President and Congress also swear to obey the Constitution and ought therefore, in consequence, to follow their own interpretation, and to disregard contrary interpretation of the Constitution. From the anarchy that would follow this logical carrying out of the theory of three coördinate powers, we have been saved by a process of mutual concessions in which Marshall's argument is disregarded. The President and Congress, in the main, have agreed to abandon their own conviction or understanding of the Constitution when it conflicts with that of the Supreme Court, their oath of office to the contrary notwithstanding. And the courts have refrained from exercising the entire power of interpreting the Constitution by calling certain questions political; for example, leaving it to the legislature to interpret the words "republican form of government" in the Federal Constitution. The distinction between political and other matters is sufficiently vague and elastic to make this arrangement workable.

The view that interpretation is exclusively a judicial function has no basis in the old common law or in the practice of any government (both Coke and Blackstone, Whig and Tory, admit the power of Parliament to expound the law). Interpretation, as Wigmore has pointed out (Wigmore, *Evidence*, 2d ed., 1923, Vol. IV, sec. 2458 *et seq*.), is essentially a process of realization, i.e., a process of translating maxims into actual human arrangements; and it is necessary not only to all who take part in the administration of law but to the legislature as well. That every department of the government must interpret the law or it could not act, was recognized by Chief Justice Parsons in Kendall v. Kingston, 5 Mass. 524, 533 (1809). The Continental view is well expressed by Barthélemy, in "Notes Parlementaires," *Revue du droit public*, July, 1908, pp. 476 *et seq*. Cf. Le Courtois du Manoir, *De l'interprétation des lois par le législateur*, 1909.

[66] Lottery Case, 188 U. S. 321, 23 Sup. Ct. 321 (1903).

[67] Allgeyer v. Louisiana, 165 U. S. 578, 17 Sup. Ct. 427 (1897).

[68] Hammer v. Dagenhart, 247 U. S. 251 (1918).

[69] Southern Ry. Co. v. United States, 222 U. S. 20, 32 Sup. Ct. 2 (1911).

[70] Adair v. United States, 208 U. S. 161, 28 Sup. Ct. 277 (1908).

[71] Lochner v. New York, 198 U. S. 45, 25 Sup. Ct. 539 (1905).

[72] Holden v. Hardy, 169 U. S. 366, 18 Sup. Ct. 383 (1898).

[73] Muller v. Oregon, 208 U. S. 412, 28 Sup. Ct. 324 (1908).

[74] Adkins v. Children's Hospital, 261 U. S. 525, 43 Sup. Ct. 394 (1923).

[75] 61 App. Div. 538, 70 N. Y. Supp. 639 (1901).

[76] See note 41.

[77] Matter of Hopper v. Brith, 203 N. Y. 144, 96 N. E. 371 (1911), holding invalid L. 1911, c. 649, sec. 12.

[78] See Rumelin, *Werturteile und Willensentscheidungen*, 1891, p. 46. For a comprehensive treatment of the problems of legal application, see Vol. IV of Bierling's *Juristische Prinzipienlehre*, 1913, especially pp. 55-58.

[79] In matter of Smith et al., 146 N. Y. 68, 75, 40 N. E. 497, 499 (1895); State v. Speyer, 67 Vt. 502, 32 Atl. 476 (1895); Potts v. Breen, 167 Ill. 67, 47 N. E. 81 (1897).

[80] For a collection and analysis of such cases see Finkelstein, "Judicial Self-Limitation," *Harvard Law Review*, Vol. XXXVII (1924), p. 338; "Further Notes on Judicial Self-Limitation," *ibid.*, Vol. XXXIX (1925), p. 221. For the establishment of a right of way through the Constitution by necessity, see Gray, J., in Head v. Amoskeag Mfg. Co., 113 U. S. 9.

[81] See preface by M. Deschanel to the volume on *Les méthodes juridiques*, 1911.

[82] See *Reason and Nature*, 1931, Book II, Chap. I. The traditional view of legal maxims is expressed by Wharton, who regards them as unalterable, "remaining the same always, as unerring principles of truth, in accordance with which all laws now and hereafter to be made, have been, and will be made, and being made, have been hitherto, and will still be, interpreted" (*Legal Maxims*, 1878, p. 8).

[83] *The Expansion of the Common Law*, 1904, Chap. IV.

[84] See Demogue's remarkable and charmingly written book, *Les notions fondamentales du droit privé*, 1911.

[85] Dicey, *Law and Public Opinion in England*, 1905; W. Jethro Brown, *The Underlying Principles of Modern Legislation*, 1912; Charmont, *Les transformations du droit public*, 1913, and *Les transformations générales du droit privé*, 1912.

[86] When I first published the foregoing views in 1914, the deans of some of our law schools wrote me that while the contention that judges do have a share in making the law is unanswerable, it is still advisable to keep the fiction of the phonograph theory to prevent the law from becoming more fluid than it already is. But I have an abiding conviction that to recognize the truth and adjust oneself to it is in the end the easiest and most advisable course. The phonograph theory has bred the mistaken view that the

law is a closed, independent system having nothing to do with economic, political, social, or philosophical science. If, however, we recognize that courts are constantly remaking the law, then it becomes of the utmost social importance that the law should be made in accordance with the best available information, which it is the object of science to supply.

THE BILL OF RIGHTS THEORY

[1] The substance of this article appeared in *New Republic*, Vol. II (1915), p. 222.

[2] *Works of Thomas Jefferson*, 1907, Vol. I, *Autobiography*, p. 121.

[3] *Ibid.*   [4] *Ibid.*

[5] Nunnemacher v. State, 129 Wis. 190, 108 N. W. 627 (1906); State v. Goodwill, 33 W. Va. 179, 10 S. E. 285 (1889); Adair v. U. S., 208 U. S. 161, 175, 28 Sup. Ct. 277 (1908). On the last see Olney, "Discrimination against Union Labor—Legal?" *American Law Review*, Vol. XLII (1908), p. 161.

[6] Pollock v. Farmers' Loan and Trust Co. (Rehearing), 158 U. S. 601, 15 Sup. Ct. 912 (1895).

[7] *Education of Henry Adams*, 1918, Chap. 10.

[8] Par. Debates, Commons (1912), Vol. 42, pp. 2230 *et seq.*; the following quotations are from *Current Literature*, Vol. LIII, pp. 629-30. The statements from the *Manchester Guardian* and the *London Chronicle* are not exact quotations.

[9] Ives v. South Buffalo Ry. Co., 201 N. Y. 271, 94 N. E. 431 (1911).

LEGALISM AND CLERICALISM

[1] Reprinted, with minor modifications, from *New Republic*, Vol. XLI (1924), p. 15.

[2] Something very close to this was stated by General Kuropotkin in his *Russian Army and the Japanese War*, trans. by Lindsay, 1909, Vol. I, p. 297.

THE PLACE OF LOGIC IN THE LAW

[1] Reprinted, with minor modifications, from *Harvard Law Review*, Vol. XXIX (1915), p. 622.

[2] Jhering, *Geist des römischen Rechts*, 1865-69, Vol. III, sec. 69; *Scherz und Ernst in der Jurisprudenz*, 1884, Chap. I, pts. 3-4; Holmes, *The Common Law*, 1881, Chap. I.

[3] Jhering, *op. cit.* (note 2), secs. 44-46, 59-68, and especially 45, 64, 65.

[4] Holmes, *op. cit.* (note 2). Note the quotation at the end of the preface, and the important place of "reasons" in the development of the law, pp. 5, 36; see also pp. 214, 219, 220, 239, 289.

[5] Wüstendörfer, "Die deutsche Rechtsprechung," *Archiv für die civilistische Praxis*, Vol. CX (1910), p. 223; Fuchs, *Die Gemeinschadlichkeit der konstruktiven Jurisprudenz*, 1909, Chaps. 1-2; Bentley, *The Process of Government*, 1908, Chap. I; Brooks Adams, *Centralization and the Law*, 1906, Lectures 1-2.

[6] Adams, *op. cit.* (note 5), pp. 39, 41, 43; Wüstendörfer, *op. cit.* (note 5), pp. 219-22.

[7] "Arbitrary discretion is excluded by the certainty resulting from a strict scientific method" (Savigny, *Of the Vocation of Our Age for Legislation and Jurisprudence*, trans. by Hayward, 1831, p. 151).

[8] Dernburg, *System des römischen Rechts*, 1912, sec. 220.

[9] Labatt, *Commentaries on the Law of Master and Servant*, 1913, 8 vols.

[10] Langdell, *Cases on Contracts*, 1871, p. vi.

[11] Bozi, *Die Weltanschauung der Jurisprudenz*, 1907; Brooks Adams and Bentley, *op. cit.* (note 5). See also note in Jung, *Das Problem des natürlichen Rechts*, 1912, p. 172.

382 NOTES

[12] Harvey, the discoverer of the circulation of the blood, said of Bacon: "He writes science like a Lord Chancellor."

[13] 188 Mass. 353, 74 N. E. 603 (1905). [14] 208 U. S. 161, 28 Sup. Ct. 277 (1908).

[15] 222 Mass. 206, 110 N. E. 264 (1915).

[16] Twining v. New Jersey, 211 U. S. 78, 106, 29 Sup. Ct. 14 (1908).

[17] Adams, *op. cit.* (note 5), pp. 20 *et seq.* And see Lewis, "The Social Sciences as the Basis of Legal Education," *University of Pennsylvania Law Review*, Vol. LXI (1913), pp. 531, 533.

[18] National Protective Association v. Cumming, 170 N. Y. 315, 63 N. E. 369 (1902).

[19] Holmes, *op. cit.* (note 3), p. 2. Cf. Boas, *Mind of Primitive Man*, 1911.

[20] Pound, "Mechanical Jurisprudence" (1908), *Columbia Law Review*, Vol. VIII (1908), p. 605; Korkunov, *The General Theory of Law*, 1909, p. 15; Bekker, *Ernst und Scherz über unsere Wissenschaft*, 1892, Chap. VII.

[21] *Brief Survey of Equity Jurisprudence*, 1905, p. 126.

[22] *Digest*, IV, 6, 19.   [23] *Ibid.*, IV, 6, 20.   [24] *Ibid.*, IV, 6, 7.

[25] Jhering, *Geist des römischen Rechts*, sec. 44.

[26] Rogers v. Burlington, 3 Wall. (U. S.) 654 (1865); Opinion of the Justices, 150 Mass. 592, 24 N. E. 1084 (1890); Lowell v. Boston, 111 Mass. 454 (1873). And cf. Parkersbury v. Brown, 106 U. S. 487 (1882).

[27] *Op. cit.* (note 21), p. 220.

LAW AND SCIENTIFIC METHOD

[1] The substance of this paper was read at the Twenty-fifth Annual Meeting of the Association of American Law Schools, December 29, 1927, and printed in *American Law School Review*, Vol. VI (1928), p. 231.

[2] See "Myth about Bacon and the Inductive Method," *Scientific Monthly*, Vol. XXIII (1926), p. 50.

[3] See *Reason and Nature*, 1931, Book III, Chap. II, "History versus Value."

[4] See J. M. Clark, "Non-Euclidean Economics," in *The Trend of Economics*, ed. by Tugwell, pp. 86 *et seq.*

JUSTICE HOLMES AND THE NATURE OF LAW

[1] Reprinted, with slight modifications, from *Columbia Law Review*, Vol. XXXII (1932), p. 352.

[2] *Collected Legal Papers*, 1921, p. 165.

[3] *Ibid.*, p. 230.   [4] *Ibid.*, p. 183.

[5] The tragic absurdity of a court's failure to understand modern industrial conditions was perhaps never so strikingly exhibited as in the opinion in Matter of Jacobs, 98 N. Y. 98 (1885). Declaring unconstitutional a statute prohibiting the manufacture of cigars and cigarettes in tenement sweat-shops, the court confessed to an inability to perceive (p. 113) "how the cigar-maker is to be improved in his health and morals by forcing him from his home and its hallowed associations and beneficent influences to ply his trade elsewhere." It is worth referring to this case because criticism of it has recently been reproved by a member of our Court of Appeals. See Crane, "The Supreme Law of the Land," *St. John's Law Review*, Vol. V (1930), p. 45.

[6] *Collected Legal Papers*, p. 184.

[7] *Ibid.*, pp. 279 *et seq.*   [9] *Ibid.*, p. 269.   [11] *Ibid.*, p. 280.

[8] *Ibid.*, p. 188.   [10] *Idem.*

[12] See especially "The Common Law," pp. 214, 219, 220, 239, 289. See also Holmes, "Agency," *Harvard Law Review*, Vol. IV (1891), p. 345; Holmes, "Privilege, Malice, and Intent," *idem*, Vol. VIII (1894), p. 1; both are reprinted in *Collected Legal Papers*,

p. 49 and p. 117. I ought to add that Mr. Frank (in *University of Pennsylvania Law Review*, Vol. LXXX, p. 48, note 73) finds in the paragraph above not a criticism of those who distort the meaning of a dictum by taking it out of its qualifying context, but—*mirabile dictu*—an adverse criticism of Holmes himself.

13 "The Place of Logic in the Law," pp. 165-183 of this volume.

14 Cf. Cardozo, *The Nature of the Judicial Process*, 1921, pp. 126 et seq.

15 *Collected Legal Papers*, p. 156. 16 *Ibid.*, p. 185. 17 *Ibid.*, p. 186.

18 Bingham, "What Is the Law?" *Michigan Law Review*, Vol. XI (1912), pp. 109 et seq.; Bingham, "Legal Philosophy and the Law," *Illinois Law Review*, Vol. IX (1914), p. 96 et seq.

19 Bingham, "Legal Philosophy and the Law," as cited, pp. 96, 114.

20 *Collected Legal Papers*, p. 224.

21 *The Common Law*, p. 106; cf. *Collected Legal Papers*, p. 198.

22 The regimental commander or the classroom teacher also has a large element of discretion. But if there is any difference between wise and unwise, loyal or disloyal use of discretion, it must ultimately be expressible in some formula or rule that gives the rational ground of the distinction. The rule need not be always explicitly formulated. But the gift of acting in accordance with it goes more often with trained than with untrained intuition. And training must consist in seeking to grasp a rule so that we may recognize old elements in new situations. Cf. the essay "Rule vs. Discretion," pp. 259-267 of this volume.

23 *Collected Legal Papers*, p. 198.

24 "A Return to Stare Decisis," *American Law School Review*, Vol. VI (1928), pp. 215, 225. Ultimately, of course, there are causes of human error and illusion, but the prospects of a well-established science that will enable us to predict when a court will misinterpret a given situation, are remote. On the whole, lawyers rely more on juristic analysis of past decisions than on any of the available methods of studying the physiologic and psychologic sources of the judge's ruling, though the art of humouring the judge is not without importance.

25 *Op. cit.* (note 24).

PHILOSOPHY AND LEGAL SCIENCE

1 This essay is reprinted, with slight verbal changes, from *Columbia Law Review*, Vol. XXXII (1932), p. 1103.

2 *Columbia Law Review*, Vol. XXXI (1931), p. 925.

3 Berolzheimer, *System der Rechts- und Wirtschaftsphilosophie*, 1904, Vol. I.

4 "The Conception of Philosophy in Recent Discussion," *Journal of Philosophy*, Vol. VII (1910), p. 401.

5 Yntema, *op. cit.*, p. 937.

6 See, for instance, Maclaurin, *The Theory of Light*, 1908, p. 7.

7 Frank, *Law and the Modern Mind*, 1930, p. 127.

8 *Idem*, p. 125.

9 Bingham, "What Is the Law?" *Michigan Law Review*, Vol. XI (1912), p. 109; "Legal Philosophy and the Law," *Illinois Law Review*, Vol. IX (1914), p. 96.

10 See p. 211 of this volume.

11 See Century Dictionary, and Lalande, *Vocabulaire technique et critique de la philosophie*.

12 "Many philosophers call their variety of nominalism, 'conceptualism'; but it is essentially the same thing; and their not seeing that it is so is but another example of that loose and slapdash style of thinking that has made it possible for them to remain nominalists. Their calling their 'conceptualism' a middle term between realism and

nominalism is itself an example in the very matter to which nominalism relates. For while the question between nominalism and realism is, in its nature, susceptible of but two answers: yes and no, they make an idle and irrelevant point which had been thoroughly considered by all the great realists; and instead of drawing a valid distinction, as they suppose, only repeat the very same confusion of thought which made them nominalists. The question was whether all properties, laws of nature, and predicates of more than an actually existent subject are, without exception, mere figments or not. The conceptualists seek to wedge in a third position conflicting with the principle of excluded middle. They say, 'Those universals are real, indeed; but they are only real thoughts.' So much may be said of the philosopher's stone. To give that answer constitutes a man a nominalist. Are the laws of nature, and that property of gold by which it will yield the purple of Cassius, no more real than the philosopher's stone? No, the conceptualists admit that there is a difference; but they say that the laws of nature and the properties of chemical species are results of thinking. The great realists had brought out all the truth there is in that much more distinctly long before modern conceptualism appeared in the world. They showed that the general is not capable of full actualization in the world of action and reaction but is of the nature of what is thought, but that our thinking only apprehends and does not create thought, and that that thought may and does as much govern outward things as it does our thinking. But those realists did not fall into any confusion between the real fact of having a dream and the illusory object dreamed. The conceptualist doctrine is an undisputed truism about *thinking*, while the question between nominalists and realists relates to *thoughts*, that is, to the objects which thinking enables us to know." C. S. Peirce, *Collected Legal Papers*, 1931, Vol. I, p. 8.

[13] See A. C. Fraser, *Selections from Berkeley*, 1891, pp. 15 *et seq.*

[14] Frank, *loc. cit.*, note 8.

[15] Frank, "Are Judges Human?" *University of Pennsylvania Law Review*, Vol. LXXX (1931), pp. 17, 44.

[16] *Idem*, pp. 46, 48.   [17] See pp. 208-218 of this volume.

[18] That the career of a decision is moulded by the treatment that later courts accord it is a proposition which Professor Llewellyn has found it possible to defend without invoking the aid of nominalistic metaphysics. *Bramble Bush*, 1930, pp. 47, 41-42, 61-66.

[19] The difficulty into which most argument as to the existence of universals falls arises from a failure to recognize that there are various realms of existence. Physical things exist in space and time. Space and time do not have such existence. Our misunderstandings and other psychic events have a temporal but not a spatial existence. The three roots of a cubic equation can be proved to exist, but such existence is neither mental nor physical. I have tried to sketch this theory in a review, "The New Realism," *Journal of Philosophy*, Vol. X (1913), p. 197.

This will answer two questions that Professor Yntema puts to me. He asks (*op. cit.*, note 2, p. 954, note 80), "Are ideals not facts?" The answer obviously is that ideals are not empirical facts, although our beliefs about them are. He goes on to ask whether I have denied existence to the ought, and thus lapsed into nominalism. My answer to this is simply that I do not deny all existence to the ought, but deny only the sort of existence that is characteristic of particular events, mental or physical.

[20] See, for instance, Simmel, *Einleitung in die Moralwissenschaft*, 1892, Vol. II, p. 16.

[21] A confusion between psychology and logic seems to me to permeate Professor Yntema's argument on the relation of science to epistemology (see *op. cit.* [note 2], pp. 938-39). The argument that scientific propositions sometimes have epistemological presuppositions is not answered by the statement that "most scientists are not epistemologists." Not the "theory of knowledge of the scientist" is in question, but the objective implications of his premises.

Similarly Professor Cook, in reviewing my volume *Reason and Nature* (in *Columbia Law Review*, Vol. XXXI (1931), pp. 725-26) suggests that some physicists today do not assume that the consequences of a true hypothesis will be true. That there may be physicists who have not expressly formulated or recognized that assumption I shall not dispute. But the assumption is nevertheless logically present in every proof or disproof of a proposition of physics.

[22] An unwarranted restriction of logic to the past seems to me to be at the root of Professor Yntema's protest that "the function of juristic logic and the principles which it employs seems to be like that of language, to describe the event which has already transpired. These considerations must reveal to us the impotence of general principles to control decision. . . . The rule can state in convenient abstract form the common element in a number of historical judicial events, but it cannot tell us whether any judicial decision, or, indeed, the decision in some future case should come within the rule" (Yntema, "The Hornbook Method and the Conflict of Laws" [*Yale Law Journal*, Vol. XXXVII (1928), pp. 468, 480-81]). Rules are impotent to control decisions only if "control" be taken in a physical sense. Rules do "control" or "govern" decisions in the sense that they describe decisions and thus are verified or disproved by decisions. A rule will be "only a mnemonic device" (*idem*) if it collects historical uniformities that are purely accidental, e.g., that all successful plaintiffs in cases appearing in Volume 48 of the *Supreme Court Reporter* employed lawyers whose names contained an "s." But a rule is more than a mnemonic device if it points to a uniformity in court decisions that is not accidental. And such rules "control" the future as well as the past.

[23] "The Process of Judicial Legislation," *American Law Review*, Vol. XLVIII (1914), p. 161.

[24] Yntema, *op. cit.* (note 2), p. 942, note 40.

[25] Lest my silence be taken as consent, I am constrained to add that there is no foundation whatsoever for Professor Yntema's suggestion (*op. cit.*, note 2, p. 949, note 67) that I am a believer in metaphysical free will, a subjective intuitionist, or in any way a follower of Geny. While I have always admired Geny's epoch-making contribution to the liberalization of the process of legal interpretation, I have never shared his diluted Catholic philosophy, and have expressed my dissent in an article on "Recent Philosophical-Legal Literature in French, German and Italian: 1912-1914," at p. 300 *supra*.

[26] Yntema, *op. cit.*, note 2, p. 942.   [27] *Idem*, p. 934.

[28] Pollock, *Essays in Jurisprudence*, 1880. It is only fair to mention that Sir Frederick changed this view in later life.

[29] Pound, "Mechanical Jurisprudence," *Columbia Law Review*, Vol. VIII (1908), pp. 605, 613; "The Scope and Purpose of Sociological Jurisprudence," *Harvard Law Review*, Vol. XXV (1911), p. 140, note 4.

[30] *Reason and Nature*, 1931, pp. 349, 447 *et seq*. Professor Yntema, in attacking my view of ethics as "subjective," confuses the data of ethics with the method of analyzing such data. The former is subjective, as are the personal observations that form the data of physics, and one does not escape this element of subjectivism by appealing, as Professor Yntema does (*op. cit.* [note 2], p. 945), from "moral intuition" to "the principle and practice of the men and women of the community whom the social mind would rank as intelligent and virtuous" or to "the scale of values" in "the social mind" or to the "book of life." But the analysis of ethical data may be objective, and as disinterested as the analysis of mathematics. Cf. Felix S. Cohen, "The Subject Matter of Ethical Science," *International Journal of Ethics*, Vol. XLII (1932), p. 397.

[31] Underhill Moore, "Rational Basis of Legal Institutions," *Columbia Law Review*, Vol. XXIII (1923), p. 609.

[32] Professor Yntema suggests that I am in "the difficult position of defining the norm

as both the actual decision and the means of its critique" (*op. cit.* [note 2], p. 951). The difficulty, however, is only for one who refuses to make a necessary distinction. The actual decision is a norm of conduct for certain individuals to whom it is addressed, but the decision itself may be judged by norms applicable to it, such as logical consistency or fidelity to established rules or to principles of communal welfare.

[33] *Op. cit.* (note 2), p. 952, note 73.

[34] The Talmud, which is an old but often shrewd law-book, somewhere declares that when he who has power to command gives permission, that permission is to an understanding man the equivalent of a command.

[35] Thus "Go to the legislature" is the typical response of the judge who feels that he cannot give effect to some social policy without violating his oath of office to obey and enforce the law.

"REAL" AND "IDEAL" FORCES IN CIVIL LAW

[1] Reprinted, with slight modifications, from *International Journal of Ethics*, Vol. XXVI (1916), p. 347.

[2] Talbert, *The Dualism of Fact and Idea in Its Social Implication*, 1910; Pound, "Scope and Purpose of Sociological Jurisprudence," *Harvard Law Review*, Vol. XXIV (1911), p. 600.

[3] Santayana, *Winds of Doctrine*, 1913, Chap. VI.

[4] Bierling, *Zur Kritik der juristischen Grundbegriffe*, 1877-83, Vol. I, pp. 66, 134 *et seq.*; Vol. II, pp. 351 *et seq.*; Bierling, *Juristische Prinzipienlehre*, 1894, Vol. II, pp. 3 *et seq.*

[5] Following the usage of sociologists I use the term "force" (when otherwise unqualified) in the remainder of this paper to denote any determining factor; ordinary usage, also, employs such expression as "the force of his arguments," etc.

[6] See Hume's *Essays*, Green and Grose, 1898, Vol. I, p. 110.

[7] Loria, *Economic Foundations of Society*, 1899; Brooks Adams, *Theory of Social Revolutions*, 1913, and *Centralization and Law*, 1906, Lectures 1-2.

[8] Burdick, "Is Law the Expression of Class Selfishness?" *Harvard Law Review*, Vol. XXV (1912), p. 349.

[9] Pollock, *Genius of the Common Law*, 1912, pp. 104-05; Holmes, "Law in Science and Science in Law," *Harvard Law Review*, Vol. XII (1899), p. 456; Dicey, *Law and Public Opinion*, 1917, p. 280.

[10] Hertz, *Principles of Mechanics*, 1899, Introduction. And see Russell, *Principles of Mathematics*, 1903, p. 482: "The first thing to be remembered is—what physicists nowadays will scarcely deny—that *force* is a mathematical fiction, not a physical entity."

[11] Pound, *op. cit.* (note 2), p. 600; *Harvard Law Review*, Vol. XXV (1912), p. 167.

[12] See "Rule vs. Discretion" in this volume, pp. 265-266.

[13] A beginning has been made by Zitelmann, *Irrtum und Rechtsgeschäft*, 1883, pp. 220 *et seq.*; W. Jellinek, *Gesetz, Gesetzesanwendung, und Zweckmässigkeit*, 1913, pp. 30 *et seq.*; H. Maier, *Psychologie des emotionalen Denkens*, 1908, pp. 636 *et seq.*, 736 *et seq.*

[14] See "The Place of Logic in the Law," pp. 165-183 of this volume.

[15] *Traité élémentaire du droit civil*, 1910-1912, Vol. I, pp. 2-3; cf. Demogue, *Les notions fondamentales*, 1911, pp. 19-20.

RULE VERSUS DISCRETION

[1] Reprinted, with slight modifications, from *Journal of Philosophy*, Vol. XI (1914), p. 208.

[2] Maine, *Ancient Law*, 1906, Chap. IV.

[3] Pollock, *Essays in Jurisprudence and Ethics*, 1882, p. 24.

[4] *Ethics*, Book V, 7.

[5] Salmond, *Jurisprudence*, 3d ed., 1910, p. 20.

[6] Plato, *Statesman*, pp. 293-300; Aristotle, *Politics*, Book II, 8; Book III, 11, 15, 16; Book IV, 4.

[7] *Rapports au Congrès International de Physique*, Vol. I, pp. 1-3 (italics mine).

[8] That judges must take part in the process of law-making, I have attempted to show in the essay on "The Process of Judicial Legislation," pp. 112-147 of this volume.

[9] See Geny, *Méthode d'interprétation et sources en droit privé positif*, 1899; Ehrlich, *Freie Rechtsfindung und freie Rechtswissenschaft*, 1903; and the various works of Stampe. Portions of these and other works in this field are translated in *Science of Legal Method*, 1917, Vol. IX of Modern Legal Philosophy Series.

[10] This is explicitly stated by the leading Catholic social philosophers of today. See Cathrein, *Socialism*, trans. by Grettelman, 1904, p. 126.

[11] *Summa Theologica*, 2a, 2ae, Q. LXI, Art. 1 and 2. For a critical analysis of some juristic first principles see Demogue, *Les notions fondamentales*, Book I.

[12] *Memories and Addresses*, 1912.

[13] Hence, also, the easy transition from radical empiricism to mysticism.

TOURTOULON

[1] The substance of this essay appears as an editorial preface to Pierre de Tourtoulon, *Philosophy in the Development of Law* (trans. from the French by M. Read, Macmillan, 1922, Modern Legal Philosophy Series, Vol. 13).

[2] Vinogradoff, *Outlines of Historical Jurisprudence*, 1920-22, Vols. I-II.

[3] Published in France in 1918.

[4] Ehrlich's *Die juristische Logik*, 1918, was not available at the time this volume was written.

[5] Act IV, Scene IV.   [6] 1914.

[7] Cf. "On the Logic of Fiction," *Journal of Philosophy*, Vol. XX (1923), p. 477.

[8] Cf. Bierling, *Juristische Prinzipienlehre*; Binding, *Die Normen und ihre Uebertretung*, 1914-22; Hohfeld, *Fundamental Legal Conceptions*, ed. by Cook, 1923; Pound, "Legal Rights," *International Journal of Ethics*, October, 1915.

[9] *Jahrbuch für Philosophie und phänomenologische Forschung*, 1913.

ON CONTINENTAL LEGAL PHILOSOPHY

[1] This essay consists of a series of reviews and comments on Continental work in legal philosophy recently published or recently translated.

[2] Reprinted, with minor changes, from *International Journal of Ethics*, Vol. XXVI (1916), p. 528.

[3] Astier, Buisson, *et al.*, *Œuvre sociale de la Troisième République*, with preface by Deschanel, 1912; Théry, *Les caractères généraux de la réglementation jurisprudentielle du contrat de travail en droit français*, 1913 (see especially pp. 234-36).

[4] See the confident assertion by the authors of the *Supplement au répertoire de Dalloz*, 1887, Vol. I, pp. vii-ix, that legal doctrine had achieved "a complete development." A striking parallel is the belief among physicists, at the time Maxwell was opening the great Cavendish laboratory, that the great discoveries of physics had already been made and that all that was left to laboratories was to perfect the determination of physical units. See Maxwell's *Collected Papers* or *History of Cavendish Laboratory*, 1911.

[5] Archambault, "Un spiritualisme social: positivisme et catholicisme," *Annales de philosophie chrétienne*, Vol. XIV (1912), pp. 363-84; Richard, "La sociologie juridique

et la défense du droit subjectif," *Revue philosophique*, Vol. LXXIII (1912), pp. 225-47; A. Levi, *Contributi ad una teoria filosofica dell' ordine giuridico*, 1914, pp. 260-83.

[6] Cf. Plastara, "Nouvelles tendances dans le droit—libertés et patrimoines," *Revue trimestrielle de droit civil*, Vol. XI (1912), p. 887.

[7] Fuchs, E., *Juristischer Kulturkampf*, 1912.

[8] Wüstendörfer, "Die deutsche Rechtsprechung am Wendepunkt," *Archiv für civil Praxis*, Vol. 110 (1913). Hostile to logical "construction" in law is also Müller-Erzbach, "Die Relativität der Rechtsbegriffe" in *Jherings Jahrbücher*, Vol. 61 (1912). In his long review, however, of Jung's book, in the *Zeitschrift für das gesammte Handelsrecht*, Vol. 73 (1913), Müller-Erzbach seems to have become afraid of the emphasis on sensibility, as opposed to logic, in law.

[9] Stampe, "Grundriss der Wertbewegungslehre" and "Aus einem Freirechtslehrbuch," in *Archiv für civil Praxis*, Vols. CVII, CVIII, CX. Stampe seems to have done the most work in the direction of actually applying the principles of the *Freirechtsschule* to the concrete subject-matter of the law.

[10] Danz, *Einführung in die Rechtssprechung*, 1912, and *Richterrecht*, 1912. See also his "Fortschritte durch Erkenntis der Lücken im Gesetz," in the *Deutsche Juristenzeitung*, 1914, pp. 7 *et seq.*

[11] Wüstendörfer, *op. cit.* It is curious that Wüstendörfer, who argues that logic should occupy a subordinate position in the interpretation of laws, should attach such great importance to a unitary method in a subject that might well admit of many methods so far as practical interests are concerned.

[12] Kohler, *Recht und Persönlichkeit in der Kultur der Gegenwart*, 1914, especially pp. 24 and 220 *et seq.*

[13] Ehrlich, *Grundlegung der Soziologie des Rechts*, 1913.

[14] Kantorowicz, "Was ist uns Savigny?" *Recht und Wirtschaft*, 1912.

[15] Heck, *Gesetzesauslegung und Interessenjurisprudenz*, 1914, is the most extensive and systematic study we yet have of the process of legal interpretation. There is some impropriety in including Heck among the *Freirechtler*, because of his rather narrow adherence to the imperative theory and his exaggeration of the extent to which the will of the legislator is determinate. But the logic of the insistence on social interests forces him to make significant concessions. Thus the judge "should protect those interests which exist at the time of the application. Only the living have rights. But each statute already belongs at the time of its application to the past" (p. 14). He also admits that Fuchs has rendered great service to jurisprudence by his warm-hearted appeals, and Kohler by emphasizing the creative function of jurisprudence (pp. 215, 277).

[16] Berolzheimer, *Moral und Gesellschaft des 20. Jahrhunderts*, 1914. Cf. also Berolzheimer, *Die Gefahren eines Gefühlsjurisprudenz*, 1911.

[17] Kohler, *op. cit.*

[18] Jung, *Problem des natürlichen Rechts*, 1912.

[19] Bartolemei, *La ragione della jurisprudenza pura*, 1912.

[20] Gareis, *Moderne Bewegungen in der Wissenshaft des deutschen Privatrechts—Rektorsrede*, 1912.

[20a] Jung, *op. cit.* (in note 18) § 7.

[20b] Ehrlich, *op. cit.* (in note 13) p. 136.

[21] For an examination of Stammler's philosophy see Breuer, *Der Rechtsbegriff auf Grundlage der Stammlerischen Sozialphilosophie* (No. 27 of the Supplements to the *Kantstudien*, 1912), and Wielikowski, *Die Neukantianer in der Rechtsphilosophie* (1914). See also Fränkel, *Die kritische Rechtsphilosophie bei Fries und bei Stammler* (1912). One of the leaders of the Fries school, Nelson, has given us a short but weighty pamphlet in this field, *Die Theorie des wahren Interesses und ihre rechtliche und politische Bedeutung* (1913).

[22] Kohler, *Archiv für Rechts- und Wirtschaftsphilosopie*, Vol. VIII (1914), p. 167.

[22a] Geny, *Science et technique en droit privé positif*, 1914, p. 96.

[23] Pp. 157-60.

[24] *System der Rechts- und Wirtschaftsphilosophie*, 1904-07.

[24a] Vol. I, pp. 429 *et seq.*

[25] A review of *Modern French Legal Philosophy*, ed. by A. W. Spencer, trans. by Scott and Chamberlain (Boston, 1916, Vol. VII of Modern Legal Philosophy Series), reprinted, with slight changes, from *American Political Science Review*, Vol. XVII (1917), p. 137.

[26] A portion of a review of Jhering, *Law as a Means to an End*, trans. by Husik (Boston, 1913, Modern Legal Philosophy Series, Vol. V), reprinted from *Philosophical Review*, Vol. XXIII (1914), p. 557.

[27] *Op. cit.*, p. 397.   [29] *Ibid.*, p. 409.   [31] *Idem*, pp. li-lii.

[28] *Ibid.*, p. 421.   [30] *Ibid.*, Introduction, p. li.   [32] *Op. cit.*, p. 389.

[33] *Ibid.*, Introduction, p. xxxi.

[34] A review of Kohler, *Moderne Rechtsprobleme* (2d ed., Leipzig, 1913), reprinted with minor modifications from *Journal of Criminal Law*, Vol. V (1914), p. 618.

[35] A review of Krabbe, *The Modern Idea of the State*, trans. by Sabine and Shepard (New York, 1922), reprinted with slight verbal changes from *Philosophical Review*, Vol. XXXII (1923), p. 97.

[36] Krabbe, *op. cit.*, pp. 46, 193, 194.   [40] *Ibid.*, pp. 8-9.

[37] *Ibid.*, p. 192.   [41] *Ibid.*, pp. 10, 48.

[38] *Ibid.*, pp. 50-51.   [42] *Ibid.*, p. 274.

[39] *Ibid.*, p. 76.   [43] *Ibid.*, p. lx.

[44] A portion of a review of Del Vecchio, *The Formal Bases of Law* (trans. by Lisle, Boston Book Co., 1915, Vol. X of Modern Legal Philosophy Series), reprinted from *American Political Science Review*, Vol. IX (1915), pp. 799 *et seq.*

[45] Del Vecchio, *op. cit.*, p. 328. Cf. pp. 101 *et seq.* on the "logical antecedence" of the concept.

[46] The study of history may at least save us from unfounded historical generalizations, e.g., the dogma that Del Vecchio accepts from Maine to the effect that all progress is from status to contract.

[47] *Op. cit.*, p. 116.

ON THREE POLITICAL SCIENTISTS

[1] This essay, in substantially its present form, appeared in *New Republic*, Vol. XXXI (1922), p. 111 *et seq.*, as a review of Fisher, *Studies in History and Politics* (Clarendon Press, 1920); Duguit, *Law in the Modern State* (Huebsch, 1919); and Laski, *The Foundations of Sovereignty* (Harcourt, Brace, 1921).

[2] Fisher, *op. cit.*, p. 197.

[3] *Studies in the Problem of Sovereignty*, 1917; *Authority in the Modern State*, 1919.

[4] Laski, *The Foundations of Sovereignty*, p. 295.

ROSCOE POUND

[1] This essay consists, in substance, of extracts from three reviews of Roscoe Pound's writings: *The Spirit of the Common Law* (Marshall Jones Company, 1921), reviewed in *Journal of Philosophy*, Vol. XX (1923), p. 155; *An Introduction to the Philosophy of Law* (Yale University Press, 1922), reviewed in *Columbia Law Review*, Vol. XXII (1922), p. 774; and *Law and Morals* (University of North Carolina Press, 1924), reviewed in *Harvard Law Review*, Vol. XXXVIII (1925), p. 1123.

[2] I am not sure to what extent Dean Pound thinks that Puritanism has also influenced

the law of England. He speaks of the age of Coke—which is the age of the Elizabethan dramatists, Shakespeare and Ben Jonson—as the age of the Puritan in England. But he gives no indication of how the English common law was modified by Puritanism.

³ Cf. Bradley's "My Station and Its Duties" in *Ethical Studies*, 1876.

⁴ Pound, *The Spirit of the Common Law*, p. 213.

⁵ *Ibid.*, pp. 17-18.   ⁶ *Ibid.*, pp. 21-22.

⁷ Wigmore, *Treatise on Evidence*, 2nd ed., 1923.

⁸ Bishop, *Marriage and Divorce*, 1856.

⁹ Churches (Scotland) Act, Stat. 5 Edw. 7, c. 12 (1905), overruling Free Church of Scotland v. Overtoun, [1904] A. C. 515.

¹⁰ Ives v. South Buffalo Ry., 201 N. Y. 271, 94 N. E. 431 (1911).

¹¹ Pound, *An Introduction to the Philosophy of Law*, p. 160.

¹² *Ibid.*, pp. 272-73.   ¹⁹ Pound, *Law and Morals*, p. 63.

¹³ *Ibid.*, p. 274.   ²⁰ *Ibid.*, pp. 80-81.

¹⁴ *Ibid.*, p. 276.   ²¹ German Civil Code, Art. 138.

¹⁵ *Ibid.*, p. 194.   ²² French Civil Code, Art. 1133.

¹⁶ *Ibid.*, p. 192.   ²³ Italian Civil Code, Art. 1122.

¹⁷ *Ibid.*, p. 235.   ²⁴ Pound, *op. cit.* (note 19), pp. 17-18.

¹⁸ *Ibid.*, p. 235.

JOHN CHIPMAN GRAY

¹ Portions of this essay appeared as a review of John Chipman Gray, *The Nature and Sources of the Law* (2d ed., Macmillan, 1921), in *New Republic*, Vol. XXXIII (November 29, 1922), Book Section, p. 4.

JEROME FRANK

¹ This essay is a review of Jerome Frank, *Law and the Modern Mind* (Brentano, 1930), reprinted with minor changes from *The Nation*, Vol. CXXXIII (1931), p. 259.

² Frank, *op. cit.*, pp. 207-21, 264-84, 289-301.

³ *Ibid.*, p. 283.

⁴ I had not supposed when I wrote this that it could possibly be interpreted as the denial of an existing fact on the ground that its consequences are inconvenient. But as Mr. Frank has so misunderstood it (*University of Pennsylvania Law Review*, Vol. LXXX, p. 26, note 22), I must point out that my argument is of the orthodox logical type, namely, that a proposition is false if its consequences are false. If the Green-Frank statement were true, if the control of subordinates by rules were impossible, then a situation would arise that does not in fact exist, hence the statement in question is false.

⁵ *Op. cit.*, p. 21.   ⁶ *Ibid.*, pp. 218-21.   ⁷ *Ibid.*, p. 288.

⁸ See *Scherz und Ernst in der Jurisprudenz*, 1885.

OLIVER WENDELL HOLMES

¹ A review of Oliver Wendell Holmes, *Collected Legal Papers*, Harcourt, Brace, 1920, first published in *New Republic*, Vol. XXV (1921), p. 294.

² Holmes, *op. cit.*, p. 30.   ⁸ *Ibid.*, p. 307.   ¹⁴ *Ibid.*, p. 159.

³ *Ibid.*, p. 306.   ⁹ *Ibid.*, p. 310.   ¹⁵ *Ibid.*, p. 247.

⁴ *Ibid.*, p. 48.   ¹⁰ *Ibid.*, p. 316.   ¹⁶ *Ibid.*, p. 32.

⁵ *Ibid.*, p. 166.   ¹¹ *Ibid.*, pp. 184, 295.   ¹⁷ *Ibid.*, p. 246.

⁶ *Ibid.*, p. 299.   ¹² *Ibid.*, p. 230.   ¹⁸ *Ibid.*, p. 29.

⁷ *Ibid.*, p. 305.   ¹³ *Ibid.*, p. 293.

Index of Proper Names

Burke, 20
Burns, 327

Caird, 248
Calder v. Bull, 376
Calvin, 13, 151, 310, 325, 332, 364, 365, 374
Cardozo, 354, 383
Carlyle, 302
Carnap, 228
Carter, J. C., 206, 376
Cathrein, 387
Cato, 161
Celsus, 378
Cervantes, 18, 87
Charmont, 20, 146, 288, 303, 304, 380
Choate, J. H., 142
Cicero, 374
Clark, J. M., 382
Cleisthenes, 73
Cohen, Felix S., 385
Cohen, Hermann, 301
Coke, 20, 74, 121, 134, 139, 256, 333, 337, 379, 390
Commonwealth v. B. & M. R. R., 172
Comte, 222
Cook, W. W., 385, 387
Copernicus, 158, 159, 171, 215
Cosentini, 299, 379
Cousin, 300
Cramner, 6
Crane, Judge, 382

Dalloz, 387
Dante, 4
Danz, 290, 388
Dartmouth College Case, 139
Darwin, 158, 292, 308, 364
Dash v. Van Kleeck, 378
Davenport, H. J., 373
Del Vecchio, 296, 317-318, 389
Demogue, 180, 303, 304, 305, 373, 374, 375, 380, 386
Dernburg, 381
Descartes, 171, 365
Deschanel, 380, 387
Dicey, 70, 146, 378, 380, 386
Dickens, 18
Dickinson v. N. R. Co., 358, 373
Digby Commission, 132
Djuvara, 278, 296
Domat, 74, 305

Domesday Book, 371
Douglass v. County of Pike, 379
Driesch, 166
Duguit, Léon, 70, 146, 188, 206, 244, 287, 288, 294, 303, 304, 319, 321, 322, 325, 352, 389
Duhem, 166
Dunlop, 378
Duns Scotus, 171
Durkheim, 275, 303

Eddington, 362
Egerton v. Earl of Brownlow, 377
Ehrlich, 189, 206, 290, 293, 387, 388
Einstein, 234
Eliot, George, 320
Emerson, 61, 155, 182
Emery, L. A., Judge, 23, 24, 25, 372
Enneccerus, 375
Esmein, 374
Euclid, 143, 175, 193, 265, 278, 279
Ezekiel, 72

Fabreguettes, 301
Federalist, 15
Fenet, 379
Fichte, 171
Figgis, 316, 325
Finkelstein, M., 380
Fisher, Herbert, 319, 320, 321, 389
Fitting, 378
Fitzwater v. Warren, 378
Fléchère, Brocher de la, 272
Foch, 189
Forbes v. Cochrane, 377
Ford, H. J., 15, 136
Forti, 377
Fouillée, 303
Fourier, 223, 229, 388
Fränkel, 388
Frank, Jerome, 203, 225, 357-362, 383, 384, 390
Franklin, Benjamin, 333
Fraser, A. C., 384
Freund, 179
Fries, 388
Fuchs, 290, 381, 388
Fuller, 120

Galileo, 171, 365
Gareis, 291, 388
Gary, Judge, 10

Thrasymachus, 249
Tocqueville, de, 374
Torah, 373
Torquemada, 14
Tourtoulon, Pierre de, 271-285, 387
Treilhard, 378
Troglodytes, 71
Twain, Mark, 18
Twining Case, 382
Tycho, 215

Ulpian, 176

Vaihinger, 278
Vareilles-Somières, 378
Vegelahn v. Guntner, 198
Vinogradoff, 20, 271, 374, 387
Voet, 74

Wach, 301
Wagner, Adolf, 373
Wahl, 378
Walter of Coventry, 20
Walton, 373

Wayman v. Sutherland, 376
Weber, Max, 82, 374
Wehli, 301
Wharton, 380
Whewell, 171
Wielikowski, 388
Wigmore, 125, 167, 335, 377, 380, 390
Willcox v. Consol. Gas Co., 377
Williams, Joshua, 42, 43
William of Occam, 84
Wilson, James, 333
Wilson, President, 15, 136, 376
Wilson, Thomas, 374
Windelband, 298
Windscheid, 92, 287, 375
Witherington, 325
Wolf, Christian, 256
Wright, 377
Wüstendörfer, 290, 381, 388

Yntema, 219-226, 228, 235-238, 240, 383-385

Zitelmann, 386

Index of Subjects

absolutism, 65 ff., 137, 278
abstractions, usefulness in law, 177, 195; abuses of, 178, 212. *See* rules *and* universals
acquisition of property, 47, 345
Acts of Sederunt, 127
aesthetics in law, 143
alienation of land, 59
America, legal philosophy in, 327 ff.
American Bar. *See* Bar *and* Lawyers
analogy in law, 124, 330, 334
anthropology, law as, 203
anti-intellectualism, 165, 194 ff., 256, 266, 290, 313, 331
anti-trust laws, 112, 160
application of law as legislation, 139 ff.
aristocracy, 48
arrêt de réglement, 127
art and science, 244
Articles of Confederation, 235
assumption of risk, 127, 330
Athenian law of contract, 73
authority, man's need for, 49
axioms and postulates in law, 174

Bar, American, 26, 158, 199, 237 ff., 352, 357; English, 184
basis of contract, 69 ff.
behaviourism, 188, 203 ff., 208; and the need of critical thought, 215 ff.; in law of contract, 94
bills of rights, 16, 35, 45, 78, 87, 148 ff., 338; and higher lawlessness, 16, 151 ff.
biologic basis of contractualism, 80
biology in law, 274
Birthright of Esau, 27 ff.
business and government, 13, 82

Calvinism, 12 ff., 75, 82 ff., 118, 151
Canon law, 83, 91, 124
capitalism, 68; and Protestantism, 82

captains of industry, 86; government by, 66 ff.
case method, 36, 170, 190
cases of first impression, 122 ff.
Catholic Church and Calvinism, 83; and European governments, 157
ceremonies, 99 ff.
certainty in law, 145, 191, 194, 203, 260, 266, 325, 333, 358 ff.
change and fixity in law, viii, 120 ff., 173, 196, 204, 259 ff., 358 ff.
checks and balances, 76, 154
child labour, 56
church and state, 157
Church of England, 83, 275
civil law and common law, 307; "real" and "ideal" forces in, 248 ff.
class, dominant, 252; interests in law, 149, 158, 201, 248, 254, 330 ff., 339, 349
classical German philosophy, 171
classification, 277; legal, 178 ff.
clericalism, psychology of, 157; and legalism, 157 ff.
Code Napoléon, 288
coercion, 46, 77, 87, 109, 204, 240, 249 ff.
commands, law as, 206, 240 ff., 249 ff.
commerce, 83; clause of constitution, 135; effect on custom and law, 71 ff.
commission, government by, 117, 264
commissions, Federal Trade, 82; Interstate Commerce, 117; Wisconsin Industrial, 117
common law and civil law, 307; pleading, 143, 276; spirit of, 328 ff.
common sense, 259; and legal theory, 98
communism, 53
competition, free, 80 ff.; waste of free, 56, 81
conceptualism, 221 ff.
conduct and legal norms, 204 ff.
confiscation, 60; abolition of slavery as, 61; prohibition as, 62

philosophy, Classical German, 171; American legal, 327 ff.; European legal, 271 ff.; French legal, 271 ff., 286 ff., 302 ff., 321 ff.; German legal, 286 ff., 305 ff., 309 ff., 312 ff.; Scotch realistic, 14, 23; Stoic, 137

phonograph theory of judicial function, 16, 112 ff., 233, 357

polarity, principle of, viii ff., 145 ff., 183, 259 ff., 263 ff.

political absolutism, 65 ff.; interpretation of law, 252; pessimism, 13, 74, 150; theory of contractualism, 74 ff.; vs. economic sovereignty, 64 ff.

poor, law and, 3 ff., 36

positivism, 94, 188, 204 ff., 232, 239 ff., 263, 281, 284, 286, 288, 294, 299, 300, 303, 307, 309, 316, 321 ff.

possession, 45

postulate, jural, 230 ff.

postulates and axioms in law, 174, 231, 343

poverty and inheritance, 28

power, property as, 45 ff., 343

practice and theory, 202

pragmatism in law, 329

precedent, 113, 122, 197, 213 ff., 334

presumptions, 126

primitive law, 167

principle of need, 52; of polarity, 145 ff., 183, 263 ff.

principles, eternal, 14, 165, 172, 175, 199, 264; legal, 122, 186; self-evident, 143 ff.

procedure, contentious, 144

procedural and substantive law, 128

productivity, 30, 52, 55 ff., 67, 81, 201

profit motive, 30, 55 ff., 64 ff., 81, 201, 367

prohibition and confiscation, 62

promises, sanctity of, 88 ff.

property, 367; acquisition of, 47, 345; and inheritance, 29; and liberty, 311; and personality, 53 ff.; and possession, 45; and sovereignty, 41 ff.; as power, 45 ff., 343; economic theory of, 55 ff., 343 ff., 367; in public offices, 61; justification of, 49 ff.; labour theory of, 51 ff., 282, 344; materialism in law of, 45; property, occupancy theory of, 49 ff., 282; real and personal, 42; rights, limitations of, 57 ff.

Protestant Reformation, 82

psychoanalysis, 357 ff.

psychology, 84, 187, 311; hedonistic, 75; in law, 215, 274 ff.; of clericalism, 157; of contractualism, 80; of judge, 123

public office, as property, 61; and efficiency, 64; policy in statutory interpretation, 131

punishment, justification of, 310; for violence, 4

"pure" law, 278, 280

Puritanism, 118, 328, 332 ff., 364 ff.

quia Emptores, 42

ratio decidendi, 214, 334

rationalism, viii, 263, 266 ff.; and empiricism, 266 ff.; in law, 217, 331

"real" and "ideal" forces in civil law, 248 ff.

realism, 248 ff.

reality, 24, 172; of rules and nominalism, 208 ff.

reason and will in law, 137, 256; in constitutional law, 139; law as, 137, 249, 251, 259 ff., 337, 339

recall of judicial decisions, 338 ff., 357

regulation of wages, 59

reliance, injurious, 95 ff., 342 ff.

religion and contractualism, 82 ff.

religion and law, 255, 308

representative government, 16

responsibility, individual, 72

restraints on popular will, 15, 18

right to contract, 87; to product of labour, 51, 282, 344

rights, abuse of, 60, 289

rights and duties, 179 ff.; bills of, 16, 35, 45, 78, 87, 148 ff., 338; limitations of property, 57 ff.; natural, 24, 57, 144, 148 ff., 184 ff., 204, 332

risk, assumption of, 127, 330

risks, contract and distribution of, 100 ff.

Roman Law, 73 ff., 114, 124, 128, 131, 137, 167, 293, 325, 332

rule and discretion, 180 ff., 259 ff., 294, 359 ff.; fellow servant, 127, 253, 330

rules and nominalism, 208 ff.

rules, diffusion of legal, 124; legal, 240; and moral, 122

saloon, 4
sanctity of promises, 88 ff.
scepticism in law, 202, 218
Scholasticism, 171, 362
school, *Freie Rechtsfindung*, 264
schools, law, viii, 36, 184, 199, 237, 352, 380
science, 25, 171, 204, 221 ff., 302, 362
science and art, 244; and law, 37, 141, 184 ff.; Greek, 167; natural, 166 ff., 170, 187, 205, 215, 236, 242 ff.
science, social, 166, 187, 215
scientific method, 128, 171, 204, 214, 219 ff.; and induction, 190; and law, 184 ff., 281; and legal procedure, 186; and positivism, 188 ff., 208 ff.
Scotch realistic philosophy, 14, 23
security, 60, 90, 102 ff., 305; static and dynamic, 53
self-evident principles, 143 ff., 165, 175, 200, 265
sense of justice, 122 ff., 182, 312 ff.
separation of powers, 114 ff., 132, 175, 286 ff., 290
Sherman Anti-Trust Act, 112, 160
sin, 72, 310, 348
slavery, 318; abolition of, 61
social contract, 87 ff., 150; control of business, 65; engineering, 337; inertia, 50; interests, 35; roots of contract, 69 ff.; sciences, 166, 187, 215; theories in law, 142
Socialism, 8, 9, 10, 57, 68, 367
socialistic jurisprudence, 118
sociology, 205; legal, 215, 242
sources of law, 293, 355 ff.
sovereign, law as will of, 137, 249
sovereignty, 249, 263, 294, 316, 323; and contract, 102 ff.; and property, 41 ff.; political vs. economic, 64 ff.
sporting theory of justice, 34
standardization of contracts, 105
stare decisis, 191, 197, 213 ff.
state and church, 157; and law, 313
statistical method, 190
status and contract, 69 ff.
statute, meaning of a, 129 ff.
Statute of Labourers, 21
statutes and contracts, interpretation of, 102; interpretation of, 112
statutory interpretation, public policy in, 131

Stoic philosophy, 137
subjective idealism, 221 ff.
subjectivism, 207 ff.
substantive and procedural law, 128
sumptuary legislation and property rights, 47
supernatural in law, 118
supremacy of law, 335 ff.
Supreme Court, 44, 45, 140, 160
Swiss law, 152, 286
symmetry in law, 123, 143

Talmudic law, 72, 382
tax, income, 21, 31; inheritance, 31
taxation, 51, 60
testamentary disposition, 28, 58
theory and practice, 202
theories and facts, 113, 160, 169, 205; social, in law, 142
tort and contract, distinction between, 96
torts, 168
transfer of property, restrictions upon, 58
transcendentalism, 237
trial by jury, 20, 150, 312
Twelve Tables, law of, 176

uniformities of conduct and legal norms, 204 ff.
uniformity in law, 275, 349
universals and legal science, 170 ff., 178, 208 ff., 221
universities, 25, 184
usury, 83
utilitarianism, 89, 307

value, and existence, 50; and history, 69 ff., 191, 318

wages, regulation of, 59
waste in industry, 55 ff., 155; of free competition, 56, 81
wealth, influence of, 48
will and reason in law, 137, 256; free, 84, 295, 309, 310, 327, 328, 332; of the sovereign, 137, 249; theory of contract, 74, 79, 85, 92 ff., 342
wills, 28, 58, 150
Witenagemot, 15
workmen's compensation laws, 22, 132, 137, 347